Please remember that this is a library book,
and that it belongs only temporarily to each
person who uses it. Be considerate. Do
not write in this, or any, library book.

WITHDRAWN

DREAM INTERPRETATION

A Comparative Study

DREAM INTERPRETATION

A Comparative Study

Edited by

James L. Fosshage, Ph.D.

and

Clemens A. Loew, Ph.D.

National Institute for the Psychotherapies
New York, New York

SP MEDICAL & SCIENTIFIC BOOKS
a division of Spectrum Publications, Inc.
New York • London

SPECTRUM PUBLICATIONS, INC.
175-20 Wexford Terrace, Jamaica, N.Y. 11432
Second printing March 1979
Library of Congress Cataloging in Publication Data

Main entry under title:

Dream interpretation.

   Includes index.
   1. Dreams—Addresses, essays, lectures. I. Fosshage, James L, 1940— II. Loew, Clemens A., 1937—   joint author. III. Title.
BF1078.F615   154.6'4   78-5874
ISBN 0-89335-048-6

To
the loving memory of my parents
Marie and Ernest Fosshage
and
the inspiration of my grandfather
Benjamin J. Ochsner, M.D.

J.L.F.

To
Gloria
whose love always encourages me.

C.A.L.

CONTRIBUTING AUTHORS

James L. Fosshage, Ph.D., Co-founder and Director of Clinical Research of the National Institute for the Psychotherapies, received his doctorate in Counseling Psychology from Columbia University and his psychoanalytic training at the Postgraduate Center for Mental Health. He is in private practice in New York City and New Jersey and is also Director of Training at the Institute for Counseling and Psychotherapy in Fort Lee, New Jersey. He is co-editor of a recent book, *Healing: Implications for Psychotherapy.*

Clemens A. Loew, Ph.D., Co-founder and Director of Clinical Services of the National Institute for the Psychotherapies, received his doctorate from the State University of Iowa in Clinical Psychology and his psychoanalytic training in both individual and group psychotherapy at the Postgraduate Center for Mental Health. He is in private practice in New York City and New Jersey. Among his recent publications are two books, *Three Psychotherapies: A Clinical Comparison* and *Changing Approaches to Psychotherapy,* which he co-edited.

Walter Bonime, M.D., received his medical degree from the College of Physicians and Surgeons, Columbia University, in 1938. He is presently Clinical Professor, Division of Psychoanalytic Training, Department of Psychiatry, New York Medical College, where he supervises and teaches in the psychoanalytic and residency programs. He was certified in psychoanalysis at New York Medical College. He is a Charter Fellow of the American Academy of Psychoanalysis, a Life Fellow of the American Psychiatric Association, a founding member of the Society of Medical Psychoanalysts (president 1963-64) and a member of the Association for the Psychophysiological Study of Sleep (APSS). He is the author, with Florence Bonime, of *The Clinical Use of Dreams* and has published over thirty-five articles.

Florence Bonime is an editor, novelist, short-story writer and ten-year member of the Writing Faculty at The New School for Social Research. Her novels are *The Good Mrs. Sheppard* (under former name Florence Cummings) and *A Thousand limitations.* She has been working with Walter Bonime on his writings for twenty-five years and has recently published collaboratively two articles, "On Psychoanalyzing Literary Characters" and "Psychoanalytic Writing: An Essay on Communication" (*Journal of the American Academy of Psychoanalysis*).

Medard Boss, M.D., graduated from the Medical School of the University of Zurich (1928) and took postgraduate training in neurology and psychoanalysis in London and Berlin. In 1925, he started his training analysis with S. Freud. A professor for psychotherapy at the Medical School of Zurich for over twenty years, Dr. Boss has lectured at medical schools in India, Indonesia, Argentina and the United States (Harvard and Langley Porter Clinic). In 1971, he received the Great Therapist Award of the Psychotherapy Division of the American Psychological Association. From 1958 to 1969, seminars were given by Martin Heidegger and Dr. Boss for the latter's students and assistants. Dr. Boss has published extensively in medical journals and has written ten books, all of which have been translated into two to six foreign languages.

Brian Kenny, M.D., graduated from Melbourne University Medical School in 1959. He was admitted to the Fellowship of the Royal Australasian College of Physicians and, for two years, was registrar to the Melbourne University Department of Psychiatry. In 1967 he began his studies of Daseinsanalysis with Dr. Boss and since 1973 has been an analyst in the Daseinsanalytical Institute, Medard Boss Foundation, Zurich.

Rainette Eden Fantz, Ph.D., is one of the founders of the Gestalt Institute of Cleveland. She is currently chairperson of the Institute's Intensive Post Graduate Training Program and is engaged in private practice of psychotherapy, work with groups, teaching and special-interest workshops. Dr. Fantz draws on her extensive background as artist, musician and actress. She did her graduate work in psychology at Case-Western Reserve University. She has written chapters about the gestalt approach in various books on psychotherapy.

Angel Garma, M.D., took his medical training in Madrid and his psychoanalytic training in Berlin at the Institute of Psychoanalysis of the German Psychoanalytical Association. His training psychoanalyst was Dr. Theodor Reik. He had a private practice as a psychoanalyst in Madrid and in Paris and, since 1939, he has practiced in Buenos Aires. Dr. Garma was the founder of the Argentine Psychoanalytic Association, the Institute of Psychoanalysis and the "Revista de Psicoanalisis." He has been a Sloan Visiting Professor of the Menninger School of Psychiatry in Topeka, Kansas, and University professor at the University of Belgrano in Buenos Aires. He is the author of eleven books, two of which deal with the psychoanalysis of dreams.

John H. Padel, M.R.C.Psych., who formerly taught classical languages and literature, is now a psychiatrist and psychoanalyst and a founding member of the Royal College of Psychiatrists. Besides practicing privately in London, he is Deputy to the Director of the London Clinic of Psychoanalysts, Lecture and Hon. Staff member of the Tavistock Institute of Human Relations, Senior Tutor at the Institute of Psychiatry and Hon. Consultant at the Maudsley Hospital, London. He has written comprehensively on Shakespeare's sonnets.

Edward C. Whitmont, M.D., a founding member of the International Association of Analytical Psychology and of the C.G. Jung Training Center of New York, is a practicing analyst in New York City. He received his medical degree from the University of Vienna in 1936 and was trained in analytical psychology in the United States and Europe. Currently, he is a trustee and faculty member of the C.G. Jung Training Center. He is the author of many articles and of *The Symbolic Quest.*

FOREWORD

MONTAGUE ULLMAN, M.D.

There is a timeliness to the idea of bringing together leading represent-atives of classical, derivative and divergent schools and having them define their positions around the theory and practice of dream work. Drs. Fosshage and Loew approach this task with a clearly defined purpose, a carefully de-veloped strategy for achieving it and the happy selection of contributors well suited to carry it out. The result is that they have succeeded admirably in what they set out to do, namely, to clarify and compare the theories and clini-cal uses of dreams as presented by outstanding representatives of six major psychotherapeutic persuasions. Working with the same set of dreams, each respondent develops his theoretical and clinical statement in a way that pro-vides the reader with a succinct summary of each point of view as well as a valid base for their comparison. This comparative assessment, long overdue, is one that the reader will be tempted to carry on by himself as he witnesses these six clinicians at work. The way is paved for this by the judicious and ap-preciative comparison and integration offered by the editors in the final chapter.

Not only have a variety of approaches flourished in recent years but de-velopments outside the clinical arena are also pressing for a fresh perspective. The normative data available from the laboratory establish the dreaming phase of the sleep-dream cycle as a regularly recurring, biologically con-trolled, universal dimension of human existence. Classical theory has had to undergo basic modifications consequent to these discoveries. The shifts and changes that have taken place have resulted in a greater accommodation to other points of view, particularly those emphasizing more active here-and-now approaches. Following Freud's enduring discovery of the clinical useful-ness of dreams, but sharply eschewing his metapsychology, these recent approaches have investigated the healing potential of dream work in their own way.

Another feature of the current scene is the growing public interest in dreams and ways of working with them. Dream books and dream dictionaries no longer suffice to meet the need of the increasing number of people who seek to connect effectively and affectively with the images they create in their dreams. The question arises as to how this need can be met by the pro-fessional strategies that have evolved in clinical dream work. Are we dealing with such qualitatively different circumstances that it would be inappropriate to expect any carry-over from the clinical to the lay scene? Might not the converse be said, that the measure of a clinical approach lies in the degree to which it can be useful to the layman and lend itself to the non-clinical pursuit of the dream? Is there a way of looking at dreams that makes sense to the non-professional as well as the professional? Can the gap be closed between clinical and non-clinical dream work? My own position is that dream theories are no more than waking metaphors for expressing, in highly condensed language, the therapist's preferred way of seeing the patient's predicament. When there is a good fit between the therapist's metaphorical construct and the metaphors of the dream imagery, there is a sense of contact between the dreamer and the therapist and the exchange has a liberating impact on the dreamer. The therapist's theoretical position is relevant only to the extent that it stimulates this dual response.

Dreams reflect current concerns. They integrate past data with recent experience and express the information metaphorically in the form of visual images. If we accept these premises we can then work with a non-technical view of the dream outside the consulting room as well as within it. Professional help is indicated when self-deceptive strategies are so intrusive that the dreamer is not open to what is coming through in his dream. Therapeutic technique provides us with an instrument for cutting through these systems of self-deception. Confusion arises in the mind of the public when these specialized techniques and the theory behind them are also looked upon as essential to dream work. Professional knowledge and technique may be a necessary precursor to effective dream work with patients. More to the point, however, is that dreaming is a natural event and that working with dreams is an ability that can be nurtured in an appropriate social setting.

The writers for this volume are all clinicians concerned with the dream as a therapeutic instrument. Freud called attention to the work involved in transforming a dream into a therapeutically useful experience. An appropriate division of labor had to be set up between dreamer and respondent. The dreamer provided the associative context. The more emotionally removed position of the respondent enabled him to see relationships that were not apparent to the dreamer and to provide interpretive comments. It is important to emphasize that a social process is essential to effective dream work. Dreams are a most private, intimate and personal experience, but paradoxically, they can be fully realized only through a social process. None of the contributors disagree on the importance of a social process to dream work. They do differ in the way they define the functional nature of that process. This stems from the way they define a single crucial issue. Are dreams disguised ways of releasing tension or are they self-confrontations, calling attention to neglected, denied or suppressed aspects of ourselves? Are the images meant to be revealing or concealing? Although several of the writers derive their views from the classical theory of disguise, most of the others have gravitated, in greater or lesser measure, toward an appreciation of the revelatory power of the images that make up the manifest content.

The role of the therapist is defined by whichever view is embraced. For those who believe that dreams are disguised messages that are difficult to decode, there is a need for an expert decoder. Working within the framework of classical analytic theory, these therapists are in the tradition of interpreters of the dream that began with the priests of old. The assumption is that certain well-defined unconscious processes have the effect of concealing from the dreamer his struggle with unacceptable wishes and impulses. These unconscious processes must be reversed in order to expose the underlying conflict. The therapist starts with an a priori frame of reference which is used as a template that allows specified meanings to emerge.

For those who believe that dreams are self-confronting, a different role is assigned to the therapist. The images have to be amplified and experienced as living parts of the self. There is no need for an interpreter. There is, however, a need for a helper or guide. The therapist works with the dreamer toward an exegesis of those aspects of the dreamer's life that are depicted in the dream but are not attended to in waking reality.

Having these views in juxtaposition in this volume highlights the vulnerability of each. In applying classical and derivative theories one runs the risk of misusing the dream in support of the theory. At the other extreme too great a concern with the sanctity of the dream state may limit the exploration of its therapeutic value for the waking state.

An important issue stemming from these diverse approaches is the role and value of theory itself in relation to dreams. We find ourselves faced with two extreme positions. At one pole psychoanalytic theory is jettisoned completely (Boss); at the other it is accepted unquestioningly and psychoanalytic therapy is considered the most favorable setting for the interpretation of dreams (Garma).

Scientific theories are often treated as established truths even though we know from historical experience that they are apt to be proven false and eventually replaced by new theories that are less false and therefore more true. Psychoanalytic theories, aspiring to scientific status, offer causal schema. Dream images, however, defy causality. They are novel effects thrown up by an infinity of circumstances and are not containable within limits set by our rational minds. They are closer to an art form than an object of scientific interest. Like a poem, a dream is a unique event. It is the embodiment of the dreamer's personal theory of his life as it is tested by a current predicament. Theoretical ideas from other sources can be only a rough guide to the dreamer's view of his own universe. The dream is painted on a canvas that is larger than waking life. Theories are derivative of a limited waking vision and no one theory can encompass all that a dream is. Unquestioned allegiance to a particular theory obscures the mystery, limits the range of possibilities and constrains the holder of that theory to settle for a partial view at the expense of openness to the whole.

The opportunity to witness multiple approaches in action bears this out. The reader will find himself facing the challenge to any single theoretical system after being witness to the therapeutic power of so many systems. Each one sounds reasonably convincing. All are different although the degree of difference varies considerably. In its own way each explicates the metaphorically expressed meaning embedded in the dream image. Each offers a different strategy for exploring this meaning. When the creative efforts of the therapist match the creatively expressed content of the dream we have a good fit. The dreamer feels this in his gut as he catches a glimpse of some of the unseen dimensions of his own life. The fact that there are many paths to this end should challenge the "rightness" of any one of them.

One conclusion to be drawn is that, regardless of theoretical orientation, dream work is enriched by a social process that involves input from diverse sources. If specific theories are not taken too literally, but are used as ways of generating metaphorically expressed meanings from the dream images, their differences can be reduced to a different clustering of metaphors offered for the dreamer's consideration. The brew is enriched by the blend, providing that we remember that it is the dreamer's taste that must prevail. New ideas about the dream images are always welcome since they increase the likelihood of the dreamer resonating to one or more of them. This exploration of the range of possibilities is an essential ingredient of any social process addressing itself to dream work.

No matter how captivated we may be by the theoretical orientation that most appeals to us, no one of us possesses the only reliable key to dream work. This view of the matter can be more rewarding than safeguarding the sanctity of individual theories. We then become more open to the richness that diversity offers. The only theory that should command our respect is the one embraced by the patient as he selects and rearranges his particular repertoire of social images in order to reflect the immediate predicament. The dreamer is the final arbiter of what is or is not right for him.

The multiplicity of approaches should not be cause for dismay. Taken separately, each approach seems like a logical, self-contained system. Considered together, each adds a significant dimension to dream work. Even though I was not in complete agreement with any one approach, I nevertheless felt enriched by the totality. Each contribution uncovered a nugget that might otherwise have gone unnoticed. If exposure to the various positions orients the reader toward greater flexibility about dream theory and tolerance for new ideas, then this book will have had a significant impact.

In practice there are probably as many approaches as there are practitioners. This would have been more apparent if the editors had chosen to select several members of one school to work on the same set of dreams. We may borrow from a theory but in its application it bears the stamp of our own individuality. Likewise, the dream bears the stamp of the dreamer's individuality. When theory commands more respect than the recognition of this individuality it is apt to intrude in an arbitrary way.

Medard Boss expresses these concerns most forcefully when he writes: "... all the hitherto current so-called depth psychology theories of the meaning of dreams do violence to our dreaming and to what appears in it. This violence is perpetrated through prejudgment about the character of our dreaming, dream beings and dream events, and the application of an abstract conceptual model for their understanding."

Regardless of whether one agrees with this statement and Boss' conviction that a phenomenological view should prevail over the "misleading theories of Freud, Adler and Jung," the question it raises concerning the applicability of theory to dream work has to be taken seriously. Working with our dream life is central to the therapeutic endeavor. Therapeutic systems may ultimately be judged by the sophistication, sensitivity and respect they bring to the task of distilling from the dream images the healing powers that lie within them. The dream is often looked upon as offering "material" for analysis. But the dream is a special kind of "material" if it can be considered "material" at all. It is totally a creation of the patient. It is an unobstructed view of the patient's universe. It is "pure patient," uncontaminated by waking state strategies of self-deception. It is unexplored territory that is easily claimed by the first theoretical explorers to stake out such a claim. Each theoretical flag that is planted, however, is planted on someone else's property, namely, the dreamer's. He may stand to gain by having this part of his psyche cut and tailored to a particular theoretical orientation, but he also stands to lose some of the unique quality of what he has created. Our goal should be to help the patient move in the direction of greater competence in working with his own dreams without stamping it with our trademark.

The consideration that each approach gives to the following issues may serve as a measure for their assessment:

To what extent is the dreamer helped to speak in his own idiom through the images he has created? Conversely, to what extent are theoretical constructs superimposed on the dream in such a way as to allow only those features of the dream to emerge that are congruent with them? Is the dream a thing-in-itself or does it become the springboard for a particular kind of therapeutic strategy? To what extent does the theoretical approach suggest ready-made answers and to what extent does it encourage a fresh empirical approach? The goal is to help the patient engage in a freeing way with the images he produces. Does the therapist allow this to happen or is this goal interfered with by the way the therapist uses a dream to validate his own theoretical formulations?

To what extent does the approach foster an expert role extrinsic to the dreamer and to what extent does it help the dreamer come into his own as the expert about his own dream? In the range of views presented here some writers rely more heavily than others on specialized terminology. How helpful is this in dream work which should speak directly to the expertness of the dreamer? The dreamer may deny his own expertness. If he does, that problem must be addressed without denying him the same degree of authority over his dream life that he has over his waking life.

To what extent does a particular approach foster a collaborative or an authoritarian atmosphere? Do we have two people in search of meaning or one person in search of a meaning known only to the other person? The feelings behind dream images surface much more readily in the framework of a genuinely collaborative relationship.

To what extent is the dream worked within a contextural vacuum, or to what extent is emphasis placed on establishing the connection between the dream images and the specific current life situation that shaped the dream and accounted for the time of its occurrence? The former leaves much more room for the theoretical projections of the therapist while the latter gives priority to the actual life experience of the dreamer.

All of the above issues may be reduced to a single question: In which theoretical system is the dreamer listened to most carefully?

The reader will have to judge the various approaches that are presented in this volume against these yardsticks, as well as others that may occur to him. If he reacts as I did he will be profoundly grateful to the editors for the sound and thoughtful way in which the material is organized and for the incisive and discerning assessment of the theory and practice of each of the six contributors.

Each of us has something to offer to anyone who shares a dream. Care must be taken not to offer too much, or too little, or become too enamored of our offering. It is the dreamer who should remain in charge of his dream images. To him belongs the excitement of seeing the images come to life as connections are made to waking life. When this happens the truths they convey become apparent and, along with them, the healing that comes from knowing the truth.

PREFACE

Dreams beckon understanding. Yet, the many psychoanalytic and psychotherapeutic schools approach dreams with different sets of theoretical assumptions, terminologies and interpretive techniques. The consequent discrepancies in understanding and evaluating dream material often appear to be confusing and irreconcilable. The paucity of communication among adherents of these different approaches prevents cross-fertilization and resolution of these discrepancies. The idea of having professionals from different psychotherapeutic orientations address and interpret the same dream series (an idea which germinated out of the senior author's, J.L.F., personal analytic experiences with both Jungian and Freudian analysts) is aimed at surmounting such barriers of communication through the clarification of the similarities and differences, as they appear not only in theory, but also in clinical application. In this way we wish to add impetus toward a new synthesis and a more comprehensive theory of dream interpretation.

This is a book on the theory and technique of dream interpretation. Throughout, we have emphasized the theory of dream interpretation, in contrast to the theory of dream formation, and its relationship to the analytic process. We hope that psychotherapists of all persuasions will find this investigation of six approaches useful in expanding and deepening the understanding of people through their dreams. We also hope that the interested lay person will benefit and potentially increase understanding of his or her internal life.

James L. Fosshage
Clemens A. Loew

ACKNOWLEDGMENTS

We especially wish to thank "Martha" for her generous participation in this project and her willingness to share her dreams.

We are most grateful to our contributors for their enthusiastic participation and for their openness in revealing their personal attitudes and working styles. Their responsiveness, often across continents, created a collaborative spirit in the development of this project. We thank Dr. Ullman for extending this spirit through his sharing of impressions and presentation of a valuable overview.

Our gratitude is extended to our fellow directors, students and faculty at the National Institute for the Psychotherapies for their interested support, and for generating an atmosphere of openness to both traditional and innovative approaches to psychotherapy.

In preparation of the manuscript, we offer special thanks to Judith Fosshage for her invaluable editorial assistance (and for her loving encouragement and support to the senior author); to Dr. Bertold Ringeisen for his able translation; to Karen Wachsman, N.I.P.'s registrar, for her gracious and efficient administrative handling of the correspondence and typing; to N.I.P.'s staff, Susan Dondey and Nancy Schulman for their ready responsiveness to typing requests; and to Andrea Miller and Joyce Romano for their most conscientious and relentless typing and proofreading of the manuscript. We extend our appreciation to Maurice Ancharoff, our publisher, who enthusiastically supported this project in its incipient stages.

Lastly, we wish to give special thanks to our analysts, who introduced us to the dream interpretive process, and in turn, to our patients who have shared with us their dreams and who have worked collaboratively with us to further the understanding of the dreaming process.

CONTENTS

DREAM INTERPRETATION

A Comparative Study

INTRODUCTION

JAMES L. FOSSHAGE, Ph.D.
and CLEMENS A. LOEW, Ph.D.

In his monumental work *The Interpretation of Dreams* (originally published 1900), Freud laid the foundation for the scientific investigation of dreams and elevated dreams to a unique position in the understanding of personality and psychopathology. The importance of dream interpretation for Freud is evident in his famous statement: *"The interpretation of dreams is the royal road to a knowledge of the unconscious activities of the mind"* (p. 608). Accordingly, dream interpretation became an essential part of the psychoanalytic process and for years served as the hallmark of psychoanalysis.

Since Freud's early work, Freudian psychoanalysis has undergone considerable theoretical change in both personality theory and technique. Other now well-known psychoanalytic schools have also emerged, such as the neo-Freudian (culturalist) and existential (phenomenological) approaches. In addition, beginning with Jung, one of Freud's earliest protégés, other widely respected psychotherapeutic camps have been established, with their respective theories, training institutes, societies and professional followers.

Throughout these theoretical evolutions and new beginnings, dreams and dream interpretation have consistently remained one of the most accessible and utilizable roads to the internal life of our patients and ourselves. Whether one maintains that dreams are the "royal road" or considers dreams to be a simple pathway, the use of dreams continues to be an important if not predominant part of the psychotherapeutic context. Accordingly, numerous publications have aimed at ferreting out the meaning of dreams, working with traditional and innovative theories, refining the old and developing new techniques for the dream interpretive process.

Moreover, an intensive physiological investigation of the dreaming state has developed. Following Aserinsky and Kleitman's methodological breakthrough in 1953, over twenty years of electroencephalographically monitored sleep studies have established a distinct physiological nonwaking state wherein most dreams occur. This nonwaking state has been referred to as REM (Rapid Eye Movements) sleep and as the D-state. REM sleep consists of "(1) rapid eye movements, (2) a distinctive low voltage desynchronized cortical EEG pattern, (3) increased variability in respiration rate, (4) increased variability in pulse rate, (5) increased blood pressure, (6) decreased muscle tonus, (7) high brain temperature and metabolic rate, (8) increased variability in arousal threshold, (9) full or partial penile erection in males, and (10) dreaming" (Jones, 1970, p. 1). However, despite the vast increase in knowledge of the physiological processes involved (for summaries of this research, see Jones, 1970, and Kramer, 1969), the contribution of the REM studies to our psychological understanding of the dream drama remains limited. Snyder (1969) makes this point:

It seems safe to agree with Kety that physiology is never likely to identify unique correlates of individual thoughts, memories, or dreams; yet I feel equally confident that we are on the threshold of learning much more about the general physical correlates of such mental events and that progress thus far made toward a physiology of dreaming is not likely to be wholly irrelevant. If I may misappropriate Dr. Lewin's conception of the "dream screen," I can conceive that in some sense the primitive biological process of the REM state periodically provides the "energy" to illuminate the screen as well as the projector mechanism to crank the film, and possibly the film itself; but that, for reasons we cannot yet comprehend, all of this would go on regardless of whether the film contained the meaningful images we call dreams. For physiological answers to such questions as how the scripts of dreams are written, or the film produced, or

why the entire process takes place, we can only wait hopefully and expectantly, but still very much in the dark
(pp. 23–24).

In light of these diverse developments there is presently a
need to clarify, compare and ultimately synthesize the various
psychoanalytic and psychotherapeutic approaches to understanding and interpreting dreams. Thus the purpose of this
book is to clarify and compare the theories and clinical uses of
dreams as presented by outstanding representatives of six major
psychotherapeutic persuasions. To accomplish our purpose we
presented to each contributor background material of a patient
in psychoanalysis together with a series of six dreams which
the patient reported during the course of her treatment. We
asked each representative to present: (1) an overview of the basic theory and techniques of dream interpretation from his
respective point of view; (2) his understanding, hypotheses or
interpretation of the patient's dreams; and (3) a description of
his hypothetical clinical use of these dreams. Since each contributor responded to the same set of dreams, a common basis
for comparison was established.

Needless to say, this is a hypothetical case for our contributors in that the patient in the flesh and the moment-to-
moment ongoing process are absent. Understandably, each contributor wanted more associations and wanted to be more fully
"there." Nevertheless, the contributors have shared their associations and hypotheses, the way they would perceive,
cognitively structure and work with a dream, all of which is revelatory of the tools they would use to approach any dream in
the psychotherapeutic situation.

Theories of personality structure, personality development, psychopathology and theories of dreams, however
formulated, affect—indeed direct—our therapeutic understandings and interventions. Yet in actual clinical practice our
diverse theories may be so modified and molded by the "moment" that therapeutic encounters may have more in common
than we would expect. By focusing on both the theories and

applications of dream interpretation we hope to clarify the actual theoretical and applied differences among these six approaches.

We selected those psychotherapeutic approaches which, in our opinion, have made significant contributions to the theory and technique of dream interpretation. The approaches we chose are: Freudian, Jungian, Culturalist, Object Relational, Phenomenological and Gestalt.

Each of these schools has its respective terminology and theories of personality, psychopathology and dream interpretation. Despite a theoretical cohesiveness, each of these approaches includes a greater or lesser variety of intraschool differences. Accordingly, no one person can totally represent a school of thought. However, our primary purpose is not to present the "exact" approach of each school—something which does not, in fact, exist—but rather to present and compare a sample of applications of the major approaches to dreams. Through clarification and comparison of these approaches we hope this book will serve in the pursuit of a new, more comprehensive theory and technique of dream interpretation.

Pertaining to intraschool differences, we decided to include separately object relations theory, although it is an essential part of Freudian psychoanalysis. Object relations theory centers on the bonds between people in contrast to instinct theory, which focuses on the need to reduce instinctual tension. British object relations theorists have stressed the importance of early object relations prior to the onset of the classical Oedipus complex. The British school had its beginnings with Klein and has changed significantly through the contributions of Winnicott, Fairbairn and Guntrip, among others. Because we feel that these contributions represent a major crosscurrent in psychoanalytic thought with significant implications for dream interpretation, we chose to include a British object relations analyst in addition to the Freudian.

We are most fortunate and grateful to have had for this project the participation of representatives who are most outstanding and well-known for their work with dreams. They are:

Angel Garma, M.D., Freudian; Edward C. Whitmont, M.D., Jungian; Walter Bonime, M.D., with Florence Bonime, Culturalist; John H. Padel, M.R.C. Psych., Object Relations; Medard Boss, M.D., and Brian Kenny, M.D., Phenomenology; and Rainette Eden Fantz, Ph.D., Gestalt.[1]

Each school offers its unique angle of understanding and working with dreams. No school can justifiably claim to have the truth. It is our conviction that any serious investigator of dreams must leave the confines of any one orthodoxy (a task which is genuinely difficult) in order to study and immerse himself or herself in the variety of approaches. Only in this way will our comprehension of dreams deepen and enhance our ability to aid the many different persons who seek psychotherapy. We hope that this book will further this pursuit.

---

[1]We have listed the approaches in an order which approximates their historical development.

REFERENCES

Freud, S. (1900). *The Interpretation of Dreams.* In *Standard Edition,* Vol. 4 & 5. London: Hogarth Press, 1953.

Jones, R.M. (1970). *The New Psychology of Dreaming.* New York: Grune & Stratton.

Kramer, M., ed. (1969). *Dream Psychology and the New Biology of Dreaming.* Springfield, Ill.: Charles C. Thomas.

Snyder, F. (1969). The physiology of dreaming. In *Dream Psychology and the New Biology of Dreaming,* ed. M. Kramer. Springfield, Ill.: Charles C. Thomas.

CHAPTER ONE

The Case Of Martha As Presented To Each Contributor

JAMES L. FOSSHAGE, Ph.D.

CASE DESCRIPTION[1]

Martha is a single, thirty-three-year-old woman who is an assistant magazine editor. At the time of her initial interview five years ago, her appearance was neat and well-groomed, her dress slightly old-fashioned. She was overweight and self-consciously attempted to conceal the fact by draping her coat across her lap for the entire interview. Her face was attractive and showed some sparkle, although it was struck with conflict. She appeared anxious and at times was tearful. Her manner was generally controlled. Her speech was articulate and that of a bright person, but painstakingly slow and careful in what appeared to be an attempt to control emotion and to be exact.

Presenting Problems

Martha sought psychotherapeutic help because "I realized that I wasn't controlling my life. I don't seem to be making decisions. I make decisions, but I don't follow through and don't have the energy to achieve what I want."

---

[1]Because the focus of this book is on dreams and what dreams can tell us about the patient, and because we wish to avoid inserting our conceptual bias, we have chosen to provide only a sketchy outline of Martha and her background, but one which will give, we think, an adequate context for dream interpretation.

In the same spirit, we have presented after each dream the patient's most immediate and spontaneous associations. Those associations achieved through exploration have not been reported.

She felt "in desperate need of help." She had been laid off from an editorial job four months earlier. She was looking, but despairing and at times not caring about finding other work. She was also enrolled in a part-time graduate program. Despite a good academic record, she complained of feeling anxious, unsure of herself and often depressed. Extreme anxiety during the preparation for and completion of a final exam precipitated her seeking help.

With intense feelings of shame and at times tearfully, Martha spoke about her compulsive eating sprees. They occurred when she was either depressed or intensely anxious. She said that when working on school assignments, anxiety became intense enough "to drive me to the refrigerator." She felt toward her eating bouts a sense of helplessness and hopelessness and perceived herself in piglike images.

Martha was approximately forty-five pounds overweight. She remembered becoming conscious of her weight as a problem around the age of eight. As an adult, her weight had varied from twenty-five to sixty-five pounds above her normal weight. Medical examinations revealed no determining factors, except that her mother and sister were also substantially overweight.

She also complained of being too emotional. Tears, anger and anxiety burst upon her for reasons unknown to her. She experienced again considerable shame and a sense of helplessness and bewilderment over these perplexing outbursts. Martha mentioned that she had a phobic fear of cockroaches. She described how the appearance of roaches terrified her into flight. Her initial fears began when she was a child living in a New York City apartment which was infested with roaches.

Family History

Martha's parents were Jewish immigrants who brought with them in attitudes and values much of the Old World. She had two brothers and one sister, and was the youngest by six years. Family ties were strong, but she felt closest to her younger brother, who is now a married, professional man.

Her father, in his mid-sixties, was a retired shopkeeper. She described him as an uneducated but intelligent man with a good sense of humor. She was repulsed by his poor personal hygiene and "boorish" eating habits. She was also often embarrassed by her father's frequent exaggeration in his storytelling.

She described her mother as evasive, overly involved and subtly intrusive. She mentioned that she avoided telling her mother anything personal, for her mother seemed to thrive on the information and would tell anyone. Her mother was easily hurt and tearful, and rarely became angry.

Demonstration of affection between her mother and father was reportedly nonexistent. Her mother was guarded and evasive when it came to discussions of menstruation and sex. In the presence of her family, Martha felt completely inhibited in showing any affection to a male.

Her first sexual experience occurred in her early twenties, while she was abroad for a year. It was an enjoyable experience in the context of a close relationship with a man several years younger than herself. She was orgasmic and felt free.

Treatment

Martha began psychoanalysis five years ago on a twice-a-week basis and is continuing presently. For the past two years she has also been in group psychotherapy.

Life Context During Treatment Period

At the beginning of treatment Martha had been out of work for four months. Three months later she successfully found another editorial position, which was, in fact, an improvement over her previous job. She has remained in this position for the duration of treatment. During the past year she for the first time began to feel genuinely competent in her work, but then became somewhat disenchanted with its financial and intellectual limitations. Approximately five months after Dream No. 6 she decided to apply to law school and has since been accepted.

During the treatment period Martha has continued to date sporadically. However, at this time she is far more open in exploring relationships with men and in expressing her desires for a relationship with a man and for marriage.

Despite some interpersonal conflicts and difficulties, she has had, before and during treatment, a number of close relationships with women.

DREAMS OF MARTHA

On the average, Martha reported a dream every other session. The six dreams selected occurred over a period of four and a half years. The criteria used for the selection of these particular dreams were:

1. The patient's first dream presented in treatment: many professionals of various orientations emphasize the importance of the first dream.
2. Dreams at intervals from seven to nine months which might indicate a direction in the patient's psychotherapy.
3. Several dreams which included the cockroach image in order to offer illumination of one of the patient's presenting complaints, namely, her

cockroach phobia.
4. Dreams 5 and 6 were included because of their powerful imagery.
5. Dream 6 was experienced by the dreamer as a breakthrough.

Dream No. 1 (first dream in treatment during the second month of therapy):

I was sitting on a rickety, shaky balcony. Everybody was dressed in period costumes with pantaloons and long dresses. I was the opposite of what I actually look like. I was tall and lanky like Katharine Hepburn, but not particularly attractive. I looked down below and there were explosions and black clouds of smoke. I was watching from the balcony. There were people jumping off the balcony and running off toward the explosions. I called out to one person not to go because it looked dangerous, but she ran off. I stayed in that chair for twenty years.

When I decided to come down, I was fifty years old and all of that activity was over. I had no emotions, and when I went down, I looked quite a distance. Before I went down, I had to get out of the chair, which was on a shaky and narrow balcony. I needed some help to get out of the chair. Everybody seems to be young and I'm regarded as old. One young man wearing an open jacket, which just now reminds me of your jacket [referring to the therapist's sports coat], graciously came up. He held out his hand and helped me to jump down. I could jump because fifty isn't really that old.

I was wearing a wedding gown. My husband [the patient is single] had gone off. The Prime Minister climbed up and asked me to marry him. But I refused.

I was now on the street walking with the people. My wedding gown was out-of-date, so I cut off a little to make it shorter. The people were nice and friendly. I asked about children and husbands, but everybody was dead. They did have grandchildren and nieces, so I was pleased.

Associations:

The only thing dangerous was the descent.

You know, being a fifty-year-old was a privileged position with not much responsibility. People smiled the way they treat someone who is older. You're indulged...treated special; it's the way I felt overseas. It's tempting.

I used to find marriage frightening, but not now. I didn't get married on two occasions, both times to foreigners. I didn't want to. All my feelings weren't there. The first time it was too soon; I would never have become a person. I barely escaped. That's one of the reasons I came to therapy. The second time was two years ago.

I think of therapy. If I didn't come now, when would I? I came when I realized I should.

Dream No. 2 (seven months later):

I came home and went into my room. My mother was in there, going through my purse. She didn't look like my mother. I didn't want this, and I told her to go away or get out. She had found a check written to you [the therapist]. I was angry and wanted to express more anger than I felt. I screamed. It never seemed to be loud enough. I grabbed her by the hair and threw her out. She landed at the bathroom door and fell. I locked my door and felt afraid that she had hurt herself. I sat down on the bed, but my mother came in again right through the locked door. She asked if I wanted anything—that was more like my mother, solicitous. The only difference is that she didn't sound wounded.

Associations:

My scream just didn't seem loud enough. It was as if I didn't have the physical capacity. I felt helpless in the face of an advancing army. When my mother starts sorting things in my room, I get angry even if I don't care what's out. There is no way to make her observe the integrity of my things.

The other day I thought that I was expressing more anger than I felt toward you [the therapist]. Each time it sounded more hollow. It was such a struggle, like locking horns. I felt that I was forcing you to answer questions and clear up the confusion.

Dream No. 3 (nine months later):

I walked into a room and my mother was standing there naked. She explained that she had told me something that wasn't true because she thought the truth might frighten me: that a cockroach had walked across her pubic hair. I thought she was right—it would have frightened me.

Associations:

I thought of my fear of cockroaches, the old neighborhood, and of a game I once played with some children a little older than I. One at a time, the girls went into a room where some boys waited. I went into the room when it was my turn. The boys tickled me and then I went out. After the game, they all laughed. One of the boys said that they had just tickled me.

Dream No. 4 (nine months later):

The thing occurred in a dream that I'm most frightened of.

I was in the bathtub and a cockroach was there. It was half dead. It got on my leg. I didn't panic. I got out. It crawled onto the wall near my bed. A girl was there and she went over to kill it, but it was too big and wouldn't quit. I took a can of spray and gave it one long spray. As I sprayed, it got bigger, turned into a chicken, then into a dog. I stopped spraying since I didn't want to kill a dog. It had some human characteristics, too. It asked to leave. I opened the door and apologized for spraying.

Associations:

I had survived the worst cockroach situation, to have one on me.

When I think of chicken, I think of my mother's Friday supper. We had chicken every Friday.

I don't like dogs. When they're near, they slobber on you. They're a threat to pantyhose. They're unpredictable and they jump even in play.

Dream No. 5 (almost two years later):

I was living with my parents somewhere. There was a fellow there who was somewhere at a nearby island. It was a different type of environment, but not too far from where I was. I was supposed to join him there in a few days for the weekend. Before he left for this island, he cut off his penis and a nipple of my breast and we exchanged them. This was supposed to be temporary. And they were supposed to reattach themselves.

I also had the razor blade. It wasn't painful. I didn't want my mother to see the razor blade and penis in my hand. If she did see, she didn't bother me. I was wearing a loose shirt. The breast was healing, but it was irritating me. If that was bothering me, he must be really uncomfortable. Was it healing right? I was supposed to join him on Friday night. I'd rather have joined him on Saturday, but I was concerned about getting the penis back for it might start rotting. I had to get it back to him.

Associations:

It was in my charge, a pressure, a responsibility. I didn't know why he had done it. It was a burden, like walking around carrying too many packages.

Dream No. 6 (six months later):

My friend Eileen takes me to an enormous building, very old and dingy. It looks like an old railroad station but is supposed to be a cultural or amusement area. Although it had been in operation a long time, I didn't know about it.

When we enter the building, we go down hundreds or thousands of feet, down many, many steps. The inside is rather like a shell, very dark, and if you fell off the staircase you could drop down to the bottom.

When we get to the bottom, it is even darker, like the basement of a big building. Some men are laying a cement floor in one room. The atmosphere is a little creepy, but I'm not frightened.

In the middle of the basement is an open place with sunlight. It seems to be an amusement area. People are there, and there are amusement park rides. I see a little girl, perhaps five or six years old. She is a pretty child, with a round full face, dark hair with bangs, and dark eyes. She may have come in spite of her mother, who tried to keep her back. I spend some time with her, and, after getting to know her a while, I say to her, "You're not evil, no matter what your mother told you."

I start back up to the ground level alone. It's a long way back up and sometimes a little dangerous. I walk cautiously but again I'm not really frightened.

When I get out, I realize that it's early and I could have stayed longer, but it's a long trip down again and it doesn't pay to go back so late in the afternoon.

Associations:

She was a solid, likable child.

When I woke up, I was struck by what I had said to the child. I felt it applied to me.

CHAPTER TWO

Freudian Approach[1]

ANGEL GARMA, M.D.

BASIC THEORY OF THE MEANING OF DREAMS

What are dreams? From the standpoint of psychiatry one defines them as "hallucinations—nearly always visual hallucinations—which occur in an individual when he is asleep." A definition of dreams from the standpoint of psychoanalysis proves more complicated, thus justifying a step-by-step approach.

Samples of Dreams

The two dreams discussed below derive from two unrelated men who had a similar conflict. During the day preceding his dream(s) each man had shown interest in a woman other than his own wife, a fact which was noticed with displeasure by the latter.

One of the dreams occurred during World War II at the time of the German occupation of Paris. A man who was married to a woman with a German name had in a previous social gathering courted a French woman. He was aware of how unhappy his wife appeared to be, which made him feel guilty and caused him to sleep restlessly. He described the following dream:

"I was in Paris and German spies watched me."

---

[1] The theoritical section of this chapter was translated by Dr. Bertold Ringeisen.

To one who knows what happened at the social gathering the dream proves comprehensible. Paris represents the French woman and the German spies represent the man's wife, who had a German surname and was very watchful and disagreeable with him during that gathering.

The dream of the second man stems from a similar, though more intense conflict situation. His attraction to a blond woman was being noticed by the woman with whom he had been living for years and whom he did not want to give up. This conflict caused him to dream the following:

"I had a smaller and gilded television set. It transmitted in colors. But I also kept my old television set, which was noisy."

During the analytic session the man narrated his dream and referred to his situation of infidelity. This led to the interpretation of the dream, in which the two television sets symbolized the two women. One of the sets was newer, gilded, smaller, and transmitted in colors—all of which alludes to the blond woman, whom he had known for a short time and who awakened in him a minor interest although she was very flashy. The old television set symbolized the other woman, whom he had known a much longer time. Its noisiness symbolized in an attenuated fashion the protests of this woman when she became aware of the man's outside interest.

When one knows the antecedents and the interpretations of both dreams, it is easy to deduce that they proceed from distressing conflicts experienced by the men in question. Their infidelity made them feel guilty. In order to better understand the dreams one must add that they felt guilt—even though not consciously—toward not only their wives but the psychoanalyst, before whom they reacted in a childlike fashion as if he were a severe father who would prohibit their amorous and intellectual liberties.

When the above-mentioned men were awake, they succeeded in repressing their guilt conflicts. But during sleep, as normally happens, their powers of repression diminished in intensity. While they were asleep, the guilt conflicts created for them a traumatic psychic (conflict) situation, entailing painful tensions striving toward the conscious level and thus a bothersome awakening. In order to prevent this, they strained in their unconscious to mask the nature of the conflicts. Unconsciously, therefore, they created dreams in which the coveted forbidden women and the harassing ones turned into something which for them was relatively indifferent: the town of Paris, the German spies, the two television sets. Then, when the painful nature of the conflicts made itself known in a masked state which consciously could not be understood, the men could continue sleeping while they benefited from an apparent tranquillity.

Terminology and Psychoanalytic Definition of Dreams

The preceding examples represent a most essential part of the psychoanalytic theory of dreams. Some psychoanalytic terms will help to better explain the theory.

Manifest content is what the dreamer perceives consciously from his dream. It is the narration of the dream by the dreamer, told as he perceived it. *Latent content* is the dream's hidden meaning and motivation, which are unconscious. It is what one discovers to be the meaning of the dream once the *interpretation* has been reached. In the latent or unconscious content of the dream are found the conflicts which have brought it about. When the individual is asleep and there is no power to repress them, the conflicts create in the unconscious a situation filled with painful tensions which cannot be resolved or adequately worked through. Because of these characteristics, such a situation is called a *traumatic situation*. In dreaming the individual disguises his unconscious traumatic situations.

In the interpretation of a dream one moves from its manifest content to its latent content. The same step, taken in the opposite direction, constitutes the disguise of the dream, or the *dream work*. This is the work the dreamer unconsciously creates—beginning with the latent content of the dream, or his *genetic traumatic conflicts*, which makes itself conscious to him as the manifest content. *Censorship* is the psychic function that impedes the passing of painful unconscious psychic content to consciousness. But the content slips through this censorship because of its disguise.

What are dreams, psychoanalytically speaking? As exemplified by the two narrated dreams above, they are conscious hallucinations of a sleeping individual which result from unconscious disguising of repressed traumatic conflicts. This definition describes the essence of the dream, but it is incomplete since it does not clear up psychoanalytically the important phenomenon of hallucination.

Genetic Traumatic Conflicts of Dreams

The conflicts which generate dreams are of a very distinct type and must always have definite characteristics. They must be of great affective intensity, and they must have repressed components. In addition, the individual who experiences them must unconsciously feel incapable of resolving them.

These characteristics indicate unmistakably that in all cases, without exception, dreams deal with psychic contents which are very important to the individual. This is true even when dreams in their manifest content may have a banal appearance and the individual may not consider them important.

The conflicts which generate dreams are always repressed conflicts or always have repressed components, that is, contents which the individual is unconsciously prohibited from considering consciously. Such is the case for those conflicts which arise from the Oedipus complex. Each individual has internal prohibitions—unconsciously intensified by the threat of castration—from bringing to the conscious level his genital desires toward his parent of the opposite sex and his death wishes toward his parent of his own sex. A similar type of internal prohibition against knowledge exists in relation to many other conflicts.

Conflicts of great affective intensity—with components contradictory among themselves which the individual can neither resolve nor work through adequately—create in the mind painful tensions which form traumatic situations. The dreams themselves constitute disguises of such traumatic situations or traumatic conflicts.

The creation of any sort of dream is initiated when the circumstances of the day reactivate in the individual a conflict with unconscious components. This is called an *actual conflict*. In the unconscious mind far fewer delimitations between the various representations exist as compared to the conscious mind. The communication and interchange among the representations are very easily established. These communications are barely comprehensible at the conscious level. When the individual sleeps (and also in part when he is awake), these possibilities of communication cause the actual conflict, activated by the circumstances of the day, to bring forth an echo of other related conflicts in the unconscious. Thus memories of previous similar conflicts are reactivated in the individual. Among these, childhood conflicts decisive for the formation of the special personality of the individual are of great importance. In this regard, one must bear in mind that these childhood conflicts are responsible for leading the individual to unconsciously seek out the special circumstances of the day which activate his actual conflict. This regressive reactivation of conflicts goes back, probably in all dreams, to the very trauma of birth.

The conscious and especially unconscious regressive reactivation of conflicts triggered by the actual conflicts that give rise to the dream brings with it many conflicts which intervene in the genesis and structuring of each dream. Therefore, these many conflicts are the ones that succeed in forming the manifest content in disguised form.

The regressive reactivation of conflicts starts when the individual is awake, but it is more intense when the individual is asleep since it is then that his mind regresses. This fact explains why in psychoanalytic treatment a spontaneous dream of an individual is much more valuable than any other product he could invent while awake.

Human conduct is determined by instinctual behavior, sexual (in a very broad sense) as well as aggressive, which has been deflected from its primitive goals by the influence of various circumstances such as the arising of relations among individuals. Herein is a source of psychic conflicts. Therefore, during the regressive activation of conflicts, primitive sexual and aggressive behavior intervene intensely in the genesis and structuring of dreams. Of this type are the derivatives of the Oedipus complex and those of the first relations of an individual with his mother.

In the constitution of the genetic traumatic conflicts of dreams, thoughts referring to death—to total death as well as to what one may call partial death—also emerge in fantasy when the individual sees himself compelled to renounce some of his instinctual desires. When this happens, the individual renounces in a triple aspect: he renounces an instinctual satisfaction, the object necessary to attain the satisfaction and a part of himself which is related to both of these. The castration complex of the individual constitutes an aspect of these representations of a partial death. In dreams representations are very frequently manifest in disguise.

An individual is pushed toward satisfaction, renunciation and modification of his instincts by the influence of his objects, of his individual and hereditary present or past which left traces in his psychic make-up. In the same way the conscience of an individual—which in psychoanalysis is called the *superego* and is largely unconscious—derives in part from the behavior of the individual's parents toward him during early childhood.

The above can also be expressed in another psychoanalytic formulation. In the unconscious of an individual there exist active representations of the real and imagined parents in childhood and also those persons who are psychically important, e.g., authorities substituting for the parents in later life. Psychoanalytically, these are *internalized parents* or *internal objects*. Such unconscious representations have great influence on the conduct of the individual and therefore on the formation of his traumatic conflicts. This explains why their presence is often repeated in the content of dreams.

Regression to the Unconscious Mind in the Genesis of Dreams

The strange aspect of dreams is determined by their construction in the unconscious, which is the active part of the mind when the individual is asleep.

The unconscious mind has its own characteristics, distinct from those of the conscious mind. It is something like a more primitive mind which is close to that of a child or a savage. Among the specific characteristics are the absence of abstract representations and the fact that the different psychic representations are more connected among each other than in the conscious mind and therefore can easily be substituted for and condensed. The conflicts with repressed components—which have been reactivated by the events of the day—emerge when the individual is asleep, because it is then that the repressive forces of the individual diminish in intensity. But also during sleep the individual abandons consciousness for unconsciousness. Therefore his active conflicts must assume aspects which are to be found in this latter state. Thus during the individual's sleep—and with it the process of regressing to the unconscious mind—the formulation of the conscious part of his reactivated conflicts must be translated into the terminology of the unconscious.

The consequence of this translation is—in the formulation of the conflict—the disappearance of abstract representations and their substitution by representations of a concrete type which stand for them. Therefore, dreams are eminently concrete. For example, an individual with instinctual urgencies does not dream that he is hungry or that he is sexually aroused—thus expressed in a general way—but sees himself concretely in front of definite food or visualizes himself caressing a woman.

This special formulation in dreams arises from the passing of representations from the conscious mind to the unconscious mind. Such a process is known as *concretization* or *dramatization*, just as in the theater any kind of abstract thesis is expressed in some concrete conflict of the players.

By the same token, as dreams are elaborated in the unconscious mind, besides being concrete they are usually short. The different contents of the traumatic conflicts manifest themselves *condensed* into few images, each containing various meanings which can even be contradictory. Thus in the second of the above-mentioned dreams a single image of a new, smaller, gilded television set that transmits in color expressed in a condensed form many considerations of an individual toward a desired woman.

In the unconscious mind temporal circumstances are taken less into consideration than in the conscious mind. Therefore—but above all because dreams express conflicts of the individual which potentially are permanently active—the manifest content of dreams occurs almost always in the present tense. In interpreting a dream one must place the genetic traumatic conflict in relation to its unleashing circumstances but without forgetting its active potentiality in the actual moment.

When an individual is asleep, he wants tranquillity. But his reactivated traumatic conflicts rob him of this, with the result that he finds them disquieting. It has already been shown that during sleep the individual is ruled by his unconscious mind and that therefore the content of his conflicts must be translated into a new terminology. In this endeavor the sleeping individual does not intend to be logical or intelligent. Nor does he try to understand himself or be understood when he later describes his dream. On the contrary, the disguise of the conflicts is attractive to him in order to best continue sleeping peacefully. Because of this motive and the fact that the individual while sleeping is thinking, in his unconscious mind, during the process of translating the conscious to the unconscious, he finds it natural to refer to illogical and unusual connections which come from the unconscious mind.

When these connections created by the unconscious mind are discovered in the interpretation of dreams, there are often comical effects. Connections of the same type are usually found in jokes. What makes one laugh is the unexpected inclusion of a type of behavior, proper for the unconscious mind, in the course of conscious logical reasoning.

Thus in the dream of one individual a fragment of the manifest content referred to a "review" and had the latent meaning that the dreamer was reviewing a matter that worried him. In a second case a fragment of an individual's manifest dream about "torpedoes" expressed his fear that one of his projects would be destroyed, i.e., that they would "torpedo" him. In a third case during the day two lady friends had been criticizing an absent person. The one who had shown herself more ruthless felt remorse during the night and dreamed about "two scissors," hers being "larger than the other"; the dream expressed in a disguised manner the traumatic conflict that provoked remorse in her for having been especially "cutting" in regard to an appreciated person. On another occasion, and proceeding from a like antecedent, the same woman had another dream in which a part referred to her "urinating"; one could deduce from the psychoanalytic session in which she told the dream that this element alluded to the conflict she experienced for having been "sh-sh-ing" ("goss-ip-ing").

The condensation which makes dreams short derives as well from the fact that the individual who sleeps wishes to dedicate the least possible time to his traumatic conflicts. The affective intensity and the traumatic situation that these create for him oblige him to occupy himself with them, but if the contents are condensed he can accomplish this more quickly. There is also another motive in the sense that in dreams various traumatic conflicts or various aspects of one and the same conflict are condensed. In agreement with the way the unconscious mind works, this type of condensation indicates that the conflicts or components of conflicts are interrelated. This provides valuable data for the understanding of the psychology of the dreaming person.

In juxtaposition to condensation is *splitting*. This also constitutes a means of expression of the unconscious mind. Splitting causes different affects, qualities or other attributes of the dreaming person or other individuals to be represented, especially if they are contradictory among themselves, through the presence in the dream of various persons or other contents, each endowed with some of the attributes. Although this representative technique increases the duration of the dream, which in principle does not result in pleasure, the dreaming person may well use it because when he splits what is distinct and even contradictory he diminishes the mental effort required for an inevitable discriminating effort.

Like the other functions of the unconscious mind, dramatization and condensation, splitting is not peculiar to dreams. One sees it, for example, in literature or mythology. Thus the splitting of an original person creates the contradictory personalities of the idealist Don Quixote and the materialist Sancho Panza, the king and his jester, Don Juan and his helper, or a god and his respective devil.

It is important to know that dreams are incapable of resolving psychic conflicts, although at times they produce such a distinct impression. Dreams limit themselves to exposing conflicts and to creating fantasies about them— arriving, at the most, at fictitious and deceptive solutions. When an individual can resolve in a certain way some of his conflicts, then they do not provoke traumatic psychic situations and therefore also are not brought up for dreaming.

Since the traumatic conflicts reactivated by the day's events are not resolved by dreaming, they continue to be active in the mind of the individual and thus present themselves in each of the successive dreams during the same period of sleep. Thus all the dreams of the same night contain the same latent meaning. Accordingly, it usually occurs that each dream approaches, disguises and even seemingly solves the common genetic traumatic conflicts in a different way. If, in addition, each one of the dreams or two or more parts of the same dream busy themselves with a distinct component of the genetic traumatic conflicts, this separation also forms a splitting.

Thanks to the successive shifts of one content to another, the formulation of the traumatic conflicts which give rise to the dreams gradually become transformed and disguised in the unconscious mind. The different psychical representations which at one moment express the conflicts are substituted by others to which the first ones are attached by connections of any type, logical as well as illogical. Among the latter, connections are established by the similarity of sound, form or the presence of a temporal or spatial contiguity. This means that these displacements occur as in the metaphor, in which the substitution establishes itself on the basis of something alike, and metonymy, in which the connective base is contiguity.

In addition, the same displacement causes the manifest content of dreams to be centered differently from their latent content. Important latent components are often represented by something negligible in the manifest content, and the contrary phenomenon also occurs. All these types of behavior indicate that to be able to reach an interpretation it is necessary to consider the manifest dream as the result of an intense transmutation of values. Therefore, in an interpretation one must tend to give to each one of the components of the manifest dream a meaning distinct from that which it seems to be.

An interesting phenomenon in the formation of dreams—and what is also a displacement—is the fact that the genetic traumatic conflicts use something that has occurred during the preceding day in order to manifest themselves. Such recent contents are called *day residue*. They can be important, such as desires or diverse preoccupations, or frequently they can be indifferent. An example of the latter occurred in the case of the television sets of the manifest content of one of the above-mentioned dreams.

The day residue can also be disguised before appearing in the manifest content of dreams and can constitute something like the clothing which gives a manifest form to the genetic traumatic conflicts. In the terminology of psychoanalysis one expresses this by saying that the genetic traumatic conflicts make their transference to the day residue, i.e., that they are displaced onto a day residue.

The fact that latent traumatic conflicts choose for their expression the indifferent day residue involves two motivations. Only something indifferent can permit an important content to be expressed through it. Something important would hold its precise meaning. In addition, by choosing the indifferent as a representative for an important genetic traumatic conflict, the dreaming person tries to diminish the importance of the latter. In this way he allows himself the possiblility of continuing to sleep peacefully.

The genetic traumatic conflicts of dreams, which are closely related to neurotic behavior patterns, have their roots in the childhood experiences of an individual that, together with his hereditary disposition, have formed his personality. They are therefore conflicts which have arisen in childhood. On the other hand, the day residue is usually comprised of indifferent impressions of the day. Thus in psychoanalysis it becomes apparent that dreams in their manifest content concern themselves with what is recent and indifferent, while in their latent content they arise from what is important and childhood-related.

Disguise of Dreams

When a person goes to sleep, he regresses from the conscious mind to the unconscious mind, from distinct characteristics to something earlier. The mere fact of this regression explains the strange peculiarities of the dreams which make their understanding difficult. But this is intensified in an unconscious way, because the individual—in order to be able to continue sleeping—seeks actively to disguise the contents of his traumatic conflicts and therefore leans strongly on all that part of the unconscious mind which differs from the conscious mind.

In order to understand the individual's intense eagerness to disguise, one must take into consideration that he has internal prohibitions against occupying himself with his traumatic conflicts beyond the fact that they cause him anguish. As indicated above, this happens in the case of conflicts stemming from the positive and negative Oedipus complex. Because of the opposition of his superego the individual must disavow his sexual desires and death wish toward his parent of the opposite sex and his death wish and sexual desires toward the rival parent of the same sex.

The emergence of the disguised genetic traumatic conflicts which arise from the unconscious mind finally penetrate the conscious mind of the sleeping person and establish there the manifest content of his dream. In this manifest content the traumatic conflicts—responsible for the dreams and actualized by the day's events—reveal themselves disguised in an incomprehensible fashion. Since in the end the traumatic conflicts are not comprehensible, due to the disguising dream work, the individual also consciously does not feel any anxiety about them and is able to continue sleeping. Thus Freud has written that the dream is the guardian of sleep.

Symbolization

A special form of displacement which intervenes considerably in the dream work is *symbolism*. The difference between displacement and symbolism is that in the first case the connection between the representation and what displaces it depends on the particular psychology of each individual, which can be distinct from the psychology of any other person, while in symbolism the displacing representation—the symbol—holds a constant meaning in the majority of persons. It is a meaning which exists in the unconscious mind of individuals. Therefore, one observes it not only in dreams but also in other psychic expressions, such as myths, religion, folklore and literature.

It usually occurs that persons dealing with dreams in analytic sessions do not view occurrences in relation to the symbolic contents of the dreams, in spite of the fact that these same symbols are easily comprehensible to them in other circumstances. For this reason Freud called symbols the *silent elements* of dreams. When they are not understood through the individual's associations, then in the interpretation of the dreams the significance which they usually have in other dreams—or in myths, folklore, religion and literature—is given to them.

The contents of the genetic traumatic conflicts which are usually symbolized in dreams are the body, parents, relatives, birth, death, nakedness and, above all, sexuality, in all their varied aspects. Since the symbols are very numerous, it would be too extensive to enumerate them in a fashion that would be demonstrative.

There are symbols whose relationship to the symbolized content is in the end easy to detect because of the presence of a certain similarity between the two. Thus it is not strange that in dreams, literature and folklore extended objects that perforate, penetrate, rise or increase in size symbolize the male genital organ, or that other objects capable of containing something or sheltering someone symbolize the female genital organ. In contrast, it is much less comprehensible that, for example, the female organ is often symbolized by paper or the number two.

In dreams, myths and or folklore, children—such as Eros and Cupid—usually represent genital organs. Birth is often symbolized by relating a person with water, as happens in the tales about Moses and the birth of Venus, or with something brilliant, such as in the popular expression "to see the light of day." The relationship of birth with water seems to derive from the existence of the amniotic fluid, and the symbolization of birth by something brilliant derives from the experience of harmful, dazzling light when the baby emerges from the darkness of the maternal womb. Clothes in manifest dreams frequently symbolize fetal membranes, and so it is possible to arrive at the supposition that it was the contemplation of the fetal membranes of the pregnant human or animal which gave to prehistoric women the idea of covering their newly born baby with something that would represent them—hides and, later, tissues made from the hair of those hides and, still later, even vegetable fibers.

In manifest dreams, persons endowed with authority symbolize the parents, and insects and other small animals symbolize siblings. Any type of activity can symbolize coitus, although some activities, such as eating or being with somebody ("cohabiting"), are more frequent symbols.

The two following examples show how genetic traumatic conflicts are expressed in dreams by means of symbols. The first was dreamed by a woman after intercourse with her fiancé during which, as on earlier occasions, she was frigid. She experienced no vaginal secretion and had no sensation of orgasm. The dream was: "I am eating at the table with my fiancé. As always, I forgot to serve him wine." In this and other dreams the table and the eating constitute the very frequent symbol of bed and intercourse. Serving wine in this dream symbolized the excitement and vaginal secretion so that the fiancé could enjoy the situation. The end of the dream expresses the woman's repetition of her frigid reaction.

In the part of a woman's dream described below, wine also symbolized a genital excretion. In this case it was the husband's semen. This woman had the dream after intercourse in which the husband did not take the contraceptive precautions which she had desired, a fact which constituted for her a traumatic situation:

> I am at the table with my husband, who holds our son in his arms. I have our daughter at my side. My husband is joyous as always. I intend to calm him. But he spills the bottle of wine and I get angry. Then I see myself in the bathroom cleaning my mouth of the cake which I had eaten.

In the dream the boisterous husband spilling wine symbolized sexual excitement and ejaculation in the wife's vagina. The two children symbolized the respective sexual organs. The child held by the husband was raised to symbolize in this manner his erection. The cleaning of her mouth symbolized the vaginal cleansing which the woman performed after intercourse in an effort to prevent possible pregnancy. Eating at the table, as in the former dream, symbolized intercourse and bed.

One must insist that symbols are not created by dreams but proceed from the unconscious mind. As already indicated, this origin makes it possible for symbols to present themselves with similar meanings in other frequent psychic productions. Thus the symbols of eating, of the mouth, and even of the process of cleaning the mouth, can be found with exactly the same meaning in a passage of the Bible (Proverbs 30:20). Here such symbols are indeed perfectly comprehensible because the passage was written with the aim of being understood. If symbolism is used, it is because one is dealing with genital contents considered punishable: "Such is the way of an adulterous woman; she eateth, and wipeth her mouth, and saith, I have done no wickedness."

Symbols usually hold common meanings in all individuals. Despite the frequency with which they intervene in dreams with a known meaning, it usually remains impossible to obtain a symbolic interpretation of a dream without being familiar with the circumstances that determined it and the particular psychology of the dreaming person. This also occurs with dreams described in literary works. They are usually of a transparent symbolism because their author wishes them be understood, but one cannot arrive at their meaning unless one knows the whole literary work or some details of the special episode to which the dream refers.

Also in literary works, dreams usually express important contents which have been repressed and which specify the psychology of characters. Thus in the dream of Don Quixote in the cave of Montesinos, the latent content indicates that Dulcinea was a prostitute and he himself impotent. This is expressed through different symbolisms such as the one in which a piece of Dulcinea's underwear is for sale and the one in which Don Quixote has insufficient money to buy it.

Secondary Revision

As previously shown, the content of genetic traumatic conflicts in dreams is disguised in the unconscious through condensation, displacement and dramatization. The successive stages of the dream work often lead to results which are not coherent among each other. In order to avoid the manifestation of these incoherencies, during the whole process of the dream work another psychic behavior intervenes to try to supress what is absurd, to reunite what is unconnected, and to round out and clarify what is not precise. To accomplish this, the individual makes use of fantasies of any kind which exist in his unconscious mind, without worrying about whether or not they correspond with the genetic contents. This behavior, called *secondary revision*, attempts to give a logical aspect or at least the appearance of a daydream to what finally becomes the manifest content of the dream. Thus it completes at any moment the work of the formation of the dream. Its activity in search of a façade of logic for the dream is more intense the closer the dreamer is to the stage of awakening, as well as when he later narrates his dream.

Wish Fulfillment

In performing the work that creates a dream, the unconscious mind of an individual generally does not limit itself to the disguise of the genetic traumatic conflicts. It needs to achieve something more, i.e., to change the unpleasant into something pleasant. The dream work makes an effort toward a "happy end." Therefore, in the course of fantasies which will constitute his dreams, the individual intends to avoid successfully his traumatic conflicts or else solve them in agreeable ways. But since he is incapable of solving the conflicts that generate his dreams—or else they would not create for him traumatic situations and he would therefore not dream of them—the individual can only fantasize fictitious solutions that are marked by infantile characteristics and are often contradictory among themselves.

The dream work conceals the deficiencies of these fictitious solutions and maintains and promotes what appears to be pleasant. Hence the happy or satisfactory aspects that frequently appear in dreams. It is these aspects that have led to expressions exalting dreams, such as the phrase "as beautiful as a dream." In no way do such expressions correspond with the reality of dreams. More accurately, one must basically consider dreams not beautiful, but rather as bothersome nightmares whose contents have been disguised in an infantile, deceptive way. Only a person who reacts masochistically (although without realizing it consciously) and derives pleasure from self-deceit can enjoy his dreams.

The fact that dreams seek to represent pleasurable contents and contain intensively instinctual subjects led Freud to decide that dreams are wish fulfillments. In this conclusion he grouped all types of wish fulfillments, even those that give origin to sufferings like those that gratify feelings of guilt or other masochistic behavior. Following this idea, Freud formulated in 1900, in his *Interpretation of Dreams,* the well-known definition that "the dream is a (disguised) fulfillment of a (repressed) wish."

In 1920 Freud described the frequent presence in dreams of traumatic situations which the individual has suffered in the course of his life. Taking these into account, he changed his definition of dreams as wish fulfillments to "the dream is an attempt at wish fulfillment." In short, despite the change he introduced, Freud persisted in the use of his initial definition.

This definition of dreams as disguised fulfillment of repressed wishes does not take into consideration all that Freud has written about, namely, the traumatic situations which create dreams. Therefore, following Freud and remaining within his teachings as has been done in the course of this exposition would make it appear more appropriate to define dreams as disguises of traumatic conflicts rather than as wish fulfillments.

Genesis of Hallucination

Freud's definition of dreams as wish fulfillments and the definition that dreams are traumatic conflicts in disguise are incomplete. Both definitions fail to mention and to clarify psychoanalytically the hallucination, which is one of the most striking characteristics of dreams.

What does hallucination consist of? While the individual is dreaming, he believes in the reality of what occurs in his dreams. Psychiatrically, this means that he makes an *erroneous judgment of reality* about what happens in his dreams. Psychiatrically, *reality testing* is the reasoning of a person who decides whether the psychical representations of a determined moment reproduce something real in the external world that is being perceived at that moment or whether they only constitute unreal fantasies.

The genesis of dream hallucination, or, in other words, the genesis of reality testing, requires a complicated explanation. Therefore, the following is necessarily detailed and contains repetitions.

In an individual any psychic representation whatsoever, e.g., the representation of a house, can have two sources. One is the perception at that moment of stimulus which proceeds from a house that really exists. That is to say, it would be a representation that is currently described as seeing a real house. By extension this representation is also called a real representation. On the other hand, the representation of a house may proceed from the fact that the individual imagines for himself a house or remembers a house, without actually seeing the house outside. In such a case the representation is not real but fantasized. Dreams are fancied representations which the individual judges to be real.

When a normal individual is awake, he knows how to distinguish whether a representation which he perceives consciously is real or fancied. When he thus distinguishes one from another, he enacts a judgment about the reality of the same. How does he distinguish them? Possibly because in his mind it is easier to manage the fancied representation rather than the real one. One way of handling the fancied representation is to reject it. Since the fancied representation has been imagined by the person—without dependence on the outer reality at that moment—it can be more easily rejected than the real representation. In other words, the reality testing which distinguishes the real representation from the fancied representation is based on the lesser or greater capacity of the individual to reject it.

This greater capacity to reject the fancied representation over the real representation ceases to exist when the individual is asleep and dreaming. During the time a person sleeps, he has no perception of real representations since he is disconnected from his outside reality. All the representations that run through his mind proceeding from his dreams are fancied representations, although in some cases they can be influenced by external stimuli, e.g., a jab. When a person is asleep, the greater facility of rejection ceases to exist in him. Indeed, the fancied representations that come from his dream are difficult to reject since they are endowed with a great affective intensity and above all since the person finds himself diminished in his capacity of rejection when he is asleep. As a consequence, the sleeping person, when faced with the fancied representations which constitute his dreams, encounters the same difficulties of rejection as when he is awake and faces the real representations. Therefore, when the person is asleep, he judges erroneously that the fancied representations of his dreams—since during sleep they are difficult to reject—are surely not fancied but on the contrary must be real representations. When the sleeping person's reality testing is erroneous, he hallucinates. When the person awakes, he becomes more capable in his mind of rejecting the fancied representations which existed in his dreams. He recognizes them as fancied and ceases to consider them as real. His reality testing is then correct. That is to say, he ceases to hallucinate and instead realizes that he has had a dream which is, like all dreams, of a fantasied nature.

If one adds these considerations about the genesis of dream hallucination to the definition of dreams already expounded, the definition can be completed in the following manner: Dreams are fantasies which occur during the sleeping stage in which repressed conflicts are dramatized, condensed and disguised; the same conflicts which create traumatic situations for the sleeping person who, in this state, cannot reject them or control them leads him to consider them as happening in fact in the outside world; and the person tries to disguise these conflicts by diverse procedures, even to the point of giving them pleasant aspects before letting them pass into his consciousness.

The preceding definition can be stated synthetically in the following way: *Dreams are fancied dramatizations of disguised unconscious traumatic conflicts which the sleeping individual considers as happening in the outside world since he cannot reject them.*

The Psychobiology of Dreaming

The discovery of the fact that dreams are constantly present during certain repeated periods of sleep (the periods of rapid eye movements [REM]) has led some researchers to put in doubt the psychoanalytical theory that dreams stem from psychic conflicts or from the need of wish fulfillment. Rather, they make them dependent on some unknown biological factor.

For some researchers the activity called REM serves the function of a sentry or guard. That is to say, it is an activity which would include more than the fact of dreaming. Dreaming would be only one of its collateral functions.

Other researchers admit a more intense relation between REM periods and dreams. Accordingly, the eye movements are the consequence of the psychic contemplation of the dream contents on the part of the dreaming person, who in this state would behave like a passive spectator of a scene which unfolds psychically as if it were taking place before his eyes. The eye movements of the REM periods are so frequent because the dreaming person contemplates simultaneously many of his psychic conflicts that are reactivated in his unconscious mind starting with the actual unfolding conflict.

What remains strange is that these revivals of traumatic conflicts occur only during some periods of sleep and that, on the other hand, in other periods of major duration the individual sleeps with great placidity.

The constant presence of REM periods with dreams during sleep indicates that the individual cannot but occupy himself with his conflicts while he is asleep. As previously shown, this occurs because the repressed conflicts continue as active ones in the unconscious mind and because while asleep the individual's capacity to repress them is diminished.

To occupy oneself with one's psychic conflicts means to recreate them, thus establishing in the individual a compulsion toward the repetition of that which is traumatic. But during the state of sleep this repetition occurs only at the psychic level, inasmuch as the individual is not an actor in his REM periods but limits himself to the contemplation of his conflicts as a relaxed spectator. That is to say, the REM periods appear to have as one of their purposes the contemplation of traumatic conflicts. In these, the individual reflects on his conflicts but does not let himself be moved by them.

The individual in the state of sleep inevitably passes through periods of REM in which he dreams of his traumatic conflicts, and when he dreams he disguises his traumatic conflicts and thus prevents his waking up. In other words, by dreaming he seeks to continue sleeping, inasmuch as "the dream is the guardian of sleep." One could state paradoxically that the individual sleeps in order to dream and dreams in order to sleep, except that the first part of the expression is not completely true. The individual does not sleep in order to dream, but sleeping—by diminishing the individual's powers of repression—makes him painfully reexperience his traumatic conflicts, the very same conflicts he tries to escape from when he disguises them in his dreams.

PRINCIPLES CONCERNING THE USE OF DREAMS IN TREATMENT

Interpretation of Dreams in Psychoanalytic Sessions

Psychoanalytic treatment creates the most favorable conditions for the interpretation of dreams. This is due to the deep knowledge which the psychoanalyst has of the person who is analyzed, to the possibilities resting in the latter to communicate freely all his thoughts, to the fact that matters mentioned by the analysand in a session dealing with dreams are normally always intimately related to the dreams, and above all to the desire of the analysand to pursue the interpretation for therapeutic progress. But it also occurs that the unconscious resistances of the analysand—which activate similar resistances in his psychoanalyst—tend to oppose themselves tenaciously to the effort to have his dreams understood, unconsciously producing disguised dreams and disallowing the associations which lead to their interpretation.

During a psychoanalytic session, the interpretative technique of dreams rests on the psychoanalyst's trust that what the analysand says is always in connection with the dreams he tells. Therefore, in the course of any session, the psychoanalyst tries to find out the unconscious relationships, which are often of an illogical and unusual type.

Dream interpretation in psychoanalytic sessions requires considerable effort. The unconscious resistances to knowing the basic meaning of the dream which exist in the analysand—and which activate similar acts of resistance in the psychoanalyst—frequently permit pursuit only of partial interpretations of the dream; after that, during the analytic session, the ideas of the analysand and those of the analyst move away from the manifest dream and also away from its latent contents. Therefore, when in the course of a psychoanalytic session no profound interpretation has been reached, it is helpful in the last part of the session to use the technique whereby the analysand considers and associates to each element of the dream separately. This technique is different from that in which, after the narration of the dream, the psychoanalyst listens to and interprets the analysand's free associations although they may appear to have nothing to do with the dream.

The dreams reported in analytic sessions always have latent contents which revolve around the psychoanalyst. They are always dreams that involve transference. At times the psychoanalyst remains satisfied when he has reached a dream interpretation, even though it may be superficial, provided that the interpretation refers to him. This tranquilizes his feeling of obligation to do justice to the theory and technique of psychoanalysis but may increase his resistance toward seeking more profound interpretations. A help in improving the interpretative task is the knowledge that every dream proceeds from eminently concrete contents and that these are always very important.

When deep interpretations of dreams are reached in the course of a psychoanalytic treatment, we feel it proceeds well. This must be so, since each dream arises from psychological circumstances which at the moment are causing conflicts for the analysand. Each dream presents to the psychoanalyst conflicts in disguise which are actual and which therefore must be urgently investigated. And since dreams are the expression of actual conflicts determined by previous conflicts which they reactivate, a thorough and deep interpretation of dreams includes understanding of the actual conflicts and their motivations. In addition, dreams narrated during psychoanalytic treatment present the actual conflicts, and those that preceded them, in the light of the transferential relationship with the analyst, so that their discovery and interpretation favor therapeutic progress.

INTERPRETATION OF MARTHA'S DREAMS[2]

In psychoanalytic treatment, a patient's dreams can be understood only in terms of what is known about the patient and the patient's associations with respect to the dream; this refers, of course, not only to the patient's direct associations to the dream but to everything else reported in that particular session, which is always connected with the dream to some extent and is therefore of great importance in elaborating an interpretation. A psychoanalyst is often quite surprised by the interpretation which emerges from the patient's direct and indirect associations, because it is not an interpretation that would have spontaneously occurred to him. This shows the absolute importance of the patient's associations if one is to make a good psychoanalytical interpretation of a dream.

In Martha's case history material, information regarding the development of her neurosis and her treatment is rather meager. Her associations, which are limited to those directly associated with her dreams, are even more meager, and there is no information about the rest of the session, which is as important as the direct associations.

It is deceptively easy to produce a dream interpretation. On listening to the dream, fantasies arise within ourselves which can be utilized in the interpretation. In a psychoanalytic session we do not produce an inter-

---

[2]This section of the paper was translated by Shulamith G. deCalles.

pretation as soon as the patient relates a dream, because we know that our own initial fantasies are not usually in accordance with the primary meaning of the patient's dream. For this reason we prefer to listen further to the patient before making an interpretation, so that he will produce his own fantasies to give us an idea of the meaning of his dream. It is also true that indications are given before the patient tells his dream, but these are not usually enough to enable us to understand the dream thoroughly.

I therefore feel that I do not possess enough material to be able to interpret Martha's dreams completely. However, I shall make an attempt at interpretation, because I believe the idea of this book, which is to make a scientific comparison of various tendencies of psychotherapy, is very worthwhile.

In interpreting Martha's dreams I shall draw on nearly half a century of work as an analyst, during which I have devoted much of my time to understanding my patients' dreams. But I should like to make it clear that I am not sure whether what I shall say about Martha and her dreams is entirely valid for the real Martha, about whom I would have to know a great deal more.

All my interpretations about Martha's dreams should and could have been made to Martha in the course of her therapy, at the appropriate times.

The content of the interpretations and the synthesized comments at the end of each dream indicate the effect that these interpretations might have had on Martha. A more detailed study would be outside the scope of this article.

Some Considerations about Martha

Martha is afraid of becoming an adult, and these fears are manifested in her feelings of anxiety, her anger and her incompetence in both her work and her emotional relationships. They are also manifested in her obesity and her intense phobic fear of cockroaches, which began when she was a child.

Her obesity probably stems from her infantile submission to her real parents and also to her internalized parents. Her surrounding fat would appear to signify her parents' surrounding her psychically, thus impeding a mature contact with her environmental objects, which she is made to feel are dangerous. Her behavior during the initial interview, when she "draped her coat across her lap for the entire interview," could signify that she was protecting herself from her therapist.

Her eating sprees were an addiction to food, theoretically signifying a regressive, oral-digestive expression of genital activity, with masturbatory characteristics, based on oedipal fantasies with objects which were both pleasant and frustrating. In other words, Martha's compulsive eating was the equivalent of masturbatory sexual activity in which she derived pleasure from digestive substitutes for her parents and submitted herself to their genital aggressions and prohibitions.

Her obesity appears to have started when her Oedipus complex began to decline and before the advent of puberty, of which she may have been afraid. "She remembered becoming conscious of her weight as a problem around the age of eight." "She felt toward her eating bouts a sense of helplessness and hopelessness," because she was submitted to her superego. Because of these submissions, she "perceived herself in piglike images." In other words, Martha devalued her genital tendencies in an anal manner.

In dreams and other fantastic tales, insects often represent siblings or a fetus. Martha's fear of cockroaches may have had the same meaning. Her phobia may have come from infantile fears which arose from fantasies of sexual play with her brothers and sister, which she felt were disgusting. Cockroaches are disgusting animals that look for food and hide in holes (vagina or anus). These incestuous fantasies occurred in the first place with regard to her parents. Martha says something about her father which might also be applied to the cockroaches: "She was repulsed by his poor personal hygiene and eating habits."

Dream No. 1

At the beginning of the dream, Martha is sitting on a balcony. This symbolizes her withdrawal from active life, particularly her aloofness from amorous involvements. Her life is spent in contemplating the love life of others. This is apparently a comfortable position ("I was sitting") but on further examination it represents mental instability ("on a rickety, shaky balcony").

In behaving thus, Martha conforms to the old-fashioned ideology of her family ("Martha's parents were Jewish immigrants, who brought with them attitudes and values much of the Old World"). Martha's old-fashioned ideology is represented in the dream by "Everybody was dressed in period costumes" and also by "My wedding gown was out-of-date." (When Martha appeared for her initial interview, her "dress was slightly old-fashioned"). The dream negates the fact that this ideological position corresponds to that of an obese person, through her identification with a "tall and lanky" actress. In fact, Martha was overweight. This deceptively gratifying identification is immediately destroyed, because in her dream Martha immediately recognizes that she was "not particularly attractive."

Her thoughts regarding a change in her behavior are expressed in the dream by looking down from the balcony. A person's mind is situated at the top of his body, and his sexual organs are lower down. Martha took "up" to mean the contemplative life and "down" to mean sexuality with all its problems. The "explosions and black clouds of smoke" which she can see below are a regressive anal expression of genital activity which she feels to be dangerous. They also represent the intense emotional conflicts which she consciously wished to avoid and which came from her repressed sexuality ("Martha also complained of being too emotional. Tears, anger and anxiety burst upon her for reasons unknown to her. She experienced again considerable shame..."). For these reasons, Martha had long preferred to be "sitting on a...balcony" rather than "on the street walking." But the consequence of her refusal to face up to her sexuality was that her contemplative position became insecure ("shaky balcony").

Sitting "on a...balcony," Martha is able to watch other people behave in a more adequate way. Those people were not afraid of sex and were searching for partners with whom they could enjoy both real and sublimated amorous activity. Martha found this very dangerous ("it looked dangerous") because of her submission to her superego and assigned to this activity the meaning of a masochistic fall, represented in the dream by "There were people jumping off the balcony and running off toward the explosions."

But the people who were jumping down also represented herself. They represented those parts of her which desired to live more vitally, to be able to enter into a deep and ample amorous relationship (with her therapist) with the possibility of greater accomplishments, e.g., to be able to have children (with the further significance also of being cured through treatment). These tendencies are opposed by others in which Martha is terrified and which are partially able to detain the others ("I called out to one person not to go because it looked dangerous"). In this part of the dream there is an ambivalent attitude toward sexual progress (which also signifies progress in her psychotherapy), in which the static tendency prevails. This ambivalence is clearly expressed in the dream: she tried to stop a person but "she ran off. I stayed in that chair...."

As I have already shown, this first part of the dream also refers to her psychoanalytic treatment. The basis of her treatment is that Martha should be adequately freed from submission to her superego, which impedes her genital progress in both the direct and sublimated sense. The different people "jumping off the balcony and running toward the explosions" represent various psychoanalytic sessions in which Martha, lying on the couch and contemplating her unstable psyche ("sitting on a chair on a rickety, shaky balcony"), decides to seek out the conflictual situations which she fears. She fears them because they are connected with her sexuality, with her castration complex and with her submission to her superego, which makes her feel it would be dangerous to stop repressing them. Her superego, i.e., her internalized persecutory parents, will not allow her to discover the truth through her treatment and threaten her with punishment and unhappiness if she insists on doing so. Because of this, Martha feels she will not be able to discover the truth, that it is too late, and that this is also her psychotherapist's opinion. ("I stayed in that chair for twenty years"; "I'm regarded as old").

This depressive content is also to be found at the beginning of the second paragraph in the description of the dream. There had been a time, of which there are still mental traces in Martha, when she felt herself capable of more ample amorous activities, but she was frightened ("Martha's first sexual experience occurred in her early twenties, while she was abroad for a year"; "I used to find marriage frightening.... I didn't get married on two occasions, both times to foreigners"). But her fear passed, and she let time go by without deciding to live more intensely ("I stayed in that chair for twenty years"). She feels that this has been going on too long and that she has grown old and become psychically castrated so that she will now be unable to have either a direct or sublimated genital relationship with anyone, or to be successful in the psychotherapeutic treatment she has just begun ("When I decided to come down, I was fifty years old and all of that activity was over. I had no emotions and when I went down I looked quite a distance"). This represents her becoming depersonalized through genital repression and being estranged from her therapy.

(This portion of the dream possibly refers as well to the time of sexual latency in Martha, when her Oedipus complex had declined, after she was five years old.)

Martha has to decide to undergo treatment, in spite of all her anxieties, because she feels insecure academically, professionally and affectively ("shaky balcony"). She has no stable emotional relationship; she has no children; she has lost her job and is afraid of her exams. It may be too late ("I'm regarded as old"), but she has to look for a change ("I had to get out of the chair").

Martha cannot escape from her contemplative life on her own; she must go to a psychotherapist ("I needed some help to get out of the chair"). Her psychotherapist is not as old-fashioned as she feels herself to be ("Everybody seems to be young and I'm regarded as old").

"Everybody" also represents that part of her which still feels young and attracted toward men and her psychotherapist. The "open jacket" of the young man, with which Martha associates "the therapist's sports coat," represents the therapist's penis, which he exhibits. (On a deeper level, it represents her parents' genital organs.) At this point the dream creates a more permissive atmosphere in which her instincts can function better, and this takes the form of orgastic acceptance of the genital relationship which the therapist is suggesting in the guise of a manual caress or even of mutual masturbation. But the hand can also symbolize the penis ("He held out his hand and helped me to jump down. I could jump because fifty isn't really that old"). As we have already seen, "jump down" symbolizes being able to attain a genital relationship.

"I stayed in that chair for twenty years" also shows that Martha thinks her therapy will take a long time and that she will be quite old before she is cured (fifty years old) and therefore not really at an age for love affairs.

The third paragraph of the dream holds the same atmosphere of sexuality as the second, symbolized first by "I was wearing a wedding gown." "My husband...had gone off." (The therapist notes: "The patient is single.") In the dream the husband represents Martha's infantile genital objects, i.e., her mother and father, on whom she is fixated but from whom, in her dream, she is able to become psychically emancipated through her sexual excitement. She is thus able to be united with her therapist, the "Prime Minister." In a monarchy, the "Prime Minister" is the person who limits the King's power. Kings here would symbolize her infantile parents. Martha makes a projective description of her therapist being sexually excited by her ("The Prime Minister climbed up [erection] and asked me to marry him"). "But I refused" signifies her anxiety about intercourse and also about progressing in her therapy, which causes her to return to her fixation on her forbidding parents. It also holds the meaning of her behaving toward her therapist as he behaves toward her, i.e., refusing her sexually.

In likening her therapist to a "Prime Minister," she is idealizing him (Prince Charming) and also mocking him. At the same time, it should be noted that there is no Prime Minister in the United States, and this means that Martha experiences her therapy as being in a foreign country where she can feel sexually freer, since she is far from her parents ("My husband ...had gone off"). Martha "didn't get married on two occasions, both times to foreigners"; her "first sexual experience occurred—while she was abroad". The foreign country also represents the unknown parts of her mind which Martha is exploring during her psychotherapeutic treatment.

"But I refused," Martha says. In the final part of her dream, Martha continues to reject a fruitful, amorous relationship with her therapist. This makes her feel a failure. But Martha denies this failure and tries to change this into its opposite. This is why the dream ends on a happy note. Yet the happy ending of this dream, as of most dreams, is deceptive. Dreams are always submission to traumatic situations.

At the end of the dream, Martha is "now on the street walking with the people." Apparently she is no longer "on a...balcony," but as free as other people. Shortening her wedding gown that was "out-of-date" symbolizes a more modern ideological approach both to sexual activity and to her psychotherapy. She feels criticized by other people and by her therapist, but the dream manifests this in the opposite sense ("The people were nice and friendly"). She feels criticizable because she feels castrated, incapable of acquiring a husband and children ("I asked about children and husbands but everybody was dead"). She then resorts to a manic deception to disguise this situation (the dead "did have grandchildren and nieces, so I was pleased"). It is interesting that she refers to "nieces" and not to "nephews" as well. This might depend on the fact that Martha was able to have "a number of close relationships with women" and rejected men affectively.

What else might be symbolized by these "grandchildren and nieces" at the end of the dream, the remants of those "dead children and husbands"? They may symbolize the cockroaches, Martha's anal objects which took the place of the forbidden genital objects of her infancy.

In synthesis, the total meaning of the dream could be the following: Martha is a person with old-fashioned ideas, who feels insecure and a failure because she is only an onlooker of adult sexuality. In order to feel better, she must go in search of a dangerous sex life for herself, and she needs psychological treatment in order to do this. However, it may be too late, and she is too inhibited. Her psychotherapist helps her and his erect penis excites her, but when she perceives that he is offering her a genital and a psychotherapeutic relationship, she rejects him. Apparently, her treatment sessions have liberated her a little, but in fact she continues to reject adult sexual objects and searches for dirty infantile objects, such as cockroaches. She tries to dissimulate this, even to herself, by pretending that sexually she is the same as everyone else.

Utilization of the Dream Interpretations

All the foregoing interpretations both can and should be made to Martha in relation to this dream and also in relation to other material where these contents can be perceived. Many of these contents refer to sexual rejection or incapacity, and when these are pointed out directly to Martha she could experience them as accusations, which would then increase her guilt feelings and her sense of incapacity. It is therefore necessary when making these interpretations to show Martha that her genital inability, and the rejection and guilt which influence her affectively, academically and professionally, are caused by her submission to her superego, i.e., her internalized, persecutory parents, who derive from her real parents but are not identical with them. It should also be pointed out to Martha that through the transference she is unconsciously experiencing her therapist as though he were her forbidding parents, i.e., as though he also were forbidding her to become genital and in consequence to progress in other ways, such as deriving benefit from her psychotherapy. I have called this negative transferential aspect of the psychoanalyst "the internal persecutory psychoanalyst" (Psychoanalytic Forum, Vol. 4, 1972, p. 183).

It is essential that Martha come to understand this transferential, persecutory aspect of her therapist to its full extent. Martha must come to be fully conscious of the fact that, if at this moment of her treatment she still has inhibitions and finds it difficult to derive benefit, it is because transferentially in her mind the analyst is forcing her to behave like this, inhibiting and destroying her well-being.

This does not alter the fact that in her mind there is also another aspect of her therapist, which derives from her genital parents, in which he is a beneficial, internal object who will help her to achieve satisfactory progress in both her direct and sublimated genitality.

The foregoing observations regarding the psychotherapist and her parents as internal persecutory objects can also be applied to the latent contents of her other dreams.

Dream No. 2

This dream appears to have two fundamental interconnected latent contents. On one hand, it symbolizes psychotherapeutic investigation of Martha's mind. On the other, it symbolizes masturbation. These two contents are interconnected because the therapist's mental investigation uncovers sexual contents and causes sexual reactions in Martha.

The dream appears to describe something that is happening in Martha's mind, i.e., in her internal fantasy world. "I came home and went into my room" symbolizes Martha turning inward to examine her mind. "My mother was in there going through my purse" is not only her mother examining her; it also symbolizes the psychotherapist investigating her mind. "My purse" clearly seems to be a symbol for her vagina, and therefore "my room" could also be her genital organs. "Room" and "purse" are thus both her mind and her genitals, in that Martha's mind is full of sexual contents.

"...into my room." "My mother was there going through my purse. She didn't look like my mother." The mother in the dream, who is also the psychotherapist, looked different because she was investigating the sexual contents of her mind. Her real mother was "guarded and evasive." The mother in the dream was more genital and incited Martha to be sexually active. This appears in the dream as "going through my purse." Because Martha identifies genitally with her mother, the mother in the dream represents Martha and her genital organs or vagina.

But the superego aspect of the mother is also present in the dream, and it is this aspect which Martha rejects. "Going through her purse" symbolizes an internal image of her mother uncovering and criticizing Martha's genitality.

The simultaneous presence of a genital mother and a persecutory mother, which are also two aspects of Martha's internalized analyst, causes Martha to retreat from fantasies of intercourse into fantasies of masturbation ("going through my purse").

In the dream, her mother "had found a check written to you [the therapist]." This check represents the excitement Martha feels toward her therapist. This excitement is sexual, and the sublimated derivation of this sexuality is intellectual, i.e., Martha's interest in her therapy. This excitement is both accepted and criticized by Martha's internal mother and therapist. A consequence of this ambivalence is that her excitement acquires the anal characteristic of money ("a check written to you").

The dream then develops under the influence of the ambivalence stemming from the acceptance and rejection of both sexuality and psychotherapy. Martha's reactions cannot be otherwise because her internal images of both mother and psychotherapist simultaneously accept and reject her genitality and its derivatives. Under the influence of her submission to these contradictory internal images, Martha feels herself unable to do anything properly. She feels she can be only partly successful. This limitation appears quite clearly both in the dream and in her associations ("My scream just didn't seem loud enough. It was as if I didn't have the physical capacity"). This held the meaning of not being able to have intercourse, only to masturbate, and also of being unable to carry out a satisfactorily deep psychotherapeutic investigation.

Martha's descriptions of her emotions in the dream are constantly ambivalent. "Anger" also symbolizes her sexual excitement, which changes to "anger" because Martha felt that her internal objects, both mother and analyst, were forcing her to reject sexuality and consciously express the opposite ("I...wanted to express more anger than I felt").

She is excited both by the genital aspects of these objects, mother and therapist, and by the genitally forbidding aspects. As she describes in her associations, she saw them as "an advancing army" before which she "felt helpless." Martha's masturbation, like that of everyone else, had the double meaning of both satisfying her genitality and destroying it. In her psychotherapeutic investigation, the same thing happens. Were it not for this contrary double meaning, Martha's fantasies would be of intercourse rather than masturbation. The contradictory double meaning which leads to masturbation is motivated by the genital and antigenital attitude of Martha's internal objects, mother and therapist. This attitude of genital rejection is the reason Martha's father does not appear either in her dream or in her associations.

Martha's attitude of both accepting and rejecting genital excitement and psychotherapeutic exploration is quite clear from her associations ("I felt helpless in the face of an advancing army. When my mother starts sorting things in my room, I get angry even if I don't care what's out. There is no way to make her observe the integrity of my things").

The act of masturbation is quite clearly represented in the dream, when it is seen that the mother, as a genital object, also symbolizes Martha's genital organs ("I grabbed her by the hair and threw her out. She landed at the bathroom door and fell"). These sentences describe Martha masturbating, her desire to achieve an orgasm and her retreat from sexual excitement when she has done so. To land "at the bathroom door" expresses once again the anal component of masturbatory excitement, but at the same time it also refers to Martha's superego causing her to evaluate masturbation as dirty, as well as something which might harm her ("I was afraid that she had hurt herself").

Martha tries to repress her hypochondriacal thoughts about hurting herself, but cannot do so ("I locked my door... but my mother came in again right through the locked door"). This expression is very significant. The fact that her mother could pass through a locked door shows that she is not the real mother, but an object of Martha's fantasy, which is thus able to overcome her attempt at repression. "...came in again right through the locked door" symbolizes a return of the repressed matter through the repressive barriers.

As I have shown, masturbation in the dream represents both direct genital behavior and also its sublimated aspect of psychotherapeutic treatment. Martha undertakes treatment in an atmosphere of favorable excitement, but she also tries to destroy it. "My mother was in there, going through my purse" symbolizes her therapist helping her to explore her mind, and this exploration excites her and encourages her to become sexually excited.

In spite of everything Martha did to her, the mother in the dream "didn't sound wounded." "She asked if I wanted anything—that was more like my mother, solicitous." This would appear to refer to Martha's treatment, in which the therapist solicitously explains the meaning of Martha's fantasies, including those which would destroy her sexuality and her treatment, without making her feel guilty but merely trying to get her to understand them. By this means, treatment will gradually help Martha to modify favorably her internal image of a persecutory mother who forbids her to achieve both direct and sublimated genitality.

Martha responds favorably to her therapist's attitude. As she says in her associations, "more anger than I felt toward you [the therapist]. Each time it sounded more hollow." Martha wants her therapist to clear up the confusion in her mind with regard to her internal objects, mother and psychotherapist, which she experiences simultaneously in contradictory attitudes, both favorable and unfavorable to her well-being. Furthermore, she wishes to behave toward her therapist as he behaves toward her; she wants him to behave in a way which will help her progress in her treatment and her genitality ("I felt I was forcing you to answer questions and clear up the confusion"). This is complicated because of her ambivalence, but it creates a strong emotional tie between Martha and her therapist ("It was such a struggle, like locking horns").

The interpretations with respect to this dream would show Martha the complexity of her mental life and the way her internal objects, one of which is her therapist, behave toward her contradictorily. This makes her behave in a very ambivalent manner, which brings with it anxiety, inhibitions and guilt.

Dream No. 3

The associations with this dream describe Martha's infantile memories of sexual play with somewhat older children who could be substitutes for her older brothers and sister. These games consisted of manual cutaneous caresses.

On the basis of these memories and other facts in the material supplied, it is possible to reconstruct the existence of an infantile era in which Martha either lived—or fantasied that she lived—in poverty, with all members of the family living in one room. She may have seen her parents copulating and also sexual play between her siblings, in which she may have taken part or have fantasied herself taking part. This sexual excitement caused her to fantasy finding satisfaction in being masturbated by her brothers or doing it herself. These fantasies were heavily criticized by the parents internalized in her superego, whose actuation within her mind must have been extremely severe, partly under the destructive influence of her infantile poverty.

This psychological situation gave rise to her phobia of cockroaches. The latent symbolism of cockroaches for Martha was the wished-for fingers of her parents, brothers and sister, a substitute for their penises, touching her genital organs and other parts of her body to excite her and make her pregnant and also to control her and punish her, in other words, making superficial, cutaneous sexual caresses, which were "dirty" like the cockroaches, by which Martha felt both attracted and nauseated.

Martha remains fixated on these unconscious sexual fantasies because of her superego prohibition of sexual progress. In her superego her parents and transferentially her internal persecutory therapist oblige her to remain fixated on these infantile sexual fantasies which give her so little pleasure.

The same sexual prohibition reduces her fantasies of cutaneous sexual caresses to a tickle ("One of the boys said that they had just tickled me"), rather like the feeling of an insect walking over a person's skin. For Martha, having cockroaches on her symbolized being invaded by sexual fantasies of the type referred to, which were forbidden to her. But she is also forbidden to pretend to abandon them and to progress toward a more mature, adult genitality.

Martha's reference, in her associations, to going "into a room where some boys waited" symbolizes penetrating that part of her mind where these fantasies lie and reactivating them. "One of the boys said that they had just tickled me" symbolizes being aware of this infantile sexual behavior, real or fantasied, and at the same time denying its sexual significance.

In the dream, the sexual significance of the cockroaches and their movements is clearly manifested, although it is projected onto her mother ("... my mother was standing there naked.... a cockroach had walked across her pubic hair"). For a little girl, the mother is the model for sexual behavior and can therefore be taken to represent her.

There is both a genital and a superego meaning to the cockroaches. In the dream, Martha's mother also appears as her superego and frightens the girl about her sexual fantasies ("... she thought the truth might frighten me; that a cockroach.... "). The mother forces Martha (the girl?) to reject and repress these sexual contents, which change into something false and unreal (... she told me something that wasn't true because she thought the truth might frighten me.... I thought she was right.... "). In this way Martha, having submitted to her superego mother, tries not to understand the latent meaning of her cockroach phobia, i.e., the sexual and superego fantasies of her childhood. Because of this, she is unable to let these fantasies develop more maturely ("Martha sought psychotherapeutic help because 'I realized I wasn't controlling my life' "). The parents images in her superego controlled Martha's life and caused her to remain infantile, which also meant that she maintained these fantasies and continued to be afraid of cockroaches.

From a transferential point of view, this dream shows the same contents with respect to Martha's relationship with her therapist. The psychotherapist, by showing interest in Martha and by making interpretations with a sexual content, excites Martha's sexuality in a forbidden way, as her parents and siblings did in her infancy. The mother in her dream is the therapist, who is baring, i.e., uncovering, the latent infantile sexual contents of her phobia about cockroaches, but at the same time, in a contradictory way which repeats her mother's contradictory behavior, the therapist makes her afraid of these contents and she feels like a little girl who is incapable of facing up to these contents adequately so that she can acquire a more adult sexuality.

Of course, the psychotherapist who behaves in this neuroticizing way is Martha's fantasied internal psychotherapist, modeled on her parents images. The interpretation of this dream would help Martha to become conscious of the transferential image of her psychotherapist as someone who makes her feel anxious about her sexuality, who forces her to remain infantile and to repress her infantile sexual and superego fantasies and be fixated on them, which makes her behave neurotically. For Martha's psychotherapy to make positive progress, it is necessary for her to become aware of the persecutory transferential aspect which her analyst holds for her.

Dream No. 4

" . . . a cockroach was there. It was half dead." The half-dead cockroach represents Martha's sexual fantasies, heavily laden with death contents or, in other words, castration. Her fixation on these causes her to masturbate and be instinctually deprived, and this in part reflects the material and psychical deprivation of her childhood.

Martha has this great fear of cockroaches because the sexual fantasies that determine her special mental image of cockroaches come from a sick sexuality. Her sexuality is sick because of the mandates of her superego. Her superego parents force Martha to renounce adult genitality and keep her tied to infantile forms of behavior such as masturbation.

In obedience to her superego mandates, Martha's love life is half dead, like the cockroaches in the dream. Martha perceives this unconsciously; it is for this reason that the conscious image of this behavior, the cockroaches, makes her so anxious. By understanding the unconscious meaning of the cockroaches, we are able to understand Martha's intense fear of them. Because of her superego mandates, Martha is unable to free herself of the cockroaches. Unconsciously, the half-dead cockroaches are the permitted sexual objects; the forbidden sexual objects are the possibility of a husband and children who could make her happy.

The beginning of the dream symbolizes these poor, sad and frightening contents very precisely. The bathtub where they happen ("...a cockroach was there") could symbolize the psychoanalytic treatment which begins to uncover them and shows their existence to be psychically both real and important. These are not secondary fantasies from which Martha can flee, as she does from the cockroaches. They are contents which are permanently present in her mind and in her genitality ("...a cockroach was there. It was half dead. It got on my leg").

The dream may indicate that Martha is more able to face up to these worrying contents ("I didn't panic"), although it may also be a negation. At the same time, it shows that these contents are becoming more and more conscious ("It got bigger....") because of her treatment.

All that part of the dream content which refers to something getting bigger may also refer to both phallic erection and to pregnancy. The dream shows that this forms part of Martha's fantasies at the present moment and also at the time when her phobia of cockroaches developed.

The dog in the dream behaves somewhat like the cockroaches, as Martha reports in her associations. If, according to Martha's associations, the "chicken" represents her mother, the dog in the dream may be her father and her father's penis—also that of the therapist—in a sexual attitude toward her ("...dogs....they slobber on you. They're a threat to pantyhose....they jump"). The sexual behavior of the therapist would be his exploration of her sexuality in the course of treatment.

These parts of her dream indicate that Martha has sexual fantasies about her parents which antedated and gave rise to those about her siblings.

The girl in the dream might be Martha feeling that she is still too babyish to be able to face up to her adult conflicts. She might also symbolize Martha's genital organs, and in that case "spraying" to kill might symbolize the opposite, the lubrication of her vagina because she is excited by a sexual object ("...a cockroach....got on my leg").

The dream would seem to indicate Martha's evolution toward more adult sexual fantasies, represented by the cockroach turning into an erect penis and a pregnancy ("...a cockroach....It got bigger"). In this positive sense, the half-dead cockroach could mean that Martha had begun to understand the latent meaning of her cockroach phobia.

The figure in the dream which gets bigger is also her psychotherapist. Martha reexperiences with him the sexual and superego fantasies related to her father. His psychotherapeutic efforts affect her more and more ("It crawled...near my bed"), and Martha does not try so hard to destroy it, although she is still reluctant to accept it ("...I didn't want to kill a dog. It had some human characteristics, too. It asked to leave. I opened the door and apologized for spraying").

The interpretations regarding this dream show Martha more clearly the latent meaning and the antecedents of her cockroach phobia. Martha is beginning to think about a more mature type of sexuality, but her internal persecutory objects still forbid this.

Dream No. 5

In this dream, Martha tries to deal with her sexuality by herself. She is making an effort to understand that the damage to her objects and her own sexual tendencies are the cause of her destructive behavior ("I also had the razor blade"). She therefore feels the need to make amends ("...I was concerned about getting the penis back for it might start rotting. I had to get it back to him").

Martha is now stating that rather than her parents having been the cause of her sexual failure, it was caused by her own castratory tendencies toward her sexuality. In this dream, her mother seems to oppose castration ("I didn't want my mother to see the razor blade and penis in my hand"). "If she did see, she didn't bother me" indicates that in the course of therapy, Martha's internal mother—who is transferentially also her psychotherapist—has become more cordial toward Martha's sex life. This gives Martha more sexual freedom ("I was wearing a loose shirt").

As the internal images of a persecutory mother and psychoanalyst grow weaker, Martha feels that she must make the effort to mature sexually. But she feels that she is not yet capable of doing so because of these superego objects ("It was ...a responsibility...a burden, like walking around carrying too many packages"). Apart from this, Martha also feels that becoming sexually mature means being able to resolve her castration complex ("...he cut off his penis and a nipple of my breast...."), and she finds this difficult, painful and complicated to undertake in her treatment ("The breast was healing, but it was irritating me. If that was bothering me, he must be really uncomfortable"). Martha would rather not make the effort, not undertake this task, nor make the effort to attain a good genital partner ("I was supposed to join him on Friday night. I'd rather join him on Saturday"). As we saw in the first dream, Martha prefers to sit and watch rather than grow more mature through treatment and become able to acquire a husband and children and fulfill herself as an adult.

In the manifest content of the dream there are "two types of environment." One of these represents the castratory environment of her childhood, where in a psychic sense she rids herself of her penis, her nipple and also her ovaries. The other "was a different type of environment." It was somewhat more genital; there the penis and the nipple "were supposed to reattach themselves." At a previous period of Martha's life, this other environment was the foreign country where Martha, far from her family, was successful in having intercourse.

At the present time, this environment is different, more genital, and corresponds to her psychotherapy. The "fellow" of the dream is her psychotherapist. The dream expresses the fact that the new environment, although "it was different," was "not too far from where I was." This signifies that Martha was reliving with her therapist castratory experiences similar to those she had experienced in the family environment of her infancy.

The similarity between the two environments can be observed in the literal description of the dream. According to her description, the "fellow" is in both environments ("I was living *with my parents somewhere*. There was a fellow *there* who was *somewhere* at a nearby island").

"I was supposed to join him there" shows that Martha feels that she must go from one environment to the other. This has the meaning of being forced to pass from the ideology of sexual castration to that of sexual reconstruction. The expression "I was supposed" shows that Martha feels the search for sexual maturity and for well-being is imposed on her by her parents and her therapist and does not emerge spontaneously from her libidinal drive. Martha still finds it traumatic to give rein to her libidinal drives because she is still submitting to her superego and her castration anxiety. This traumatic situation gives rise to the dream and appears in a disguised form in the manifest content.

Dream No. 6

Martha associates that the little girl in the dream represents herself. She feels the little girl is "solid, likable," a flattering opinion of herself which disguises her castratory anxiety.

The fact that the little girl in the dream was five or six years old indicates Martha's opinion that she was normal at the zenith of her Oedipus complex, that she considers herself basically a normal person, thus again denying her castration complex.

In the dream that occurred six months earlier, Martha seemed to express the feeling that her sexual failure was her own fault and not caused by the prohibitions of her parents and, transferentially, her therapist. In this dream she reacts differently. She again lays the blame for her guilt and sexual failure on her parents and psychotherapist ("I see a little girl.... She may have come [to the amusement area] in spite of her mother, who tried to keep her back.... I say to her, 'You're not evil, no matter what your mother told you' ").

The building where Martha and her friend go down the steps appears to symbolize the female genital organs, especially the vagina. It is probably Martha's own vagina and also the "enormous" vagina of her genital model, her mother ("... an enormous building.... an old railroad station.... The inside is rather like a shell.... we go down.... an amusement area.... there are amusement park rides.... ").

They symbolize genital organs, but there has been mental repression regarding their activity ("although it had been in operation a long time, I didn't know about it").

On the basis of these interpretations, we can suppose that owing to the therapist's work Martha is beginning to feel a sexual rebirth. She reactivates fantasies of genital exploration, of masturbation and intercourse, and finds them interesting and pleasant, although also very dangerous ("... if you fell off the staircase you could drop down to the bottom"). Falling is a pejorative evaluation of genital activity. The word "fall" also indicates that Martha relates the control of her sexuality with sphincter control, i.e., the involuntary loss of excrement.

"In the middle of the basement is an open place with sunlight." I have made a detailed study ("Present thoughts on Freud's theory of dream hallucination," *Intern. J. Psycho-Anal.*, Vol 50, 1969, pp. 492–94) of the meaning of the shiny details to be found in some dreams. I believe such details symbolize the memory of being dazzled by extrauterine light at the moment of birth, when the fetus "first sees the light of day." If this is the case, then the above part of the dream, in its context, could symbolize the capacity of the female genital organs to produce children. And in its sublimated aspect, it would symbolize psychotherapeutic ability to "clear" the mind and help an individual to be positively fulfilled.

Indeed, this dream also symbolizes the fact that Martha's treatment penetrates the depths of her mind. These depths are full of conflictual sexual matters, thus connecting this interpretation to the previous ones. In the dream, as in psychotherapy, one must penetrate deeply ("... we go down hundreds or thousands of feet"). They go down many steps, which symbolize the many sessions of therapy.

Eileen, who accompanies Martha, may represent the psychotherapist. She may also symbolize Martha's genitality and that part of her mind which during psychotherapy investigates another part of her mind.

According to Martha, the further down you go—or, symbolically, the deeper you investigate the mind—the darker it gets ("... it is even darker ...."). Increased resistance could be indicated here, and this, as we shall see, crops up again further on. "The atmosphere is a little creepy"; it gets creepy because the repressed contents seem creepy or sinister when they emerge from repression.

"Some men are laying a cement floor" could signify increased repression as psychotherapy delves deeper.

Martha says in her dream "but I'm not frightened," yet this does not seem true. On the contrary, the fact that in her dream she comes back to the surface too quickly seems to indicate that she is afraid of the depth to which the psychotherapist investigates her sexuality. This early return to the surface probably represents what Martha does in her sessions. At times, and especially toward the end of her sessions, Martha probably refuses to delve deeper into her psyche. She feels that her therapist does not accompany her in her resistances, so at this point of her dream she is alone, without a companion. This makes her return dangerous, because it implies a rejection of the well-being which her therapist could bring her ("I start back up to the ground level alone.... sometimes a little dangerous.... When I get out, I realize that it's early and I could have stayed longer....").

"...but it's a long trip down again and it doesn't pay to go back so late in the afternoon." This part could signify, among other things, that it is an arduous task to penetrate the depths of the mind, full of upsetting sexual contents. "...so late in the afternoon" appears to refer to her age. It may be that at the end of this dream Martha is saying that at thirty-three it is already too late for her to normalize her sex life, too late for her therapist to help her to improve even further.

This is a phobic reaction to the possibilities of further progress in her therapy. It stems from her superego fears and her castration complex. This phobic reaction could make her abandon treatment too early, just as it brings her back to the surface before the end of her sessions, unless this latent content is interpreted to her adequately whenever it appears in her sessions.

In synthesis, on a superficial level in the latent content of this dream, Martha feels herself to be quite capable both in her sexuality and in her psychotherapeutic progress. This signifies that she realizes how much she has improved, but it also reinforces her resistance to further improvement. On a deeper level, to which Martha has more resistance, she is afraid because she feels threatened by her persecutory parents and by her therapist when she undertakes sexual and psychotherapeutic activities and hopes to improve. These fears could make her interrupt her treatment too soon. She can do this either by stopping treatment or by making sure that her sessions are not productive.

REFERENCES

Garma, A. (1970). *Nuevas Aportaciones al Psicoánalisis de los Sueños*. Buenos Aires: Paidos.

————— (1974). *The Psychoanalysis of Dreams*. New York: Aronson.

CHAPTER THREE

Jungian Approach

EDWARD C. WHITMONT, M.D.

BASIC THEORY OF THE MEANING OF DREAMS

The dream as the experience of an involuntary psychic process not
controlled by the concious outlook presents the inner truth and reality as it is; not because I presume it to be thus, nor as I could wish it to be,
but simply as it is.

The dream describes that inner situation of the dreamer the truth of which
the conscious position fails to acknowledge or acknowledges only
grudgingly.

The dream rectifies the situation. It supplies that which properly belongs
to it and thereby improves the attitude. This is the reason why we need
dream analysis for our therapy.

—Jung, *Psychological Reflections*, 1961, pp. 49–50

In Jung's approach the dream represents a superior, if archaic intelligence which can offer a meaningful new attitude to life. The dream directly
presents an objective reality, external and/or internal, that corrects and compensates our subjective distortions and blind spots. The dream is not a
product of pathology or repression. The seeming illogic of the dream is not
the result of censoring unacceptable wishes or of inferior reasoning, as the
psychoanalytic approach holds, but is an expression of a preconceptual psychic stratum that operates in terms of images rather than thoughts. Allegories
and symbols which appear foreign and absurd to our conceptual reasoning
have an uncanny precision of insight when we understand their imaginal
logic. In marked contrast to a view of dreams as pathological symptom for-
mations, the dream is a function of a self-healing balancing process. It relates
a message that is unknown to the dreamer but is of vital importance, in that it
compensates the one-sidedness of the conscious position and its

deficiencies.

Association, Explanation and Amplification

We attempt to make the dream's image logic accessible, in part at least, to our conceptual frame of reference by putting the dreamer's associations and explanations into the context of the images. For instance, a young man dreamed that his pocketbook was stolen by an unknown person in Puritan dress. With his pocketbook he associated his means of personal identification; it contained his driver's license, etc. With the Puritan garb he associated an outdated and rigid religioethical system; clothes are means of protecting oneself and adapting to external climates, and they typify the way we present ourselves to others. The dream can be conceptualized, then, as showing that an unknown, i.e., unconscious, aspect of his personality characterized by rigid religious and cultural bias, an outdated way of presenting himself to others and to the world, robs him of the means of establishing his personal identity. By inserting associations and explanations in place of the images, a conceptual meaning is reached *in part*. Conscious and unconscious dimensions are now in connection. This is the essential experience for therapeutic change.

I stressed "in part" because often in genuine symbolism the unknowable is touched and a single correct understanding is not possible. In many instances, no complete or final formulation of the dream's meaning can be found. The layers and facets of its symbolism may seem inexhaustible. The aspects and feeling tones with their associations, explanations and amplifications have to be "felt," meditated upon, attuned to by consciousness until some relevant insight evokes an "Aha!" reaction.

Hence the interpretative approaches are highly individual, influenced not only by the material and conscious context of the dreamer but also by the personalities and interactions of dreamer and interpreter. No dream symbol ever bears a fixed meaning. Associations must be provided by the patient, explanation and amplification by dreamer and therapist. Together they provide the indispensable basis for interpretation.

Associations are the thoughts, feelings or recollections, whether logical or not, that arise in the dreamer's mind as the dream is recalled. For instance, *Automobile:* "Each time I played with toy cars my brother tried to take them away."

What I call explanations are functional definitions of a dream image or object. They are largely consensual and objective. For instance, *Automobile:* "A means of 'getting there';" pen: "A means to express one's thoughts by writing." Although primarily objective, explanations are modified by associations and emotional predispositions. To one person a car is simply a means of locomotion; to another the stress is on the pride and prestige to be gained by the make of the car; to a third it is a way to prove driving skill and ambition. When the image is a person, the emotional coloring of explanations may be at a maximum. A policeman is a public or collective enforcer of the law. This is the explanation of the policeman image. The feeling tone of the associations tells us whether he is trusted or feared or ignored. Explanation alone would tell us only that the dream message is about this person's relationship to authority. Associations alone would tell us that the dreamer has a given attitude toward some aspect. Explanation modified by associations shows us this person's attitude toward authority.

Amplification enriches a dream image with the meanings of that image or motif in myths, religion, fairy tales, art and literature. These are the traditional associations of mankind, the historical understanding and explanations of archetypal symbols. Associations, amplifications and obviously explanations are preferably limited to the immediate context of the dream image. Free association is usually not considered helpful since it tends to lead away from the direct message of the image. Because the dream does not conceal or censor but reveals the "situation as it is," the image in its immediate allegorical or symbolic context presents the meaning directly. No censor needs to be circumvented. The images need to be related to feeling or conceptual patterns.

Object and Subject Level

A dream may be interpreted in terms of an outer "object" reality, or on the "subject level," in terms of inner psychological reality. Which of the two approaches offers more insight into an unknown yet important situation is a matter of clinical judgment. Usually after a helpful object level interpretation more relevant insight into the psychodynamics underlying the situation may be achieved by a subject level interpretation of the same material.

A dream of seeing oneself or another dream figure disregarding lights, cutting recklessly in and out of traffic and finally being knocked down may point toward a tendency to behave this way in actual traffic, but foremost it points to a basic attitude. On the object level it warns of the effects of inconsiderate or ruthless behavior which eventually will result in getting "knocked down."

But primarily the dream describes a willful ego hypertrophy which fails to regard the inner warning signs and the feelings of others. Probably these are repressed for the sake of ego goals, and hence this person is ruthlessly cutting in and out of "interpersonal traffic" and "psychic traffic" (the autonomous flow of biopsychic energies). Driving oneself without regard to physical or emotional needs and capacities may lead to the threatened knock-down in the form of a somatic or psychic breakdown.

In practical terms, these two interpretations are likely to be synonymous, for such an overbearing ego attitude will lead to this behavior both in actual traffic and in interpersonal relations. Even if such a person controlled himself and avoided such behavior in the object world, the subject level interpretation would give insight into the motivations and projections which may or may not bring about the analog of the dream in external situations.

In subject level interpretation, every object or person of the dream represents an aspect or dynamism of the dreamer's unconscious psyche. Even the dream ego represented by the dreamer himself may exhibit attitudes of which the waking ego is not aware.

A patient's dream of being taken advantage of by Mr. X, his business partner, and responding naïvely would first be reality tested. Is Mr. X actually engaged in unsavory practices which the dreamer has managed or preferred to overlook? Is it possible that the dreamer has such a high yet unjustified opinion of his own skill in handling the known machinations of Mr. X that he has naïvely become a sitting duck for exploitation? The blind spot is compensated by pointing out Mr. X's character or, if this is known already, by pointing to the dreamer's own naïveté, or both.

If, on the other hand, the dreamer has no illusions about Mr. X and his own ability to handle him effectively, the dream would merely restate a situation already known when taken on the object level. In such a case, or when an object level interpretation obviously makes no sense from the outset or fails to reveal anything new, or when the dream deals with people or situations of no current relevance (such as the candy store owner of one's childhood), a subject level interpretation is directly called for. Mr. X then would be taken as an inner partner, the dreamer's own unrealized dishonesty or manipulativeness, naïvely identified with high-flying ego ideals, which gets the better of him. The actual Mr. X may be innocent of those shady qualities ascribed to him by dream and indeed even by the dreamer. The dream would be pointing up the nature of projections upon Mr. X. (In Jung's definition, projection is not a deliberate defense but an original choiceless illusion caused by unconsciousness. Whatever complexes operate actively while we are unconscious of them appear to us as though they adhered to external objects or persons.) The associations and explanatory descriptions proffered by the dreamer in respect to Mr. X (dishonesty, manipulativeness) would also be directly applied to the dreamer as descriptive of his own unconscious complex.

These need not be only negative, of course. We can be as unconscious of our better sides and capacities as of our faults. The dream may also compensate an unawareness of potentiality. A young woman laboring in indifferent and boring jobs dreamed of her father making her a birthday present of a pen. To her a pen meant writing, and she considered her father a gifted writer. The dream then points not to an incest situation but to the fact that she has writing ability and that writing is her birthright, a talent which is also an obligation.

The structure or make-up of the dream itself does not indicate whether or not an object or subject level interpretation should apply. Jung felt that there is no hard-and-fast rule or generally valid method for dream interpretation. The criterion is whether the particular way of dealing with a dream or, for that matter, with a clinical situation is compensatory and has a healing effect.

However, when people or situations in a dream evoke strong affect in the dreamer, they tend to show up projections and hence call for subject level interpretation, regardless of object level relevance.

The subject level is more rewarding generally, since there is all too often little we can do directly to change outer situations. But insights into our own functioning can bring about changes in our own approaches to those situations and thereby change at least the effects of outer circumstances upon ourselves.

Image, Allegory, Symbol

The language of emotion-charged imagery, of allegory, symbol and myth, is the language of metaphor. Both allegory and symbol are pictorial, analogic "as if" descriptions and are concerned with "meaning." Both offer cognition by means of image rather than concept or abstract thought. Allegory is a representation of an abstract or spiritual meaning through concrete forms. It refers to facts or situations that in principle can be fully grasped by the reasoning mind. A symbol in Jung's definition is

not an arbitrary or intentional sign for known and conceivable fact, but an admittedly anthropomorphic—thence limited and only partly valid—expression for something suprahuman and only partly conceivable. It may be the best expression possible, yet it ranks below the level of the mystery it seeks to describe.

Allegorical descriptions widen and correct our view in respect to personal and mentally accessible facts which we have overlooked or preferred not to see. The imaginal form of representation is merely an expression of the fact that the message comes from the "image seer" in the psyche. The message—even though it may use poetic license and dramatic exaggeration—can, in principle, be rationally interpreted and understood. Its subject matter is directly observable facts, external or psychological, even though unconscious, outside of the dreamer's awareness. These are constituents of what Jung called the personal unconscious.

Symbol and myth, however, mediate a rationally unknowable world of transpersonal reality, a stratum comparable to that which a physicist described as one in which we find

> nature behaving so entirely differently from what we observe visible and palpable bodies of our surrounding that no model shaped after our large scale experiences can ever be "true." A completely satisfactory model of this type is not only practically inaccessible, but not even thinkable. (Schroedinger, 1951, p. 25)

Physics had to design its own symbolic or mythological "as if" language for this dimension, e.g., particles juggling around central nuclei. This reference is not meant to call upon physics to explain psychology but rather to illustrate the heuristic validity of the symbol-making function of the psyche by the analogy of an exact science which has shown less hesitation than psychology to accept symbols for the sake of penetrating aspects of reality inaccessible otherwise to the rational mind.

Symbols, by pointing to the not fully knowable, imply a transpersonal dimension of reality. By emphasizing the symbolic, the Jungian approach thereby accepts such a dimension as a basic concern of psychic life. The symbolic dimension is a therapeutically significant expression of a need for meaning in life over and above the satisfaction of instinctual needs. The dream may confront the dreamer with his instinctual needs in the form of allegory and with new dimensions of meaning when read symbolically or mythologically. Human life is motivated by an urge for meaning and purpose, to be discovered in individual personal existence as well as in interpersonal relationships. This need for meaning demands satisfaction over and above the needs of material security, sexuality and aggressive assertion. It may be considered a "fifth" to be added to Lorenz's "big four" drives (fear, hunger, sexuality, aggression) when considering human as opposed to animal motivation.

V. Frankel has described how survival in concentration camps depended not so much on physical stamina and the satisfaction of physical needs as on the capacity to find a sense of meaning to existence even under grimly destructive conditions. The most difficult and tragic situations can be tolerated if they can be found to "make sense" in relation to "ultimate reality." Neurosis or psychotic breakdown occur when a complex situation makes no sense and therefore cannot be integrated into some life outlook of world-self affirmation.

Symbols, as they spontaneously arise from unconscious depths, are potential guides to psychic health because they point to such contexts of meaning. Thereby they offer new creative possibilities in situations consciously viewed as meaningless chaos.

A middle-aged businessman in a state of depression dreamed:

I was in bed with a young girl and had just finished intercourse. Then I heard a voice saying in Hungarian—my mother tongue—that I did not deserve the *fa* or *fasz*. I was not sure which, perhaps both.

In Hungarian *fa* means wood, *fasz* means penis. Taken on the personal level, allegorically this dream might show the dreamer that he undervalues sexuality, does not trust—perhaps even represses—his sexual potency or his masculine aggressiveness. This level of interpretation should be checked out first in every case; often it will apply.

But in this instance it did not. There was no question of any repression of sexuality or masculine aggressiveness. Moreover, in the dream the man had performed the sexual act quite satisfactorily. The dreamer was a self-confident and successful go-getter and felt himself quite deserving of his successes both in and out of bed. On a purely personal sexual level of interpretation, a therapeutic bias could have been foisted upon the patient. Further, the mythological implication—the archetypal equation of penis and wood—would go unheeded. Often the seemingly irrelevant or irrational details of a dream supply the most helpful pointers for its interpretation. In terms of associations, the wood motif drew a relative blank from the patient. He liked wood as a material and as a youth had tried his hand at wood carving.

Viewed symbolically, however, as a best possible representation of a transpersonal, essentially undefinable reality, the dream opens a new dimension of understanding. Archetypal symbols are images which appear in similar forms in dreams and fantasies and mythologies of past and present: the World Father, the Great Mother, Mountain, Cave, Abyss, Hero, Child, Redeemer, Search for Treasure, Water of Life, Death and Renewal, Monster, Serpent, Bird, etc. Archetypes are defined as *a priori* motivational energy configurations which express themselves in typical representational images, typical emotions and behavior patterns characteristic of the human species, analagous to the instinctual patterns observed in animal behavior.

Archetypal images appear most often in contemporary form, not in historical costume. One can recognize them by their thematic analogy to myth, fairy tale, religious tradition and artistic imagination. When images that are identifiable as archetypal appear in dreams and no mythologically resonant associations occur to the dreamer, the therapist has to draw upon his knowledge of mankind's associations, that is, the collective historical understanding of those symbols.

The phallus that is also wood is a widespread cult object. At the spring festival Indian men dance with wooden phalli. In ancient Egypt the wooden phallus represented the generative power of Osiris, restored to life by Isis from death and dismemberment; his natural phallus was lost and Isis substituted a wooden one by means of which he begot the child, Horus, on her. The wooden phallus, then, is not naturally, unconsciously and automatically grown but deliberately created. It signifies creativity that is not of the flesh, of natural being, but of the striving of the spirit, of immortality. An analogous image is found in the phallus carved upon antique grave monuments bearing the inscription *Mortis et vitae locus* (the place of death and life). Purportedly this is a replica of the phallus which Dionysus, the god who dies and is reborn, erected before the portal of Hades.

This amassing of analogous images is an example of amplification. Amplification is essential for interpretation in such a case, but, equally important, it appeals to the dreamer's feeling imagination rather than simply to an intellectual understanding. The symbolic significance of the image cannot be grasped without such an involvement of feeling and intuition. It is to the mystery of spiritual renewal that the symbol of the wooden phallus points, and in respect to this, not to overt sexual prowess, the worthiness of the dreamer is questioned by the dream.

The validity of this assumption seems borne out by the associations and descriptions of the young lady, the bed partner in the above example. She was an acquaintance whom he described as a grossly opportunistic go-getter, an unscrupulous success hunter whom in actual life he found quite repulsive.

On the subject level she is an unconscious aspect of the dreamer's psyche, representing (allegorically) the opportunistic tendencies with which he is so deeply involved (depicted by sexual union) as to become almost incapable of a creative renewal in his life.

Objective Psyche and Compensatory Function of the Dream

The "objective" or transpersonal psyche is defined as a psychic "field" prior to and independent of ego and ego consciousness. It operates in terms of a meaning of its own, only part of which is in accord with the goals of ego consciousness. It includes and may subsequently contain elements that were once conscious and have become unconscious again through repression. (This Jung calls the personal unconscious; together with the ego it constitutes the subjective psyche.) The transpersonal psyche may be likened to an unconscious background personality or personalities. These unconcious background patterns are as though related to an unconscious center which Jung called the Self and are what is depicted in the persona, shadow and animus-anima figures of the dream. The Self appears like an organizing totality of a person's given potential, an a priori wholeness potential or gestalt principle from which originates the drive toward individuation, toward becoming what one potentially "is" or is "meant to be."

Psychic health rests upon a dialectic, mutually cooperative relationship between the unconscious self and the ego. The relationship depends upon whether the ego can remain sensitive to the unconscious self of which it is but a particular manifestation. When the ego's frame of reference is too far removed from its unconscious psychic roots, dissociation and psychopathology may ensue.

This tendency is compensated by the dream. Dreams then register the nature of the dissociation and attempt to convey to the ego a maplike survey, in images, of the critical situation as seen from the position of self.

ℝ The dream is a perception of inner or outer facts, registered by the transpersonal psyche, conveyed to and picked up by the ego consciousness in more or less fragmented pieces. (We rarely if ever remember a dream in its completeness.) A dream may be read as if saying "Self addressing ego: A blind spot in your view of a situation is herewith recorded by us as though . . . " The imagery of the dream follows.

In addition to clarifying personal psychopathology, the dream may compensate defects and distortions in our life orientations, as well as our views of our relation to life, world and cosmos. In addition to showing superego standards, a genuine inner conscience is expressed which may or may not be in agreement with superego or ego standards. Apparently our attitude to existence is of importance to the autonomous steering center, the self. The need to discover an ethical orientation arises from the unconscious transpersonal non-ego center that demands a psychological orientation toward meaning and purpose in life. The capacity to feel responsible for ethical wrong is an aspect of the archetypal need for meaning, referred to previously, which differentiates human from animal psychology. This ethical sensitivity opens one to the experience of conflict and necessitates individual choices in conflict situations. The necessity to make choices builds individuality. Conscience, one's unique "inner voice," is a dimension of meaning, a demand upon the ego, no less than the demands of the superego. Ethics and superego morality both are part of the social and cultural web because they arise in the human psyche, rather than being imposed upon the psyche by a culture envisaged as divorced from psychic functioning. The cultural demands of the superego do not fall from heaven but are expressions of a collective psychic functioning to which the individual psyche relates like branches or leaves or roots to a tree. Superego demands are precipitates of collective psychic development. A continous flux in unconscious dynamics expresses a life current which evolves into new forms and increasing differentiations of organism and consciousness. Thus the internalized collective superego standards are polarized by variations, complementations, modifications and oppositions arising in the psyches of the individuals who make up the collective body. The relationship between individual and collective psyche is a dialectical one of complementary polarization. The individual's uniqueness is found through discovering his own "synthesis" between the "thesis" of superego demands and the "antithesis" of one's intrinsic values and needs, the inner voice, conscience. Through this dialectic *Auseinander = setzung* between individual and collective values, one's life meaning, one's unique selfness is approached.

Moreover, the individual antitheses to the collective themes are challenges that eventually call forth an evolution and renewal of the collective standards. These new standards become the superego demands for the following generation, or generations, to be complemented and opposed by new antitheses of individual conscience.

Conscience expresses an individual's necessity to "become what he or she potentially is" by discovering and living up to an intrinsic ethical integrity. This is to be carefully differentiated from the superego, to which it can stand in a polar, antithetical relationship. An adequate conscious relationship to this value-setting individual center is as vital for one's sense of integrity, self-respect and trust in the meaning of existence as is the satisfaction of biologic instinctual needs. Our attitude toward existence and toward our fellow human beings is a matter of concern to the autonomous steering center, the self.

A young man narrated a dream in which a policeman attempted to stop him from entering a beautiful orchard. Enter he did, but when he was about to pick a piece of luscious fruit he was scared off by a cobra or rattlesnake coiled around the branch. He pulled back in terror, the snake struck and he awoke. In alluding to the myth of the Garden of Eden a general fact of human existence is restated for the dreamer's benefit. "Knowing," growth of consciousness or maturing must be paid for by travail and even suffering, at any rate by losing our paradisical easygoing innocence. Throughout all cultures prior to the Judeo-Christian tradition, the snake represented a symbol for healing and renewal, poison as well as medicine, the paradox of danger and renewal within living. Our dreamer is thus offered a piece of existential philosophy from the universal storehouse of mankind: difficulties are not necessarily expressions of failure or ill luck poised just to plague him of all people, but are unavoidable stepping stones to a growth in awareness and maturity, the other side of joy and fullness of living.

The dreamer's resistance to risking himself in a more courageous living is shown to arise from two sources: the policeman, whom he manages to bypass, and his own fear of the snake, which proves fatal. The policeman to him represented unquestioned obedience to law and order, a collective superego value, a piece of Puritan heritage in his case that forbade any deviation from established rule and profoundly mistrusted joy and pleasure and sexuality. In his conscious trying the dreamer, a member of the counter-culture, defied that prohibition. He was "liberated," or so he thought. Yet the dream shows him that his own fear of taking risks, of risking involvement, of wishing for the easy simple way out, leads to an escapism which but invites the troubles which he fears and hopes to avoid.

Ordinarily, when not bothered, a snake will not deliberately attack. In dreams behavior which is contrary to realistic expectation marks a significant dynamic. Also in dreams, when one event follows another, a causal relationship is often to be postulated. These two indications, combined with a feeling in the dream that the pulling back elicited the attack, lead us to conclude that the dreamer's avoidance provokes exactly what he fears.

The superego says, "Stay away," but the life will, which could be likened to the genuine conscience, says, "Risk!" and by implication "Wake up!" A message such as this, when it grows out of the amplification and explanation of a mythological motif that arose from a dreamer's own unconscious psyche, rarely fails to score a therapeutically effective impact. Partly the reason for the impact is that its appearance in the dream times it. At this particular juncture there is a readiness and need to assimilate the message. A point has been reached where the particular message is needed as a compensation to restore psychic balance.

Adequate interpretation frequently can be offered only when the "blind spot," the deficiency or one-sidedness of outlook in the conscious position, has been located. Hence the conscious position of the dreamer in respect to subject matter involved and outlook must be known before a dream can be adequately understood. Rarely if ever does a dream merely restate a known event or an already established attitude. An interpretation that adds nothing to what is already known is probably inadequate.

The seeming absurdity of some dreams is accounted for by compensatory exaggeration. What consciousness underrates, the dream is likely to overemphasize in like proportion. A person or issue that we unduly minimize may appear in our dream blown up to gigantic proportions, and vice versa. In dreaming of oneself as committing some dastardly deed, one's overblown notion of goodness may be compensated. A dream of impending disaster may compensate one's overoptimistic or careless evaluation of a situation, or, in terms of subject level interpretation, it may confront the dreamer with his hitherto unrealized pessimism or alarmism. The optimal interpretation is determined by establishing the dreamer's opposing exaggerated position and by the nature of the associations and explanation offered. Familiarity with the dreamer's life situations, conscious attitudes, value systems and ideas, as well as associations and explanations, must obtain before adequate interpretation can be attempted.

Also, interpretation will invariably be colored by the interpreter's attitudes, feelings and intuitive capacities. The more adequate the therapist's relation to the world of his own inner images, the more likely will justice be done to the patient's. This is because interpretation comes out of sensitivity to one's own spontaneous nonrational responses, which are not available to one who is not related to his own unconscious. Even more important, what is unconscious inevitably gets projected. The therapist's unconscious complexes will color his perceptions of the client's material.

Dramatic Structure of the Dream

It is frequently helpful to perceive the structure of a dream in terms of the basic elements of classical drama. Perhaps dream and drama, both, embody an inherent archetypally structured way in which human development is viewed in terms of inevitability of conflict and conflict resolution.

The basic elements are exposition, plot or complication, crisis, peripeteia and lysis or catastrophy. Particularly in involved dreams these structural elements help one grasp the basic message rather than get bogged down in detail. Any elements may be more or less developed or absent in a given dream. The exposition points up the principal characters, starting positions, subject matter and location of the story about to evolve. Hence some dreams cannot be adequately understood unless the opening setting is well considered.

In our last example the exposition is "dreamer in front of orchard." The theme the dream is about to treat is "How is he to deal with the good things of life?" The complication is the encounter with the policeman who represents his superego, the puritanical conviction that if something feels good and joyful there must be something wrong or forbidden.

After this complication has been by-passed, the real crisis is encountered in the threat of the snake. The moralistic taboo hides the critical weakness, to be met by conscious awareness—his fears of living and risking.

The peripeteia is the way he deals with or, here, fails to deal with the impasse—turning his back. Lysis (solution or catastrophy) refers to likely outcome—in this case, the shock effect intended to wake him up. The snake now strikes. What he dreads, he brings about by running and looking away.

Thus in terms of dramatic development this dream can be quickly scanned and summed up as saying, "By failing to courageously face the dangers of life you bring about what you most dread."

In every dream exposition and complication refer to the present. Lysis or catastrophy indicates future potentiality, ways in which the situation can or should be resolved. The crisis may be present or imminent, depending on the facts of exposition and complication. The past is referred to in dreams only inasmuch as it still affects present reality.

Sexual Symbolism

Sexual images need not necessarily refer to overt sexual or genital activity. Sexual imagery is one of the oldest forms of archetypal (mythological and religious) imagery. The psychoanalytic approach explains images in mythology and religion in terms of a repression of sexual feeling or behavior. This is a metaphysical bias that the basic human concern is with instinct gratification and that spiritual concerns are derivative. Such a position denies symbolic reality as a primary motivation. Male-female polarity, the contrast of the Yang and Yin of Far Eastern philosophy, has always been the way in which the basic polarities of energy activity have been symbolically expressed. A gestalt called "Maleness" is depicted as outgoing, active, aggressive, analytic, separative, abstractive and creative, and is concretized by phallic images including penis but also spear, sword, gun, tower, eagle, hawk, and by heaven, lightning and thunder, and spirit and reason. Femaleness represents the indrawing, introverted, receptive, containing, gestating, nourishing, preserving and playful aspect of energy, represented by hollow, cave, womb, vessel, container, house but also dove, cat, cow, and by earth, water and nature, and emotion, to mention but a few examples.

I wish to emphasize that male and female as indicated here refer to archetypal symbolism or gender and not to sex in the sense of men or women. Jung was the first to draw attention to the fact of psychological bisexuality for either sex—to the anima, the repressed femininity in men, and the animus, the unconscious masculinity in women. Conscious assimilating of the psychic contents of anima and animus constitutes a basic stepping stone toward individuation. (Further details of this most important aspect of Jung's contribution would be beyond this study. The reader is referred to the extant literature.)

Thus on the object level sexual images may indeed point to sex and/or relationship problems (for relationship always rests upon encounter of opposites and therefore archetypally comes under the female-male heading). But on the subject level they reveal the impetus to a needed union of separated or opposed psychic elements. Sexual symbolism hence is relationship and individuation symbolism, a partial aspect of which is genital sexuality.

Homosexual imagery, in particular, frequently points to the inner need to assimilate adequately the qualities of one's own sex specifically pointed up in the qualities associated to the object of the homosexual attraction. No overt or actual homosexual tendency need be adduced, even though it should first be checked out on the object level.

Transference

What has been said about sexual symbolism applies equally to dreams dealing with the therapist and the dreamer's relationship to him. On the object level such dreams may uncover repressed feelings or sexual wishes toward the therapist.

But on the subject level they show attitudes to the therapy process, projections upon the therapist or the relation to the "therapist within," an adequately or inadequately functioning self-awareness, therapeutic attitude and healing power within the psyche.

A young woman dreamed, "I am in Dr. W's office. A noisy teenage crowd romps around there and I cannot come near and touch Dr. W." This dream made most sense on the subject level. She could not get in touch with an adequate awareness of herself until her teenage attitudes (expecting always to have a good time and be supported without responsibility) were gotten out of the way. Neither could she relate to the therapist, of course, as the overt dream image would depict. But the subject level interpretation is more inclusive than the interpretation, which would limit the problem to the person of the therapist.

PRINCIPLES CONCERNING THE USE OF DREAMS IN TREATMENT

In Jungian practice dream interpretation is the chief therapeutic modality. The dream, particularly an initial dream, also helps the therapist evaluate diagnosis, prognosis and psychodynamics. Contrary to earlier, widely held assumptions, the Jungian technique is as useful for the unraveling of specific personal problems as it is for the understanding of archetypal constellations.

A dream like the one with the snake at once allows a differentiation between superego inhibitions and the deeper layer of existential fear, thus permitting the therapist to focus upon the more essential issue instead of having to wait for the slow disentanglement by free association or pursue his own more or less correct guesses. Such direct diagnostic use of the dream can be an invaluable tool for situations where brief psychotherapy is indicated.

Equally important can be the warnings of fragile ego structure or threatened psychosis, where anything more than ego supportive therapy might be dangerous or impossible. For example:

Walking in the desert valley with but little water available I found a stream of water in a deep chasm. But the descent to the water would be over vertical and brittle rocks and I saw that a single step was likely to loosen a rock avalanche which even if I did not slip would destroy me.

Such a dream or dreams of destructive volcanic outbursts or destructive floods from which there is no escape are warnings to stay away from the unconscious.

In turn, variations of the above themes that show the dreamer unharmed or able to master the danger are prognostic encouragements, indicating that the going is likely to be rough but manageable.

The most important use of dreams is as guides for insights—indeed, as directors of the therapy process. It was Jung's contention that since the patient cannot know and the therapist must beware of assuming that he knows what is wrong, the healing instinct within the unconscious psyche is to be looked to as a guide. This autonomous center of the personality directs development, integration and healing. Dreams singly and in serial connection seem to provide running commentaries and consistent developments of such themes as are essential for motivational insight. When a dream journal is kept through the course of an analysis, it becomes obvious that a consistent goal-directed personality development is being directed by the dreams. Dream 1 may raise an issue; dream 2, another; dream 3 may link them; dream 4 may elaborate a side issue tangentially referred to by dream 1; and so forth. Often one gets the impression that, for example, Dream 6 hints at or creates a basis for what it "knows" dream 86 is going to elaborate.

This Ariadne thread of dreams through the maze of unconscious motivations and interactions thus provides a map showing what issues need to be raised and when they safely or successfully may be raised. The experienced therapist will bide his time and not touch upon sensitive issues until and unless a dream does so. It is not only the understanding but also the emotional impact of wrestling with the dream symbolism that has a therapeutic effect. This effect is nonrational and seems to operate through the emotional and intuitive level.

Hence the course of a Jungian analysis rests chiefly on work with dreams. The analysand is asked to keep a dream journal in which dreams are to be recorded immediately upon waking, no matter how fragmentary, absurd or irrelevant. In the analytic session they are then discussed in the context of external current life events as well as their subject level inner dynamics. As the ego position is modified by the insights induced by the dream, the following dreams respond to that modified position. They elaborate, reiterate or correct erroneous interpretations. A dialectic to and fro is thereby induced between ego and unconscious in respect to which the analyst's role is one of participant interpreter who supports the client's journey.

Jung emphatically insisted that the therapist give up pretensions to superior knowledge and all authority and desire to influence his patient. The therapist must adopt a dialectical procedure of comparing his findings and impressions with his client's. Every stance of the patient is considered tentatively valid unless challenged by the unconscious itself through a dream.

Jung unequivocally states that every and any resistance is justified. If a client refuses an interpretation, it indicates that the therapist's approach is inappropriate if not in content then at least in timing, attitude or emotional stance or insufficiency of rapport. The validity of an interpretation is affirmed by a subjective deep sense of "Aha!" or "Touché!" on the part of the dreamer, regardless of his intellectual reservations and indeed even emotional resistance. Only this "Touché!" experience confirms that the message or at least a part of it has registered. Until this assent by the patient is gained, it is well for the analyst to consider even the best and seemingly most appropriate dream interpretation invalid.

This fact constitutes a severe limitation in discussing the clinical material of part two. An adequate interpretation without the dreamer's associations, explanations and subjective reactions of assent or refusal, without personal rapport and without detailed insight into the concrete life and therapeutic situation which gave rise to the dream, is next to impossible.

The best that can be offered are theoretical speculations of what the dream might point to, what sort of questions might have to be asked, what assumptions might be made, what conclusions might be drawn—perhaps.

After all that is said and done, the reader must be reminded that, like all healing, dream interpretation remains more an art than a science.

INTERPRETATION OF MARTHA'S DREAMS

Theoretical Understanding

Dream No. 1

The first dream reported in a course of therapy (initial dream) usually offers a diagnostic and prognostic summary of the overall situation and, in terms of crisis and lysis, points toward specific problems and attitudes to be dealt with for therapeutic resolution.

This one presents us with an image of the dreamer in an "elevated" and isolated "shaky and narrow" position, watching "from above," a world which she perceives as utterly dangerous; looking down at life as explosive and dangerous from an exalted but inherently unstable, indeed rickety position—a picture of alienation and inflation, most likely owing to an identification of self with unrealistic exalted ideas and ideals. Yet, unconsciously and in spite of herself, there is a pull to get involved; dissociated elements of her libido are shown to be drawn toward the explosion (people jumping off the balcony and running toward the explosion). If not consciously (through therapy) and voluntarily, she would be compulsively and unconsciously involved in the explosions. It should be elicited whether her objective life situation is dangerous, given her present psychological structure, or whether the danger is imaginary. In the latter case, the explosiveness appears projected upon the outer world. In the first case, a fragmentation and breakdown of the personality may be warned against.

The period dresses refer to a perhaps romanticized but certainly outdated external adaptation. Clothes—the garment, mask or uniform one wears (the persona in Jung's terminology)—are the means of presenting oneself to, as well as protecting oneself from, the external world. Judging from implications of the other dreams, the outdated adaptation is probably in terms of rigid sexual and respectability standards of past generations. The therapist would have to request the dreamer to characterize the values and standards of the period to which these clothes belong. Also, more specific information about the attitudes or qualities that impress her about Katharine Hepburn should be elicited. From what we know about the figures which Katherine Hepburn used to impersonate there emerges the likely image of a "lady" who is "above it all," a bit of a tomboy and a snob who does not wish—indeed is afraid (see Dreams 2 and 3)—to be touched by emotion or passion, lest she "explode"; and all of this dressed in outdated sets of standards. The adherence to outdated sexual standards and the Katharine Hepburn identification compensate an inferiority feeling centered upon a self-image of unattractiveness either in outer appearance or as an "evil" person (see Dream 6).

The motif of remaining in her stance of passive detachment for twenty years requires associations to twenty. What significant events inner or outer are recalled from her twentieth year or from twenty years ago? This may elicit traumatic events, conditionings or expectations which continue to be instrumental to her detachment.

Her association to fifty-years-old as a privileged position, and all activity being over when she finally comes down, points to her expectation of being assured a privileged position with not much responsibility and relative noninvolvement in the struggle of life as a prerequisite for "coming down" and "risking involvement." It is a self-defeating paradox, and "coming down" under the conditions she anticipates makes her miss the boat. Everybody of her own generation is dead. She misses out on contemporary life, as long as her coming down is conditional on the above expectations. Here an archetypal or mythological theme is struck. There are many stories, fairy tales and legends of the youth who allows himself to be seduced by the song of the sirens or the Lorelei into the world of the naiads or by the elves in the hill into the fairyland of unreality, only to find when he returns as an old man, after what seemed a short sojourn, that life has gone by. No one knows him any more, his kin are gone and dead. Everything is changed from what he knew, and the world he has returned to is strange. He no longer fits.

The archetypal motif always addresses itself to the general human theme. A general temptation and its dangers are stated. The urge to withdraw from life is alluded to as a regressive enticement from the depths of the un-conscious, a form of a death urge or a primitive readiness to remain with the call of the deep. The enticement of the unconscious here may be inferred by amplification of the archetypal context in which missing out on life happens because one is tempted by the unconscious. If and to the extent she succumbs to that temptation, life is missed. While a pull to the unconscious may be vital and called for after adequate ego development, in her situation, characterized by withdrawal and a rickety pseudo-ego and by allusion to the motif of miss-ing out on life by withdrawal, such a pull is regressive.

If and when she resists it and attempts to come off her chair and balcony, she needs help from the therapist or therapy. The association to the therapist in terms of his clothing emphasizes the need for the contemporary (sports coat) way of meeting reality presented by the therapist. The reference to the need for the therapist's help as early as in the initial dream may be compensa-tory to the therapeutic resistance alluded to in Dream 2 and perhaps 6, and should alert the therapist to discuss reservations about the necessity of thera-peutic help.

The themes of wedding and Prime Minister are in need of further clari-fication by associations. What does she find frightening about marriage? Probably it is the need for emotional commitment, but it could also be the dread of what it may represent to her in terms of her outdated traditional standards.

Marriage, as a joining of opposites, is one of the oldest symbols of the in-dividuation process, of becoming a whole person. I would explore this archetypal subject level interpretation, in addition to object level concerns about actual marriage, because of the Prime Minister's involvement. He pro-poses to replace the legitimate life partner and is a modern equivalent to king and prince of fairy tale, a glamorous figure. On the object level this would al-lude to an overglamorous expectation of the prestige marriage could provide. On the subject level it points to being caught in an unrealistic frame of refer-ence of an inner figure—in this case, that one ought to live in a context of glamour and prestige. In response to this expectation, she would have to be a Katharine Hepburn type person. The glamorous Prime Minister seeks to re-place the realistic life expectations (the ordinary husband who has left in the dream). Her refusal of the Prime Minister is prognostically promising. It makes possible a lysis which is merely hinted at here. She does manage to touch ground—even though belatedly, it seems. She shortens her out-of-date wedding gown, cuts down her outdated, exaggerated and pompous expecta-tions and so does find a new adaptation of sorts.

Yet the lysis is ambiguous because of the implication of "too late," of having missed out on her generation. Something is achieved, but something vital seems lost or missed.

I cannot comment upon what this might be without more associations (children or grandchildren?) and probing. Perhaps it has to do with "not staying long enough" (Dream 6). The exploration is not sufficiently deep. She is satisfied with adaptational rather than profound personality change. In summary, the initial dream describes the overall situation as characterized by a life attitude of alienation and romanticized ideas, of detachment motivated by fear of responsibility and involvement. Crisis and peripeteia point to the necessity of "coming down" to a reality "street" level, of joining the human family, through therapy and by resisting the siren song of glamour. The lysis puts this as within reach, but with an intimation of something missed.

Dream No. 2

Here we deal with the intrusion of the mother, who is not her real mother and cannot be gotten rid of by efforts of will. In presenting a figure who is not the actual person it purports to be, the dream points to an entity "like mother" from the outset, that is, to subject level significance. It refers to "mother in her," to whatever qualities, values or attitudes the mother engendered in her. The mother's standards or feelings in her are the intruders in her "room," her personal inner space or individuality. The purse (ask for associations!) frequently also connotes personal inner space. It contains personal means of identification as well as money (energy or libido). Here, the mother concerns herself with a check for the therapist. The implication is that she intrudes upon or questions the libido given to therapy. Perhaps the mother's value system considers analytic work to be an indulgence or immoral. This again is speculative. One would have to ask what the mother believed in and how she would feel about therapy. At any rate, an ambivalence if not outright resistance is intimated.

Martha characterizes the mother as solicitous and having no respect for the integrity of her things, for the contents of her inner space, an attitude that attempts to dominate and manipulate by worry and spoiling. Perhaps this engenders the "princess" attitude, and lack of trust in her capacity to accept responsibility in life, described in Dream 1.

From Dream 6 we can also assume that the mother's standards intrude upon her individuality by discrediting her feelings and instincts, notably pleasure and sexuality.

The dreamer's attempt to deal with the issue by anger and force are unsuccessful. She gets angry at herself and tries forcibly to overcome the results of the mother's conditioning in her. This is an attempt to change by force of will and by forcing emotional responses; neither is usually successful in the long range, in the transference or in life. The problem comes back as overt solicitousness. Here one might ask the patient, "Where and how are *you* over-solicitous? Toward yourself, toward others?" This solicitousness, in whatever form she answers, needs to be consciously confronted.

Dream No. 3

The cockroach motif touching upon phobic anxiety points to a basic factor of her disturbed dynamics. Frequently, clinical symptoms have symbolic significance. Animal phobias often express fear of instinctuality; the repressed drives in turn exert obsessive pressure resulting in phobia and creating a vicious circle. Cockroaches (personal associations and explanations ought to be asked for) usually are associated with dirt. They are animal life, drives, that are to be hidden from the light and feed on refuse—psychologically, on what is "refused" by consciousness, instinctual urges that are considered dirty. Often the allusion is to sex. In view of the context of this dream (pubic hair) and of the indication of forbidden play in Dream 6, the reference to sexuality in its playful aspect would probably apply.

The frightening truth is that the mother is "touched" by "dirty" sexuality. But what does this mean? The patient would be asked for reactions and associations to this question. Lacking these, only speculative possibilities can be considered. On the object level, did the mother present herself as untouched by sex, thereby setting an exemplary standard that good women do not allow themselves to be stirred in their depth by sexuality?

The mother also embodies the archetypal Feminine and becomes an unconscious paradigm of feminine adaptation to the daughter. On the subject level, the frightening truth is that "dirty" sexuality and femininity *do* touch, are insolubly connected, and that the daughter cannot find herself as a woman while discounting her deepest emotional responses to her sexual experiencing. Concretely, how does she discount them? Most often it occurs through separating sex from feeling. Yet we are not told here.

Dream No. 4

Dream 4 repeats and elaborates the cockroach problem. Dream themes are repeated when their implications are insufficiently or wrongly understood or assimilated. The repetition of a dream theme may be a response to wrong interpretation or the expression of a need for further elaboration. This dream shows an unsuccessful attempt to deal with the roach problem by doing away with it by willful repression. This reminds us of Dream 2. Mother and cockroach are accorded the same treatment. (Does she identify the mother with a cockroach? Is femininity repulsive like a cockroach?) At any rate, there is a tendency to substitute willed and rational control over her instinctual and feminine responses. Conditioned by the mother, she sees femininity as solicitousness and perhaps domesticity (chicken). She wants to control life.

Chicken and dog are hidden components of the cockroach complex. They reveal themselves and move nearer to consciousness (the progression from insect to humanoid animal) as she unsuccessfully tries to fight it. This progression is accompanied by a shift in attitude toward greater willingness to accept these aspects. If associations were obtained to the girl that tries to kill the roach, we could know by means of what attitudes she tries to control the situation. Again, we need more associations to chicken and dog. Evidently, the issues are "bigger" than they seemed at first! They seem to include fears of how she appears to the collective view (pantyhose), how she will be seen and judged as a woman, and matters of religious and cultural tradition (Friday supper in Jewish homes is loaded with religiocultural or family tradition significance).

The dog (perhaps also the chicken) may refer to the "hungry" aspect of her instinctuality, which she fears to be uncontrollable. It would make her overdependent and overemotional (slobbering) if let loose and thus ruin her neatly controlled external stance (pantyhose are the "proper" covering for the legs, one's proper stance). Evidently, the dreamer's life style is one of maximal self-control and minimal risk of exposure and spontaneity. This would be consistent with Dreams 1 and 6 and her stated intent of wanting to control life.

Dream No. 5

Dream 5 calls for familiarity with archetypal symbolism and, obviously, the subject level interpretation. The theme of dismemberment and rejoining occurs frequently in religious and alchemical symbolism. An example was already given in the dream of the wooden phallus (in the theoretical part of this essay). Another example is the crucifixion of Christ, the rending of his garments (as a substitute for his body) and the resurrection of a new, spiritualized body.

The underlying theme is breakup and reunion in a new form, analysis and synthesis, termination of unviable states for the sake of reorganization and renewal. In this dream the reorganization involves a temporary exchange between the dreamer—the conscious personality who is still in the world of her parents' attitudes—and the unknown man on the island. He is in a "different environment," an as yet unknown orientation. An island, solid ground separated from the larger continents by water, depicts an autonomous personality fragment in the midst of the unconscious, an autonomous complex. The male on the island is a consciousness potential within this complex, an animus figure. The animus represents those drives in the feminine psyche that strive for assertiveness, positive accomplishment, discernment and rational judgment. (In the man's psyche, his unconscious femininity, the anima, refers to the potential for receptiveness, adaptability and the capacity to convey and master sentiments and moods.)

The penis she receives refers to an assertive or discrimination potential that needs to be actualized. This again is merely a general statement, without the specific qualities associated to this man or a person resembling this man.

The phallus is also, as in our previous example, an image of creative renewal. Lacking specific associations to breast and nipple, one might speculate in general archetypal terms that by renouncing her identification with the mother's attitude she may avail herself of her phallic assertive potential. By getting away from being the "mother's daughter", who shuns the risks of living, she can assert herself and rely upon her own mind and power of judgment.

But eventually the phallus is to be returned to its rightful owner if she is to receive back the integrity of her breast, that is, to find her own femininity. This I take to refer to the necessity of relating to the animus as an autonomous function of the non-I rather than identifying with it. It means being responsive to the impulse for assertion and discrimination—but in a woman's way as opposed to a male's, deliberately or unconsciously. A more detailed explanation of this can be found in Whitmont (1961, Chapters 11 and 13). I cannot deal with the allusion to Saturday versus Friday without more associations.

Dream No. 6

This dream features the classical archetypal motif of the descent into the underworld of the unconscious which enables the dreamer to confront a core problem and thereby attain a degree of liberation. The issue focuses upon the six-year-old in the area of amusement which is also an "open place with sunlight." Evidently, at age six or thereabouts, perhaps in connection with going to school, the mother's restrictive expectations managed to quench her "sunlight." This would have to be verified or modified by memories or associations. The liberating experience rests upon conscious awareness of these oppressive restrictions upon the child and her ensuing ability to substitute her own value judgment for her mother's. Yet the descent is perhaps terminated too soon.

The figure and implication of Eileen deserves attention. Eileen serves as a guide like Virgil in Dante's descent into the underworld in the *Divina Commedia*. She represents a particular set of attitudes which adequately or inadequately led her to this beginning and perhaps prematurely aborted confrontation in depth. Associations are required to clarify what these attitudes are. (How do you see Eileen? What is she like?)

The old building which serves as the portal of descent might represent the old structure of her cultural tradition, but it also might lead to a purely personal emotional complex depending upon the associations, memories and explanations. It reveals itself as containing a potential for renewal, if one goes far and deep enough into its unconscious contents.

The unconscious contains not only products of repression and the chaotic urges of the "id"; it is also the source ground for a creative growth and an expansion of consciousness and individuality. In its depth we are joined to our social and cultural community, past and present, by which our mind is conditioned. Restructuring of the personality cannot disregard collective premises of the personality which modify the unfolding of the inherent individuality. Associations would have to be elicited to identify what collective premises need to become conscious for a deeper restructuring of Martha's personality.

The ending of the dream appears to imply that more could have been assimilated. She "could have stayed longer" but it does not pay to go back again. Is this an insufficient willingness to work upon her development in depth, perhaps as a result of the mother's (in her) interfering with therapy as foreshadowed in Dream 2? We can only speculate; the answers would have to arise out of a personal confrontation of therapist and client.

Clinical Use of the Dreams

The above understandings, confirmed by feeling "right" to the dreamer, pinpoint problem areas and help the client experience them in terms of imaginal descriptions rather than as abstract speculations of the therapist. Imagination is a more powerful modality for affect mobilization than is abstract thought. And the dream "knows" where the outsider can merely conjecture.

Martha's initial dream would enable the therapist to gain a preliminary overview of the disturbed dynamics and alert him to areas in need of attention. Depending on the assessment of Martha's capacity for insight and ego strength, treatment can focus immediately on discovering where and how she operates in terms of Katharine Hepburn and the Prime Minister fantasies and identifications. Therapist and client can explore by what means and rationalizations she holds herself aloof and avoids conflict, involvement and commitment. One need not wait until free associations or the therapist's theoretical speculations lead to those issues, if they ever do.

Dreams 2, 3 and 4 likewise draw direct attention to Martha's relation to mother and to the mother's attitudes as part of Martha's own make-up. The latter is particularly important since it is so readily assumed that conscious opposition to the behavior, affect, pattern and value system of a significant person protects us against psychic infection or being conditioned by them. What we have to fight, we introject as effectively as what we willingly identify with. This initially opposed conditioning occurs unconsciously, overriding the resisting will. It mobilizes strong affect and may be more powerful than a conscious identification, as our limited experience with brainwashing has shown.

Thus our likeness to the persons or objects which we tend to oppose and resent is easily overlooked. In protesting outer difficulties and past injuries, we overlook our own corresponding complexes which perpetuate them by our unrealistic behavior, affect, reactions and distorted perception. The subject level interpretation of affect-charged dream figures and objects points directly to the dreamer's distorted areas and therefore is of invaluable importance.

Martha's Dream 2 tells her loudly and clearly that in spite of her conscious effort her own resemblance to the ways she experiences the mother interferes with her development and even with her therapy. The dream would be used to explore the ways the mother might feel about therapy and then to look for a similar set of feelings in Martha.

Dreams 3 and 4 would lead to an exploration of feelings and valuations about sex in terms of the mother's influence but also in terms of cultural and religious values. The dreamer's ideas about herself as a woman, her feminine adaptation and her fear of losing control over her emotions would be explored.

Dream 5, beyond emphasizing the need for positive assertiveness, is also prognostically significant. It points to the existence of a growth and assertiveness potential. This dream may also be used to assuage possible fears on Martha's part that a more assertive stance would be incompatible with her stance as a woman. It can be pointed out that the nipple is eventually returned to her.

Also, Dream 5 indirectly sheds light upon Martha's original presenting problems of being unable to control her life and making decisions which she cannot follow through. This impasse is characteristic of an ego dissociation from the unconscious dominants of the personality which in this dream are represented by the animus figure of the man on the island who lends her his penis in exchange for the nipple.

Ego attempts to control, regardless or in direct disregard of one's unconscious drives and personality patterns, result in willful directives and decisions which fall flat, owing to unconscious lack of cooperation or even outright sabotage by the objective psyche. The exchange in Dream 5 depicts that this split might be healed by putting Martha's femininity at the disposal of the assertive needs and realizing that these (the phallus) are not hers. They are not to be subject to ego whims and arbitrariness; they belong to a deeper layer of the personality which seeks expression either in cooperation with or at the price of interfering with the ego system.

Dream 6 raises the issue of conscious self-acceptance which might need further discussion and deepening. A differentiation of her own judgments from the mother's might also be explored. Once this separation is accomplished, the mother as a person need no longer be fought and resented. Affection and love may become possible. Attention might be drawn also to a need to explore her religiocultural conditionings and the ways in which her personal values could be reconciled with hitherto unexplored facets of this tradition. The Hebraic tradition was originally matriarchal and not at all as restrictive in terms of play and sexual morality as it has become through the Middle Ages. This may be one of the implications of what is to be found in the depth underlying the old ramshackle building. Perhaps in being her own person she need not alienate herself from her tradition and family. And, of course, the significance of the perhaps premature ending of the search would be raised for discussion.

The quality and degree of the use of dreams depends on the personalities of therapist and therapee, both unknown here. There is a range of possible style of use from direct interpretation and confrontation to expectant waiting and encouraging the client to meditate upon and feel out the imagery. As required, nonverbal, particularly artistic approaches also can be used to "get into" the dream experience. Jung encouraged painting of dream images and figures and used them as starting points for "active imagination" development. Modeling and dancing have also been used by Jungians and, in recent years, gestalt and psychodramatic enactment as well.

Yet no matter which particular technique is used for the purpose of concretizing the dream's images, the innovative and practically most significant contribution of Jung's approach is the subject level approach to the dream. It shows what needs to be and can be safely confronted at what particular time.

REFERENCES

Jung, C. G. (1945). *Psychological Reflections*. New York: Harper Torchbook, Harper & Brothers, 1961.

———— (1958). *Psychology and Religion: West and East. Collected Works*, Vol. 11 York: Pantheon.

Schroedinger, E. (1951). *Science and Humanism*. Cambridge: Cambridge University Press.

Whitmont, E. (1961). *The Symbolic Quest*. New York: Putnam (to be reprinted by Princeton University Press).

CHAPTER FOUR

Culturalist Approach

WALTER BONIME, M.D.
with FLORENCE BONIME

BASIC THEORY OF THE MEANING OF DREAMS[1]

Dreaming is a state of consciousness that has become more and more difficult to define. During the last quarter-century, research in the sleep laboratory has discovered that everyone dreams cyclically and that dreams occupy roughly a fifth of our sleep time. The new data make it impossible for us to say, as we° used to say, "Where there's a dream, there's a problem,"

°*Regarding the author pronouns "I" and "we" etc.:* All of the clinical psychoanalytic work on which this chapter is based was done by Walter Bonime. In the full and clear communication of the ideas, Florence Bonime collaborated throughout. To avoid confusion, the initial discussion will use the plural pronouns "we" and "us" but this switches to the singular "I" when the material moves ahead to clinical processes. (The communication of ideas in the behavioral sciences is the subject of a collaborative article by these authors which appears in Vol. 6 of the *Journal of the American Academy of Psychoanalysis.*)

[1]There will be no effort here to summarize the recent research (more than two decades) into the physiology, psychology and sociology of the dream state. My comments will make only scant allusion to some of this work. For excellent presentations the following references are offered: Jones (1970) and Breger (1969). An important text on the dream as an expression of a problem ("focal conflict") is found in French and Fromm (1964). A valuable research paper correlating dream content with waking concern has been written by Kramer (1977); see also Kramer et al. (1976). On "consciousness" there is Tart (1972); Ornstein (1974); and Ullman et al. (1973). Finally, texts on culture and dreams are by Von Grunebaum and Callois (1966) (expecially chapters by Eggan and Bastide) and Ullman (1960, 1973).

because this implied that the problem caused the dream to appear. Now we know that there is always a dream, whether or not the dreamer has what we call "a problem."

Most dreams are not remembered, and of the remembered dreams few are reported to anyone. The context of a dream experience differs from the context of a waking experience in at least two significant respects: (1) compared with waking life, there is minimal sensory input; and (2) there is no necessity to regulate behavior, to think rationally or to engage in verbal communication. There are many other physiological and psychological variables, but the two we have mentioned are the most relevant to a study of the use of dreams in psychotherapy.

We view waking thought (unless one is at work on a concrete problem) as random, exploratory and associative. It is evoked, interrupted, propelled, redirected by internal and external perceptions and sensory stimuli, and by adaptive needs and operations. The act of noticing our thoughts tends to impel us to organize them into rational and verbally communicable form. When we stop noticing them, they return to the free-associative style—which may also exist, at a subliminal level, during the rational and communicative periods. Our minds are continually at work.

Most of what we experience in a dream is nonverbal. Sometimes words or sentences occur, but they may be neither coherent nor obviously purposeful, as our waking utterances try to be. The dream mode is symbolic, imagistic and affective. Language is, of course, also symbolic, but symbolic in the service of communication, whereas dream symbolism seems to serve a different purpose, perhaps an integrative purpose. We cannot state with assurance that dreaming has an integrative function, but there is theoretical and empirical support for that concept. Empirically, when working with dreams, we capture a portion of a continuing process which involves construing, correlating, reevaluating, modifying, feeling and creating. Theoretically, the integrative function has been spelled out by neurophysiologists and psychologists, and we shall quote one from each of these disciplines.

Neurophysiologist Hernandez-Peon (1965), who posits continous personality structuring through constant active circuitry within the brain, says: ".. . during dreaming the Conscious Experience System processes some of the information which has been stored without awareness, so that the most relevant items can be selected by a variety of types of associations with memory tracings consciously available, and thus be utilized for future adaptive behavior—it may explain many examples of ideational problem-solving occurring during dreaming."

The concept of dreaming as an integrative function is expressed by psychologist Louis Breger (1961): "... the possibility remains that even as private, unrecalled events, [dreams] may serve the function of integrating aroused information into existing structures." We accept this concept of the integrative function of dreams—not in isolation from waking life, but as part of the totality of life processes. Behavior, thoughts and feelings when awake are affected by dreams, and in turn affect our dreams. Life is a continuum (Robbins, 1960; Bonime, 1961).

The above statements are hypothetical. We cannot ask of our so articulate brains, Why do you dream? What is a dream? Why this image, that sound, those colors? Even with the new technology, we have no glimmer of an answer, but many exciting possibilities exist. The brain hemisphere research, now hotly pursued, is establishing differences between right-hemisphere and left-hemisphere functioning (Ornstein, 1974), and as this research continues it may in time illuminate more of the psychological and physiological purposes and processes of dreaming; but our knowledge of the determinants of any one dream can at present be only partial and speculative.

As an empirical base for the following pages, we can safely say that the dream is not a communication created to impress another; it is an unguarded symbolic expression of self. In its nakedness it reveals, or makes possible our tracing of the true nature of the dreamer's personality. The dream is not a disguise, but probably the most authentic presentation of personality.

We say "authentic" because the experienced dream embodies attitudes, feelings and intuitions which the dreamer is unable or afraid to recognize about himself in his waking state. At an inchoate level, however, there is some knowledge of these attitudes, and that is why clinicians and their patients are able to discover them in working with dreams.

Dream symbolism is a way of knowing, of combining cognitive and affective responses, and presenting them to oneself in the "representational" mode. The manifest dream does not directly *tell*—it *presents* to the dreamer accurate information about his own attitudes, in the form of oneiric images, actions and emotions. We regard the latent content of the dream as all the attitudes represented in the dream which the individual, in the waking state, cannot yet recognize in himself.

The associative thought process described above becomes our exploratory method for discovering the latent content of the manifest dream symbolism. We do not regard the manifest dream itself as a disguise, so we have no need for the concept of "censor." It is the awake patient who disguises his own feelings and thoughts, trying to hide them from others and from himself, in order to maintain his self-image—a painful, often bankrupt process which has brought him into therapy.

In reporting the dream, the dreamer must convert the experience into a linguistic description. The discursive mode, which is syntactical and therefore logical, must necessarily alter the original nonlogical experience. The dreamer's vocabulary and style of speech are part of his existing life pattern and are limited to what is permissible in the maintenance of self-image. To that degree, the report is affected by his existing personality, including all its disguises. But there is also the inherent difficulty (even with the most candid and honest intentions) in translating from one mode of thought to another. We have no verbal language adequate to the awesomely condensed and accurate symbolic language of dreams.

These remarks are an attempt to express briefly the perennial wonder, and some hypotheses, as to what dreams really are and why indeed we dream at all. Although we can not satisfy our curiosity at present, we can nevertheless make good use of our dreams.

PRINCIPLES CONCERNING THE USE OF DREAMS IN TREATMENT

Any expression of the mind, awake or asleep, under any physiological influence, can be taken as a point of ingress to examine the personality.[2] A dream has certain advantages. Because of its unfamiliar symbolic and metaphoric modes of expression, its seeming illogic, its frequent violation of temporal and spatial limitations, a dream lends itself more readily to the unaccustomed disjunctiveness of associative activity. Work with dreams serves particularly well to induct the patient into free association—and, while learning free association, the patient also becomes involved in collaboration.

Since the collaborative approach is the backbone of my contribution, I will interpolate at the outset my reasons for participating in this type of comparative study. There is an obvious discrepancy between my credo in clinical practice and the one-sided speculations I will engage in later. My written "work with Martha" is done apart from this patient and is necessarily very different from what it would be in collaboration. In actual interchange, my focusing on Martha's responses and her focusing on any hunches of mine that resonate within her would be followed and elaborated within her. Her experience and my experience, my increasing knowledge of her and her increasing ability to use free association, our continuing exchange—all of this combined would produce, for the patient and for me, a richer, more accurate, more meaningful and useful understanding of her dreams and her personality.

In the present context, there will, by design, be extensive speculation and

---

[2]The clinical method discussed here is fully developed in the authors' *The Clinical Use of Dreams* (New York: Basic Books, 1962). Page footnotes, unless otherwise identified, will refer to this book.

no exchange. As an exercise, nevertheless, I believe that this comparative study will be heuristically useful and that a technical emphasizing of collaboration should be represented among the approaches to be compared.

The Culturalist's Orientation

One additional explanation is in order. The term *"culturalist"* means to me that interpersonal experience is the dominant force in the development and dynamics of personality. Constitutional factors are codeterminants (Thomas et al., 1968), but I do not employ the classical instinctivist theories. Environment, particularly social environment, and personality, in reciprocal interaction, continue throughout life to determine and modify the structure and function of personality.[3]

This orientation developed for me through early work with Horney (1937, 1939) and Robbins (1955, 1956, 1960). To Robbins, the term *unconscious* referred to those aspects of the individual's value system that remain expediently unknown at a conceptual level but which betray their presence in activity.

In this framework (which is my framework), the broad spectrum of emotions which we call love, hate, grief, sorrow, despair and guilt, as well as other feelings, some of them nameless, are highly complex experiences, developed during intricate and long-elaborated social interactions, predominantly after early infancy.

Words such as "culturalist" and "collaborative" will acquire more shades of meaning in the pages ahead. Both are consistent with a fundamental premise that "personality evolves through interpersonal experience and is modified through interpersonal experience" (Preface, p. xxii).

Starting the Patient in the Use of Dreams

All we know when we hear a dream is that it is a personally novel expression, and we surmise that it was set off by a recent affective experience stirring memories. The dream becomes a point of departure in a search for the nature of the dreamer's personality. Free association, which is a groping, floundering and risking activity, can be used clinically to dip into the patient's ongoing processes of thought and feeling. Without preconceptions, we

---

[3]The clearest statement of the evolution and nature of the culturalist orientation is that of Ullman (1962b). For an excellent, more recent paper on the subject, see Rubins, 1975.

can collaboratively seek out the idiosyncratic connotations of the dream elements of each patient.

The free-associative style of thought (as mentioned in the previous section) is probably a continuous waking human mode, though we seldom notice it. When we do, we tend immediately to dismiss or rationalize it, or we are quickly diverted from it by other stimuli. When focusing on a dream in psychotherapy, we try not to dismiss or rationalize; we allow the free exploratory process to continue unhindered. Associations range freely over present events, thoughts and feelings, as well as remembered events, thoughts and feelings, including all fantasies, until linkages begin to emerge and are noticed by patient or therapist. The linkages may lead to a tentative interpretation, speculation or hypothesis. If the therapist speculates aloud, his speculation may simply not "ring a bell." On the other hand, it may surprise and stimulate the patient to continued associations and linkages of his own which may confirm, modify or replace the therapist's hypothesis.

The development of collaboration in working with dreams proceeds along many paths. It can be used to engage the patient in the therapeutic process (Bonime, 1969b). It is often necessary to reengage and reengage the patient. The patient eventually feels more at home in this new activity, acquires an inner readiness and openness toward associative activity and eventually may precede the therapist in seizing the implications of a dream.

One must bear in mind that the reported dream is not the experienced dream. The reported dream has been translated from the symbolic mode into the discursive mode and therefore is unavoidably a distortion of the experienced dream. The listener hears the reported dream in accordance with his own personality, so that the dream as perceived by the analyst's consciousness is again changed. We have a rough approximation of the patient's dream experience to work with—but it is enough.

The length or brevity of the reported dream is unrelated to its richness and usefulness. We never know whether or not the patient has remembered all of the dream or only a fragment of it. Very brief dreams (such as Martha's third dream below) may have widespread significance. Martha's first and sixth dreams were both long, and both significant, but dealt with very different levels of readiness for self-recognition. At times a long dream may be like a rambling anecdote, with little discoverable value. The length of a reported dream, therefore, gives us no clues.

The dream experience can express internal chaotic inconsistencies and contradictions in symbols that are simple, compressed and powerful. Dreamer and therapist, either or both, can sense the power of the symbol while the meanings it contains remain obscure and baffling.

In pursuit of meanings the therapist initially explains free association to the patient, who may or may not immediately accept or understand it. I explain to the patient that one often wakes from a dream while lying in bed and that disconnected thoughts flow through one's mind; and I suggest that the patient can try the same experience now, letting thoughts and feelings, no matter how disjunctive or trivial they seem, flow through his mind.[4] I explain that we will be looking for possible significance in these random thoughts and that he can help himself, and help me, by expressing aloud every memory, feeling, fantasy or fragment, of any kind whatever.

When the patient actually begins to associate, the disjunctiveness, the apparent inappropriateness or seeming triviality may appear embarrassingly stupid or silly. The extraordinariness of most dreams, however, makes the extraordinariness of this suggested procedure more acceptable.

The Analyst's Associative and Interpretive Activity

If the analyst can offer a correlation of any fragments or associations, his own or the patient's, with part of the dream, and if these correlations resonate within the patient, the patient is usually intrigued by the process and tends to enter into it.

This educational event has great importance for the interpersonal situation during therapy. The analyst has risked the expression of a possible absurdity, a complete mistake, and he has been (or should be) ready to accept correction or rejection of his concept. His offering can be the beginning of the dissolution of the hierarchical barrier and the start of a cooperative tie. If his suggestion is not helpful, there is a shared bafflement, and the patient may begin to feel the need for more reciprocity.

The patient's humiliation—his sense of being "a defective" in the presence of "an expert"—starts to fade. Collaboration, a curative process in itself, is nurtured. A committed patient and an alert, attentive therapist can often together find linkages in the associative pieces, then move ahead to discover the symbolic implications and eventually achieve coherent cognitive statement. In this continuing process, both members of the dyad expand their

----

[4]If a timid patient has not been able to use the couch, this explanation may help him to try it, even if only on an experimental basis. If a couch is not available, reversal of the patient's chair will serve. The basic reasons for avoiding face-to-face seating are: to facilitate preoccupation with internal associative, mnemonic and affective experience and to eliminate as much as possible any editing that might result from efforts to calculate (by studying the therapist's appearance) the ongoing effects of the communication.

understanding of the patient's personality.

I try to cultivate in the patient the ability to report his first association, which many patients tend to discard. For this reason I do not allow long silences but instead very soon ask the patient to say what he is thinking, what he has thought during the brief silence and, if possible, to say it in the order in which the thoughts came.

While there are occasional situations in which a suggestion from the therapist may be useful in initiating reactions to a dream, it is usually important for the therapist not to offer at once his association, empathic response or interpretive hypothesis in order not to contaminate or steer the spontaneous train of thought, memory and feeling of the patient. If we later discover an identity of association, this may constitute a consensual validation and be of great value.

The therapist may at times say to the patient, "I have some associations and speculations about this dream, or part of it, but I don't want to interfere now—go ahead and we can compare later." If there is a good working alliance, the patient will welcome the respectful challenge to pursue the problem independently, believing in the therapist's eagerness for the greatest productivity, trusting his readiness to speak out later, to compare and openly correlate their contributions.

There are also times when, after the analyst has expressed an association or an interpretive hypothesis, the patient will acknowledge having had the same thoughts moments earlier, or at some time between the dream and the session. Such an occurrence can enable a patient to recognize his own resistance—and also, as indicated above, to simultaneously appreciate the usefulness of reciprocal activity.

A holding off by the therapist is not always productive. As at all other junctures in psychotherapy, technique varies according to the particular patient and the state of the therapeutic interpersonal relationship.

Dreams that are brief and vivid provide their own focus. Some dreams (such as Martha's first dream in the following section), however, are long and crowded, and a focus of attention must be provided. Early in therapy it is commonly the therapist who must establish a priority and a focus. (When the patient takes over the major responsibility for these roles, he is demonstrating a degree of commitment to dealing rationally with his problems that indicates one of the criteria for termination.)

The therapist's action in establishing a priority arises out of his own subjective consciousness. His subjectivity is a factor to be kept in mind at all times. The patient's dream sets in motion, in the therapist, intuitive and memory processes related to this patient, to other patients and to his own life experience. These stirrings are the sources of his questions to the patient and to himself. Every increment of cognitive-affective information about the patient can serve to stimulate questions and associations, and further to probe and synchronize the related idiosyncratic memory store of both patient and therapist. The process is reciprocal, but the focus of attention should not waver from the dream itself.[5]

Cultural Referents

So far I have mentioned referents that are subjective, idiosyncratic, within the patient and within the therapist. There is also a store of referents that are shared by members of the same culture (such as the cultural competitiveness which will come under discussion later).

Nevertheless, there is always the question of how "common" for everyone in it any culture can be. How much background can be shared by an upper-class Irish Catholic Boston analyst with an Orthodox Jewish patient who is twenty years younger or older and of the opposite sex? How much cultural commonality is there between a poverty-born Jewish Chicagoan analyst and a small-town Southern Baptist now a millionaire mill operator? What makes the commonality within "Western culture" itself—and then where is the commonality between the Middle Eastern, Far Eastern, African, whole cultures that may make difficult the penetration in either direction?

Such questions have no single definitive answers, yet we know that in the therapeutic situation the barriers come together at an interface and that the interface can be penetrated by collaborative activity and mutual learning.

But let us return to the differences of cultural connotation within one culture. We have idiosyncratic differences of emotional connotation even when the dream symbol is identical for several people and even when the first association to it is also identical. An apple, for example, dreamed of by a Swiss woman, might evoke first the William Tell legend, and next she might think of manly courage, the attribute of the national hero, which she might finally romantically apply to a new male acquaintance. Another Alpine person might also think first of William Tell, but might then go on to his envy of people who have such consummate skill. In the dream of a young Swiss boy who suffered intense hostility from his father, the apple might at first elicit William Tell but then might quickly move on into anxiety about his father's homicidal aim.

---

[5]There are circumstances of pressing immediate concern which may have a higher priority than the dream (Bonime, 1966a). Furthermore, a particular association may provide an overriding focus.

An elderly American who remembers the Depression years might dream of an apple and think of formerly financially secure men selling apples on street corners, then go on to anxiety about a possible business reversal. Or the oneiric apple could denote a nostalgia for rural living.

Examples of differential interpretation of symbols can go on endlessly. Enough has here been suggested to indicate that the symbolism of dreams cannot be universal, even though some of it may refer coincidentally to a common heritage and experience.

Affect in Dreams

In the effort to achieve the fullest possible understanding of dream symbolism, I find that the pursuit of emotions, both felt (experiential) emotions and symbolized emotions, is the most productive path to follow (pp. 31–48). Unless spontaneous associations come immediately, I usually ask, "What were your feelings during the dreaming?"

There are several reasons for the pursuit of emotions. Primarily, the *experienced* feelings cannot be known to anyone except the dreamer.[6] Secondly, the recapture of feelings that occurred during the dreaming often results in the recall of additional portions of the dream. Where the patient has an uncrystallized memory or a dim memory, attention to feelings can help him to get back more, or the first clear elements, of the dream.

Some patients repeatedly omit the experienced feelings from their reports of dreams. This omission is caused by the dreamer's dim subjective sense that his disavowed feelings (often naked in a dream) can damage his self-image. The analyst's persistence in this area, however, eventually becomes a patient's own discipline, and even a spontaneous tendency.

Sometimes a patient, honestly puzzled, may say, "There didn't seem to be any feelings at all." If I follow up with something like "Were you anxious? Or angry, perhaps?" I may elicit, "Oh, no, as a matter of fact I was feeling just, well, confident. And pleased," or some other contrasting expression of the mood I had suggested.

Naturally, one does not follow up feelings exclusively before proceeding with other questions, but the nature and quality of the affect must be explored all along. Bearing in mind the great distance between dream

---

[6]In the psychotherapeutic situation, the patient is always the resource person concerning emotion. The therapist's empathy can never do the job. To have value, his empathy must be corroborated by the patient.

dream experience and dream report, we find that pursuit of the affect results in more completeness and eventually more clarity.

A tangential profit from the careful pursuit of dream (and waking) emotions is greater clarity even about reported feelings. The patient may be using a kind of pseudo-communication—a fuzzy terminology such as "upset," which can have meanings as disparate as angry, disappointed, embarrassed, frustrated, disheartened, enraged. Other imprecise terms are "funny" and "strange" (pp. 96–98). More precise examination of such affective terms can help both patient and analyst to detect emotions actually experienced in the dream.

Affect is usually multiple: emotions are present not as a single note but as a chord. Patients reporting experiential feeling in a dream usually report just one feeling, and that one only if it is strong. For example, a man may say he was mad. He may, however, have been at the same time chagrined over revealing his anger to his friends, embarrassed by acknowledging anger to his therapist, humiliated because he remembers his wife's frequent accusations that he hid his hostility. Simultaneously he might experience a modicum of pride at having made some progress in "expressing his feelings."

In addition, the analyst can only conjecture, and the patient, left to himself, may not examine closely enough to perceive the multiplicity of feelings and perhaps also the contradictoriness of all the affects embodied in the dream. A dream about a funeral, for example, may suggest deep personal loss, angry sense of abandonment, release from a tormentor, vindictive pleasure, welcome competitive advantage, compassion for another's release from suffering, anxiety about one's own mortality. Any of these, in any combination, and still other emotions could predominate. Actually, the whole "funeral" could refer to the metaphoric "death" of some quality within the patient or in his environment. The dream funeral could be evaluated variously by the analyst, rationalized or glibly interpreted by the patient. In contrast, careful exploration of affect could discover a whole new aspect of the patient's personality or perhaps give crucial confirmation of an attitude that might theretofore have been only suspected.

Patients who become awakened to the depth and complexity of their own emotions usually develop more alertness to them, but for a long time they may continue to require outside activation. Eventually, during the continuum of analysis, greater readiness to deal with the reality of self (rather than maintaining the illusory self-image) is accompanied by greater readiness and ability to discover, delineate and communicate the complex feelings within the dream. (All of these considerations apply equally to sleeping and awake effect.)

Hypothetical Nature of Dream Interpretation

One moves from affect to the dream as a whole. Sometimes with honest puzzlement the therapist may have to ask, "What's this all about?" This kind of question is an invitation to engage in interpretive activity.

All our "interpretations" of dreams are hypothetical. There is an enormous amount of material to be sought beyond the reported dream. Sometimes this is already shared information based on a long period of work together. Individual dreams develop personal glossaries (p. 32 and Index) from previous dreams and previous experiences. These are idiosyncratically derived in work with the patient—terms, phrases, symbols of intricate but established dynamics, elements densely and exquisitely charged with communicative power within the psychotherapeutic dyad.

A patient's own personality attribute is often represented in his dreams by another individual. His own tyranny may be symbolized by the presence in the dream of a domineering person whose behavior the dreamer, when awake, abominates. A dreamer's own unacknowledged timidity may be represented in his dream by a coward.

A patient's characteristics may also be represented by nonhuman (animal) or inorganic elements or combinations of these. An unresponsive quality in the dreamer may appear as a granite statue; a servile, adaptive trait, as a thermometer; the unhappiness of an efficient employee, as a weeping robot.

Not all the oneiric individuals and objects, however, necessarily represent the dreamer. In his waking state, the dreamer may be reluctant to acknowledge certain qualities in other people and may reveal his rejected perceptions of these others by intuitively accurate oneiric symbols (pp. 4–8).

An interpretive effort, whether it comes from the patient or the therapist, has grown out of persistent collaborative pursuit of the patient's continuing fantasies, impulses and activities, and the interpretation can be authenticated, expanded or modified through the same kinds of collaborative pursuit. If patient and analyst have similar associations and interpretations, this may, as noted earlier, become a kind of consensual validation. If this occurs while the patient is beginning to see a part of his own personality that is difficult to accept, the spirit of collaboration diminishes self-consciousness and shame, and facilitates freedom and trust; a great deal can be risked by both patient and therapist; the patient's shame, embarrassment or anger accompanying the report can be acknowledged and become valuable added affective data.

Obstacles to Effective Work with Dreams

So far, I have talked about an optimal situation in which skills and freedom in associative and interpretive activity are learned and increasingly used;

trust is engendered; the patient makes progress. Now I will address myself to obstacles in the therapeutic process: the therapist's role in interfering with the progress of therapy, and the patient's anxiety and resistance.

The subjectivity of the therapist has been discussed as a necessary and effective contribution to the work on dreams, but his subjectivity may also cause him to resent his patient's independent efforts, to become authoritarian, to be impatient for closure and intolerant of new discoveries that did not arise from his own work. He may designate the patient's increasing participation and developing skills as "resistance" to his own "insights." He may have obsessive tendencies toward certainty which accelerate and then rigidify his translation of symbols, and this urgent search for certainty may steer him away from some dream material which would otherwise be extremely productive for the patient. I think we may safely say that no discipline is immune to obsessive and tyrannical personalities, that such traits may be not at all obvious and that they bear watching, each therapist for himself.

The patient may detect this domineering tendency in a therapist not only in the office interaction but through the appearance of the therapist in a dream. This occurrence is traditionally regarded as "transference" of feelings the patient had in his formative years toward parental figures. In my own dealing with such phenomena, I regard reactions to me as immediate to the ongoing situation and do not consider myself a surrogate. When the patient reacts to the therapist, he is responding with his own personality to the personality of the therapist. The patient may be misperceiving or misinterpreting the therapist, but he also may be responding to a warp in the character of the therapist. The concept of transference can become a strategy of denial on the part of a therapist who seeks a surrogate as a scapegoat. The transferring may be a phenomenon of the therapist rather than of the patient.

This may result in a serious distortion of the therapeutic interpersonal relationship and an undermining of the entire process. It may accentuate in the patient all his anxieties, resistances, distrust. Therefore, every so-called "transference" response and its reflection in dreams should be examined for potentially revealing data about the therapist himself and about the interpersonal activity that is happening right now, rather than in some historical stage of the patient's development.

There is no intention in these cautionary comments to locate the major source of resistance in the personality of the therapist. Let us suppose that the therapist is the best of all possible therapists, mature and flexible, and with no stake in being "first" or "right." The patient will still have abundant anxiety in sensing the need for, and even the process of, personality change—and this anxiety will give rise to a variety of forms of resistance.

At this point one must think a moment about the culture in which we all operate. The collaborative method runs counter to our prevailing "free enterprise" ideology (not an exclusively American or Western phenomenon), with its emphasis on competition and status. The prevailing cultural competitiveness, even within close-knit families, can be seen everywhere, often coexisting with love, between good friends, between husbands and wives, among siblings and between generations (Bonime, 1966b). In the business and professional worlds, where openness and trust are scarce and somehow limited even among colleagues and co-workers, collaboration in work is often confined to the immediate task and has an impersonal and cautious quality beneath the outer camaraderie.

In this unfavorable cultural climate, the culturalist fosters collaboration, aims to create a climate of openness and trust. The aim is not to encourage the patient's trust in everyone: it is to enable him to make distinctions not only between people who are more trustworthy, or less trustworthy, but also between different degrees of trustworthiness, at different times and under different pressures. There are human limitations and human strengths, and a maturing individual can acquire complex recognitions of many possible variables.

To return to the patient's anxieties: He comes into therapy with the personality he has been developing throughout his life and with accustomed modes of functioning which have been failing and causing him great misery. In the course of therapy, he begins to learn how his own behavior contributes to (or creates) his own misery. But such learning cannot be easy. The patient has a sense of being alive, is familiar to himself, when functioning in the old ways. A threat to the old ways is subjectively experienced as a dissolution of his "sense of self." (Bonime, 1973, 1976a). He therefore, regardless of the pain of maintaining his accustomed mode of living, adopts many maneuvers to preserve the only "self" he knows.

Dreams, being the reflection of the whole personality, reflect also those elements of interpersonal functioning by which the individual seeks to avoid the influence of others, including the therapist. His recurrent, anxious efforts to disengage from the collaborative effort are characterized by the common cultural elements referred to above: competitiveness and cynical mistrust. The patient may withold his dreams, severely edit them or offer them at the very end of a session. He may report dreams in such abundance that he fills the hour by filibuster, leaving no time for explorations and associations, and depriving himself of the potentially revelatory gleanings of the night.

A patient may subjectively sense that a dream will expose a quality that is incompatible with his self-image (see above). He may report the dream, yet be unwilling at that point to associate to it. "I don't think of anything—nothing comes to mind" is often a decision rather than an accurate report. A dozen billion brain cells cannot remain dormant—a good fact about which to remind a patient on occasion.

The patient may be competing with the therapist, trying to force from him the first commitment. (This may result from the patient's own previous private associations that were too revealing to be tolerable.) Or he may seek to nullify his own thoughts by saying, "I know what you're thinking." It is important for the therapist not to enter the fray. The patient's possibly competitive avoidances can be simply overlooked. If the therapist speaks his own thoughts, such intervention may be a partial illumination of the dream, for which the patient is basically grateful, and there may result a reengagement in the therapeutic alliance.

Pursuit of the anxiety that gives rise to such resistances can be a productive therapeutic course (Bonime, 1959). Questions asked in connection with anxiety-provoking dream elements may bring back numerous waking experiences of anxiety. By correlation, these may give clues to the nature of anxiety-provoking life circumstance for this patient and augment the immediate sensitivity to other moments of the dream.

There are endless variations on the maneuvers an anxious patient goes through to avoid painful self-recognitions. Fears connected with surrendering the old ways gradually diminish in therapy, however, as the patient acquires more and more fragmentary experiential evidence, more and more recognition, that it is possible and safe for him to change—that he has healthy resources.

Relationship of Insight to Change

This raises a further question: If the insights should prove to be valid, can we feel assured that the patient will change? That is, of course, a fundamental question in psychoanalysis. Insight itself does not produce basic change. It provides the option for change (Robbins, 1960; Bonime, 1961). Until the patient knows what motivates him he is in a poor position to change his behavior. Insight provides a second chance, an opportunity for the patient to determine the form of his personality. If his insights are applied in life situations, the result will be a salutary alteration in attitude and function, more satisfying experiential consequences and a new perspective. In therapy also, new practices are made possible by the options that open up as a result of insight. Having produced evidence of healthy resources, the patient's efforts in working with his dreams can be considerably strengthened (Bonime, 1958).

There may, on the other hand, be situations in which an individual is disbelieving or hostile to signs of change. Change may be experienced by the patient as a sign of competitive defeat. Dreams may simply reveal more growth than a patient is willing to acknowledge.

A patient may be profoundly ambivalent about emergent health, with its unfamiliar sensations and behavior, its fragile masteries which are in conflict with the long established pathology. The anxiety or the rebellion against progress, coexisting with the progress itself, results in a disturbing ambivalence—but this should not be regarded simply as pathology or as resistance alone. Ambivalence is often an achievement.

Reassurance prompted by dream evidence (or waking evidence) is a particularly delicate activity for the therapist. Unjustified or mistaken reassurance is therapeutically injurious. It may give the patient a small initial "lift," but if there is no qualitative change in feeling and performance, if the patient is merely engaging in a ritualistic display of a "new" spirit accompanied by "new" gestures, and if there has been no development of the patient's potential, there will be an inevitable letdown which, in turn, will attenuate motivation for engagement and change.

Reassurance is even more difficult to deal with in the depression-prone patient. Depressives reach avidly for help from the resources of others, rather than from their personal resources (Bonime, 1976b). Calling attention to genuine achieved progress may be sensed by the depressive as a demand upon him, or perhaps a discontinuance of support. It is essential to make clear to him both the evidence of healthy change and his complete autonomy regarding the further use of insight.

Sources of Associations

To return now to the reciprocal process when it is moving ahead without too much interference—it is useful to bear in mind that associations do not arrive "out of nowhere." In my opinion, any association of patient or of therapist is a fragment of an already existing inchoate concept. Associative activity, then, is already the inception of interpretive activity. The anecdotal and affective material preceding the report of a dream, during its recounting and following its communication, is all part of an associative mix out of which a hypothesis is derived. The item which leads to, "Oh, I had a dream!" (the moment of association) (p. 11 and Index) is a particularly significant clue to the dream's meaning (a precious bit of data for the therapist to note, even by writing it down). The dream is suddenly recalled as an association to the moment's recollection. All the associations are fragmentary at first, but illumination begins to develop as the patient and analyst begin to recognize certain harmonies, dim connections among them. There is an uncrystallized cognitive matrix out of which all the associations come—an area of knowing without being aware. The association comes because it is relevant.

Crystallization of the dream and its associations into a meaning may occur with the sudden arrival of a crucial element, a process somewhat similar to a foreign body's effect in a chemically supersaturated solution—that wondrous moment in which there is an instantaneous shift from liquid to solid crystalline state. This crystallization is what we call *insight*, and it may be the result of something insinuated during associative activity by patient or therapist. Regardless of who has contributed the element that brings meaning out of the associative process, the insight arrives because some association has been recalled or been generated out of a previously inchoate cognition. Each associative fragment is an element of that incompletely structured framework of understanding.

Evolution of Insight

The newly discovered meaning or insight may be in need of qualification or even total rejection in favor of a more authentic meaning. We continue to pay intense affective and cognitive attention to all the elements in the dream, in a continuing process that will support, expand, modify or nullify the "insight" contained in the dream. This may proceed sporadically for weeks or months, and a more fully correct meaning of the dream may arrive even years later, in a momentary clinical or other life context.

The arrival of profound understanding of a dream is for the patient, as well as the analyst, an exciting, rewarding, often aesthetic experience. This is true for the patient even if the insight is frightening or otherwise disturbing.

Because it is so important that insight be as full and as correct as it can possibly be at that point in therapy, caution is necessary to avoid premature closure. As mentioned, premature closure can result from the therapist's infatuation with a theory or with his own previous "insights." It can also be desired by a patient who urgently wants to drop the subject. At such moments the therapist needs to reactivate his awareness of the patient's resistances and his own.

Symbols

I believe I have made clear (by so far omitting sexuality from this discussion) that sexuality per se is not basic to my concept of personality symbolism. The appearance of a snake or a tube would not turn my mind to sexuality unless the patient's associations created that meaning. Sexuality does not determine character—rather, it is the nature of a person's character that determines how he behaves sexually. Physiological and psychosocial determinants and expressions are intricately intertwined. These observations apply equally to masturbatory fantasies (Bonime, 1969c). Overtly sexual images or completely nonsexual images can equally implicate sexual or nonsexual disturbances of personality. The dream metaphor may, furthermore, deal with both kinds of disturbances simultaneously.

The precise and idiosyncratic meaning of the dream symbols of any patient can be reached through reciprocal efforts. But, once understood, the symbols must still be observed for signs of mutation. (In the case of Martha, the mutations of symbolism appear to be clearly traceable.)

For each patient certain symbols remain as continuous themes until personality begins to change. At that point the dream symbols may alter or mutate in conjunction with changes in attitude, behavior and feelings of the patient. Herein can be traced the progress, resistance to progress or loss of previous gains. This holds true for a single dream with various episodes, different dreams of the same night or the progression of dreams over a period or over the total course of treatment. The modification of dream symbols reflects the changing ways in which the patient responds to, perceives and interacts with other people and with circumstances.

Affection for the Analyst

The optimal result of clinical collaboration is achieved when the patient has developed new capacities for cooperation and honesty; when he has increased his awareness of his own emotions, attitudes and values; and when he deals with his life problems and his interpersonal activities in more rational and feeling ways that perpetuate his personal growth.

These favorable developments may cause the awakening of a new feeling: affection for the analyst. This phenomenon is potentially a valuable gain, but it may cause unnecessary pain for the patient. The patient's way of life has so changed that there is more enjoyment and more promise in life, and this has come about through mutual effort. The conditions exist in which the patient may feel a strong and genuine love for the therapist. But the therapeutic situation, unlike everyday life, does not permit mutuality of this emotion. The therapist has provided a situation which is unique for each patient, but this situation is necessarily one-sided. The therapist's work has been reciprocal, but he does not have the same life situation, needs and feelings, does not find the same kind of fulfillment in relation to the patient and does not fall in love.

At that point the patient has, often for the first time, achieved the capacity for loving. If this experience is dealt with as pathology, serious damage can be done. It is essential to differentiate with the patient between the achievement of loving and the demand to be loved. The demand for reciprocation can lead to an angry sense of rejection, of betrayal (often vividly imaged in dreams), a competitive misinterpretation of having been defeated and humiliated, a desire for revenge. There may be a resurgence of cynicism and of disbelief in the most trusted of all current human contacts. All these emotions will show in dreams and be reflected in waking behavior. This clinical situation requires the most sensitive handling, involving the therapist's delineation for the patient of the actual conditions of the therapeutic alliance and how that alliance differs from the relationships of everyday life. If this is accomplished with thoroughness, tact and honesty, that process itself constitutes significant work in the therapy, which can then move ahead even more productively (Bartlett, 1973).

INTERPRETATION OF MARTHA'S DREAMS

Dream No. 1

Preliminary Remarks

The temporal occurrence of the first dream report in analysis can be related to the emphasis placed on dreams by the therapist. I have often heard a dream in an initial session simply by asking, "What did you dream last night?" The patient may not recall a dream from the previous night, but may volunteer one, or a fragment of one, from the past. The importance of dreams has then been at least suggested, and often the therapeutic process can be significantly initiated (Bonime, 1969b).

There is a question as to whether this was the first dream Martha remembered or whether it took more than a month for her to risk reporting one. She suffered from a need to control, entered analysis stating, "I realized that I wasn't controlling my life," and her therapeutic contact was precipitated by a period of uncontrollable anxiety. She may have delayed, wondering if she would be enough in control of the therapeutic situation if she revealed her dreams. She had already described feelings of shame, helplessness and bewilderment in connection with her own emotional outbursts—surges of fear, anger and anxiety—and her first dream appears to be suffused with a wide variety of affect.

It is also noteworthy that those dream emotions which might in waking life have become unmanageable, and which she probably preferred not to recognize, are *symbolized*, while the more pleasant feelings are *experiential*, at least as she reported them. Altogether, a great deal in this dream appears to reflect the patient's presenting problem—anxiety about lack of control over her life and emotions.[7]

Interpretive Hypotheses[8]

The dream report displays affective symbols of insecurity. The "shaky

---

[7]In actual practice, I establish no interpretations without the collaboration of the patient. Every interpretive offering in this section is a speculation and a hypothesis, unilaterally conceived.

[8]The hypotheses here presented are related to the protocol and to Martha's first dream. The same subheading, and the same qualification (as in previous footnote), will be applicable for each of the following dreams.

balcony" is the dreamer's position in life—elevated, but not solid or safe. "Everybody was dressed in period costumes...."; the human environment has a note of unreality and of temporal dislocation. Martha was described as appearing "slightly old-fashioned." How much unsureness about herself is indicated by the temporal dislocation and by the Rip Van Winklish twenty-year wait in the dream? Twenty years possibly also represents her concept of the period from her menarche to her avoided but wished-for awakening to mature womanhood.

One of her spontaneous associations after telling the dream was "I used to find marriage frightening...."—another reference to insecurity. In the dream not even her body is her own, and while she seems to reach for a more feminine self-image by taking on, in place of her obese body, the litheness of Katharine Hepburn, she is still "not particularly attractive." Her insecurity is expressed also in the dream symbols of explosions and black clouds. She "stayed in that chair for twenty years." How long has she held back, fearing the dangers of going with the crowd? Finally she woke up to her predicament. "I think of therapy. If I didn't come now, when would I?" That is her spontaneous association with descending from her uncertain perch.

Her association between waiting for twenty years, then getting up and entering therapy, is implicitly her interpretation.

When she "decided to come down," she "had no emotions...." How much of her insecurity had developed from her unsuccessful efforts to control her feelings by denying them?

So far all the indication of emotion has been symbolized and indirect. The explosions and black clouds are at an indeterminate distance. Are these the dangers of intimate contact, the experiences of ordinary people below her level? Are they instead, or also, explosions of present anger which endanger her by being uncontrollable? Are they angry, jealous contempt for those with a possibly fuller life who live down to earth, not on her higher but disturbingly shaky level?

The explosions may also represent the anger such people would evoke in her if she moved more among them. The anxiety connected with losing her tenuous superiority is expressed in her statement "The only dangerous thing was the descent."

Besides the diffuse insecurity in the dream, and the suggestion of anger, there are indications of grandiosity, depression (another aspect of anger) and competitiveness. Grandiosity may be guessed from the start of the dream when she has the physical appearance of a famous actress, Katharine Hepburn, and later when she is sought by the Prime Minster. Then, after hibernating (staying aloof?) in a chair for twenty years, she finds herself quite spry and able to jump down. At her oneiric age of fifty, she enjoys a "privileged position with not much responsibility...indulged...treated special."

On the other hand, while only fifty, she has already outlived all her contemporaries from the start of the dream. This last feature implies her competitiveness.

Another element of the broad array of pathological emotions in Martha's personality in this dream is symbolized depression, suggested by the explosions (a fitting symbol for her own frightening angry outbursts) and also by the black cloud, an apt description of a depressive attack. The depressive hostility may also be represented in her dream scenario when she saw her peers running off into the dangerous milieu. The explosions and black clouds, as angry mood metaphors, and her later expressed appreciation of "a privileged position with not much responsibility," together make up a major part of the constellation of depression (Bonime 1976b; 1979, in press).

Looked at collectively, Martha's anxiety, her unreal self-image, her grandiose goals in the dream, the uncertainty of her dominance, the self-defeating practices of the depressive (staying behind for twenty years)—these symbolized emotions augment the initially emphasized theme of insecurity (anxiety) as a major characteristic of the dream.

In addition to the pathological elements, there are also evidences of healthy affect. Martha perceives the "warm and friendly" nature of the offspring of her former peers, and is glad to be with them. She is resourceful in dealing with an overlong wedding dress. That gesture possibly signifies a desire to get along with others after lagging for twenty years.

Important among her positive feelings is the exhibition of trust toward her therapist and gratitude for his assistance in getting her moving. There is a healthy hopefulness concerning personal growth. In spite of her age handicap in the dream, she accepts only the necessary amount of assistance—without expecting to be lifted down, she jumps and lands on her own feet. This (like the altering of her dress) suggests a readiness to use her personal resources of strength, resilience and adaptability. The healthy aspects of the dream may be correlated with her waking recognition that she needed help and her action in seeking out analytic help.

The foregoing hypothetical interpretations could be extended by attention to additional items, such as the people jumping instead of taking steps off the balcony; the nieces, without mention of nephews; the presence of a Prime Minister (British) rather than a Cabinet member (American); Martha's possession of an instrument with which to shorten her wedding dress. Any of these disregarded items might have developed significance if they had been discussed.

Without interchange one cannot know how ready the patient is to face anxiety-provoking material—embarrassing, self-degrading, self-inflating, nonsensical items. How much trust of the therapist has she acquired? Does she fear evoking from the therapist a hidden scorn, dislike, open criticism, rebuke? In the protocol Martha seems cooperative and verbal, yet without meeting her one cannot guess how much of her dream experience she reported and how much she was awarely or unawarely editing.

What did she emphasize, how did she vocally inflect her report? Was the dream affect pursued? As I mentioned above, we never achieve full knowledge of the dream experience, and I cannot emphasize too strongly that accuracy is particularly diminished if we are lax in exploring affect.

Questioning the Patient[9]

I have already speculated about the basic nature of Martha's symbolized emotion—her feelings of insecurity symbolized by the rickety balcony. But if she does not *say* that she felt insecure, unsafe and anxious, it would be necessary to ask. My first question would probably be "How did you feel sitting on the balcony?" If the reply were evasive ("Nothing special . . ."), or if she referred only to being intrigued by the costumes, I would try to sharpen the focus by inquiring how she felt specifically about the ricketiness of the balcony. The inquiry might serve to evoke associatively other insecurities, either in the dream or in her waking life.

In the protocol Martha said, "The only thing dangerous was the descent." A moment later she spoke of fears connected with getting married and of her final decision to get into therapy. But between "the descent" and " . . . I came to therapy" there is reference to her two near-marriages and her feeling that she had *barely escaped.* This opened up therapeutic opportunity. One might speculate that the pleasing deference she felt as a fifty-year-old woman was like the esteem and special privilege she may have enjoyed as an American woman courted in a foreign country. The dreamed costumes of an earlier era may have augmented the dream mood of romantic enhancement of women. The courting may have fed her grandiosity, and she may actually have been in love not with the man, but only with the courting. In any event, she "escaped" before marriage could materialize.

---

[9]The questions to follow typify the specificity I would try for. As given here, the questions may seem so numerous that the patient would be deprived of time to think or feel or speak spontaneously. It must be remembered that I might not get beyond, or even get *to* the first question. As the patient gains experience he comes more and more to use his dreams spontaneously and intensively, and his participation might anticipate, preclude, or replace all my suggested questions for each of the dreams.

We have no knowledge of what was going on at this time between Martha and men in her life. Was she heady about some attentions she was receiving? Was she fearful of the intimacy, reluctant to take on social responsibility, anxious lest she become controlled by a man? All these possibilities are suggested by the protocol and the first dream.

I might ask related questions: What are these men like (the men you see now)? How do they treat you? How do you feel toward them? Do you enjoy sex? Are you frightened about it? Did you want sex or submit to it because of other factors in the relationship? Have you been orgastic during intercourse or in response to other stimulation? Why did you break off the earlier relationships? What do you mean by "all my feelings weren't there"? What do you mean by your possibly never becoming a person? What were the circumstances and your feelings when you "barely escaped"? How do you feel about marriage now? What about the affair two years ago? (The foregoing questions apply to the two men she nearly married, and also to other less serious affairs she may have had before or since.) In what way was your relationship with men a reason for coming to therapy?

These questions relate to sex, grandiosity and anxiety. They might lead into areas concerning control through sex—the enjoyment of controlling men who loved or desired her, and her fear of being controlled once married. Since Martha had had anxiety about being unable to master feelings of anger, she may have feared being controlled by the obligations inherent in a wife's role and her own resultant uncontrollable rage. Such concerns might have been intensified even more in the man-woman mores of another culture (both suitors were "foreign" and may have represented, in addition to greater courtliness, a higher level of male domination).

Anxiety might also relate to the possibility of her own overpowering sexual impulses. Masturbatory fantasies, if asked for, might prove helpful regarding the whole area of sex (Bonime, 1969c).

More questions arise involving Martha's feelings about having children, her confidence or diffidence about motherhood: Could she control her children? Would she feel controlled by the demands of children? Or, if she waited too long, might she lose control of the possibility of ever getting married and having children?

In the dream her husband had "gone off." How did she feel about his absence? What were her emotions when proposed to by the Prime Minister and when she refused him? How did she feel in that long bridal gown, and what were her feelings in shortening it? She said all the people she inquired about were dead, and she was "pleased" with their grandchildren and nieces. But what were her reactions to the deaths?

Obviously, all these questions could not be asked within a single session. It would become necessary to focus on a particular area, and this would be done by starting with the rickety balcony because of my subjective sense of its symbolic value as a focus for probably numerous insecurities. Many of the questions proposed above must be asked in later contexts, even in the context of later dreams or later life events. But at the first report of the dream I would consider the possible points of focus and try to move in a direction leading to the greatest possible engagement and fullest productivity.

I would remember that anxiety about an examination brought Martha into treatment. There are striking images of insecurity and anxiety in the dream, and in the protocol a number of events suggest insecurity—her flight from marriage, her cockroach phobia, her hypersensitivity to her mother, her depression about her job loss. There is also Martha's stated need to control feelings and a reflection in her dream report of a desire to deny feelings altogether. I would therefore probably move toward Martha's presumptively major problem, her anxiety about control, probably best referred to at this point as insecurity.

I would have in mind that this dream might well engage the patient in the therapeutic process (Bonime, 1969b) and might be the beginning of the development of her "personal glossary." As an example, one might imagine "rickety porch" becoming a useful designation of her feelings in precise situations in which she feels isolated and elevated above the crowd. The elaboration of the meanings of "rickety porch" would have to be developed through work on Dream 1.

Having explored this first dream, the question may arise: What's the use of all this? What potential help is there in eliciting so much material, exploring all of it for meanings and trying to formulate interpretive hypotheses? Martha already knew she was often angry and unable to control her anger. She was aware of her insecurity and her anxiety *before* the occurrence of this dream. So why work so hard on the dream?

In the course of exploring the dream, we would begin to establish connections between dream elements and personality elements. In making these connections, some causes of Martha's everyday behavior and experience might come into view. Correlations between seemingly unrelated events in her life might begin to reveal a pattern of functioning. Martha may not have been aware, for example, of her own competitiveness and grandiosity. She may also have been hardly aware of some of her genuine capabilities, because they fell short of her grandiose self-image, and her unawareness of her genuine capabilities would then contribute to her insecurity. Possibly the anxiety about the examination derived in part from jeopardy to an exalted concept of her own intellect . . . the large amount of studying may have been in alarming contrast with her expected quick comprehension.

In spite of evidences of grandiosity, in her daily life she may have feared that it was growing late for marriage for herself. She might have begun to discover certain unacceptable attitudes connected with her breaking off relationships before reaching marriage. To attract men, get proposals and then withdraw may be connected with a competitive sparring for control.

That tentative insight might also provide an explanation of her eating binges, that is, the eating binges as a competitive maneuver against her mother. But the binges might also be despairing attempts to fill the sensed emptiness within because she lacked meaningful relationships.

The report of this first dream, with its spontaneous associations, taken together with the protocol, indicates that Martha is a patient who can speak articulately and with some degree of openness, and will be reasonably ready to explore crucial personality difficulties. Examination of the dream has suggested opportunities to discern previously unrecognized attitudes (such as grandiosity), behavioral patterns (such as competitiveness) and related unsuspected emotions (such as vindictiveness).

Dream No. 2

Preliminary Remarks

In comparison with Martha's first dream—complex, filled with shifts in setting, unidentified individuals, multiple events and emotions—this dream seems simple and limited to one angry involvement with her mother. Yet examination of this brief dream reveals considerable complexity and a wide variety of feelings. The dominant feeling is anger, and the major problem appears to center on control of her mother and of herself. The clearer identification of the interpersonal relationship, and the sharper focusing on and recognition of feeling, all indicate therapeutic progress.

Interpretive Hypotheses

One is struck by the fact that this nearly thirty-year-old woman, employed in a responsible position, is still living at home with a mother who treats her like a child.[10] The dream mother is intrusive. Possibly the dream mother "who didn't look like my mother" resembles a kind of person Martha would not like to acknowledge as her mother. If she can avoid seeing what her mother really is like, or her true feelings about the woman, perhaps she can more readily justify to herself that she still lives either at home or closely

---

[10]It is possible that she was not living at home, yet felt as though she were still there under her mother's scrutiny.

tied to her mother, and always under observation.

In the dream Martha enacts her presenting problem: inability to control her own feelings. But, in addition, she cannot control her mother. This failure leads to irrepressible outbursts of impotent rage. There is a clear crescendo: "...I told her to go away or get out.... I was angry....I screamed....I grabbed her by the hair and threw her out. She landed at the bathroom door and fell." This is a progression toward a murderous rage over her inability to control her mother's attitude or behavior. It is also an "outburst" that Martha cannot control within herself and an anger whose real intensity she prefers not to recognize. "I wanted to express more anger than I felt." (She might have been trying to say, to herself and to the analyst, "This is not really me—I was putting it on a bit.")

A great value of the dream's action lies in its depiction of a physical attack on her mother. The action in the dream was not a pretense, and her screaming was not histrionics. "My scream just didn't seem loud enough. It was as if I didn't have the physical capacity." She yelled her utmost, and it was still not enough. It is likely that the dream anger, rather than being less than she felt, was more than she was willing to acknowledge.

Though Martha was afraid the mother was hurt, she did not bother to investigate and instead locked the door of the room. She reported that the mother "had hurt herself," thus evading a clear statement that she, Martha, had hurt the mother. This shielded her from facing the full intensity of her own rage. It is my hunch that Martha's shock was not at her mother's possible injury, but at the intensity of her own rage.

The mother is then depicted as coming right back "through the locked door," a beautiful visual metaphor for the insidious, indomitable quality of her intrusiveness.

And there is much more implied about this relationship. There is an intimation of a competitive battle between daughter and mother which may, perhaps, be the secret of Martha's helplessness and her reason, despite so much misery, for remaining within her mother's orbit. Her mother hypothetically controls Martha through solicitousness; she stoops to conquer. Possibly Martha cannot resist her mother's material favors.

This solicitude may also be experienced by Martha as an avenue for her own control over her mother. Despite the daughter's enraged attack the mother remains servile. Despite the daughter's muted sarcasm—"like my mother, solicitous,"—Martha nevertheless stays close. There may be a mutual enslavement in the relationship, and this would be a crucial insight into the intrafamilial environment.

Summarizing up to this point: The second dream confirms Martha's expressed problem of her inability to control her anger. An important hypothetical cause of the anger—her mother's intrusiveness—is established.

There may also be a basic dynamism of mutual enslavement. The spectrum of emotions includes frustration, rage and physical violence; anxiety, scorn and feelings of helplessness. There may also be an aloofness bordering on cruelty (locking the door after the mother fell with possible serious injury). This is a considerable spectrum.

There are also indications of Martha's tendency to denial (a protection of self-image): she said associatively that "the other day" she had expressed more anger toward the analyst than she actually felt. Toward her mother in the dream, though her hostility approached murderous proportions, she said similarly that it was "more anger than I felt."

Furthermore, the dream mother "didn't look like my mother." Might she have been hiding from herself a revulsion more intense than anything she was ready to acknowledge?

Beyond the anger and the reciprocal battle for control, there is another connection that can be made. As I visualized the mother "coming through the door," I had a sudden association to the patient's presenting complaint, her cockroach phobia. How intrusive and intractable cockroaches are! How much emotional connection might there be between the anxious struggle with her mother and the phobic battle with cockroaches?

Martha is single at twenty-nine and apparently limited in her relationships with men. During the evolution of her personality, she seems to have developed neurotic problems of control connected with intrusiveness and (presumptively) with fears of intimacy. There may be strong connections between her problems with her mother (and possibly with men) and her cockroach phobia.

One thinks of how easily a cockroach enters a locked room, how ineffective are one's revulsions and even one's ultimate murderous crushing! Still they come—"like an advancing army." And this phobia leads me to speculate also on Martha's battle to control her own rage. How fearful had she become of treating others as savagely as she would treat a cockroach? How scornful and dehumanized could she be, and how often had she come close to violently attacking not only her mother but also others in her life? Her fury at those who made her impotent (who were uncontrollable by her) might lead not to a physical attack, but to a more indirect attack: as she defeated her mother by becoming obese and temporarily failing to find a job, perhaps she defeated men by veiled scorn or lateness, or more subtle means of conveying indifference or dislike.

Martha's fury appears to be the outstanding emotion in this dream and seems connected with her problem of control. One may speculate that her mother strained to the utmost Martha's efforts at controlling not only the mother's behavior, but also the mother's attitudes. Martha could not force respect for her privacy.

It is possible that Martha subliminally sensed a connection between her hostility toward her mother and her eating sprees. Despite mortification over lack of self-control, despite possible self-scorn in her resemblance to an uncouth father and perhaps resemblance also to the obnoxious food-bound cockroaches, she may also have felt that she could at least deprive her mother of a married daughter and grandchildren. Martha thus had contradictory internal pressures defeating her efforts toward self-control, and she had thereby much for which irrationally to hate her mother.

Affectively, in addition, Martha's competitiveness is clearly revealed in the therapeutic session where Martha describes her own desire to control the therapist by "forcing [him] to answer questions" and by "locking horns."

Questioning the Patient

Although various questions might arise from the foregoing hypotheses, my questioning would focus on the presumptive chief problems: anger and control. I would ask Martha about her anger at her mother and would not be surprised to hear a long list of complaints about interferences, suggestions, attempts at regulation, interrogation, snooping and criticism.

There might also be a repetition of her earlier denial, i.e., a statement that she often acted angrier than she felt. I would inquire about the fury depicted in the dream—flinging her mother by the hair, then locking her out despite possible injury. Did Martha ever feel like beating her mother? Did she ever slap or push her? My questions would pursue the intensity of the anger: What fantasies had she ever had about attacking her mother or about her mother being injured in some other way, perhaps by being mugged, hit by a car, killed in an airplane crash? Positive answers might follow, accompanied by qualifications: Such fantasies are rare; everyone has them at times; anyway, they are absurd or exaggerated.

The object of such questions would be to help Martha find in her waking life whatever corresponded to the ferocity of the dream, so that she would begin to recognize that the dream is her own product, a reflection of the woman she actually is.

The next category of questions would have as their object the exploration of the actual life circumstances which provoked anger. These questions would not be confined to her mother. A new emphasis would be developed—that control is a basic problem and that anger is connected with inability to control. Martha already knew that she was alarmed by the uncontrollability of her own outbursts—now this helplessness could be explored in situations in which she couldn't get her way. Probably a correlation could be made between her inability to control her own anger and her hostility toward others who were not amenable, who remained independent of her.

Also, did she get angry when people or circumstances made demands upon her? Did she feel annoyed when the analyst said the session was over? Was she provoked by criticism? Did criticism seem like a demand, or an instruction to change what she was or what she had been doing?

All of the foregoing questions could not be brought up in a single session. Moreover, the very first inquiry into her feelings about her mother might evoke a torrent of feeling and memory that would fill the rest of the hour in a way that would not justify interruption. A similar flood might result from a query regarding her feelings about her own temper. The list of speculation-based questions might arise in various sequences or contexts during many successive sessions. New dreams, and new incidents in Martha's life, might create in the analyst many associations to this reported dream, and might reinforce or modify the foregoing speculations and prompt new questions in a new context.

To return to the theme of denial, I would call Martha's attention to her saying, after describing the physical attack on her mother in the dream, that she was afraid her mother might have "hurt herself." I might tell her of another female patient who, in one dream, resented her mother's interference with her cooking. That patient, though describing her feeling in the dream as "annoyed," gave her mother an impatient "get away" jab with her elbow and was surprised when her mother, as a result, was hurled across the kitchen where she landed in a heap.[11] I would suggest to Martha that if she was not aware of the intensity of her feelings, she could not be aware of her own activities, frequently painful to herself, resulting from these feelings—such as ostentatiously suffering loneliness, self-contempt, uncontrollable eating sprees, all in some measure aimed against her mother. Becoming aware of such feelings in herself would give her a stronger and healthier control of her own life.

The parallel between Martha's hostility to her mother and her spontaneously associated hostility (locked horns) toward the analyst also offers an opportunity to discuss with Martha the singleness and unity of her own personality. In her relationship with her mother Martha tried to force her to stop being intrusive; in her relationship with her analyst she tried to force him to answer questions. There is one Martha, battling two separate and unrelated

---

[11] This would be an association of mine while "hearing" Martha's second dream and would be a useful instance of making Martha aware of the therapist working through his own free associations, emphasizing the parallel functioning and thereby fostering collaboration.

people. Competitiveness and controllingness are pervasively present, dominant aspects of her personality.

I would point out also that she appeared to me to be denying her true feelings toward me when she said, "I was expressing more anger than I felt toward you," and that it was possible that, like the mother in the dream, Martha in that session herself felt like an advancing army.

This dream shows therapeutic progress since the time of the first dream seven months earlier. Martha's dealing with the dream indicates her spontaneous independent focusing when she correlates her own dream activity (forcing respect from her mother) with her remembered activity in a previous session (forcing answers from the analyst); Bonime (1968).

Because of the achieved progress, there would be an opportunity to point out to Martha the connection between her controllingness and her misery. I would explain that her misery might be very durable, without ever being lethal. She did not *have* to change. That would open the way to some discussion of the parallel between the therapeutic relationship and her relationships with her mother and others. This could lead associatively to some recognitions of the ways in which her pathology (controlling and avoiding control) retarded clinical progress, and there would be a chance to clarify therapeutic goals. Some of the "curse" of the analyst's unwelcome but necessary influence could be ameliorated.

The "curse" is the patient's concept of the therapist's influence, subjectively misinterpreted and experienced as coercion. It could be clearly affirmed to Martha that she did not have to give up seeking control. No force on earth could make her give up this pursuit. She would have to recognize, however, that she could not avoid the consequences of her own behavior. She could not change her mother's attitudes nor avoid her own reactions when her attempts to do so were frustrated. Also, to the extent that her eating sprees and her cockroach phobia might be generically related to her search for control, she could not help herself with these problems. By her modes of seeking control, I would suggest, she actually produced the opposite. She deprived herself of a considerable degree of currently possible and potential mastery of her own life.

At this point in her therapy, where there seems to be a fair degree of collaboration and understanding, Martha has also a degree of ripeness for such formulations and the opportunity to gain from hypothetical insights that have been distilled out of examination of her own life experience.

Dream No. 3

Preliminary remarks

In the second dream we were able to identify Martha's relationship with her mother as a probable source of much of her anxiety and hostility. Now, after one and a half years, Martha is again (still?) focused on her mother, with whom the cockroach seems specifically and perhaps synergistically connected.

What is the meaning of the mother's previous concealment that a cockroach had crossed her pubic hair? It might represent that the facts of life (father's "cock" penetrated mother's genitals to produce Martha) had been hidden from Martha. Did the withholding occur because that action represented to the mother, and perhaps also to Martha, something base, forbidden, repulsive? One may speculate about the influence of an evasive milieu on the growing child and adolescent. The roaches, it was earlier suggested, may have represented various elements in Martha's life that were uncontrollable. But the meanings of symbols gradually change. At some stage of Martha's growing up, the roaches might have been the sperm that initiated the frighteningly uncontrollable process of pregnancy. Was the urgency of the excited "cock" another of the uncontrollables and did that contribute to keeping Martha at a distance from men?

Did she hate and feel repelled by the "cock" because her own uncontrollable sexual urges "degraded" her to the level of other women? other human beings? Did this leveling threaten her grandiosity? Did the roaches symbolize also the unbearable boorishness of her father and the debasement of her mother? And were those connotations of helplessness and humiliation, then, precisely what her mother sought to spare her?

This last possibility could be the source of her feeling of agreement in the dream and her appreciation of her mother's candor, even though her mother lied to her at an earlier time. There is now, however, a more accepting attitude toward her mother, in contrast with the violence of Dream 2. This interesting shift of feeling appears in a dream involving two symbols (mother and roach), presumptively connected with feelings of rage and terror. The emotions evoked are nevertheless gentle, empathic and trusting. The changed feelings suggest the possibility of new insight and maturation.

Interpretive Hypotheses

The moment one "hears" this brief dream, the change of tone is apparent. The woman who has been her enemy, and the creature which has been her phobia, are there together, and no intense feeling erupts—no rage, no revulsion. There is, instead, an acceptance of good intentions and a feeling of agreement. Her mother, instead of being an intrusive, enraging ogre, is presented as well-meaning and candid. There is, of course, the contradiction that she is telling Martha a frightening fact that she declares having (previously) spared her. Nonetheless, Martha interprets her mother's decision as correct, as though the mother had really protected Martha. (Here again we may be witnessing only another example of denial.) The incident is reminiscent (my own association) of the mother's failure to discuss sexual matters with her daughter, an omission that almost certainly caused considerable pain and confusion for Martha.

Martha's associations following the telling of the dream give some confirmation of these hypothetical possibilities. She recalled the childhood game with other children. She had taken her turn, going alone into a room full of boys. Was she confused, aroused, humiliated by the treatment she received? "One of the boys said that they just tickled me," she reported. Did the tickling involve breasts, pubis—was it a disorienting experience? Or was she perhaps humiliated that they had "just" tickled her but had done more to the older girls? Was she left feeling like an immature fool? Did the mother's dream avoidance of sexual information represent the mother's real attempt to protect the child Martha from the sexual realities of the childhood game, even though this avoidance left the child socially and emotionally disoriented?

Was this a more mature and generous evaluation of the mother's earlier evasiveness about sex in general? Was Martha now able to consider that the mother's sexual uncommunicativeness was part of an effort to spare her daughter sexual terror?[12]

Since Martha suffers from compulsive eating, possibly the image of cockroach and pubic area produce for her a combination of sensations connected with quick satisfaction, i.e., food hunger and sexual hunger. Eating binges and masturbation both lend themselves to quick gratification, and these activities, if they are represented by this condensed symbol, would produce both shame and a haunting sense of lack of control.

Questioning the Patient

The foregoing passages, predominantly in the form of questions, represent interpretive hypotheses. Out of this extensive matrix I would first question Martha about her feelings toward her mother in the dream. A beginning might be: Do you enter your mother's room while she is naked? What were your feelings in the dream at seeing her naked? I would extend this line of questioning toward explorations of Martha's feelings and experience with

---

[12]Because of Martha's more tolerant attitude toward her mother, one suspects that by this time Martha has dealt more firmly and successfully with her mother's intrusiveness.

sex: In the dream you agreed that you would have been frightened. How did you feel in the dream after you learned about it? What are your feelings now about your mother's evasiveness in the past? What was your experience at first menstruation? At bodily changes? How do you feel now about your body and about sex, and how did you feel as you grew up? How did you learn about sex? What were your feelings during and after masturbating? What were your masturbatory fantasies?[13] Tell me about your initial and later experiences with boys, with men, with intercourse. Just say all that comes to mind about sex. Why do you keep so close to your mother now, and how much do you talk with her intimately? How does *she* feel about your relationships with men? Do you think there has been a change in your feelings toward her in the last few months, last couple of years?

All these questions are obviously in pursuit of Martha's sexual development and current sexual life, combined with an exploration of her feelings toward her mother. The inquiry comes up because of what appears in the dream to be a relaxation of her former hostility and the linkage of this relaxation with patent sexual connotations.

As I suggested earlier, there may be some connection between roaches and her father. Little reference to the father appears in the protocol, except, on the positive side, to his uneducated intelligence and to his sense of humor; on the negative side were his repulsiveness because of poor personal hygiene and his "boorishness in eating." I would examine with Martha other aspects of her relationships with her father and two older brothers.

With so much focus on her mother in the second and third dreams, however, there seems to be a good opportunity to investigate the mother/daughter relationship, especially its connection with sex, uncluttered for the time being by her relationships with the three male members of her family. The mother-oriented inquiry might at any point lead Martha to feelings and memories connected with father and brothers, but unless that spontaneous shift occurred I would pursue the course first described with this dream of the mother's pubic cockroach.

There is an opportunity to help Martha see that the dream reveals an enhanced self-image, containing the qualities named above—more acceptance and greater maturity.

---

[13]These can be as significant as dreams and can serve the same function (Bonime 1969c).

Dream No. 4

Preliminary Remarks

Martha's first dream expressed a broad spectrum of emotions and a fragile, insecure personality. After more than two years in analysis, emotionality continues to characterize her dream state and she seems to carry forward a salutary development from the dream of nine months earlier. There is a degree of mastery of her phobia, an absence of rage, a transformation of feelings in the direction of humanity and compassion. All this is set forth as experiential and also as symbolized feeling, with striking imagistic mutations. There is, overall, the aura of an integrating personality.

Interpretive Hypotheses

It is interesting that Martha starts telling her dream with the statement, "The thing occurred . . . that I'm most frightened of." The diminution of her fear is clear in what follows. While she was in the bathtub, naked, a cockroach "got on my leg." But the roach "was half dead." This may reflect (except for the possibility of denial) her feeling that its power to terrify her is half dead. Possible confirmation comes: "I didn't panic." That this long-standing anxiety-producing symbol does not bring on panic can be seen as her own recognition of the attenuation of her anxiety. The cockroach followed her when she went to her bedroom and was on the wall by her bed. This may imply feared lack of control of sexual, including masturbatory, impulses. There is another girl who tries to kill the roach. This second girl may be Martha trying to suppress sexual impulses or uncontrollable anger, such as she had toward her mother's cockroach-like intrusiveness in the earlier dream. On the other hand, the girl may be a now more sturdy, less fragile Martha, attacking the problem instead of fleeing from it in terror. The second girl is then replaced by the real Martha tackling her problem in a more self-contained fashion—using an insect spray. She gave it "one long spray." This may possibly refer to her awareness of taking a good long look at her own problem of wanting to control.

The succeeding dream events may at some level represent what has already happened in the course of analysis through the deliberate pursuit of certain difficulties.[14] As she continues to spray, *the problem expands and takes*

---

[14]This is a characteristic phenomenon in analysis.

on new forms and connotations: " ... it got bigger, turned into a chicken ... "
Her spontaneous association is to her mother's Friday chicken. This may be
placing her mother (in contrast with the intrusive insect) in a more common-
place maternal role, which would be further evidence of Martha's maturing.
It may imply Martha's developing capacity to see others as more than insects,
more than obstacles and problems with which she must contend. As she continues to dream, and perhaps to recognize what has been happening in her
analysis, the problem takes on still greater dimensions—the confronted creature turns "into a dog." But there is something remarkable about this dog. It
"had some human characteristics." Was this additional recognition of the nature and needs of other people? Has the once intrusive mother been
recognized as an individual with feelings, who wants to be freed from her
daughter's attacks? "It asked to leave," and Martha complies and apologizes.

There are, of course, alternative interpretive possibilities. The Friday
night chicken dinners may represent an oppressive family ritual. The spraying of the chicken may indicate a continuing desire to get rid of certain
aspects of the mother. The dog may represent a "slobbering" quality of men,
commencing wi and none is a valid hypothesis until authentication, in the
form of associations and emotions, comes from the patient during collaborative investigation of the dream.

Questioning the Patient

With so much change in affect, and so wide a range of symbolic possibilities, many questions arise. Martha's responses might quickly eliminate
some and produce still others. I would start by asking about Martha's feelings
while in the tub with the roach on her leg: "You didn't panic, but what were
your feelings?" My guess is that there would be some anxiety, even though
there is diminution of her phobia.

"What is the first thing that pops into your mind when you think of the
girl who appeared in the dream?" This may produce some evidence of
change in Martha's feeling about herself. She might have a flash of association
to a recent incident in which she or someone else acted with independence or
self-respect. Her recurrent episodes of self-esteem–damaging behavior would
make emerging evidence of self-respect of great importance regarding self-
image and an added motivation for therapeutic efforts.

How did she feel about the roach being "half dead"? "Say all the
thoughts that come to mind, and all your feelings about that single little fact."
"How did you feel later when it was on the wall near your bed?" "What was
your reaction to the girl? Say whatever comes to mind as you picture her.

Describe her, both her physical appearance and her movements[15] (p. 233), and mention anyone who flits through your thoughts as you try to tell about her."

"How did you feel when you 'gave one long spray'?" "How did you feel as the cockroach got bigger? As it changed into a chicken? Was it a live chicken with feathers or one ready to be cooked? What were Friday chicken dinners like at your mother's?"

I would continue in this vein: How did she feel during all of the mutations? How about the dog, how did she feel as she became aware of its human qualities? What human qualities? "What other reactions come to mind, all your feelings about dogs?" (Martha probably has many feelings about dogs that apply equally to human beings, perhaps especially to men, but which she can more readily identify with respect to dogs.) "If what comes to mind seems trivial, irrelevant, embarrassing, say it anyway."[16] "What do you mean when you say they're unpredictable? Say everything you feel about their unpredictability."

How did she feel as she became aware of the dog's human characteristics? When it asked to be released? When she released it? When she apologized? For what was she apologizing? "Focus very hard on that and say all that you're reminded of."

I would not be surprised if Martha talked compassionately about her mother. If she did not mention her mother, but talked compassionately about another person or people, I would speculate aloud that Martha may have developed more understanding of her mother. That would be a therapeutic risk I would take. Martha might pick up this suggestion through some internal resonance with it and move ahead in that vein. Or she might drop it—in which case I would tell her that to me the dream seemed to indicate a greater awareness of the needs of others, a greater responsiveness to human characteristics and regret for having been so attacking in the past. I would reiterate also that the healthy aspects revealed in this dream were just as important to recognize as her pathology (Bonime, 1958).

This suggestion might produce a reaction toward the therapist like Martha's description of dogs—as though the analyst were uncomfortably unpredictable, jumping and repellently slobbering. I would watch for evidence

---

[15] I would mention *movements* because a kinetic image often awakens feelings that help to identify people not otherwise readily recognized in the dream.

[16] This kind of precautionary reminder must often be repeated, even long into the analysis.

of having been quite wrong, or perhaps inappropriately persuasive, and be ready to acknowledge error.

The session in which the dream was presented was, of course, too short to explore this dream satisfactorily, but it is the kind of dream that is likely to recur associatively in the context of many sessions because it is so vivid, richly charged with affect, elaborate in metaphor and presumably signaling critical personality change.

Dream No. 5

Preliminary Remarks

Four years into her analysis Martha is apparently dealing with her relationships with men, with problems of intimacy, sexuality and commitment. The element of compassion, which appeared in her third and fourth dreams, seems involved here in her relationship with men.

A maturing sexuality is suggested, even though it is oneirically represented in bizarre fashion.

Interpretive Hypotheses

While the total dream suggests intense physical involvement with a man, specified in genital and mammary terms, and although there are plans for her to live with the man over a weekend, Martha's lingering immaturity is indicated by her conceiving of herself as still, or again, residing with her parents. Her continuing insularity from men is implied in her boyfriend's being "somewhere at a nearby island." Her ambivalence about venturing too far from her familiar ways is indicated by her description of the man's island as being different, "but not too far from where I was." Does this mean not too far, developmentally, from where she is? Not too far (any longer) from the "security" of life within the encirclement of her parents? Does it promise imminent change?

In preparation for the weekend there is the bizarre sexual arrangement: the man's cutting off his penis and one of Martha's nipples, and their exchanging of the severed parts. She quickly adds, when reporting the dream, "This was supposed to be temporary. And they were supposed to reattach themselves." This may have indicated commitment or, alternatively, a desire for detachment from the carnal aspect of the relationship, but with a recognition that the detachment could not continue. "I also had the razor blade" may imply some recognition of her own part in creating distance between herself and men. She may have symbolized release from an intimacy which we know she has eluded throughout her adult life (her withdrawal from two potential marriages), and which she revealed in her first dream of an essentially husbandless wedding. "It wasn't painful" makes one wonder if she is again denying. On the other hand, the absence of pain may have implied some dim anticipation of her release from a puerile kind of existence.

Now she is presumably more independent, not embattled with her mother, and is arranging to go off with a man. While she says she "didn't want my mother to see a razor blade and penis in my hand," she nevertheless felt that "if she did see it, she didn't bother me." She has credited her mother with being discreet, a quality which she may have helped cultivate in her mother by overcoming her own outbursts and by appropriately demanding her mother's respect for her new maturity. Furthermore, noticing the mild irritation of her breast, she becomes aware of her boyfriend's probably greater difficulties (from sexual detachment or involvement): "If that was bothering me, he must be really uncomfortable."

From this empathy Martha then appears to leap to mature awareness of the consequences of her behavior: Relationships can deteriorate as a result of detachment (and possibly also from excessive demand for commitment). Is this what she feels when she thinks that procrastination from Friday to Saturday might be too long, might lead to rotting? Is the rotting a destruction of interest, a decay of desire? She holds the razor—is she responsible?

There is, of course, ambivalence about the responsibility. Martha says about the penis in the report of the dream, "It was in my charge, a pressure, a responsibility. I didn't know why *he* had done it." (Italics mine). She was nevertheless collusive. "It was a burden like walking around carrying too many packages." This dream ending again brings to mind Martha's "escape" from two relationships and the husbandless wedding of the first dream. An independent and empathic sexual relationship is possible, but she finds it a bloody and burdensome prospect. Growth may be, and frequently is, welcome and at the same time dangerous and repellent to confront.

Questioning the Patient

I would expect Martha to speak of the strangeness of the dream, to recognize the centrality of sexual concerns and to express some repulsion and bewilderment. At this point in her therapy, I would move directly to particularities in the dream that she might hope to avoid, e.g., an intensive exploration of the severed penis. "What comes to mind as you think of walking about with the man's penis in your hand?" It is likely that she would begin to recall fragments from her sexual affairs. There might be unrecognized or deeply unwelcome recollections of cock-teasing experiences. Any analyst working with this patient for four years would have many associations to specific incidents in her life. There could be an exchange of associations, some of them probably identical, perhaps including Martha's thoughts of having "cut off" earlier opportunities for marriage. I might offer to Martha the hypothesis that the surgery represented detachment from sexuality, and a great deal might then become possible in exploring other detachments as well. We could examine together the present state of her insularity, the state of her problems of control of emotions, and perhaps her depressions and their underlying angry feelings of deprivation (Bonime, 1976b). One would sense interrelationships among these problems and the opening up of a broad area of therapeutic opportunity.

Martha would be able to pursue with occasional determination some of the pathology blocking her fuller participation in intimacy.

"What was this fellow like, the one living at a nearby island?" "What was your relationship? How did you feel about him? And how did he feel about you?"

"Tell me, Martha," I would say, "what was the environment like, where you were living, and how was it different where the man was living?" I would hope to learn something of Martha's feelings about living with her parents and about the kind of "different environment" toward which she was heading.

"I'm confused about the cutting off of the penis and the nipple," I would say. "Did you watch him do it to himself? And what were your sensations during the experience? You said it was not painful but you may have had some thoughts or emotions about his action. Say anything that flits through your mind as you recapture and describe how he cut off your nipple. Was it very bloody? Frightening? Casual? Perhaps there was no blood and it seemed weird, or even perfectly natural. What was your idea of how the nipple and penis would reattach? What do you think when you say they were 'supposed to'?"

These questions would be asked one by one, with time for reply after each. There would be a great deal coming from Martha in response to the questions, any part of which might preclude further inquiries until a later session. With such a bizarre and significant dream, I would recommend that she jot down any thoughts or feelings related to it during the intervening days before the next session.[17]

There are additional lines of inquiry. "You bring your mother into this.

---

[17] I regularly recommend that my patients write their dreams; even that they sleep with pad and pencil at bedside and a flashlight handy if necessary. Associations and feelings (especially affect during the dreaming) should be noted and if possible added to if they occur before the next session.

You didn't want her to see the razor blade or penis in your hand. Why not?" I'd want to know what her relationship with her mother was at this time. I'd also ask about her father—did she have any feelings about his seeing what she carried? Did either of them notice blood on her shirt, or the absence of her nipple? What did all this have to do with her parents' attitude toward her having boyfriends? "Did your mother know about your affairs?" "What kind of exchanges did you have with her about your affairs?" I would ask if her mother was discreet about seeing the penis and razor, or was it more likely that the mother had not seen them at all. I would pursue this type of questioning or encourage Martha's spontaneous pursuit, in an effort to clarify whether she was becoming defiant, indifferent to or closer to her mother.

It would be important to learn the basis for Martha's procrastination. "Why did you wish to delay until Saturday, instead of meeting the man on Friday?" I would pursue whatever explanation she gave but also tell her that I had suddenly recalled her first dream in analysis, in which she procrastinated for twenty years.

At some point (connecting with this problem of procrastination) I would bring up the question she had raised by referring to pressure and responsibility. "You said, Martha, that it was a burden, like walking around with too many packages. Do you feel this way about participating more fully in life? Do you connect this with your depressions?"

I believe that all these inquiries would foster productive pursuit of the problems which brought Martha into analysis. She might be able to delineate and tackle her sense of the burdens of maturity and the contributions she made to bringing on depression and anxiety. She might recognize more clearly the limitations she herself imposed on her enjoyments.

While Martha brought in many dreams, one such as this could provide the source of fruitful therapy through many sessions—by itself and also through its connections with numerous successive dreams and experiences.

Dream No. 6

Preliminary Remarks

Some reported dreams suggest a meaning at once. Others have a latent period of mixed connotations which later, during the associative and interpretive activity, evolve into recognizable meaning. Still other dreams produce in the listener an initial reaction of utter puzzlement. The sixth dream (like the first) produced in me an initial chaotic response. As I read it, many fragmented associations swirled in my mind. I began to feel I would not be surprised to learn that there had been a recent discussion of termination at the end of the analytic year (the following June or July).

I had serious questions as to how far Martha had gone in her capacity to develop relationships with men. That seemed to be the area in which work had still to be done. The length and danger of the climb, down and up again, suggested to me some anxiety about imminent drastic change. There appeared also to be connotations of greater courage in exploring herself, a discovery of potential pleasures in the "depths," and the suggestion of a new, firm basis for further development. The general impression was, in brief, that Martha had come a long distance in analysis and that the outlook was promising.

Interpretive Hypotheses

There would be uncertainties of interpretation and a likely presence in Martha of much ambivalence. The dream starts with a recognizable peer, "my friend Eileen." (This is in contrast with Martha's first dream, in which all her peers were undefined and eventually dead.) The two women go to a "very old and dingy" building. There is some insecurity, but it is combined with courage. Martha explores deep into the building, going down hundreds or thousands of steps, "and if you fell off a staircase you could drop down to the bottom." But she proceeds anyway. Eileen may symbolize the analyst or even a new aspect of herself. The "enormous building, very old and dingy," may be her old obese self. It is "a cultural or amusement area. Although it had been in operation a long time [perhaps all through her life?] I didn't know about it." Is she on the brink of discovering unknown potentials and pleasures? "The inside is like a shell, very dark," she reports, and this suggests the limbo of alienation in which she may feel she had been living. There is implicit mild anxiety in "It's creepy," but she seems nevertheless ready to go on, saying, "I'm not frightened."

Possibly, instead of courage, we may be hearing another manifestation of denial, which has been pervasive in the presumptive personality of Martha. She may be experiencing both courage and anxiety.

At the bottom "it is even darker," but something significant is taking place: "Some men are laying a cement floor." This could have as a referent some activity dissociated from herself or may refer to her sense of her own progress, her own constructive work. The men may represent actual men who have become meaningful to her, as well as her therapist.

The presumptive positive trend may be represented further by the image "in the middle of the basement is an open space with sunlight." This suggests a possible awareness that by plumbing the "dark" depths of her personality, in spite of "creepy" anxiety, she is finding new illumination, a more crystallized insight. All is not pathology. There are pleasures and solidity to be found. Men do not have to be threatening—in fact, they can perhaps help to make a concrete base for her life.

A new world opens up—one that she hadn't known about, "although it had been in operation a long time...." Before entering the building, it looked like "an old railroad station," perhaps implying a place from which she might travel.

Altogether, there is hopefulness. A new, young Martha, "a little girl, perhaps five or six years old," is coming into existence, a new personality emerging from nearly five years of analytic work. I would hypothesize confidently that Martha is seeing herself in a new light, with youthful potential. In the dream the "solid, likable child" has come "in spite of her mother who tried to keep her back... and after getting to know her... I say to her, 'You're not evil, no matter what your mother told you.' "

Associatively she later reports, "I was struck by what I had said to the child. I felt it applied to me." This spontaneous association indicates Martha's sense of her own progress. There is also ambivalence, indicated in the dream by her getting away earlier than necessary. "I could have stayed longer...." This reminds one of how often a patient may look at his watch, long before the end of the session, when difficult material is being examined. Or this may mean that Martha is frightened (partly depersonalized) (Bonime, 1973) by her new sense of herself and therefore wants to terminate analysis prematurely.

Questioning the Patient

Martha's early departure from the concrete basement and the likable child, and the sunlit interior, may be an indication of her remaining desire to escape the responsibilities of involvement with others. Thus the questioning here requires considerable care. If the speculations of forward movement hold, associative activity of both Martha and analyst would revive much experiential confirmation in current data from Martha's life (including the recent year or two of analysis). Much would depend on Martha's capacity to identify and differentiate among her hopes, her reluctances, her commitments, her self-confidence and her anxiety.

At this point many of the following questions would be anticipated by Martha and dealt with spontaneously. My first questions might simply be "What do you think this is all about?" and then "What was your reaction to it when you woke up?"

I would want to know: "Thinking about Eileen, who crosses your mind? What is she like? What are your feelings about her?"

Many questions would come to my mind, and I would try to make sure that Martha's own discussion included answers to the following: What were her feelings at first sight of the railroad station and on entering it? What were her feelings about its dinginess? What did she mean by "cultural center," and did she mean to use that interchangeably with "amusement park"? (I wondered whether the interchangeable use of the two terms implied a correspondence between an adult's excited anticipation when entering an art museum, theater or concert hall and the excitement of a child approaching an amusement park. If there is a correspondence, it would suggest a rising interest in what adult life offers.)

Regarding the long descent, I would want to know how Martha became aware of the great depth, since it was "very dark" and at the bottom "even darker." Was this knowledge simply an oneiric "given," or was there a metaphoric affective connotation? Was it connected with the implied anxiety, the danger of falling, the risky sensations of descent into the unknown—and what would this mean concerning Martha's possible feelings about further analysis and commitment to a new life?

"What was your response to the sight of men laying cement? How many men? What kind of men? What occurs to you about their work, and about its happening in only one room?" (I would be interested in comparing my association that the one room might be law school, which she was just beginning.)

"What was your feeling when you saw the sunlight and the amusement park?" "How much did you participate?" "Was it for yourself or for the sake of the little child, or for both?"

"Tell me more about the child, all the details that come back, such as her bangs. Say anything that crosses your mind. Say more about your feelings toward her while you were dreaming." Since Martha had already spontaneously established an identity between herself and the child ("what I said to the child, I felt it applied to me"), the questions are an attempt to make this identification more specific and more revealing.

I would address the question of Martha's leaving earlier than necessary. "What impelled you to leave? How did you feel as you went back up the stairs? What comes to mind when you recall the thought, 'I could have stayed longer'?"

I would want to know if she had had ambivalent fantasies of ending analysis, or perhaps of wanting to extend it. I might return to her feelings about the descent into the dark, the many steps, the possibility of falling, and more about her creepy feeling. My emphasis on this theme derives from Martha's changed sense of herself. I would want to know the effect on her of this sense of change (Bonime, 1973).

Discussion of this dream might occupy or recur during a number of sessions. If possible, I would try to arrange for one or more double sessions. It is difficult to end an hour in the middle of a highly charged interchange, especially during a transitional period, in this case possibly leading toward a terminal phase.

All the detailed inquiry into Dream 6 leaves us with tantalizing questions and speculations. I will conclude with a brief commentary comparing the *first* and *sixth* dreams.

Important information and recognitions of Martha's growth toward a healthier life can be gained from a comparison of the two dreams. As in any patient, "progress" and even "readiness for termination" does not require eradication of the presenting or the later uncovered problems. In the course of Martha's treatment, however, we have a marked decrease in the intensity of her problems and a salutary change in her manner of dealing with them.

She seems to have achieved a more purposeful and hopeful mode of life. Her pathological desire to control is less evident. (Pathology sometimes actually disappears in therapy, or the impulse toward it becomes recognizable in dreams and in waking life before the patient acts—and can therefore be curbed.)

Dream 1 showed her great insecurity, her anxiety about controlling her emotions, and her desire to avoid involvement in ordinary life. Instead of moving off her rickety balcony to examine the distant explosions (possibly her angry outbursts), she stayed behind and waited (slept?) in her chair for twenty years. In Dream 6 she went almost fearlessly into an exploration of her self and her current life—going down a great many steps, even though there was still insecurity in doing so with no apparent protective banister.

In Dream 1, she trivialized her analyst—he was a nice young man. She was ambivalent about ordinary marriage; her own marriage was seemingly husbandless and was immediately followed by a proposal from a VIP, the Prime Minister. In Dream 6, the men at the bottom of her exploration were laying a concrete base that may have symbolized a new view of her analyst and of other men—as human beings who helped her to create her life's solid foundation.

In Dream 1, Martha became a fifty-year-old "old lady" who had stayed in a chair for twenty years. In Dream 6 (even though she left the situation, perhaps anxiously, earlier than necessary), she had found herself to be a solid and likable "child," with life ahead of her.

The problems of fantasy-self, and of insecurity about her ability to control, might still be there in Dream 6. Was she leaving analysis early because of grandiose impatience and overconfidence? Did she fear that too much change had already occurred? These questions cannot be answered here. But there was obviously a marked improvement in her view of herself. The prognosis was favorable. Martha's spontaneous interpretive activity indicates, in addition, that she had acquired a valuable tool in dealing with her future life—a growing independent capacity to use her dreams.

REFERENCES

Bartlett, F. (1973). Significance of patient's work in the therapeutic process. *Contempory Psychoanalysis, 9, 4:405–17.*

Bastide, R. (1966). The sociology of the dream. In *The Dream and Human Societies,* eds. Von Grunebaum and Callois. Berkeley: University of California Press.

Bonime, F. and Bonime, W. 1978 (in press). Psychoanalytic Writing: An Essay on Communication. *Journal of the American Academy of Psychoanalysis* Vol 6 #3.

Bonime, W. (1958). The use of dream evidence of evolving health as a therapeutic tool. *Psychiatry,* 21, 3:297–99.

———— (1959). The pursuit of anxiety-laden areas in therapy of the schizoid patient. *Psychiatry,* 22, 3:239–44.

———— (1961). Intellectual insight, changing consciousness, and the progression of processes during psychoanalysis. *Comprehensive Psychiatry,* 2, 2:106–12.

————, with F. Bonime (1962). *The Clinical Use of Dreams.* New York: Basic Books.

———— (1964). Role of dreams in psychoanalysis. In *Science and Psychoanalysis,* Vol. 7, ed. Masserman. New York: Grune & Stratton, pp. 185–92.

———— (1966a). Disregard of dream data in psychotherapy. In *Science and Psychoanalysis,* Vol. 9, ed. Masserman. New York: Grune & Stratton, pp. 170–73.

———— (1966b). Competitiveness and cynicism as factors in personality distortion. In *The Etiology of Neurosis,* ed. Merin. Palo Alto, Calif: Science and Behavior Books, pp. 152–58.

———— (1968). Marital conflict, analytic resistance and therapeutic progress. In *The Marriage Relationship,* eds. Rosenbaum and Alger. New York: Basic Books.

———— (1969a). A culturalist view: the dream as human experience. In *Dream Psychology and the New Biology of Dreaming,* ed. Kramer. Springfield, Ill. Thomas, pp. 79–93.

———— (1969b). The use of dreams in the therapeutic engagement of patients. *Contemporary Psychoanalysis,* 6, 1:13–30.

———— (1969c). Masturbatory fantasies and personality functioning. In *Science and Psychoanalysis,* Vol. 15, ed. Masserman. New York: Grune & Stratton, pp. 32–47.

———— (1973). Depersonalization as a manifestation of evolving health. *Journal of American Academy of Psychoanalysis,* 1, 2:109–23.

———— (1976a). Anger as a basis of a sense of self. *Journal of American Academy of Psychoanalysis,* 4, 1:7–12.

———— (1976b). Psychodynamics of neurotic depression. *Journal of American Academy of Psychoanalysis,* 4, 3:301–26. (also 1966, in 1st edition *American Handbook of Psychiatry,* Vol. 3, ed. Arieti. New York: Basic Books, pp. 239–55.)

————, with F. Bonime (1979, in press). Depressive personality and affect reflected in dreams: a basis for psychotherapy. In *The Dream in Clinical Practice,* ed. Natterson. New York: Aronson.

Breger, L. (1961). The function of dreams. *Journal of Abnormal Psychology, Monograph 72: 1–28.*

———— (1969). Dream function: an information processing model. In *Clinical Cognitive Psychology,* ed. Breger. Englewood Cliffs, N.J.: Prentice-Hall.

Eggan, D. (1966). Hopi dreams in cultural perspective. In *The Dream in Human Societies*, eds. Von Grunebaum and Callois. Berkeley, Calif.: University of California Press, pp. 237–66.

French, T., and Fromm, E. (1964). *Dream Interpretation*. New York: Basic Books.

Hernandez-Peon, R.: A neurophysiological model of dreams and hallucinations. *Journal of Nervous Mental Disease, 141*(6):645, 1965. 632-646

Horney, K. (1937). *The Neurotic Personality of Our Time*. New York: Norton.

———— (1939). *New Ways in Psychoanalysis*. New York: Norton.

Jones, R. M. (1970). *The New Psychology of Dreaming*. New York: Grune & Stratton.

Kramer. M. (1976). Dreams as a reflection of immediate psychological concern. In *Sleep Research*, Vol. 5. Eds. Chase, M. et al. Brain Information Service/Brain Research Institute, Los Angeles, Calif.: University of California Press, p. 122.

———— et al. (1976). Do dreams have meaning? An empirical inquiry. *American Journal of Psychiatry, 133*, 7: 778–781.

Ornstein, R., ed. (1974). *The Nature of Human Consciousness*. New York: Viking.

Robbins, B. S. (1955). The myth of latent emotions: a critique of the theory of repression. *Psychotherapy* 1, 1:3–29.

———— (1956). Consciousness: the central problem in psychiatry. *Psychotherapy* 1, 2: 1956.

———— (1960). The process of cure in psychotherapy. In *Current Approaches to Psychoanalysis*, eds. Hoch and Zubin. New York: Grune & Stratton.

Rubins, J. L. (1975). The relationship between the individual, the culture, and psychopathology. *American Journal of Psychoanalysis, 35*: 231–49.

Tart, C., ed. (1969). *Altered States of Consciousness*. New York: Wiley; Anchor Doubleday, paperback.

Thomas, A., Chess, S., and Birch, H. (1968). *Temperament and Behavior Disorders in Children*. New York: New York University Press.

Ullman, M. (1960). Social roots of the dream. *American Journal of Psychoanalysis 20*, 2: 18–196.

———— (1962). Foreword, *The Clinical Use of Dreams*. New York: Basic Books.

———— Krippner, S. and Vaughn, A. (1973). *Dream Telepathy*. New York: Macmillan.

———— (1973). Societal factors in dreaming. *Contemporary Psychoanalysis*, 9, 3.

Von Grunebaum, G. E., and Callois, R., eds. (1966). *The Dream in Human Societies*. Berkeley: University of California Press.

CHAPTER FIVE

Object Relational Approach

JOHN H. PADEL, M.R.C.Psych.

BASIC THEORY OF THE MEANING OF DREAMS

For a psychoanalyst of the British Society to contribute a chapter on the object relational approach to dream interpretation raises a curious problem. Harry Guntrip (1974) writes that Fairbairn "would have disapproved of any attempts to create yet another school of theory." Guntrip himself told me that he deeply regretted the subtitle to that work "The Fairbairn-Guntrip Approach." Winnicott, describing his own clinical and theoretical approach, once said "It's a whole system," but he also claimed that all his work was nothing more than an attempt to translate Freud's method into English. (He spoke and wrote paradoxes.) The cultural difference between Britain and the United States is such that, while this American book is planned on the principle of different approaches, the British would be more likely to consider the *individual* differences of the writers than to regard them as representing different schools of thought and more ready to look for what they shared than how they differed.

I cannot claim to write as a Fairbairnian or as a follower of Winnicott or Guntrip, or of Balint, Brierley, Milner, Rycroft, Sutherland or Khan, to mention only those from whom (after Freud and Abraham) I personally have learned most. They have never formed a school, and, although they have in my opinion maintained in common a certain basic approach to psychoanalysis, it is far easier to say what central tenets they have never accepted of the 'Kleinian dogmata on the one hand' or of Anna Freud's views of psychoanalytic theory on the other, than it is to formulate their shared principles and opinions. In fact, I believe they would all have consciously rejected the idea of a commonly defined approach; for one thing, they have not freely used one another's terminologies or discussed their usefulness or otherwise, and rarely have they dealt with the meaning of one another's central ideas. Khan is perhaps the person who has made the biggest effort to interpret these thinkers in the Society and so to one another; Rycroft has emphasized the central function in psychoanalysis of human communication and of factors that hamper and facilitate it, so defining in his way both the method and the object of analysis. His *Critical Dictionary* is a sustained attempt to explicate and to relate the various terminologies.

I doubt whether all these thinkers would have called themselves object relations theorists, yet all have put at the center of their inquiries the nature of the psychological bonds between people who are close to one another and the problem of choosing the best ways of describing the processes that occur between them. And they have done so without making important use of classical metapsychology, although they have used Freud first and foremost. Fairbairn overtly tried to eliminate from psychoanalytic theory certain terms and metaphors which he felt had become more of a hindrance than a help. For example, while Hartmann was soft-pedaling the superego, Fairbairn was proclaiming that both superego and id should be dropped as concepts, that their component concepts should be made more explicit and that the *relation-ships* implicit in each of them (quite explicit in many of Freud's writings) and in the ego should be featured.

Fairbairn, Winnicott and Guntrip have been the three most concerned to describe personality development and personality structure dynamically; for all of them the relationships actually lived in the family and the personalities of the adults present in the child's formative years accounted for all the personality structure that was not the outcome of his own creativeness and his own refusals. It was the stuff of which he made his education, his career, his symptoms and his new relationships.

The main outlines of the object relations theory of emotional development are soon told; from it any theory of dreams derives.

The infant who is mothered well enough deals with all failures in the mother-self relationship by internalizing and by keeping separate (splitting off, repressing) those instances which are deeply unsatisfying or disturbing; these he keeps detached as images ("bad object relationships"). They are unsatisfying or disturbing for alternative reasons: they imperil his security and his integrity, either because they prevent or punish spontaneous libidinal approaches or because libidinal behavior seems to be attended or followed by chaos or abandonment; when libidinal experience seems vitally necessary, the obstacles to it are felt to be bad; when human presence and care seem crucially important, libidinal spontaneity and excitement may seem disruptive and bad.

The infant who is mothered well enough has no problem with all the instances of mothering which are deeply satisfying. He does not need to keep such moments of fulfillment detached from consciousness; on the contrary, they have confirmed his sense of security and furthered his sense of completeness. Whatever tensions he experienced during the processes that ended in satisfaction were resolved in such a way that he felt no ultimate contradiction between his sensual excitement and his need for his mother's presence to ensure comfort and continuity.

Those experiences laid down the pattern of good relationship, based on the mutual acceptances of each other's rhythm. No doubt they were internalized because there were times of tension, even acute although comparatively short-lived. But whereas we postulate a *memory* of such experiences, serving to define the elementary standards of goodness, we contrast such experiences of remembered goodness with the internalization of failures, which led to division of the "bad" mother-self images from the idealized ones made and kept by effort and ultimately even by a turning away from libidinal activity on the one hand and from anger over the failures on the other.

The images of the idealized mother, self and mother-and-self are superficially closely associated with the memories of the satisfying moments of fulfillment, which have after all provided the models for their fashioning. Yet insofar as they are maintained by effort and have unconsciously associated with them the "bad" images of failure, they are not freely available to enrich the range of behavior toward figures in the world. External figures are now sought as needed and treated as potentially satisfying or as fostering security, but there attaches to them a deep wariness which inhibits absolute spontaneity. It is perhaps a necessary ambiguity in terminology that the terms "ideal object" and "idealized object" cannot always correspond to definite psychological distinctions.

Thus two kinds of relationship are clung to yet suppressed from consciousness ("primarily repressed"), one in which control is all-powerful and one in which libidinal excitement is all-important. These are related to each other owing to the fact that the relationship of control exerts its greatest power over the relationship of libidinal excitement, more deeply suppressing it from consciousness ("secondary repression"). These two repressed relationships become categories of thought and feeling on the extreme edges of daily relationships, which mostly proceed free from either kind of threat (anti-libidinal deadness and libidinal chaos); but any important relationship does contain both threats at its edges, and, since both libidinal excitement and secure control are features essential to living, any child will explore each of its parents for both capacities. Clearly each "object" (of feeling; parents and siblings) will at this stage appear intensely ambivalent, offering unlimited excitement yet refusing to allow it, encouraging and threatening, tantalizing yet crushing. The child's natural solution is the Oedipus relationship: distributing the excitement and the control between his parents, he enrolls one parent as his good object, the other as his bad ("good" and "bad" are here used in a libidinal sense). This frees him (for a time) from ambivalence, which will nevertheless return to plague him if he cannot reverse the Oedipus relationship and so experience *each* parent now as ambivalent and now as a refuge from his ambivalence toward the other and from the other's ambivalence toward him.

Living out the double Oedipus situation constitutes a long period of transition, a time in which the child has passed the stage of dependence that is unconditional and absolute owing to helplessness and to needs that are imperative, yet has still not fully passed the stages of ambivalence, has not yet reached the stage where he is ready to engage in relationships of mutual dependence on equal terms. That capacity is something that develops while good and more independent relationships multiply at school, before and after puberty, and is usually achieved only after some critical period in adolescence and finally after periods of courtship.

The repressed relationships, libidinal and anti-libidinal, are not usually so split off from one's personality that they leave one's daily and new relationships unaffected. Far from it: they are the resource of one's new experience and the guarantee of one's self-control if things go well; otherwise, they are the source of anxiety, of one's self-defeating, and of destructiveness to oneself and to others. Those repressed object relationships cannot be kept out of any developing external relationships, whether at work or in love, in situations of two individuals or in group situations; they ensure the quality and the features, the meaningfulness or the pointlessness of new relationships. Still less are the repressed object relationships kept out of dreams, of which they provide the structuring, the two threats (of deadness or helplessness and of chaos) accounting for the polarization of dream activity. (Martha's Dream 2 provides a short example: on the one hand, she is at her mother's mercy, she cannot keep her out of her room or her purse; on the other, her mother is at her mercy, flung by the hair at the bathroom door.)

Owing to the fact of primary identification with his object at the beginning of life, the infant's first *perception* of his object is something that he cannot at all differentiate from himself (for the return of such nondifferentiation, such confusion, cf. Shakespeare's sonnets Nos. 39 and 62); his first perception is of a self-object relationship (Freud, 1914, p. 88; from the beginning each of us has two sexual objects, himself that is suckled and the woman who nurses him). That ultimately uncertain differentiation of self and object characterizes all later relationships of childhood, adolescence and adult life but is especially marked in the repressed libidinal and anti-libidinal relationships. As these repressed relationships become reinforced and less repressed in psychotherapy, thanks to the enduring and developing relationship with the therapist, the patient will experience the emergence of figures (most clearly in dreams) with whom he is closely identified and whom he will need to consider now as self (or an aspect of himself), now as another, e.g., as an important person from his past (Freud, 1923 pp. 120–21). Martha's Dream 6 provides examples of this that are not yet worked out: Eileen has something of Martha in her and the little girl has something of Martha too, yet is clearly more complex than just a past self-image.

It is upon the need to repeat (or to hold on to the possibility of repeating) such experience, in which self and object cannot be finally differentiated, that Winnicott (1951) based his theory of *transitional* experience; the *transitional object* is that possession which can stand for self or mother and can do so because it symbolizes the relationship that was already there when memory began. Upon the need to repeat such experience is based also the notion of therapeutic regression.

Since some people will have lived through failed relationships very early in infancy (e.g., because there simply was not a good enough mother, with all the various possible meanings of "not good enough"), before self and object were at all clearly differentiated, the basic disaster that threatens their later relationships will appear as loss of self, a schizoid experience; since others will date their greatest insecurities from a little later (e.g., when her child's hate and anger become too much for a mother), once ambivalence has set in but before the three-person relationship begins to offer a real alternative security, the basic disaster that looms for such people will be loss of object (or destruction of object), the central feature of depression. Yet at each of these stages "self" and "object" have the double aspect of self-and-object (Freud, 1914). Only the three-person situation of the Oedipus period helps to disentangle the "self" from the "other" and therefore to provide insurance against either disaster or the repetition of failures. So important is father!

From this time onwards the context in which a relationship is lived is an essential component of the experience of the relationship itself. Of course, this was true from the start, yet at the very beginning of our lives we can take for granted, if we are lucky, the lap and the arms that hold us and concentrate on the supply and its source. Once the world has in it a cast of three or more, the relationships of the context must afford at least a minimum assurance so that the relationship of sensuality may proceed; all persons in the immediate environment are regularly tested out for reliability as well as for the opportunities and supplies they offer.

More and more, from this time on, there can be detected an alternation between two modes of thinking and perceiving: one in which the contextual relationships impinge—for good or ill—with no less vividness than the relationship of need satisfaction (this may be called the "ternary mode," because there is experience of at least two others besides the self) and one in which the context is assumed to be reliable and forgettable, as in good sexual experience and in deeply satisfying concentration upon an aesthetic awareness (this may be called the "binary mode," when there is—temporarily, at least—no room in one's attention for more than oneself and one other).

The writers I have mentioned appear to have shared the traditional approach in the understanding of dreams. Fairbairn worked a great deal through dream interpetation, taking dreams to represent, first, statements about the present lives of his patients, second, situations from the past—especially the oedipal period—and, third, the "state of affairs" of the inner object relations. His most important papers about dreams and their significance are those of 1944, of 1954 and of 1958. He pointed out that dreams are schizoid phenomena *par excellence;* the observing ego is remarkably detached from the two aspects of ego involved in the repressed relationships, libidinal and anti-libidinal.

It was a patient's dream that provided him with the material for his final theory on mental structure. This dream

> consisted of a brief scene in which the dreamer saw a figure of herself being attacked by a well-known actress in a venerable building which had belonged to her family for generations. Her husband was looking on but he seemed quite helpless and quite incapable of protecting her. After delivering the attack the actress turned away and resumed playing a stage part which, as seemed to be implied, she had momentarily set aside in order to deliver the attack by way of interlude. The dreamer then found herself gazing at the figure of herself lying bleeding on the floor; but as she gazed, she noticed that this figure alternated between herself and this man until eventually she awoke in a state of acute anxiety." (Fairbairn, 1944, p. 95)

From the dreamer's associations to that dream Fairbairn derived three sets of interpretations: one in terms of the dreamer's current life situation and marital relationship; a second in oedipal terms, describing her libidinal relationship to her father as an identification with him and her relationship to her mother (the actress) as both masochistic and, by identifying with her, as sadistic toward the male; and a third in structural terms, finding in this dream "a basic character which entitles it to be regarded as the paradigm of all endopsychic situations."

Briefly, Fairbairn distinguished three egos, each related to a special kind of object: the central (observing) ego linked with an ideal or idealized object (the helpless husband of the dream); the libidinal ego (the figure of herself being attacked and then lying bleeding) linked with a libidinal object (the man with whom that figure alternates); and the anti-libidinal ego (the actress-self that conformed with her mother's pattern) linked with an anti-libidinal object (in this dream the actress-mother fused with the actress-self). The three links of being separate-but-like, of being incompletely fused but alternating, and of being completely fused may be seen as different stages of object-relationship. Fairbairn's diagram (1954, p. 105) representing these structures and their relationship should be compared with Freud's diagram of the psychic personality (1933, p. 78). Fairbairn perhaps never realized that *they are the same diagram* with two exceptions: (1) Fairbairn's makes *explicit* in the diagram the components which Freud had described of the superego and the components of the repressed libidinal relationships; (2) where Freud puts ID, Fairbairn leaves a blank, though in his text he describes, as filling that space and then absorbed into the central ego, the idealized object from which the libidinal and anti-libidinal objects have been split off. For Fairbairn energy was adequately represented in the bonds of attraction and repulsion uniting bor keeping separate the different egos and their objects.

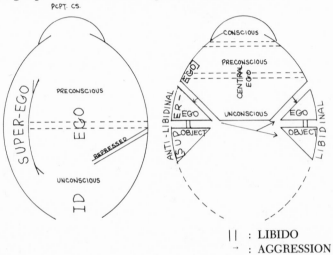

| ┃   : LIBIDO
→   : AGGRESSION

FREUD: NEW INTROD. LECT. 31   FAIRBAIRN: OBJ.-REL. THEORY OF
(S.E. VOL. 22, p. 78)   PERSONALITY (1954), p. 105

MODIFIED:

(a) CHANGED SHAPE OF OUTLINES

(b) FAIRBAIRN'S CHANGES IN
    TERMINOLOGY AND [SUPER-EGO]
    WRITTEN IN

(c) (DOTTED LINE)
    IDEAL OBJECT
    (ACCEPTED OBJECT)

©John H. Padel, 1973

In amplification of the modified diagram of Fairbairn on p. 131 I add the follow-ing notes. The structures (ego + object) called libidinal and anti-libidinal are often represented in dreams and in other experiences as fused, but ego and object of each kind may appear separately. Fairbairn insisted that primary direct repression is ef-fected and maintained by aggressive activity and an aggressive attitude toward the object, perceived as "bad"; secondarily, a part of the ego is repressed closely associ-ated with each repressed object, so closely that there is often a state of fusion or semifusion.

Perhaps Fairbairn did not emphasize fully the way these states of fusion, one of which we watch becoming loosened in the dream he quotes, account for the loss or recovery of parts of the self as fused with an object. (Winnicott's "true self" would be such an internal libidinal system dissociated from the central ego, which is then a "false" or "caretaker" self.) Fairbairn's 1931 case paper describes the recovery of parts of the self as personifications, a mischievous preadolescent boy and a vivacious young girl.

Sutherland has aptly referred to the internal structures as "systems," a primitive need system (libidinal) and a primitive control system (anti-libidinal).Each subsidiary ego is, in Fairbairn's sense, a *structure* and must have appropriate objects internal to it; so also each subsidiary object is a *structure* and has been experienced as such, not only by projection but by objective perception. A child from an early age has a real-ity sense that recognizes in his parents greed and irrational anger directed not only toward him but toward each other.

It needs to be clearly stated that the repressed objects cannot be experienced as "bad" *at the moment.* The libidinal object (and ego) is "bad" if it is overstimulating or imperils the continuity of coherence of the central ego or of its relationships; the anti-libidinal object (and ego) is then felt to be "good" if it exercises automatic con-trol, even if this is inhibiting to the whole personality. The anti-libidinal object is "bad" if it rejects, witholds, impedes or attacks the libidinal experience, without which life is empty and futile; libidinal experience is felt not just as "good" but as vitally necessary, whether it be shared or solitary, straight or perverse, direct or symbolic. Thus the anti-libidinal ego, fused with its object, maintains an aggressive opposition, even an implacable hostility, against the libidinal object with which its portion of ego is fused; this is indirect repression (the ego has borrowed the strength of the father to repress the primary libidinal object choices—"an energetic reaction-formation against those choices").

Then what of the id, the system unconscious? The system unconscious is repre-sented (1) by the four repressed structures and a large area of the central ego, made, as Freud stated, out of abandoned object relationships (incidentally, this allows for lines of cleavage under stress or after loss, separation or rejection) and (2) by the sym-bols = (libido) and ⁻ (aggression); these are all that remain of the instinct theories, whether of the component instincts, of sexual *versus* ego instincts or of life-and-death instincts. Energy is not absent in the structures themselves but it can be left unrepre-sented, since the distinction between ego and object components that have been absorbed into the personality would be artificial. Some of the energy at the disposal of the central ego is, of course, represented by the arrows symbolizing direct repression, including what Freud called the maintenance of counter-cathexes.

Fairbairn's sentence "There is no Id" means that he could not subscribe to the confusion of categories that Freud made when he lumped together sexual and aggressive *instincts*, repressing *forces*, and repressed *images* and experiences in a "seething cauldron." In the diagram I have represented by a dotted line the acceptable, accepted and accepting object from which the repressed object portions have been detached. This is only in his text (not in his diagram) because he regarded it as absorbed in the central ego and so available for forming and maintaining good object relations with figures and institutions in the outside world (Stierlin, 1970).

The diagrams also reveal two symmetries: the symmetry about the horizontal axis indicates the relationship between self and object (it shows the self-object relationship as forming at the *unconscious*, not at the *conscious* pole); the symmetry about the vertical axis indicates the close correspondence between the sensual need system and the primitive control system. The only asymmetry, the divided arrow symbolizing indirect repression (aggression against the sensual need system), comes from a structure even more tightly fused with its object than the sensual; this suggests that the mother-child bond of security, as Bowlby (1969), using ethological findings, has argued, is even more fundamental than the bond of supply or gratification in excitement; both bonds are represented by the sign =, because they are, as shown in *Beyond the Pleasure Principle* (1920), ultimately libidinal. The "aggression" of maternal rejection and of reaction to it proceeds from a self-object system for which, as Winnicott also showed, the *environment is ultimately responsible*. Fairbairn argued that the splitting process, the schizoid position, and the resulting structure were fundamental and normal and that they patterned all relationships, including those of the oedipal period, when first one parent (or sibling) and then the other is identified as the exciting or libidinal object and the parent not so used is identified now as the secure base and guarantor of control, now as the rejecting or anti-libidinal object. In fact, the diagram can be used to transform what Rickman and Balint called a one-body psychology into a two- and three-body psychology, into a psychology of interpersonal relations. In the process of defense the ego is split into three, but this itself makes object relationships possible—and complicated.

For clinical purposes Fairbairn and others who base their work on his assume that dreams are representations of endopsychic situations over which the dreamer has got stuck (fixation points) and often include some attempt to move beyond that situation. In dream or in real life any person who offers or encourages the fulfillment of need is liable to be seen as libidinally exciting and sets into action also the primitive control system (anti-libidinal); with the help of a figure like the therapist, whose interventions lead to the patient's distinguishing between past and present components of his anti-libidinal figures, the bonds both of repulsion and of attraction may be loosened and the object relationships newly abandoned may be established appropriately in the central ego, providing each time a little more learning by experience.

I find it extraordinarily interesting that Karl Abraham, whose elaborate phase theory Fairbairn most vehemently rejected, had described a very similar dream (Abraham, 1924) of horse-drawn carts, each with a man slung underneath, and had clinically interpreted it in the same way, describing the same three kinds of relationships outlined by Fairbairn twenty years later. Both analysts operated easily with the notion of identification alternating with object relationship.

Winnicott, in his clinical use of dreams, looked out for that element in which the *transitional* was most apparent. I offered above an account of what Winnicott meant by his term "transitional." Here it may be redefined as any element which has a markedly ambiguous quality, an ambiguity in its status of existence: it is at one moment part of the self, at another part of the central figure in the world beyond the self. In a child's series of drawings Winnicott once pointed to a detached bunch of loops that looked like a complexly tied shoelace and occurred on each page as a minor element. He said, "They could be representing the child's own fingers during thumb-sucking or a bow on her mother's night-dress." Rycroft (1960) has described the importance of decoding symbols, especially those occurring in dreams, according not only to their conventional meaning, but also to the meaning given them by their context. Khan (1972) has made most explicit the idea of dream space and insisted that it too can be *transitional* in the same sense as Winnicott's *transitional object*, i.e., that it characterizes the dreamer's inner world and also the inner world of the dreamer's mother. Like all transitional phenomena in psychotherapy, it needs to be considered (and perhaps interpreted) first as the space of the dreamer and then as the space of the mother. Martha's sixth dream will show an excellent example of this.

PRINCIPLES CONCERNING THE USE OF DREAMS IN TREATMENT

I do not believe that there is a difference in principles between an analysis based on the theory of object relations and one based on the classical approach insofar as they use dream interpretation. Freud's advice is followed not to concentrate on dream interpretation but to deal first with what is uppermost in the patient's mind. Nevertheless the dream is the royal road to the unconscious. Perhaps we now recognize more readily in the dream and also interpret more readily the features of the current transference relationship. We look less for the wish underlying the trains of associations than for the attempts to deal with bad or threatening object relationships and to put right what once went wrong. (Martha's words to the little girl in Dream 6 provide a fine instance).

It is still the analyst's task to get the patient working or, I should say, *playing* with the ideas (from dreams or other sources) that preoccupy him. The main principles of achieving this will have been gathered not only from the therapist's own personal psychotherapy or psychoanalysis but from his education, his upbringing and his pleasurable pursuits, expecially but not only those shared with other people. Free association is best thought of not as a technique to be acquired but as the capacity to play in thought with words and images arising spontaneously or evoked by other people and events. The special value which most patients attach to their dreams appears to be due first and foremost to the fact that dreams are their own productions and secondly to the fact that their therapists seem to appreciate them. (There is, of course, a danger in the latter, since dreams can be and often are produced to slow down the therapist's work, much as the throwing of each golden apple effectively slowed down Atalanta, who could not resist picking it up.)

Winnicott's own greatest contribution to technique has been to get therapists to think of their patients as people who in childhood or adolescence forgot or never developed the knowledge of how to play and who now need to play. The therapist has the resources of example, of interest, of encouragement and of silence, all of which at different times serve as effective stimuli—and at other times as inhibitors. Aristotle in different works defined both the best interpreter of dreams and the best user of metaphor as somebody who most readily could see the similarities between things. To Winnicott and Aristotle I will add only Freud, who offered ten pearls of wisdom which make it unnecessary to extend this section of my chapter (Freud, 1923). The most succinct and telling summary I know is Chapter Five of his "Outline" (Freud, 1940).

Psychoanalysis has tended in Britain to rely more and more on transference analysis; this has often been fruitful but it has two dangers which are related: the first is of prolonged regression; the second, of a prolonged dependence upon (even enslavement to) the analyst, from whose opinion about the transference it is hard to make an appeal on objective grounds (yet he is himself only as capable of objectivity about the transference as his own personal analysis has enabled him to be). Dream interpretation is a technique as productive as transference interpretation and as essential, if one aims at maintaining an equal relationship. A dream provides that objective third term, equally available to patient and to analyst and offering the patient an opportunity to judge his analyst's competence and limitations. Dream analysis also ensures that repression is as far as possible undone whereas transference analysis, if unrelieved, sometimes leads to greater repression, from compliance to the wise and powerful analyst, and to the moral defense that Fairbairn described—an intensified, even delusional sense of guilt as a defense against too powerful bad objects.

As for practical advice, I have found most helpful of all Freud's 1923 paper "Remarks on the theory and practice of dream interpretation". Fairbairn's clinical papers are rich in examples, as are several of Abraham's (especially 1924). Technique becomes a matter of operating with the *transitional* and of recognizing the repressed object relationship emerging in the transference and in dreams, but first and foremost of respecting the creativeness of the patient.

INTERPRETATION OF MARTHA'S DREAMS

Theoretical Understanding

To have undertaken the evaluation of Martha's dreams is in a sense to have accepted an invitation to put myself in her therapist's place, to interpret in a provisional way her dreams and her immediate associations and to decide early on in each of the six sessions how to help her to explore them, predicting the future on the basis of my experience. But there's the rub; her therapist has had a growing experience with Martha, shared experience, and for him prediction becomes increasingly based upon that experience of her responses to his contributions, upon knowing her as a person. Therefore, with each dream it becomes progressively more impossible for me to put myself in his place and to make meaningful predictions. The first dream should give me the greatest opportunity to do this. On the other hand, since I have read the other five dreams, I have most after-knowledge of Martha when I evaluate the first dream, whereas he had least experience of her; so I am now in a position least like his at the time.

Considerations of this kind lead me to reverse the order of the dreams in my interpretation, so as not to pretend to a freshness of approach toward the earlier dreams but to use first the freshness that I have toward the last or last two dreams. After that, I can consider all six chronologically from a practical point of view.

Dream No. 6.

I fully share Martha's own appreciation of this dream as a breakthrough. Whatever techniques may have led to it have been justified by the fact of the dream experience and its quality. In the dream the relationship between the patient and her friend, Eileen, makes the exploration possible and not terrifying. I remember that in the first dream there were explosions and black smoke *down below* and that a female friend joined the people running toward them and was warned by Martha of the danger. "Down below" now has a different and fuller meaning; there is still risk but Martha is taken by her friend to the very bottom *and comes up alone*. Both the unknown friend who ran to see in the first dream and Eileen in the Dream 6 represent aspects of Martha's ego (see Freud, 1923), but the different use made of this maneuver indicates that the self-splitting can now be used constructively and is far less compulsive; independence has grown.

Whatever associations to Eileen Martha may have, I should assume that the pun on her name is significant, the name signifying dependence. But Eileen appears to represent other aspects of femininity as well; she knows that things inside are important, inside the body and stored inside as memories of the past; she is prepared to act on curiosity and to take Martha to find out. So Martha of the descent (Fairbairn's *central ego*) is probably identified with her therapist, who is taken for an exploration of Martha's inner world.

Here Winnicott's notion of the transitional object and transitional phenomena (1951) seems most helpful. I define the *transitional* operationally as "that which needs to be interpreted (if interpretation is appropriate) in two different ways, as a part or aspect of the mother and as the self or an aspect of the self." As a symbol it represents a dim memory of the composite unity of self-and-mother before it was differentiated into the two separate individuals; it is therefore used to facilitate switches in identification. I referred to the space explored in the dream as "Martha's inmost world," but since I regard it as having that characteristic transitional quality, I should also consider it as the space of Martha's mother's inner world, the space of her person. The creepy reminds me of *The Uncanny* (Freud, 1919, especially p. 245), characterizing an approach to our place of origin—the maternal genital. One of Fairbairn's ideas is helpful here, namely, that transitions (he used the word ten years before Winnicott in a slightly different sense but referring to the same developmental stage) from one defensive technique to another, particularly to a developmental stage of greater independence, are often symbolized in dreams by crossing a chasm or by other actions in which there is a risk of falling a long way.

I think of Dante's descent with Vergil into Inferno and wonder if Martha knows it. I have a passing curiosity about the difference between hundreds and thousands (of steps); does she switch so as not to know or reveal the total, like Catullus and Lesbia their shared kisses? Is it the difference between multiples of 10^2 and of 10^3? Is it a memory of Hundreds and Thousands, those chocolate drops covered with tiny colored sugar seeds?

Men laying a concrete floor is a good constructive symbol for the anal aspect of Martha's parents' intercourse. How creatively she has used her memories of her father's "poor personal hygiene!" Wet concrete has the homogeneous, mushy, gray-brown qualities which make it a fairly common symbol for feces; also, from the child's point of view, men get fascinatingly dirty as they lay the concrete.

An area of sunlight in the middle sounds promising. Father's potency penetrates even as far as this and ensures that the area has been and can still be used for amusement and not only for cultural activity (the latter I interpret as the *procreative* aspect of sexual intercourse).

But all this is preliminary to the episode with the little girl of five or six. Martha's insight that what she said to the child applied to herself makes it possible to interpret the child as representing at least a split-off (forgotten, repressed) aspect of herself (and I hope Martha will be able to talk more freely about her relationships at home and at school when she was five and six). Winnicott's *true self* comes to mind and also Fairbairn's early paper in which he tells of split-off relationships recovered *via* dreams about two complementary figures, adult and child (Fairbairn, 1931). I hope we shall discover with whom the patient is identified in speaking as she did to the girl: perhaps an early schoolteacher (an elder sister figure) represented by someone in her concurrent treatment group. If the dark eyes and the bangs are not mainly symbolic, they will have important associations.

I understand the discovery of that child and the play with her, getting to know her, as representing the main undoing of the split (the repression), so that the journey to the surface is made without the dissociation that was necessary for the descent. The mild contradiction about the time of day—"early" yet "so late in the afternoon"—reveals different ways of viewing her stage of life now that treatment is drawing to its close. "Early" means that she has enough time left for making something of her life but "so late in the afternoon" means that being in her late thirties she can't afford to spend longer on her self-analysis (if she's going to have a family), however enjoyable it has been. It is good to discover that the solid child has become an imaginative woman—"of imagination all compact"—through the constructive use of her anal sexuality and through playing. I assume that the regularity of her sessions, the production of dreams and other experiences, and her need of her therapist's attention, care and restrictions have all recalled to her more and more readily different features of her toilet training; they will have let her realize the importance of her own rhythms and initiative, and have brought out a knowledge of her own powers of originality, immobilization, destructiveness.

Dream No. 5

By my reckoning Martha had had about six months of group therapy when she had this dream. I guess that her therapist would not have sanctioned or encouraged it concomitantly with the individual therapy if it had not seemed to him and to Martha that she was hanging back unduly on a heterosexual experience, avoiding the implications of sex differences and resting upon the symbolic equation of breast = penis. In other words she had been avoiding the interior aspects of the female genitals, both vagina and womb (that is why exploration of the interior is such a breakthrough in Dream 6), and emphasizing the exterior. If the young man on the island (another pun?) was not representing the therapist, I should look first toward a male in her therapeutic group, particularly as Martha holds both razor blade and penis under her mother's eyes. Presumably a brother is hidden behind the figure of that young man.

The symbolism of the dream is extremely compressed. The razor blade can stand for the gums and teeth of the infant, for the fingernails in infantile masturbation and for the vagina when intercourse is envisaged. My main interpretation is of a masturbation fantasy in which the penis is appropriated and internalized; concern for the male is marked; the patient has probably had some urethritis or vaginitis. The fecal stool seems to have stood for the penis and to have been an object both of pride and of guilt. Although there is marked *displacement upwards*, I think this happened upon the background of very early experience in which the nipple or the bottle teat was regularly withdrawn too soon, so that there was a strong fantasy of biting it off.

I like the way in which Martha becomes more able to accept her penis envy through envisaging the man's envy of female organs. I notice that her readiness to postpone heterosexual relations a bit longer comes up as "I was supposed to join him on Friday night. I'd rather have joined him on Saturday .... " Perhaps this also refers to her reluctance to depart from the Sabbath observation appropriate to her Jewish background.

Fairbairn's ideas on the *moral defense* are applicable here. Who had done the cutting? The young man—but the patient had the razor blade (and in Dream 1 the patient had cut her wedding gown herself). Although it is true that this represents her ego split and her preference for making the male responsible, the reverse may be important here—namely, that sexual initiative and aggression by an older male (perhaps her brother, cf. "I didn't know why he'd done it") can have been regarded by her defensively (i.e., delusively) as her own doing; "better to be a sinner in a world ruled by God than an innocent in a world ruled by the Devil." This may account for the sense of pressure, responsibility and burden. I should guess that *"carrying too many packages"* stands for a long period of constipation and reluctance to empty her bowels: the depressive defense consists in taking on the burden of others' failures or misdeeds.

Dreams No. 4 and No. 3

Although there is clear progress from Dream 3 to Dream 4, since in Dream 4 Martha faces her phobic object and the object changes and gives rise to quite different lines of association, both dreams are remarkable for the strong defense against entertaining serious thoughts of male sexuality. (I am not surprised that concomitant group therapy was started two years after Dream 3.) The main point of this defense would be to make the therapist responsible for thoughts of male sexuality and to keep females (especially Martha's mother and herself) innocent and unaggressive.

The hysterical personality split is shown in Dream 4 when it is the other girl, a disowned aggressive side of herself, who starts killing the cockroach. Passivity and helplessness appear to be particularly associated with the bath and less with the bed. A sign of recovery is taking the can and giving the creature one long spray. As so often with an hysteric, recovery seems to start from recollections of initiative and independence over urination. I would interpret one phase of her masturbation in this sense but the cessation of it as due to the alternatives she was faced with in fantasy: oral attack on the breast or urinary attack on the penis (chicken and dog, respectively). I wonder about her attitude to her therapist's interpretations over this time. I expect him to have lived through many sessions in which he was acutely frustrated by her apparent naïveté, by her failure to take up and use his interpretations and by responses to him such as "That's what *you* say" or "So what?" His interpretative potency during this time is likely to have been scorned or shunned, or treated as of no use to her or beyond her powers.

Dream 3 seems to have been useful both in bringing Martha face to face with her mother's sexuality (also their joint shrinking from acknowledging it) and in recalling the memory of the boys. She suspects that she was left uninitiated because she was littler than the other children, but she also puts the onus of initiation and of witholding it upon the males. The word "just" recalls both that others knew and felt more, and that Martha herself avoided knowing and feeling.

The cockroach in both dreams has a transitional quality; also, it is a devourer, it is dirty, and it is lively—characteristics of oral, anal and phallic sexuality, respectively. But what is it that the mother won't tell and that the girl doesn't wish to know? Not the role of the male but the female's *own* sexual activity, so that the cockroach stands both for the labia and clitoris and for the fingers. The defense against knowing this is very strong, and, once the cockroach phobia is dealt with, its transformation will be the razor blade and the fear of her mother's comment.

Dogs have similar oral, anal and phallic characteristics. Dogs that jump up are indeed a threat to pantyhose, but the paucity of associations and the fact that Martha opens the door and apologizes to the dog suggest that she holds fast to her virginal primness. I very much doubt whether she has yet experienced penetration. In fact, I imagine that this first occurred not long before or soon after Dream 6. If it happened much earlier, Martha retained her psychological virginity only by means of marked dissociation; this is less likely.

Dream No. 2

The transitional quality of Martha's bedroom as a symbol for her person is shown by the way in which it is equally accessible to her mother and to herself. The purse seems to be a female genital symbol but is as much anal as genital; the check for the therapist indicates Martha's old secret that she felt close to her father because her stool could be equated with his penis. Martha's repressed anger and violence toward her mother, presumably over toilet control and over suppression of early masturbation, does need interpretation, especially since her growing feeling for her therapist will be resurrecting her early devotion to her father and her brothers, but it is a good sign that she recalls how she has recently treated her therapist: she admits that she has acted toward him (investigating and trying to get things out of him) as her mother had acted toward her; presumably it is also the other way round, and she regards the sessions as putting pressure on her to part with her contents at times not of her own convenience or choosing. The symbol of locked horns states that her insistence on equality and on stubbornness will make the treatment long.

Potency is represented both by the personal possessions and by the scream that isn't strong enough (its later transformation is the spray). Martha's physical violence runs the risk of being too strong. Hair is quite important to her: I would take throwing by the hair as a masturbation fantasy; this may have been acted out with a female partner in an attempt to deny the underlying anger and violence. Throwing her mother against the bathroom door indicates the place in which the main traumas occurred; the sense that there was no way to make her mother observe the integrity of her things indicates the nature of the traumas. Even at the first interview Martha was well aware of her mother's intrusiveness; she is now beginning to be aware that her own relationship to the males of the family did not develop enough because it could not go unobserved by her mother.

The stage of this dream is crucial because Martha indicates that she will fight to avoid the maternal transference. (I wonder if Dream 3 could be used to get Martha to realize it.)

Her sense of threatened helplessness in face of an advancing army shows what Guntrip always believed to be the central feature of pathology—a sense of helplessness and weakness. Although he expressed this by means of a concept which I think is inaccurate ("a split in the libidinal ego"), I am sure that he was right about the tendency to regression in the face of enforced passivity and about the use of self-imposed passivity as a defense against powerful control by parent figures.

Dream No. 1

This is a rich opening dream, yet it is well-organized, not chaotic. It announces Martha's problem as hysterical in its preoccupation with the past (period costumes), in her marked identification with an older woman and in the fantasy of being proposed to by a man of great importance. It declares the pathology to have begun mainly in anal experience (the explosions and the black smoke) and to have been coped with by a phobic maneuver of avoidance as well as by adoption of the attitude of passive looker-on and by identification with the older, supposedly postsexual woman (aged fifty). Martha also acknowledges her warm acceptance of her therapist's help and her preparedness to "come off it," to give up her false identities and her passivity, and to put herself on an equal footing with other people.

I infer a delight in fairy tales and nursery songs when she was little. I think of the little woman who fell asleep and had her petticoats cut all round about by a peddler: "Lawks-a-mercy on me, this is none of me!"—a nice opening for an identity problem! I think also of Rip Van Winkle and interest in making connections between progeny and people formerly known. (This would make a nice entry for early interest in babies and marriage.)

What I find most striking about the dream is first Martha's announcement of "being the opposite of what I actually look like" and second the number of pairs of opposites she manages to establish: (down, over there; up here, above; on a level with) (then; now) (sitting watching; running, walking, jumping) (alone; together with) (old; young) (rickety; safe) (barren; fertile) (unmarried; married) (really dangerous; dangerous in fantasy). All these pairs of contrasting terms indicate two things: on the one hand, a fertile and imaginative mind; on the other, a deep cleavage both between herself and other people and between two aspects of herself. Martha has failed therefore to integrate her active and her passive experience and has difficulty in moving from one to the other. She also establishes the close association between excitement and danger, and promises to use the new kind of relationship to face the dangers of excitement. She gives a warning that "being treated special" may be so gratifying that it will play into her defenses and also that one of her main defenses is the anal one of postponement. Becoming a false personality if she undertakes a sexual relationship prematurely is the Scylla (a female monster with ravening dogs around her pubis) opposite the Charybdis (a deadly whirlpool) of postponement until too late; both risks are serious, and like Ulysses and his crew she must steer narrowly between them.

Clinical Use of Martha's Dreams

The precise manner of gearing interpretations to associations cannot be specified here because it would depend upon the personalities of both patient and analyst.

Dream No. 1

My chief aim would be to establish two things:

(1) Martha's spontaneous observation that she thought in opposites; and
(2) her need for and readiness to use a secure relationship in order to make changes that she felt she had already left for too long.

I would also hope that we could reach a preliminary statement both

(3) of what changes she hoped to effect; and
(4) of what the obstacles to change and development had been, i.e., what kinds of danger she had represented in the dream.

Finally I should like her to realize that she had used two ways of avoiding change:

(5) postponement by being the passive spectator rather than the active participant; and
(6) identifying with an older woman, which she knew brought big yet unsubstantial gratifications and deprived her of real achievement.

Of course some of these points will have been covered in the sessions of the first few weeks of therapy, but as her therapist I would take the opportunity to acknowledge that she had made a dream that referred to the ones we had talked of and which also pointed ahead to things she meant us to discuss.

My first approach to the use of the dream would be through her talk of marriage and the two opposite dangers she mentioned: (1) a precipitate inappropriate marriage which would leave her less than a person and (2) indefinite postponement of the problems.

My second approach would be through the imagery of the dream, nursery song, and story; by playing with the thoughts of earlier sessions and with the images and memories of childhood, she had made a coherent dream which seemed to be full of meanings and allusions.

Whatever her responses to these two statements, I should be on the lookout (probably at the next session) for her to enjoy the making and telling of dreams, and I should gently raise the question whether this might not also be a way of postponing instead of effecting change—being the passive spectator again. But I should take care to use the next dream positively and not only as a warning. If I thought that a warning given so early might discourage her unduly, I should wait until some dream itself incorporated the alternatives of active participant and passive spectator, and I should use that dream to state the antinomy that each role served an indispensable purpose which could be achieved in no other way.

Dream No. 2

I should interpret Martha's efforts to keep her mother out of my consulting room, i.e., her fear that she or I would be bound to play the part that her mother had played in the past and that this could happen at any time; I should point out how dangerous she felt this likelihood or certainty to be, since if her violent feelings came up outside she might act so as to damage others or herself; if they came up in my room she might damage me.

If Martha herself did not raise the question what her excess of anger was about, I should do this and in particular suggest that the purse and the bathroom seemed to allude to body contents and their removal. I should also acknowledge that she regarded her relationship with me as a private possession which she apparently wished to keep unscrutinized by her mother, as she had perhaps wished to keep her relationships with her father and with her brothers and sister free of her mother's scrutiny and control. But I should state that the dream alluded not only to the past but also to the future; it signified Martha's hope that her mother *would* discover the fact of her therapy as a relationship that she could not control; it might even signify Martha's wish to talk to her mother about her therapy so as to triumph this time. Triumph and defeat seem to imply wounds, but Martha does appear to envisage a relationship in which, despite her anger, mother and daughter are concerned for each other without wounding one another.

Any interpretation of the not-loud-enough scream as a symbol of impotency or of an elimination that is too dangerous to go to climax would depend upon whether we had begun naturally to use the decoding of symbols. But I should certainly set the struggle on equal terms with myself (locking horns) in opposition to the triumph-or-defeat issue of a struggle with her mother. I should say that Martha appeared to think that an equal and animal-like struggle with me would be a more satisfactory way to express her anger over scrutiny and over parting with private facts. For one thing, there seemed to be less risk of being overwhelmed as by an advancing army.

If masturbation had already been talked of, I should interpret that the hair on the head represented body hair and that Martha's violent anger over being controlled was something that powered her masturbation fantasy of a struggle to retaliate against her mother or me.

Dream No. 3

This dream seems very useful for eliciting the grounds both of Martha's passivity and of her mother's preference for being hurt rather than for hurting.

I should first take up the way Martha implies that, because she was little, she had missed some fuller initiation that the older girls could have had from the boys. I should hope that Martha would suggest what the fuller initiation might have been—seeing, touching, being touched, and being displayed. If she avoided this, I should point out that her avoidance was a way of trying to get me to initiate her and of putting the onus of activity on the male. I should in any case interpret that she and her mother seemed to collude over avoiding sexuality by leaving to males the responsibility for any unpleasantness of initiation. Then I would say that the presence of the cockroach suggested something else which Martha and her mother both wished to avoid, namely, the idea that the female is also an animal just as devouring, dirty, excitable and passionate as the male. They would both find it easier to pretend to each other that it represented the male or the male organs rather than the female organs, but they would then both be left having to accept that they could only be the passive recipients or victims of male sexuality.

I should hope to establish from this dream that the cockroach could represent female sexuality—the female genital parts and female sexual activity, whether of masturbation or of contact. It would be important to point out that two females might wish to avoid acknowledging this if they were anxious about homosexual feelings or contacts.

Then I should say that the boys seemed more scared of the female sexual animal than the girls of the male, since the boys were in a group and introduced the girls only one at a time, whereas the girls dared to go in alone to face the boys. (I hope Martha would puzzle over Kipling's line "The female of the species is more deadly than the male.") I should suggest that Martha and her mother both avoided "the truth" because they dreaded the power of female sexuality and that the girls had preferred to face the boys alone for the same reason.

Dream No. 4

Martha's associations are encouraging. She can now face the worst not only in its symbolic form but also the worst about herself. I should say so and then tell her that she was now using the cockroach to realize her violent reactions to something that she had experienced with terror but had never yet been able to put into words. Her sense of passivity and helplessness was more associated with the bath than with the bed, where someone—a more active version of herself—can get on with the job she'd begun before the dream's apparent beginning, the job of killing the cockroach. When she takes over the spraying (and I should now interpret that it represents the sense of power she had felt both in urinating and masturbating), the creature changes first into a chicken, associated with her mother, and then into a dog, which seems like a threat to her purity and is therefore linked rather with the males of her family. I should expect Martha to associate the dog with her father, particularly because of its slobbering and because of her original comments about her father's poor personal hygiene and boorish eating habits. I should account for the growth in size of the object sprayed with the growth in size of the genitals when stimulated.

Then I should interpret the cockroach that grows first as her own genital that swells and then as the sexually combined parents (the "two-backed monster" of Elizabethan and Jacobean literature); I should interpret her masturbation as a mortal attack on them because of the terror she had felt at the notion of being present when they copulated. Her feelings of guilt become evident once the parents have separated (the dog leaves through the open door).

Whether or not to interpret further at this time would depend upon the extent of our working together. This dream would make it possible to offer a reconstruction (Freud, 1937) of a situation to account both for the cockroach being on her leg and for the deep anxiety connected with the bath. This is that during the period when she was still being breast-fed (mother's Friday chicken) she had felt terror and excitement together and had soiled her legs; the bath would have been linked with the experience, either that it happened in the bath or that there had been terror over being cleaned up. "Opening the door" and releasing the dog with an apology would stand for later conformity over defecation.

Dream No. 5

Because of the strong imagery of this dream, I should expect Martha to be sensitive to her therapist's understanding of it and wary of his interpretations, yet much would depend upon whether or not they had already worked with this kind of imagery or whether it occurred unexpectedly. In either case, Martha would be greatly relieved to find convincing reasons for her use of it.

I should interpret her reluctance to accept sex differences, perhaps reminding her of the struggle with locked horns associated with Dream 2 (but only if this image had been enough used then and later); that struggle had implied bodily equality. I should relate her reluctance to a sense of being at a disadvantage as compared with the male because her most important sexual organs were inside and the inside was not only unseen and undisplayable but was also regarded as dirty. She opposed nipple to penis partly because she could not conceptualize her vagina as an organ that could contain the penis as her rectum contained the penis-shaped stool.

I should expect Martha to want to imagine what the man might feel like with a clitoris (the nipple) in comparison with her possession of a penis. It would be important for Martha to face her anxiety that if she really let herself go in intercourse, she might capture the penis and damage the man. "Walking around carrying too many packages" does seem like a way of remembering a period of constipation, of representing premenstrual tension, and of imagining pregnancy. I should refer to pelvic fullness.

But it would be important to take up the words "I didn't know why he'd done it," first as perhaps referring to some sexual behavior of an older male (a brother) which she hadn't understood when she was little and could have felt irrationally guilty about, then as indicating her uncertainty as to whether other people felt separation acutely and tried to mitigate it by exchanges, and whether she herself could have missed the breast and longed for the nipple as intensely as grownups feel sexual desire.

Dream No. 6

It might be unnecessary to interpret much over this dream. I should hope that Martha would lead me to anything she needed to have interpreted. I should have an explicit statement that the exploration is of her own inner world and of her past (she is already convinced of this, since she realizes that the words she says to the girl playing apply to herself) but that it also represents the exploration she wanted to make, when she was little, of her mother's body, of the womb from which she came. She wanted to discover what her father actually did in there (men laying a concrete floor conveys the notion that feces could be used constructively; the penetration of the sunlight is the main image of procreation). If Martha did not make the link herself, I should make sure that we both accepted that the dream of exploration referred to the main business of the therapy as completed. I should hope that Martha would announce some experience of sexual intercourse.

If there was a quiet opportunity, I should ask her if she had read the *Inferno* and should wonder how she felt now about her father's exaggerations in storytelling—what meanings she now assigned to it.

From then on, I should look out for opportunities to help Martha deal with her feelings about ending treatment and about leaving.

REFERENCES

Abraham, K. (1924). Stages in the development of the libido. In *Selected Papers*. London: Hogarth Press, 1927.

Bowlby, J. (1969). *Attachment and Loss: Vol. I Attachment.* New York: Basic Books.

Fairbairn, W.R.D. (1931). Analysis of a patient with a physical genital abnormality. In *An Object Relations Theory of the Personality.* New York: Basic Books, 1954.

————— (1944). Endopsychic structure considered in terms of object-relationships. In *An Object Relations Theory of the Personality.* New York: Basic Books, 1954.

REFERENCES

———— (1954a). *An Object Relations Theory of Personality*. New York: Basic Books.

———— (1954b). Observations on the nature of hysterical states. *British Journal of Medical Psychology*, 29, 2:112-127.

———— (1958). On the nature and aims of psychoanalytic treatment. *International Journal of Psycho-analysis*, 39:374-385.

Freud, S. (1914). On narcissism. In *Standard Edition*, Vol. 14. London: Hogarth Press, 1957.

———— (1919). The uncanny. *Standard Edition*, Vol. 17. London: Hogarth Press, 1957.

———— (1920). *Beyond the Pleasure Principle*. *Standard Edition*, Vol. 18. London: Hogarth Press, 1955.

———— (1923). Remarks on the theory and practice of dream interpretation. *Standard Edition*, Vol. 19. London: Hogarth Press, 1957.

———— (1933). New introductory lecture 31. *Standard Edition*, Vol. 22. London: Hogarth Press, 1959.

———— (1937). Constructions in analysis. *Standard Edition*, Vol. 23. London: Hogarth Press, 1959.

———— (1940). *An Outline of Psychoanalysis*. *Standard Edition*, Vol. 23. London: Hogarth Press, 1959.

Guntrip, H. (1974). Psychoanalytic object relations theory. In *American Handbook of Psychiatry*, ed. S. Arieti, 2nd Edition, Vol. 1: 828-842. N.Y.: Basic Books, 1974.

Khan, M.R. (1972). The use and abuse of a dream. In *The Privacy of the Self*. London: Hogarth Press, 1974.

Padel, J. (1973). The contributions of W.R.D. Fairbairn to psychoanalytic theory and practice. In *Psycho-Analysis in Europe*, Bulletin 2.

Rycroft, C. (1960). Beyond the reality principle. In *Imagination and Reality*. London: Hogarth Press, 1962.

———— (1968). *Critical Dictionary of Psychoanalysis*. London and New Jersey: Thomas Nelson.

Stierlin, H. (1970). The functions of "inner objects." *International Journal of Psycho-analysis*, 51:301-9.

Winnicott, D.W. (1951). Transitional objects and transitional phenomena. *Playing and Reality*. London: Tavistock Publications, 1971.

CHAPTER SIX

Phenomenological Or Daseinsanalytic Approach[1]

MEDARD BOSS, M.D.
and BRIAN KENNY, M.D.

BASIC THEORY OF THE MEANING OF DREAMS

For two reasons, a new theory of dreaming—and not merely any new theory but a specific "daseinsanalytical" or "pheonomenological" one—has become necessary. First, all the hitherto so-called depth-psychology theories of the meaning of dreams do violence to our dreaming and to what appears in it. This violence is perpetrated through prejudgments about the character of our dreaming, dream beings and dream events, and the application of an abstract conceptual model for their understanding. Second, increasing numbers of practicing psychiatrists and psychologists have begun to discover the degree to which the therapeutic efficacy of "dream interpretation" is vitiated by the conceptual violence done to the dream content. Nevertheless, there could be no new daseinsanalytical theory of dreaming if Freud, Adler and Jung had not made their decisive and epoch-making concrete observations. Yet the dream theories of these pioneers were from the outset misleading. They took it for granted that all beings and events encountered by a dreamer are mere "unreal," intrapsychic "images," produced and projected outside itself by the dreamer's mind. The dreamer's own experience, however, totally contradicts this degradation of the beings of his dream world with only a very small number of exceptions. To him the givens of his dream world usually show themselves—as long as he is dreaming—as things no

---

[1]A glossary is available following the text.

less "real," actually optically perceptible and no less physically palpable than the things he encounters when awake. Therefore, to call the dream phenomena self-made "inner images" means judging something from a point of view outside its proper realm; in this case, qualifying dreaming from waking. Furthermore, this way of dealing with dream phenomena presupposes a previous and clear understanding of what "reality" is in itself. How else could anyone be in a position to qualify something as being "unreal"? Modern dream theories, though, are far from being capable of defining what reality actually means.

Moreover, there is and was another pitfall. All so-called depth psychologies still refer to *the* dream as if it were something that could be had or possessed; indeed, the French language knows "the" dream as something which the dreamer "makes." Thus dreaming, a definite mode of human existing, is reified, is made into an objectifiable thing—which it certainly is not. In fact, there is no dream had, or made, that is an object which can be grasped or possessed. There is always only the dreaming human being. At one time he exists as a dreaming being; at another, as a waking being. Waking and dreaming are two equally autochthonous, though different possibilities or modes of existing of an ever-integral and whole human being. For this reason, an adequate understanding of the basic constitution of human existing is a prerequisite for any serious theory of dreaming.

Our existing, whether it happens waking or dreaming, reveals itself directly as a primordial being-in-the-world. Any human being who reflects on himself as Da-sein discovers himself always and only as already having been thrown into a world. Of crucial importance is the way in which the little word "in" of this human being-in-the-world is understood. The human being is never merely "in" his world in the way that clothes can be hung in the space within a wardrobe and so be "in" there. Such nonliving things can only be placed within the hollow space of the interior of some other bigger nonliving thing. The clothes in a wardrobe know nothing of their being "in" the inside of a cupboard. They are "in" the world merely by occupying a definite volume of space at a particular point in space at measurable distances from other nonhuman things.

The "in" of human being-in-the-world is, however, of radically different character. When we look carefully at the way we, as existing human beings, are "in" the world, we discover ourselves as beings to whom the most manifold living and nonliving beings, always and from the beginning, address themselves in their significations as that which they are, from their own particular places out there within the open realm of our world. This means that we are also, always and from the beginning, in a thinking, responsive relationship to what is encountered, in a way that corresponds to the perceived meaningfulness of its address. Integral with this discovery of the way we are "in" the world, a still more fundamental feature of our existence—of its waking as well as dreaming state—discloses itself to us. There could not possibly occur any understanding relationship between man and what he is encountering as meaningful items out there in his world were not that which lies in-between the former and the latter of an open character, of a kind of clearance into and through which our human being can enter, cross it, expand itself, fill it and keep it luminated by its understanding nature, similar to the way beams of sunshine need an open space into which they can shine. The decisive difference between beams of physical light and the possibilities of human relationships lies in the fact that sunshine knows nothing of itself or of that which it is illuminating. Human existence, however, consists primordially of an understanding of itself, as well as of an understanding of the meaningfulness of that which is encountered but which does not belong to that particular human existence. We are, then, never present to ourselves as some encapsulated subject present somewhere at a definite point in physical space, a subject which among other properties also possesses the property of being able to perceive and respond but otherwise remains an unknown X. Rather, we span the world openness from which we are addressed by beings *as* a realm of openness, a realm of seeing and perceiving, extended as far as the most distant beings that address us. At times while dreaming, we experience most vividly this basic fundamental constitution of the human being, when we are nothing but a realm of seeing and perceiving, in which beings—living, nonliving and human—appear and events occur. At such moments, we are not aware that we may also be seen and handled as bodies present at a point in space. As human beings, as Da-sein, we consist of nothing other than a world spanning open, a clear realm constituted of the ability to perceive beings and events in their significations. As such, we provide that realm in which beings and events can *be* at all. Further, we consist of the ability to respond actively to what is being perceived in a way appropriate to its significations—we may eat an apple, a carpenter may make a table out of a tree trunk, an artist may succeed in revealing truth in his work. In our active responses to the beings and events encountered, we may and are claimed to help them to unfold their being as far as possible. All of this is not simply an additional property of the Da-sein. To reiterate, we *are* nothing other than a perceptive, seeing, hearing and actively responsive world openness.

This ontological insight into the basic feature of human existence motivated the German philosopher Martin Heidegger to reserve the term "Da-sein" as an exclusive designation of man's existing. The meaning given to this term by Heidegger cannot adequately be translated into English by any one single word. Already in its original gestalt, the "Da" in "Da-sein" was given an unusual significance by the father of Daseinsanalytic philosophy. The ordinary, everyday meaning of "Da" is "here," signifying a definite place in space, in the immediate vicinity of the speaker, as distinct from "Dort," "there," "over there." In Heidegger's use of the term "Da-sein" as the title for human existence, however, the "Da" comes to mean that which has just been described as the fundamental feature of human being, i.e., the whole realm of clearance, of understanding world openness which is existed by man. Therefore, "Da-sein," literally translated as "here-being," can best be defined as the "Sein *des* Da," i.e., as "the being, *the* here," "existing *the* here." Thus "Da" and "here" would mean—to repeat once more—the whole realm of the understanding world openness *as* which man is basically existing.

All ethics of mankind are intrinsically based in this fundamental condition of our existence. In order to be true to our fundamental nature, we must be at the disposal of everything that is and has to be. We must exist as the world openness so that we may be claimed by this everything as that realm of seeing, of perceiving, of "sunshine," into which it may appear, shine forth out of a primordial hiddenness, out of nothingness and so stand revealed in its meaningfulness and referential context, i.e., that it may *be*. If there were no seeing world openness, no clearance, no light such as is actualized by human being, then there would be no realm into which the beings of our world could appear and so *be*. The human being, then, bears responsibility for his own being, and for the beings and unfolding of the beings which are encountered, whether living or nonliving or human.

In that each human being exists from birth as a unique, but totally unreifiable fabric of possibilities of perceiving and responding, he is always and primordially *by* the diversely meaningful beings he encounters in a common world. The "in" of our being-in-the-world is then to be heard in the original meaning of "by" or "at." Once more, human existence can be compared, to a limited extent, to physical light. This light, too, is already at or by the things that shine forth in its luminousness. With our whole being, then, we are always already "outside" *by* what we encounter so that we dwell in the relationship of being addressed meaningfully by it and indeed exist *as* these perceptive, responsive relationships to things. One can never perceive, grasp and understand something unless one is already by it, at it. For this reason, the "outside" was put in quotation marks. There can only be an "outside" in distinction from an "inside." However, our existing knows no "inner life" conceptualized in the usual sense of our dwelling in our thoughts by the representation of an outside world in the inside of a conscious capsule. If this were the case, it simply would not be possible for man to realize that there was an outside world. Nor has anyone ever been capable of showing that there actually are intrapsychic representations of objects of an outside world inside a "psyche." We cannot dwell—in the sense of being perceptively, seeingly, understandingly related—*by* something that cannot be demonstrated. Rather, we are always "outside" by the beings of our world, at those places of the world where they are present. This is so even when their mode of being present is that of being visualized, remembered, planned, fantasied or hallucinated, and not that of being sensually perceptible.

An unprejudiced simple seeing reveals that both modes of existing—waking and dreaming—are equally characterized by this basic constitution of human existence. Only so can we while dreaming believe that we are fully awake. It is also for this reason that any momentary state in which our dreaming as well as our waking existence appears is to be defined by exactly the same criteria. Two questions must be posed:

(1) To what beings and events is a human being at any given moment, waking or dreaming, sufficiently open, free and attuned in order to allow them entry to that worldly realm constituted of his extended receptivity for and responsiveness to the meaningful address of what is encountered?

(2) In what way is he perceptively, responsively, emotionally related to what he is able to encounter?

If all dream phenomena are approached with these two appropriate questions, then the coercion to mental acrobatics, imposed by the unverifiable suppositions and abstract conceptual models of the depth psychology theories of "dream interpretation," disappear.

However, this sameness of the basic constitution of human existing, whether it be waking or dreaming, does not exempt us from the difficult task of considering the momentous differences between these two modes of existing. Indeed, their distinction is a prerequisite for the best possible therapeutic application of an understanding of dreaming. Both the questions of the fundamental existential constitution of waking and dreaming existence, and the search for the characteristic differences that distinguish dreaming and waking, are directed toward discovering the basic character or essence of a thing. They are then both philosophical, ontological questions, for which the philosophers are properly responsible. We all know that dreaming and waking are somehow different, or better, we know it until we have to thinkingly define this difference. As soon as the specific question is thematically and explicitly posed, even the philosophers are at a loss.

Almost two and a half thousand years ago, Tschung-tse wrote poetically of an experience of his own that illustrates the difficulty of the distinction: "I, Tschung-tse, once dreamt I was a butterfly, a butterfly fluttering hither and thither. I knew only I was a butterfly, following my butterfly whims. I knew not that I was human. Suddenly, I awoke. I lay there. I—once more 'myself.' Now I do not know: was I then a man who dreamt he was a butterfly, or am I now a butterfly dreaming I am a man?"

Little has changed since then. The words of the modern thinker Pascal ring similar. He felt compelled to admit that we would be unable to distinguish waking from dreaming if the events of the latter observed the strict regular sequences of happenings. With similar resignation, Schopenhauer had to confess that the sole distinction he could discover was the empirical experience of awaking. Awaking, however, is not a characteristic of dreaming as such. He could only conclude: "If both waking and dreaming are judged from an objective viewpoint, then there is no definite difference to be found. We have no choice but to admit the poets are right when they say that life is but a long dream."

If we attempt to examine phenomenologically the basic character of the human dreaming state, it would first seem that when we dream, we dwell in a more open, broader, more free, less constricted world than when we are awake. Compared with the beings of our dream world, are not those beings by which we dwell in our waking state mostly rigidly fixed objects made up of ponderous inert masses that can only be changed or mutated with the greatest difficulty? By contrast, the beings we encounter while dreaming are often of a fleeting and mutable character, like mere cloud masses blown in the wind. Cannot a dream mouse suddenly become a lion, a bare railway waiting room an imperial palace, the black-and-white projection of a battle on a screen a colorful battle between men of flesh and blood?

In fact, the reverse is true when we direct our attention to the breadth, the freedom and the openness of our being-in-the-world. Provided we do not suffer from a neurotic or psychotic disorder, we are able, waking, to choose the existential relationships in which we dwell, exist. We may dwell in far or close relation to sensually perceptible presences of the present, to things of the present or past that we are merely visualizing "in our thoughts," and to that which still has to come to be present from the future. Waking, we are able to dwell from moment to moment, relatively free in the totality of the time-space field of the understanding openness of that worldly realm that we ek-sist, that we hold or bear open and free. On the other hand, what appears to us out of the openness of our dream world appears predominantly—not exclusively, but to an incomparably greater degree than in waking—in that mode of being present of an immediately sensually optically, auditively perceptible, temporally present presence, as distinct from visualized presences, remembered presences or expected presences. This is so even when those presences of our dream world are of a more mutable character than are those of our waking world.

The much extolled occasional hypermnesia of the dream state does not negate but rather confirms that the openness of the dreaming existence is largely limited to admitting only the sensually perceptible presence of what is encountered as being temporally present. Freud saw correctly in this hypermnesia a further argument against the degradation of dreaming to a disturbed state of mental existence. It actually happens that we repeatedly dream of people and things of whom we no longer know anything when we are awake. But do we really remember them? This would be the case when what we dreamed of was present as something that once, at some given time, had been. In truth, however, that which has long disappeared from our waking world confronts us in our dreaming world as an immediately sensually perceptible, temporally present presence.

There is a second and equally fundamental distinction between the worldly realm open to understand the significations of the encountered as existed by the waking human being and that by the dreaming one. What appears to us in dreaming is not exclusively but incomparably more frequent than in waking, revealed in the mode of sensually perceptible temporally present presence—materially visible things or the equally sensually visible bodies of human beings, animals and plants. As such, the beings of our dream world, in their immediate sensual visibility, come impressively and at times uncomfortably close to us. Waking, we are "seeing" beings also in a second sense, that of "insight." This has only peripherally to do with the "seeing" of the sensually, perceptible "external" characteristics of materially present objects. It refers rather to the thematic perception and recognition of the immaterial basic character of things, namely, their significations and referential context, and the equally immaterial inobjectifiable existential behavioral possibilities of human beings in their encounter with the world. This distinction between waking and dreaming necessarily gives rise to a third. The significations and referential context (the totality of interconnecting significations) that constitute our dream world address us predominantly from "external" beings, which we ourselves are not. Dreaming, we rarely reflect on ourselves in the attempt to gain insight into our existential state. It scarcely happens that we perceive from ourselves our own existential condition, that we perceive of what inobjectifiable, "immaterial" behavioral possibilities we are constituted.

The following short example vividly illustrates the three described distinctions between waking and dreaming:

A young woman dreamed that she was together with her best woman friend, and this friend was suffering from a serious heart disease (which is not at all the case in her waking world). The friend had an advanced stenosis of her heart valves. Waking, this young dreamer was already—though as yet to a very limited degree—aware of "heart trouble" in a metaphorical sense. In her waking state she had fallen in love with her analyst. She herself suffered in waking some emotional pain as a result of the inevitable frustration of this love but did not want to admit it. Dreaming, her existence was still much less perceptive than in her preceding waking. Dreaming, she perceived not the least of her own suffering in her "love sickness." The meaningfulness of ailment and pain addressed her, in her dreaming state, solely from a disturbance of the material, bodily heart of another woman.

At this point the dreamer gradually woke up. In the course of the unusually slow process of her awakening, the dreamer herself became aware of an amazing kind of opening up of her existence. She noticed a sharpening and farther reaching out of the perceptiveness and responsiveness of which she consists. Within the more clear-sighted and farther reaching realm of her awakening existence she came to realize ever more succinctly that she herself and not her friend was suffering terribly from a "heart-sickness." But as her friend's bodily heart disease, which had disclosed itself to her so distinctly within her dream world, transformed itself by and by into an ailment of herself, it also changed its form completely. The basic meaningfulness of trouble, the meaningfulness of ailment, remained nevertheless the same. The more she awoke, however, the more completely this meaningfulness of pain addressed her in the form of an emotionally painful affection, arising out of her frustrated love for her analyst and no longer from a material bodily organ.

This self-observation of a slowly awakening dreamer gives particularly convincing evidence of the way in which a dreamer's existence, as perceiving and responsive world openness, had been dimmed and restricted in comparison with the realm of understanding which then constituted her following waking state. In her dreaming state "heart trouble" had disclosed itself to her existence's understanding only from a bodily sphere, from a diseased heart organ. This certainly is a more peripheral and distant region than is the "heart," in the sense of the core and center of one's feelings. In addition, it had not even been her own heart which had been sick while she was dreaming, but the much more remote organ of another woman, although this woman was her closest friend. Her dreaming existence had become completely blinded to her emotional suffering from her frustrated love, although it had already been present to a certain degree in her previous waking state. And more than only this: her hurt feelings did not exist at all within her dream world; they had totally fallen out of it. Nothing whatsoever justifies the assumption that her emotional "heart-sickness" nevertheless continued to be present in her dreaming state as a "psychic being" but was only temporarily "symbolically" hidden behind the "dream image" of a diseased bodily organ. Any dream theory which pretends to know of those kinds of psychic mechanisms is committing the inadmissible logical mistake (long since called a *petitio princiii* by the classical philosophers), i.e., putting into the presuppositions that which would have to be deduced, demonstrated and proven as a result of logical thinking.

On the other hand, the diseased bodily heart of her friend, which was sensually perceptibly present as long as this patient existed in a dreaming state, as soon as she awakened changed its mode of being present into the mode of being of a "having been dreamed presence or phenomenon." This is, by the way, one more example of the manifold modes of being present.

By far more important practically, however, is the above-mentioned statement that the daseinsanalytic understanding of the dreaming state clearly no longer has anything to do with the hitherto commonly assumed "symbolism" of the different dream theories of the so-called depth psychologies. To the contrary, it discloses the fact that all those who pretend to know of any "symbolically" deceiving and veiling, perpetrated by "the dream," have first to believe in the existence of a most fantastic superdemon within a dreamer's personality. This allegedly ever-present superdemon within a dreamer's mind would have to be able to perform a threefold miracle. First, he would have to know much more than the dreamer himself does. Second, he would have to be capable of deciding what of his additional knowledge he wants to let appear before the dreamer's eyes. Third, he would have to dispose over veiling mechanisms which could transform the things to be hidden into completely different objects and then to project them outside into the dreamer's world.

Actually there is no need at all for such a hypothetical superdemon, if the phenomena of the dream world are not arbitrarily qualified beforehand as being deceptive and as not being "actually" that as which they show themselves to the dreamer. No factual dream phenomenon itself, however, lends any justification for assuming a separate symbolizing veiling agent within a dreamer.

All that can actually and scientifically be observed is that our existence is predominantly open to the perception of one kind of phenomena in its waking state, whereas the realm of openness—called "world"—that is breached and inhabited by the meaning-understanding human existence in its dreaming state allows mainly different entities to enter its clearance, to shine forth there and thus to be. But all those beings shining forth into the world-wide expanded openness or clearance of understanding as which man exists neither "mean" nor are they "in reality" anything other than what they reveal themselves directly to be. There is no reason to be found why this statement should not hold equally true for the waking as well as for the dreaming states of human existence.

Denying the actual existence of a hiding, deceivingly "symbolizing" agent within the dreamer, the daseinsanalytic dream interpretation need not be concerned at all with "undoing" the hypothetical work of a "dream censor" as assumed by the modern dream theories. To the contrary, daseinsanalytic or phenomenological dream "interpretation" accepts all phenomena showing themselves in a dreaming state as being nothing but what they reveal themselves immediately to be. It leaves them all to stand in their own right. The daseinsanalytic dream interpretation, therefore, "simply" consists in unfolding and in differentiating ever more clearly and succinctly all the significances and references of meaningfulness which make up the essence of a given dream thing or person, and of which a patient may not have become thematically aware at first sight. A wooden table, for example, within a dream world is *not* simply a heap of isolated, chemically defined molecules with measurable spatial extensions and weight as little as a table perceived in a waking state. A table as such and in itself is above all something to be used as a thing on which other things can be put. Furthermore, in itself a dream table refers to the earth on which it is standing, as well as to the tree out of which it was made and to the carpenter who made it and so on. Finally, a dream table may even address a dreamer as being that particular table at which he sat with his father ten years ago when he was severely rebuked by the latter for being too lazy in his studies. This reference of meaningfulness also belongs to the table's own properties and is far from being a merely subjective "symbolic content originating out of the dreamer's mind and then secondarily projected by the latter onto the table."

Our waking world is made up of a richer more manifold totality of beings, present in the most diverse modes. This world appears day for day after each new awaking as the same and familiar, endures through the whole waking state and guarantees the much more comprehensive historical continuity of our waking constitution. At one with this, it guarantees a greater world openness. As a result, in each more waking state, we discover one realm of meaningfulness more than we knew in that state, which from the vantage point of a more waking state we recognize as dreaming. Moreover, when the many possibilities of awaking, going to sleep and dreaming during dreaming are considered, it is to be seen that the basic distinctions discriminating dreaming from waking become more marked in each state that is "more" waking than the preceding dreaming one. It follows necessarily that the greatest possible unfolding, maturing and freedom of our Da-sein can be actualized in the "most" waking state. So it is that the waking mode of existence assumes the highest rank.

In the final analysis, the startling fact that we can *a*wake (*er*wachen) from a dream state into waking existence but can never say, in an analogous way, that we *er*träumen—that we "*a*dream," "awake into dreaming"—is grounded in this hierarchical relation between dreaming and waking. The German language as such allows this point to be vividly illustrated. The prefix "er-" in unaccentuated combination with a verb is the weakend form of the prefix "ur-." This "ur-" belongs in turn to the Indo-German adverb "aus," and "aus" means "auf etwas hinauf" ("upward toward something"), "aus etwas heraus" ("coming out of something"), "hinauf zu" ("upward to"), "empor zu" ("high up to"). This basic meaning of "aus," from which "ur-" and then "er-" are derived, is present in such words as "Ursprung" ("origin, original source"), "Ursache" (commonly used as "cause" but originally meaning the "basic ground of a thing"). Primarily, though, the prefixes "ur-" and "er-" designate the primordial or original state, the basic constitution of a matter, or the setting-in of a happening, the attaining of something. The "a" in awake (as distinct from the "a" in many other words of the English language) is related to the German prefix "er-" (*Oxford Dictionary of English Etymology*, p. 1).

Accordingly, it is our awaking (*Er*wachen) and only this awaking which leads out into the full unfolding of being, out of the unfree dimensions of a dreaming being-in-the-world, up to the greatest possible freedom of our most waking mode of existing, and so to the attainment of the proper meaning and purpose of our "Da-sein."

PRINCIPLES CONCERNING THE USE OF DREAMS IN TREATMENT

At first sight, any attempt within the daseinsanalytic or phenomenological perspective to use dreaming in the treatment of a waking person appears hopeless. As was shown previously, the phenomenological research method reveals the fact that every phenomenon, whether perceived in the waking state or in the dreaming state, stands for itself in its own right and for nothing else. No justification whatsoever can actually be brought to light for the assumption that most dream phenomena do not mean what they seem to be, but are "in reality" deceptively and symbolically veiled completely different things and therefore have to be "interpreted" in the sense of replacing them by the allegedly corresponding "really meant" ones.

If there is no such "hide-and-seek" connection to be found between the worlds of dreaming and of waking, is there any other relation existing between the two states as the necessary prerequisite for a therapeutic application of the daseinsanalytic understanding of dreaming? There is nothing less than the decisive and undeniable fact that it is always one and the same human existence that is at one moment in its dreaming state and shortly afterwards again in its waking state. Both are ways of being, belonging together in one existence and in which this one human existence is carried out at different times. This being so, it is more than likely that at a given time the basically same fundamental existential structure shines forth in waking and dreaming, though—as was extensively pointed out—through different kinds of phenomena. More than this: exactly that peculiarity of dreaming which we have shown to be privative, deficient and constricted in comparison with waking allows a skilled therapist to utilize dream happenings as a highly effective means of healing. Certainly, the existence modus of the dreamer is in general more constricted than that of the waking person. Notwithstanding, it often happens that previously unknown significations and referential contexts address the human being and become existent for the first time during dreaming. To be sure, these appearing significations are revealed during dreaming mostly from sensually perceptible present beings and events outside in the dreamer's world. Not only do these significations often address the dreamer for the first time in his life from the dream beings and events, but they do so in a massive and ineluctable way exactly as sensually perceptible, material presences. Due to this specific character of dreaming, the dreaming existence is of decisive therapeutic importance, even though it is less open and free. The practiced therapist, in appealing to the clearer sightedness of the waking existence of the former dreamer, can often utilize what has been dreamed to lead the dreamer toward a clarification of his own waking existential state.

Practically, the daseinsanalyst has first "only" to ask his patient over and over again to describe the phenomena which had addressed him during his dreaming state, ever more succinctly, as to all the particular features and meaningful references which immediately belong to what was perceived by the dreamer during his dreaming state. The dreamer must continue this phenomenological endeavor until he and the analysand have become fully aware of all the whereabouts making up the dreamer's worldly dwelling place. For example, when one dreamer has to stay in a locked cell of a prison or a lunatic asylum, and another is a king in a huge palace, who feels free to do whatever he, himself, chooses to do, this suggests a very great difference in the world openness also of the waking existences of the two dreamers. The patient must also describe the general mood he found himself in when perceiving all these dream "givens," as well as all the particular kinds of emotional relationships to them in which his existence was engaged while he was dreaming for the attunement of an existence is a sure indicator of the existential freedom a human being has already gained. Any existence whose important possibilities of relationships are still covered up is essentially, and therefore always attuned, in itself, to a depressive mood, whereas an existence which is free enough to dispose overall its possible relationships is, in itself, attuned to happiness. For this reason a patient has to state whether he was afraid of what he was encountering as a dreamer or felt very much at ease with it, whether he fled from it or embraced it, or whether he was disgusted by it. Once he has become fully aware of the structure of his dreaming state of existence, he may then justifiably be asked, on the basis of the above-mentioned daseinsanalytic understanding of the two modes of human existence, "Do you now, in the more clear-sighted waking state, become aware of one or another as yet not fully realized unobjectifiable, immaterial, "mental" possibilities of relating to something—a possibility which shows in its basic features an analogy, even a sameness with the essential meaningfulness and signification of one of the sensually perceptible, material objects which addressed you during the dreaming state of the past night?"

If the patient still remains blind, the therapist may be more waking and see more than the patient. He may then dare to make some suggestions in the form of questions such as: "Does not that big old chest of your dreaming, with its heavy iron edges and its huge lock, speak to you, whenever you let it address itself to you in its full character, about the meaningfulness of being closed and walled in? Could it be that now, in your waking state, you become more aware than you were while dreaming of a corresponding being-walled-in of your own existence, and not merely of being-walled-in by a chest and iron material locks outside yourself but by your own neurotic immaterial existential attitudes?" Or, "Is it not remarkable that of all possible things of this world it was just and exclusively an old chest with extremely thick wooden walls and heavy locks which stared at you during your dream state?"

Another dreamer may be asked: "Does it not strike you that you found yourself, in your dreaming state, standing high up on a shaky iron scaffolding, clinging in terror to its iron shafts lest you fall down to your death? Do you perhaps have an inkling now, in your waking state, of an analogous position? Do you feel any similarity between your bodily position high up on the scaffolding in your dreaming and your neurotically precarious existential condition in which you are constantly shaken by anxiety?"

These examples show what kinds of dream elements the therapist has to pick up first of all and to what kinds of questions they may motivate him. To the dream elements with which the therapist has to deal first belong those ways of a dreamer's behavior which, on the one hand, consist of being afraid of something or someone, of flight from something or someone, of being disgusted by something, of meeting barricades of some kind or other. The common denominator in all of these modes of behavior is a warding off or a resisting against closeness with something or someone, a definite lack of courage and of freedom against being claimed by what approaches the dreamer. On the other hand, the patient's attention has also to be drawn to those dream elements of his which are characterized in themselves, and as themselves, by a feature of coercion, of walling in, of hiding, protecting or destructiveness, of animal life in its aggressive form such as wild lions, of curtains or heavy castles of the Middle Ages.

With patients who suffer from marked inferiority feelings, however, the therapist is well advised never to fail to point out to such analysands first of all any if ever so small signs of some courage and freedom which have shown up in his dreaming. For example, he may comment on them by telling his patient: "At least in your dreaming state you already have had the courage to hit back at your enemy." Or, "You had the freedom to sail out into the open ocean." He may then continue: "To be sure, you still had to be very much afraid of the dog"—and so on. If the therapist fails to proceed in this way with these patients, he will simply lead them into a depression in which any analytical work will stop for at least a long time, if not permanently.

When asking a patient in this manner, the therapist also must take care that he choose only those questions among all the possible ones which he is sure that the present mental condition of his patient and the actual quality of his patient's emotional relationship with him can well bear.

In the further process of making a patient understand his dreaming phenomenologically and of using this understanding in treatment, the therapist li?ccloseness in which they have shown themselves to the dreamer.

INTERPRETATION OF MARTHA'S DREAMS

How They Can Be Understood Daseinsanalytically or Phenomenologically and How This Understanding Could Have Been Used in This Particular Treatment

Dream No. 1

First, a simple description of the dream events, highlighting the meaning they possess and the context of references in which they belong. In her first reported dreaming during therapy, Martha's worldly dwelling place is a chair on a rickety balcony above the face of the earth. It is outside any solid house, without a secure foundation of its own. Martha is raised above the happenings on the earth below her, and yet her isolation from them is precarious—the balcony is unsafe and does not guarantee a secure abode in a familiar world. Should this abode collapse, then her existence, as she knows it, could plunge, perhaps to its destruction. She is not alone. There are people dressed in period costumes with pantaloons and long dresses. Their clothing, that which first strikes attention, takes its determination from a past age. The past speaks clearly in the way Martha is open to perceiving her fellow human beings. She is then not existing as a human being actively engaged in the events occurring on the earth, committed in her relationships to her contemporaries. Spatially, she is situated insecurely isolated above the world, passively viewing it as a spectator. Temporally, her world is incongruous. It is so much influenced by the past that this past is able to dress her fellow human beings in period costumes.

She herself appears bodily as the opposite of what she looks like in her waking state. She is tall and lanky like Katharine Hepburn, but not particularly attractive. Dreaming, she experiences the bodily possibility of existing differently. Bodiliness is nothing but that particular sphere of a person's existential relationship to whatever he encounters, perceptively and responsively, at any given moment, which lends itself to measuring, weighing and computing, like any nonliving, nonhuman material thing. These natural science procedures can never comprehend it in its essence. To judge by her films, Katharine Hepburn is a highly temperamental, active, energetic, courageous woman capable of committing herself fully in her relationships. Martha's similarity to her is exhausted, though, in the realm of bodiliness. She does not live out the nonreifiable existential possibilities of her own, which resemble those of Katharine Hepburn, even though these possibilities appear in her world as potentially her own in her bodily resemblance to this other woman.

Ensconced in her chair, Martha exists as a distant spectator of what goes on below her. Even her view is obscured by black clouds of smoke. Ongoing worldly events can be experienced by her only as dangerous explosions, whose nature and significance she does not know. Instead of plunging into these obscured and veiled events, she remains sitting in her chair for twenty years, aloof from active life, indifferent to the call of world. Nevertheless, she is open to another way of behaving, but only in the way of seeing it from others. People jump off the balcony and run toward the explosions. Except for her watching other people's activities, Martha remains passive. Not only does she not make these active relational modes of others her own, she even tries to warn others against engaging in them.

Martha does not dare leave her elevated refuge from worldly affairs and relinquish her distant spectator mode of existing until all *that* activity is over and she herself is at the age of fifty, empty of all emotions. All "danger" of close responsible engagement in her relationships has already disappeared. It matters little to her that, in refusing to carry out most of her possibilities of relating to other fellow human beings, she loses twenty years of her life in a monotonous never-changing present.

"I had no emotions." She speaks as if she possesses inside herself feelings or affects which are then attached to the "intrapsychic" representations of the objects in the "external or extrapsychic" world. She understands herself in terms of the current psychological conceptual model of the human being, a model based on unfounded artificial constructs. What she is describing though, is the particular way in which her whole existence is attuned to, and so correspondingly open for, the perception of her world. The state of her perceptive, responsive openness to the things and fellow human beings of her world is such that she at her dream age of fifty encounters them with an existential attunement of indifference and lethargy. She is touched neither by them nor by the horrendous fact that she herself has spent the twenty potentially most fruitful and productive years of her life in a state of stagnation, lethargy, indifference and unfeeling passivity, aloof from others. It does not pain her that everybody seems young and that she is regarded as old, without her having lived out her years. She even comments, "Fifty isn't really that old." It fails to dawn on her that the significance of a woman's being fifty does not consist primarily in her having lived a certain number of years or whether she can still jump. It is rather that at fifty one's reproductive capacities are usually over. The time for her to have a sexually active husband, children and establish a family is past. She has not used the time span allotted to her existence in actualizing herself.

Martha finally decides to go down from her balcony but is not able to put her decision into practice without help. Alone, she cannot get out of her chair. Her dependency and helplessness appear clearly. Her dream world is sufficiently open to allow the approach of a young man who is ready to help her. She is "protected" from him in that she is already fifty and regarded as old. The encounter with this manly being is exhausted in his helping her jump down. Nevertheless, this is a decisive event, in that Martha's mode of being-in-the-world as a passive, indifferent, lethargic spectator changes to that of a woman who chooses to descend to the earth and to use her own two feet to carry her among the people there.

At this point, a word about Martha's comment on the young man's jacket resembling that of the therapist. According to the traditional depth psychologies, the temptation would be great to "interpret" this "association" as indicating a "transference" phenomenon, viz., that the young man "in reality" represents the therapist. The young man and the therapist have something in common—they are both male and both are helpful. It is probable that the waking process of analysis has attuned Martha's existence to the meaningfulness of being helped by a man, and that this attunement and the perceptive responsive openness bound up with it persist into her dreaming state. It is significant, though, that this dream helper is clearly not the therapist but a previously unknown young man who offers nothing but a physical aid in getting out of a chair and jumping down from a balcony. There is no question at this point that Martha, in her dreaming state, is not perceptive of and responsive to her analyst, who is helping her, in her waking state, in other than physical ways, viz., in the existential discovery of herself, her world and her inborn possibilities of relating to it. To interpret the young man as the analyst would be to overlook the human distance which Martha still maintains from him. Only if the unknown young man is allowed to remain what he is—unknown—does it become visible how the behavioral possibilities of a young man, as being helpful and gracious to a woman, have hitherto been unknown to her, except the peripheral touch of acquaintedness in form of the recognized coat of her analyst.

In the dream Martha is wearing a wedding gown. A woman wears a wedding gown for the ceremony in which she declares her readiness and resolution to spend her life in union with a man of her choice. Human society ratifies this union and gives it its blessing. The wedding gown is laid aside, and the couple comes together in consummation of the most intimate, sensuous and bodily, loving closeness, which marks the beginning of their union and the formation of a new human family. Martha spends twenty years in a wedding gown which remains in her case a mere superficial adornment. There is no question that she opens herself in existentially loving, sensuous intimacy to her husband and grows, together with him, to the full maturity of a woman. He goes off, while she sits in a chair on a balcony and loses sight of him. Even dreaming, she is not able to maintain even a most peripheral relationship with a husband.

"The Prime Minister climbed up and asked me to marry him, but I refused." The Prime Minister is the first among the men of his land, a man of the highest authority. He holds the powers of government in his hands and is, moreover, socially the first. The man who seeks Martha's hand is characterized not by a deep personal familiarity with her but by investment with high political office, which does not require any particular human characteristics other than an excellent political sense. Tender, loving feelings or a deep, binding commitment to her play no part. Her dreaming existence is attuned not to love but rather to matters of status in society, to externals that determine the hierarchical position in public life. Not only this: Martha experiences herself as being above such a man—he has to climb *up* to her. Her narcissistic self-love and estimation appear also in her refusing him.

Toward the end of her dreaming, Martha, still wearing her wedding dress, is walking on the street among the people. She realizes that this gown belongs to an earlier phase of her life, is out-of-date and belongs to the past. She attempts to remedy this by cutting off a little. Here is an active attempt to make good one result of her twenty-year stagnation. Her realization of the terrible significance of her stay in the chair touches only the periphery. In comparison with the loss of her twenty most fruitful years, what is made good is trivial. Certainly, Martha's relationship to her world and the people in it has changed. She is walking on a street, a public place and not an intimate dwelling place for human beings, among people who are nice and friendly. She even speaks to them. Nevertheless, her relationship to these hitherto unknown people is casual and noncommittal. She is not dwelling in deep, enriching, intimate human relationships, rooted in a common past and expectant of a common enriching future. Her concern consists of asking whether they have children and husbands. She learns that they are all dead. Everything that would have had to do with the twenty years between thirty and fifty in the life of a woman—having a husband and children—has withered away from Martha's world. She is pleased, though, that the *other* women of her dream world have grandchildren and nieces.

The "associations" that Martha offers are of two kinds: those clarifying the dream events and those that give information about her waking existence. The first association is descriptive of dream events. The descent was dangerous. In that Martha knew herself in this dreaming as a passive lethargic spectator and as nothing else, to give up this mode of existing seemed like giving up existence itself and hence was dangerous. This indicates what little inkling Martha has of her own existential potential, not to speak of her having made other modes of behavior her own.

The second "association" elaborates what it meant for Martha to be fifty years old—privileged and not responsible. From a waking point of view she adds how she is tempted by such an indifferent, irresponsible mode of existence. This comment does not reveal anything of how the dream events are to be understood. However, it does draw attention to something that will in all likelihood be a recurring theme in the course of her therapy—the questions of engagement, commitment and responsibility.

The third "association" likewise contributes nothing to our understanding of the dream events. It is, though, important in that Martha waking is aware of difficulties in the realm of marriage and her relationship to men.

The fourth "association" suggests that Martha realizes something of what these dream events reveal about the sorry state of her present human condition and the necessity for change.

Therapeutic application of the existential understanding of the dream events. In the course of an analysis, it is usually necessary that the analysand be "shaken to his roots," that his predominant, rigid, stagnant and, for him, matter-of-course, current ways of seeing, thinking, feeling and behaving be shattered, that his resistance and defensive attitudes be dissolved. If Martha could grasp the full significance of these dream events and their context of references, such a convulsive reorienting of her existence could be initiated. In the dream events themselves, though, the indications show that it will not be easy to reach and touch her. She exists as a distant spectator who "has no emotions," who lets nothing touch her. The therapist has to be prepared for a long and tedious analysis.

Almost every dream event could be usefully explored and applied therapeutically, and yet to deal with each event as if all were of equa! import would be to reduce the impact of the most significant ones. The first step would be to have Martha describe her dreaming once more, to encourage her to clarify and elaborate each detail with particular emphasis on her feeling and her motivation for her various modes of behavior. Only when she has re-visualized these events and described them as precisely, differentiatedly and vividly as possible, should the therapist proceed to draw Martha's attention to the intense pathological restrictions in her dreaming existence. The therapist could reflect to his patient her spectator role, her passivity and lethargy, at the same time making her aware of the reverse modes of behaving, emphasizing that she herself sees such modes in others, which is in itself very positive, but does not make them her own. She perceives in her dreaming that it is possible for the human being to leap courageously into an engagement and commitment with the world, even when it seems explosively dangerous. The further questions would be appropriate: "Is it not striking that all possible activity on the face of the earth discloses itself to you only as being dangerously explosive? Waking, could it be that you live in the expectation that danger lurks around each corner, especially in a metaphorical sense, for example that every human encounter is threatening?" "Do you really think it has to be so?"

Most important, these dreaming events reveal to her the urgent necessity for deep change. "In your dreaming state, you exist in a continuous present of monotonous, barren stagnation. During your twenty years between thirty and fifty, your fellow human beings appear in the garb of a past age, their appearance taking its determination from the past. During this time there is no glimpse of a future, only a monotonous, never-changing present. Your persistence in this state bears the consequence that you remain dormant during those years in which you could fulfill your destiny as a woman in having family and children, in loving union with a man. It is no less than horrifying that you have no emotions at a moment when the deepest sadness and despair would be appropriate, as you realize that you have lost the twenty most productive years of your life and, with them, the most important part of your life." The therapist could proceed with the question, "Are you waking more clear-sighted than you are dreaming? Are you able to see any analogy between your dreaming and your waking state, behavior and immediately realizable, accessible possibilities of existing? Could it not be that you are also, waking, a mere spectator of life? Could it not be that in your present state you can only expect a future of barren stagnation?"

Of course, such a massive confrontation presupposes that a therapeutic relationship to the therapist has already developed. Martha's readiness to accept help from the young man in her dreaming is one hint that she is also, waking, able to accept help and support in her attempt to live more fully. It would also be appropriate to emphasize the positive elements in this dream. First, she is becoming ever more deeply aware of her present miserable state, and this is a first step toward changing it. In her bodily otherness, the possibility of a totally different way of existing is indicated as being potentially her own. Her dream world is open for the actualization of other more fruitful modes of behavior—to be sure, *at the moment*, only by others. She herself does come down to the earth and walk on her own two feet. Not only that, she is open to the address of three men: one, a young helper; the second, a disappearing husband; the third, the Prime Minister himself, who sues for her hand. She is still, though, very distant in her relationship to them. At this point, it would be too early to place in question the pathological limitations in the address of the Prime Minister. Such a comment could easily discourage her in further encounters with men. On the other hand, it could be helpful to point out the hitherto unknown character of the helpful address of a young man.

Dream No. 2

Martha is in more familiar surroundings. She comes home and goes to her room, where she finds her mother going through her purse. To understand the full significance of this, it would be necessary to know whether Martha's room was in the home of her parents or whether she had tried to leave her parents and establish an independent dwelling of her own. In any event, her mother is present in her room and has access to her purse. For a woman, her purse has a special significance. She keeps her most intimate and personal possessions here—money, bank card, identity card, passport, keys, cosmetics, picture of a loved one, "the pill." Traditionally, the purse is regarded as a symbol of the female genitals. However, if we leave the purse as a purse, we see that it refers, of itself, to the most diverse spheres of the intimacy of a woman and not merely to her physical genitals. This intimacy is raped by Martha's mother, and Martha is helpless. She can attempt to defend this intimacy with violence, to establish barriers of walls and locked doors between herself and her mother, but all to no avail. She succeeds only in throwing her mother to the bathroom door, where her mother then lies between her and that room of a house where a human being is most intimately concerned with bodily self. Her mother does not remain lying but passes unscathed through all barriers and is once more present in Martha's intimate realm. Martha's dreaming state is then that of a little child in the presence of an overwhelmingly powerful mother. She exists in the relationship of daughter-mother—and indeed a daughter-mother relation not characterized by loving concern and respect of the mother for the integrity of her daughter's person and intimacy. Martha's existence is rather at the mercy of her mother. She exists as a dependent, helpless person, subjugated and imprisoned in a daughter-mother world relation from which adult free behavioral modes are excluded.

The dream events reveal many subtleties in the form of this daughter-like, childlike way of existing. In the first instance, Martha's mother does not look like her mother. When her mother behaves in the way of raping Martha's intimate sphere, she appears bodily different. The phenomenon of bodihood is but the carrying out of human existence in the sphere of body. As such, it refers immediately and directly to the totality of the existential relationship. That the bodily appearance of the mother is strange and unfamiliar indicates that Martha does not recognize this behavioral modus as belonging immediately to her existential relation to her mother, in which she herself exists as a helpless, defenseless daughter. This is surprising when we think of Martha's first "association" in which she reports exactly analogous behavior of herself and her mother. It would seem that Martha has not wakingly recognized what her tolerance of this behavior of her mother means for her, nor how much of her independence and personal integrity she looses by her submission and helplessness to this relational mode.

The concerned, solicitous behavior of the mother is nevertheless familiar, and, in harmony with this, the mother appears bodily like her mother. Missing are the signs of her having been wounded by Martha, those signs provocative of guilt feeling. There is an incongruity in this behavior. Martha takes her by the hair and throws her out. She is humiliated and treated violently. Instead of responding openly and directly, she returns seductively, concerned and solicitous. Martha experiences her impotence in her struggle to free herself from a mother relating in these ways.

In these dream events, Martha's angrily and violently defensive behavior is also provoked by the mother's penetration of her relationship to her therapist. Indeed, this penetration touches something only peripheral to the relationship, namely, the therapist's bill, which refers to her having to pay in order to be able to see him. Whether this is also peripheral for Martha is not described. We do not know if she understands this deepest and most intimate relationship of analysand-analyst as some material thing that can be bought and sold. At any rate, it appears so in the framework of Martha's daughter-mother relation. Nevertheless, Martha wants to keep this relationship for herself and not betray it to her mother. In her dreaming state, she dares for once to defend a more grown-up, independent selfhood.

Here, Martha is concerned solely with her relationship to her therapist, and to no one else. This specific relationship is penetrated by her mother. There is no justification for designating Martha's dreaming of her analyst's bill and her mother's discovery of this bill as a "transference dream" in which the analyst "in reality" means her father and the dream events represent the "oedipal constellation." Such an "interpretation" would not be an interpretation of the dreaming, but rather the arbitrary substitution of one thing for another. In the dream events, there may indeed be parallels to the kind of relationship that Martha had to her mother and father when she was small—perhaps five or six years old. Nevertheless, in her present dreaming, it is the relationship to the analyst that is penetrated by her mother. It is not that the analyst represents her father, but rather that Martha has stagnated so that she still exists as the childlike "field of seeing" as which she has already existed as a child. Consequently, she is able to perceive only the paternal and maternal traits of grown-up human beings and possibilities of relating to these grown-ups only as a child even in her present dreaming. If these dream events were simply "interpreted" as a replay of past events in masquerade form, their impact for the presently living Martha would be greatly weakned. She would be distracted from experiencing fully her actual and concrete emotional attachment to her therapist. On the other hand, when she becomes aware of the childlike character of her present existing, those events of the past speaking in her present relational modes will begin recurring to her with full relevance.

But to return to Martha's responsive behavior to the mother. She is angry and wants to express more anger than she feels. She screams, but it never sounds loud enough. Here is a strange discrepancy. It is not that she wants to show fully the anger she feels, but that she wants to pretend more anger than she feels. Does Martha somehow recognize that she has reason to be more angry than she feels, or does this wish reveal something not genuine and false in her, that she wishes to appear other than she is, angrier than she is? We would have to ask her. Her second "association" deals with another example of a discrepancy between her feelings and what she reveals of her feelings. Does she attempt to manipulate others with a show of feeling that she does not feel?

Martha is afraid her mother has hurt herself. What is she afraid of? Is she afraid of guilt feeling, of having transgressed that "commandment" whereby children owe absolute respect and deference to their parents? Is she afraid of losing her mother's solicitude and concern? Is she afraid of retaliation? We do not know, but we do know that Martha had every right to defend herself from this rape of her intimacy. What did she do? She sat on her bed and waited—she was passive. We are reminded of her long, passive stay in a chair on a shaky balcony.

Therapeutic application of the existential understanding of the dream events. As with the first reported dreaming, a full recognition of the content of meaningfulness could further a shaking up of Martha's present state. Once more, it would be advisable to encourage Martha to describe the dream events in the greatest detail, to visualize them again, to allow her feelings to appear—her anger, fear, resignation, impotence and despair. Through exploration, the therapist could illuminate the character of her anger and fear, and make her aware of the discrepancy between her feeling and what she shows of her feeling, dreaming and waking. He could then call her attention to how she exists as a dependent, helpless little child knowing nothing about defending her realm of intimacy, how her dream world—and with it her own dreaming existence—stands under the domination of her mother. "Can you recognize, waking, that you exist in an unfree, dependent, childlike state, dominated by fear and guilt, unable to have an intimate realm of your own—that even your relationship to me can be penetrated by outside influences? Is it not strange that you still allow your mother to have such overwhelming power over you?" These questions would not only refer Martha to the pathological restrictions in her existing, but would at the same time hint to her that contrasting ways of existing are also possible. It is then also an encouragement for her to discover these free ways of existing and to make them her own. It may be necessary to state this expressly. The questions—as questions rather than statements—allow Martha more freedom in the exploration and discovery of herself and her innate potentialities. The authoritative and suggestive power of the analyst's words is lessened, and exactly this power could easily be irresistible for such a childlike, easily dominated person as Martha appears in her dreaming—as irresistible as her mother's.

Dream No. 3

"I walked into a room and my mother was standing there naked." What sort of a room was it? Where was it? How did Martha come to be there? What did she want there? Was she simply there without knowing where she was, how she came there, why she was there? We do not know. It would have been necessary to ask her these questions. We know only that her dream world was restricted to the four walls of this room, and in it stood her mother naked. Once more, we see vividly how Martha is oriented toward her mother, how she exists as a daughter, i.e., as a dependent being who takes her cue from a parental authority. In this instance, Martha perceives the possibility for a woman to stand naked, revealing her physical bodily womanliness, which is an immediate indication of the possibility of living out fully the existential potentiality of a grown mature woman. To this potentiality belongs the possibility of union with a man, becoming pregnant and harboring within her own body, in maximum safety, another human being, of bearing a child, of nourishing this child from her own body. Martha looks only toward her mother and does not see that she herself possesses all these possibilities, even if they are not realizable at the moment.

Martha experiences her mother as having practiced a deception in that she had withheld a truth from her. Out of her captivity in a daughter-like mode of existing, Martha is denied access to truth. Another decides what she shall see and what not. The reason for this denial is the mother's intention to spare Martha having to accept anxiety and fear about this truth. Martha's response to this dream event is directed solely toward her mother's motivation for it. There is no trace of bitter indignation and resentment that she was cheated of access to a truth and that it was thereby made impossible for her to orient herself to this truth, become familiar with it and decide how she will behave toward it. She accepts being under tutelage, having nothing to decide for herself. Not only that: in her eyes, her mother's behavior was "right."

Martha does not concern herself further with "the truth" that is at last revealed to her—all the more reason that we ask what it means when a cockroach walks through the pubic hair of a woman. The pubic hair belongs to bodily sexual maturity. It grows in the immediate vicinity of the genitals. What appears here and makes its way through the pubic hair? It is not a loved and loving man, but a cockroach. Now, a cockroach is a very specific kind of beetle. As a beetle, it is far removed from a human mode of existence. It is cold-blooded. It is bound to limited instinctive, unfree modes of behavior in relation to what it encounters. It is a beetle that has preserved its bodily form unchanged since the earliest phases of evolutionary development, successfully resisting all pressures to change. It has a hard, resistent shell around it, protecting it from its environment. It lives hidden from sight in dark cracks, corners and cupboards. Since time immemorial, it has plagued human beings, bringing disease and spoiling stores. In every age and on every continent, it has been hated and held in contempt and disgust. When the French want to insult the Russians, they call them cockroaches and vice versa. Northern Germans call cockroaches "Schwabenkäfer"—"Swabian Beetles."

Of all the possible forms of life that could appear in connection with the pubic hair of her mother, it had to be a cockroach. How much Martha knows about cockroaches would have to be explored, but in any event she certainly knows them as bringers of plague and disease, as strange, distant, unfamiliar beings living in secret nooks and crannies, as things invoking panic. In her dreaming state, Martha's existence is open for the perception of mature womanly sexuality only from the bodily appearance of her mother, and then only in the closest connection with all those characteristics and significations properly belonging to a cockroach.

The one "association" to these dream events hints at a connection between Martha's relation to cockroaches and a harmless sensuous game of her childhood. It throws no further light on the dream events. The connection between the "association" and the dream events is quite obscure—many different things, past and present, unconnected with the dreaming itself could have given occasion to such reminiscences.

Therapeutic application of the existential understanding of the dream events. First, it would be advisable to emphasize the dominant role of Martha's mother in her dreaming. "In your dreaming you are oriented solely toward your mother, perceiving something of womanliness and sexuality from her, but you remain oblivious to your own possibilities. Do you see any similarities between your waking relationship to your mother and your own perception, or lack of it, of yourself as a woman? In your dreaming you are so fascinated, mesmerized by your mother that you lose sight of yourself. Are you, waking, blind to your own existential possibilities as a woman?"

Second, Martha accepts her mother's withholding a truth from her in order to spare her anxiety. This reveals something of Martha's attitude toward truth. It would be fruitful for her to hear of her therapist's astonishment that she was not wrathful about her mother's cheating her of a truth and so cheating her of the possibility of self-discovery in relation to this truth. A further pertinent question would be "Could it be that you, as a waking young woman, are practicing, out of anxiety, a self-deception about yourself, your world and your relationships to it, especially in relation to sexuality? Could it be that you 'keep your head in the sand,' ostrich-like, not wanting to see?"

Up to this point, we have applied this existential understanding of her dreaming in a way meant to highlight her resistance and her defensive, evasive attitudes, and to put them in question. This may be enough, and indeed it can be harmful to draw attention too early to what is being evaded, warded off. Simply on the basis of the dream, it is difficult to tell whether it is time to proceed to the "truth" that was withheld. Here it would be helpful to know more of the course of her therapy. Nevertheless, the question of sexuality appears "naked," and it would seem possible and fruitful to confront Martha with it directly. As a first step in this undertaking, the therapist would have to help her see the meaningfulness and referential context of her dream beings and their behavior. "Now that you understand more of the meaning of a naked woman, her pubic hair, a cockroach, are you able to see more clearly how you wakingly exist as a woman and what your attitudes to sexuality are? Is there anything stagnant in your development in this respect, something with its roots in the past and encased in a hard shell, something that appears only momentarily in the light of day before scuttling off into darkness again, something that awakes disgust, contempt and fear?" "It is characteristic of an animal—a cockroach, too—that although it is living and vital it is totally unfree in its encounter with other beings. Such modes of unfree but live and vital behavior also belong to the existence of human beings. They are frequently designated as 'drive determined,' and sexual behavior in particular is usually regarded as such. Do you recognize such modes in yourself? Think of your fear of cockroaches. Is there any such fear in your attitude toward your own animal-like ways of behaving?"

Dream No. 4

This dreaming of a cockroach is radically different from the first and shows definite progress in the therapy. Here, this living being concerns Martha directly, in the moment when she is engaged with her own bodiliness and nakedness. No longer does she have to perceive it only from a mother outside herself, while she just looks on. Her own relation to this being of her world is in the foreground, even though it is half dead. She does not panic, contrary to what would have been expected at a similar waking encounter with a cockroach. She retreats from the bathtub, from her intimate concern with her own bodiliness and nakedness, and thereupon the cockroach leaves her and goes onto the wall near her bed. Martha remains a passive spectator while a girl—that is, a young, not yet mature female—attempts to kill the cockroach, which proves to be too big and hardy for her. It will not die. Martha attempts to take things into her own hands and gives the cockroach one long spray. It is not chance that she takes a highly technical tool to her aid, one that allows her to maintain distance and not touch it.

At this point, there is a strange turn of events. During the spraying, during Martha's own attempt to rid herself of the cockroach, it grows, turns into a chicken and then into a dog that has some human characteristics. "I stopped spraying. I didn't want to kill a dog." In a few dramatic moments the openness of Martha's dream world changes. In the wake of her encounter with the cockroach, albeit a hostile encounter, her existence as world openness expands to such an extent that it allows ever more differentiated animal forms of life to shine forth into it and come to be present. A living being that is absolutely stagnant in its evolutionary development undergoes first change to a chicken and then to a mammal—to a dog, "man's best friend." Martha is prepared to let this living being go free in her dream world and even shows regret at having tried to kill it. She is, though, still far from welcoming the immediate presence of this warm-blooded animal and becoming familiar with its bodily intimate and playful but unpredictable behavior. In her encounter with the dog, she is free enough to willingly permit an animal form of life to remain in the openness of her existence. This is far different from her response to animal ways of beings when they could only disclose themselves to her from the ever-disappearing, hated and despised cockroach. Now that they can appear revealed to her from a dog with human characteristics, they come much closer to her human existence, even though a considerable aloofness still remains.

Each of the "associations" to this dream has to do with Martha's waking attitude to the dream events and beings—in itself of great importance for understanding Martha and for deciding how to utilize the dream events therapeutically. In themselves, however, they contribute nothing to an understanding of the dreaming. On the contrary, as long as Martha does not go further than the sensually perceptible beings, their observable characteristics, and her past and present waking understanding of and attitude toward these things, her understanding of her existential state remains stagnant. To expand her vision, her world openness, she has to grasp the full meaningfulness and context of references of everything given to her in her dreaming. Rather than inquire about "associations," the therapist must encourage her to examine her dreaming to the last detail, to make her descriptions as differentiated and precise as possible. He has to discover what specific and peculiar significations each dream being and event has for her and to indicate the constrictions and distortions therein, so that a freer and fuller understanding can develop. To achieve this, it may even be necessary to direct her to avoid contaminating her dreaming with extraneous associations. Alone, the insight gained through such an exploration of the dream events may be enough to explode the limits of her present existing as she becomes aware of possibilities of which she previously knew nothing. A further step is to inquire whether she is not, waking, able to recognize analogies between her existentially understood dreaming and her waking world happenings and behavior.

During this dreaming different animals appear. Most characteristic of an animal in distinction from the human being is that its modes of behaving toward the encountered beings of its world are very limited, predetermined and unfree. It has to respond in conformity to the character of the address of the encountering being. Among the many more free possibilities of relating to his world, the human being is also constituted of unfree possibilities similar to those of animals. As already mentioned, we designate these possibilities as "instinctual" or "drive" behavior. Dreaming, Martha only becomes aware of these animal-like possibilities of behaving from animals outside herself. She has no inkling that animal-like "instinctual" ways of behaving also belong to her own existence.

Therapeutic application of the existential understanding of the dream events. After allowing Martha to explore her dream events and helping her to see their meaningfulness, the therapist could ask, "Waking, are you not perhaps more clear-sighted and thus able to see in your own behavior something of an anxious flight from your own unfree, animal-like behavioral modes? Could it be that you have existed in an immature girl-like state in which you knew nothing other than to attempt to eradicate in yourself these ways of behaving? Could it be for this reason, that you encounter only a half-dead cockroach in your dreaming? Nevertheless, these modes seem to have endured and persisted despite your hostile attitude toward them. Could it be that you, as a grown woman, have tried to eliminate them through the distance of a cool, intellectual handling of them, analogous to your using a poisonous spray which incorporates principles from the natural sciences of physics and chemistry? Is it not, though, an occasion for rejoicing that, despite your dream unwillingness, your dream world allows of an evolutionary development of the rigid animal life appearing in it? After the cockroach, a chicken appears. It is warm-blooded and much more differentiated than a cockroach. At last, a dog with human characteristics appears. It has already more, richer and freer ways of behaving than a 'real' dog. It has wishes of its own and seeks a wider, more free world than the narrow confines of your bedroom. You are able to allow it to go, to roam at will, as long as it is not too close to you. You maintain distance. You do not greet it with joy and enthusiasm, savoring its playfulness and unpredictability. Waking, do you have an inkling that your own accessible animal-like possibilities have undergone an evolutionary-like development? At least dreaming, animal-like possibilities no longer have to disclose themselves to you only from a loathsome cock-roach, with its remoteness from human existence. They can already present themselves to you in ever more 'humanized' form, finally as that well-known friend of man, a dog—and indeed a dog with some human characteristics. But still, even in your dreaming, a tendency toward separation between you and such animal-like behavioral modes appears. You no longer want to kill the dog, but it wants to leave, as if the confines of your world are too narrow. You courteously allow it to go. Do you notice anything stand-offish and distant in your waking attitude toward your own such possibilities, analogous to your cool courtesy to your dream dog?"

Dream No. 5

Matha is still living with her parents. Where there are parents *as* parents, there are children. Martha remains, then, in a parent-child way of existing in relation to her world, not as a grown, mature woman with her own independent dwelling place. As such a childlike being, she again takes, in her dreaming state, her orientation from the parental authority in her world. She does not knowingly and deliberately choose her whereabouts and her acquaintances. Rather, she is thrown into an unknown, unfamiliar region chosen by her parents. Somewhere, at some nearby island, there is a fellow. Who is he? What sort of a fellow is he? In what sort of a world does he move? It is a world different from Martha's but not too far away. As an island, though, it is surrounded by water, isolated from the mainland.

At some future time, Martha is supposed to join the fellow for a weekend on the island, but, not yet. The temporary separation from her parents is post-poned. She is *supposed* to meet him. What is the significance of this supposed? Has she freely and deliberately chosen to leave her parents for a time and go to him? We would have to ask her. The suspicion arises that she has not freely and wholeheartedly chosen this course but is doing what "one" does, what is expected of "one."

Even while still living with her parents, Martha has had "sexual inter-course" with the "fellow." With a razor blade, he has cut off his penis and a nipple of her breast, and they have exchanged them. How different is this "in-tercourse" between Martha and "the fellow" from a loving union in which a man and woman discover each other in the mutual abandonment of the most intimate, sensual, bodily closeness, and so participate in each other's specifi-cally manly and womanly possibilities of existing, attaining to that unity of male-female which is the highest goal of human sexual love. For Martha, "loving intercourse" with a man consists only in a mutilation of the involved partners and the exchange of separated-off parts of the body. The penis is not a symbol of the "fellow's manliness. In itself, it belongs directly and immediately to what constitutes the basic character of the being of a man as distinct from the being of a woman, and at the same time refers to the deepest relationship to a woman. The penis belongs immediately to the existential possibility of a loving union with a woman, *as* the bodily sphere of this relationship. At one with this, it allows a man to take a place in the history of the human race. He is a vehicle for the evolutionary development of life. He gathers the history of mankind in himself and offers it to the future. In this moment, he participates in the "divine" and the "eternal." Likewise, the nipple of a woman's breast belongs to the existential possibility of her being erotically aroused by a man's caressing it, of her nourishing a new human being from her own body. This piece of a bodily organ belongs, then, to a most specific and rich possibility of womanly existing.

None of these significations could as yet enter the "realm of seeing" or "world openness" *as* which Martha existed at the time of her dreaming. Her existing as such an "open realm of seeing" is still so narrowly constricted that of all the richness of loving union with a man, she could perceive only the possibility of a mutilating exchange of fragments of bodily sex organs. All sensual pleasure was lacking, not to speak of the experience of happiness.

Strikingly, though, Martha feels no pain when her nipple is cut off, nor is there any report of her partner's suffering when he severs his penis from his body. Pain is felt when the existence is mutilated or damaged, whether this be in the sphere of body or soul or spirit. Although Martha's "intercourse" with her partner is mutilating, the lack of pain suggests that Martha does not experience it as damaging her existence—a gentle hint to her that intercourse with a man need not necessarily be mutilating but could be "wholesome" and enriching. Indeed, in the exchange of fragments of bodily organs with such rich significations and referential contexts, there is a direct—but from Martha totally hidden—hint at the possibility of a man and a woman sharing in each other's specifically manly and womanly existential possibilities through intercourse with one another.

Martha is very, very far from perceiving directly these possibilities. While dreaming at this time, the consequences of her extremely privative "intercourse" with a man are burdensome and bothersome for her. Instead of experiencing any erotic lust, she feels only a sense of responsibility, and from her comments on her first dreaming we know that she does not like responsibility. Here, she is responsible for her partner's severed penis. The burden of responsibility is almost too much for her. She also suffers from her own contribution to the exchange. The "intercourse" involves a temporary bodily loss of her nipple. The wound is irritating and leaves her preoccuppied with worry as to whether her breast is healing right. Is it possible that this intercourse has caused damage to her that she did not anticipate?

At the end of her dreaming, Martha is supposed to join her friend on

Friday night but would prefer to postpone her joining him and stay another night with her parents. Is her joining her friend something chosen and wanted? Or is this more mature, adult behavior somehow blindly imposed? At any rate, Martha would clearly prefer to postpone leaving her parents for a man. The child-parent relationship is preferable to a man-woman relationship. Nevertheless, she feels duty-bound to return the penis to its owner; otherwise, it might rot. If she chooses to remain longer with her parents, it is possible that the whole realm of existence gathered in the significations of that one bodily organ may decay out of her world. Her concern with this organ has to do with conscience. There is an awakening awareness of what she owes her fellow human being, though there is still little awareness of what she owes her own existence. Waking guilt feeling about her neglect of her existential possibilities would be appropriate.

Another indication of Martha's childlike, dependent state appears in her veiling the signs of her intercourse as well as her womanly contours behind a loose shirt. More particularly, her wish to prevent her mother from seeing the razor blade and penis in her hand belongs to her not being able to openly admit and stand up to what she has done.

The one "association" to the dream events contributes important information for understanding how Martha felt about having the penis in her possession. This has been dealt with in the description of the dream happenings.

Therapeutic application of the existential understanding of the dream events. The vivid, compelling character of these dream events allows them to speak clearly and unmistakably to the dreamer as soon as she has recognized the meaningfulness and the peculiarities of the referential context of the dream beings and events. In one, this would reveal to her the narrow limits of her understanding of a mature, loving, sexual, man-woman relationship, and at the same time reveal to her that something vastly different and richer is possible.

Once more, the ever-recurring theme appears: Martha's obstinate persistence in a childlike, daughter-like mode of existing and her tendency to avoid responsibility for herself and others in her constantly seeking dependent modes of existing. The catastrophic consequences of this for her existing as an adult woman are indicated.

Here, though, it is of greater importance to deal explicitly and thematically with the question of Martha's relationship to men. The therapist would do well to show her his joy that in these dream happenings a relationship to a manly partner is open to her. A prior confirmation of the positive features is of great value for a person like Martha, who has so little sense of personal worth, self-confidence and self-reliance. On the other hand, the therapist would then have to continue that the dreaming relationship is still a long way from a full, loving relationship between two mature partners. "Do you not notice, yourself, how many aspects of this relationship are reduced? Dreaming, you are able to allow entry into your existence's light of only an unknown man, who lives somewhere on an island, isolated from the mainland. Further, you have no longing of your own to join him as soon as possible. It is merely expected of you, by some unknown agent that you go to this man in the near future. You would even prefer to remain in a childlike, daughter-like mode of existing in which you do not have to bear responsibility for yourself and others."

Last but not least, the therapist would have to draw Martha's awareness to the fact that obviously a short encounter with a man had already taken place in her dreaming state but that the full richness of an encounter between a mature, loving man and woman, carried to fulfillment in mutual abandonment in the most intimate sensous bodily closeness as well as in the merging also of all nonbodily spheres of two existences, is reduced in Martha's case to a mutilating exchange of certain sexual parts of the body only.

Moreover, the therapist would have to ask his patient whether she did not think it rather striking that her motive to go to her "fellow" was not a loving longing for him but a feeling of responsibility for his isolated penis only?

Dream No. 6

Martha is no longer in the company of her parents, but of a friend, Eileen, who conducts her to a place, a building of which she previously knew nothing, although it had been there and functioning a long time. She discovers something new about the surface of the world in which she lives, something that had been there but which she had not seen. The building itself is anything but inviting. It looks like an old railroad station—old and dingy. It seems, then, like a public place where people hurry anonymously past one another, not a place where human beings habitually tarry in order to meet one another in fruitful encounter. Nevertheless, it is supposed to be a cultural center or an amusement area. This is a striking confusion, for the two are very different. The first provides a human being with a possibility of expanding his existence through education in the arts, while the second gives him the opportunity to be distracted by the technical apparatuses constructed for the amusement of anonymous masses. In common, they both have little to do with the deeper feeling states of the human being and his intimate personal encounters with others of his kind.

Martha follows her friend into the building, entrusting herself to her. They descend hundreds or thousands of feet, down many many steps. The descent is dark, not without danger of falling. They reach the bottom safely, where it is even darker, like the basement of a big building. Some men are employed cementing the floor of one room. Here is a constructive element. Manly beings are engaged in consolidating the floor, the fundament of the building. The atmosphere is unfamiliar. Martha is not used to going to the fundament, to "getting to the bottom of things," to constructive manly activity. But she is not afraid.

In the middle of the basement is an open area with sunlight. It seems like an amusement park. People are there. Contrary to the "laws" describing geometric, physical space, this open space deep within the earth is lighted by the sun. The sun supports all the activity and all the life on the face of the earth. It governs the seasons and the weather, directing growth and crops. It gives us warmth. It gives us night and day, determining the rhythm of our lives. Most conspicuously, it lights our world. It allows the beings of our world to appear before our physical eyes so that we may see and, seeing, understand what is revealed in its light. Of course, this physical seeing is to be distinguished from that way of seeing "with the inner eye" that we call insight. This latter refers to that specifically human way of existing as a realm of openness constituted of the ability to perceive the encountered beings of its world and to respond to them actively in accord with their significations.

This space in the dark basement of an old and dingy building has the characteristics of space in the specifically human sense, even if it defies the laws of physical space. According to these laws, sunlight could never shine so deep below the surface of the earth. In contrast, then, to physical space, there is in the basement of the building an open, clear realm into which beings of the world can appear illuminated by the light of the sun, revealed in their meaningfulness and significations. In this realm, there appears to Martha a pretty child with whom she spends some time, getting to know her. An intimate encounter with another human being takes place, albeit an encounter strictly limited to a given place as well as in duration. "She may have come in spite of her mother, who tried to keep her back." Not only that: Martha perceives something else of the greatest significance. " 'You're not evil, no matter what your mother told you.' " Once more a mothering influence appears in Martha's dream world. It does not appear as an influence fostering a child's growth to independence, letting it experience itself so that it achieves a sound, healthy state of self-confidence and self-reliance. Rather, the reverse: here is hindering independence and a healthy development of the self. Indeed, Martha's comment to the child would suggest that this mothering influence had tended to let the child believe it was evil.

Martha undertakes the ascent to the surface of the earth alone and despite a little danger is not afraid. It seems a matter of course that she leave this realm of light, where an intimate encounter takes place. Martha's world relationship in these dream happenings are such that her "getting to the bottom of things," reaching the fundament, occurs far away from the place where she habitually dwells on the face of the earth. The question of staying does not occur to her, which is surprising when we compare these two worldly dwelling places, the one barren and comfortless, the other bright, open, lighted by the sun—a place where she discovers a child. Martha just goes back to her old habitual abode. Not until she is outside again does she realize that she has not used her available time to the best possible advantage. She could have stayed longer in the open, lighted realm where an important human encounter took place. Rather than undergo the hardships of the return to this realm, she chooses to remain comfortably on the surface of her world. Martha's passivity and lethargy come once more to the fore.

Therapeutic application of the existential understanding of the dream events. The therapist would once more do well to emphasize the positive aspects of Martha's dreaming, at the same time indicating how they open new possibilities to her. He would praisingly point out to her that she is not dependent on and dominated by her mother as in her previous dreaming states. Nevertheless, she has not undertaken this voyage of discovery on her own initiative. She still requires the guidance of a friend, but one who is of her own age and behaves as an equal partner. The therapist would then hint to her that she still has much to do before she is able to exist as she was meant to, according to her given innate possibilities. It would be necessary to refer to her behavior at the end of her dreaming, to her tendency to complacent, languid passivity:

"Except that you are in the company of a friend and not of your parents, the surface of your dream world is barren and does not foster your personal growth in an understanding of yourself and in the discovery of ever more fruitful, feeling human relationships. Only when you dare a long, dangerous descent and penetrate into the depths of the earth do you discover a lighted realm in which a highly significant personal encounter can occur. Waking, could you be more clear-sighted than you are dreaming? Do you now know anything of another way of penetrating the hidden depths of your world, where you discover a clear, bright, open realm whose brightness is other than that of a physical light? Have you begun to suspect new ways of seeing into the fundamental state of your world and your own condition? Could there be a hint in the dream events as to what it means for you to get to the bottom, to the fundament of your own existence? There it has to do with seeing, discovery of influences on behavior and personal development, how to encounter these influences, and the discovery of hitherto hidden potential. In your dreaming, all of this began in the moment when you committed yourself in the encounter with another human being . . . But let us proceed to a consideration of what you encountered in the clearness, brightness and openness of this realm under the earth. It is a pretty, healthy child who is able to make decisions for itself and penetrate alone to such depths despite its mother's prohibitions. You engage yourself in the encounter with this child and discover something astounding. 'You're not evil, no matter what your mother might have told you.' This highly significant being is a child, but one who has begun to assert itself as an independent human being, that can resist the crippling prohibitions of a pathogenic mother. After spending time with her—mark you! Not just watching her for a fleeting moment from a distance— you can impart her knowledge that could radically and fundamentally influence the future unfolding of her human potentialities. You told her she is not evil. You resist the deforming, crippling influence of her mother on the development of a sound, healthy self-esteem and self-love, both of which are essential for the formation of a reliable selfhood.

In your more open waking state do these dream events lead you to discover anything new not only about another human being, but also about *your* selfhood, about the influences determining *your* existing, about *your* relationship to your *own* mother, past and present, about what is still childlike and unspoiled in *you*, and so still warm, spontaneous and full of developmental possibilities?

Lastly, you have experienced these dream events as a breakthrough. Immediately after waking, you felt your comment to the child applied to you. You are immediately aware that these dream events are significant for you and that they can help you to the discovery of your own, genuine selfhood as distinct from that crippling view of yourself imposed by your mother. However, it is sad to have to realize that you did not use your time to the fullest . . . . 'it's a trip down again and it doesn't pay to go back so late in the afternoon.' Does not this attitude belong to the complacent passivity and languidity that pervaded your first dreaming in therapy? Is not the stay in such an open, clear, bright realm as that which you discovered worth every effort and hardship? Did you not perhaps renounce it too easily and lightly, endure it too short a while? Were you not too quickly prepared to return to the usual barren surface of your existence?"

Conclusion

Has anything happened with Martha in the course of her four and a half years of therapy? Can her dreaming tell us anything relevant to this question? We shall now compare the dream events from different phases of her therapy, in terms of the two criteria defining human existence as Da-sein as formulated in the theoretical part of this paper.

(1) The human being exists at any given moment, waking or dreaming, as a perceptive world openness for the meaningful address of what is encountered. The degree and the attunement of this openness determine what beings

and events can at any given moment be perceived. Concretely, an art dealer may look at the Mona Lisa, and this picture may disclose itself to him as being nothing but a piece of merchandise of inestimable value. Another more open human being may be aware of a beautiful woman whose enigmatic smile leaves him pondering the nature of womanhood. Our question, then, is: For what beings and events is the human being at any given moment in his waking or dreaming existing open and free? What beings and events can enter into that worldly realm that is constituted of his ability to perceive the meaningfulness and the significations of the encountering beings and events?

(2) In what way is the human being, as perceptive world openness, actively responsively related to what he encounters?

The first and sixth examples of Martha's dreaming contrast sharply with one another. *Where* does the world openness, as which Martha exists, happen? In the first, she is spatially above and isolated from the world below her, but nevertheless unsafe. Her worldly dwelling place has no firm foundation of its own. It is just an appendage, a balcony, attached to the outside of a house. When she comes down onto the face of the earth, it is as a woman shorn of the possibility of realizing her specifically womanly potential. In the sixth example, she reaches to the secret depths of her world, arriving at the fundament, discovering light there and perceiving significations that could reveal to her what it means to come to the fundament of her own existence. These matters are dealt with in greater detail in the body of the description of the different dream happenings. Between the first and sixth, Martha's worldly dwelling place becomes ever more personal, stable and open in a specifically humaj way.

In the first dream events, the immediate appearance of other human beings takes its determination from the past. Martha herself lives a monotonous, never-changing present of twenty years' duration, in which no glimpse of future appears. In the last dream events, there is, in the form of the solid, likable girl-child, a promise of a full womanly future. Martha sees it only from outside herself, but nevertheless it appears in her dream world. Temporally, the dimension of future is vastly more open, and the determining influence of the past is put in question.

In the first described dreaming events, Martha responds to her world as a passive, languid, anxiously shrinking spectator. When she eventually comes down to the earth, she remains disengaged, noncommitted and irresponsible. In the sixth, she penetrates actively into the depths and commits herself in a human encounter, even though this encounter remains limited in character and duration. Again we see a maturing in her behavior. At the same time, though, she still has a tendency toward a complacent, languid passivity and indifference.

Once more, we reiterate that Martha, like all human beings, whether waking or dreaming, exists as a perceptive world openness, as a realm of seeing and perceiving of the beings and events of her world. This is vividly clear in those dream happenings in which we are nothing other than a seeing realm in which beings appear and events happen. At such moments we are not present to ourselves as anything but this seeing realm. The ability to perceive or "see with the inner eye" is not physically "objectively" constant, as is the ability of a camera to take up light. Rather, this ability to perceive may be so constricted and distorted that only certain privative beings and events may be discerned or, in other words, be admitted to this realm of seeing, as which the human being exists. On the other hand, this ability may be so highly developed and mature that beings and events appropriate to the highest state of human existence may appear. The dreaming state is especially suited to reveal how open and discerning a human being is at any given moment. In Martha's first reported dreaming, the events present themselves as distant, dangerously explosive and obscured behind clouds of smoke. In her later dream happenings, the events are ever more differentiated and personal. This change in the general character of the events of her dreaming indicates a maturing of Martha's Da-sein.

What appears in Martha's world? At first, the people are all anonymous, indicating a great human distance. There, where husbands, children and families were to be expected, was nothing. Everything that had to do with the realization of specifically womanly potential was conspicuous for its absence. Among the beings of her dream world Martha understands herself as a woman living absolutely monotonously, until she is fifty years old and without any possibility of realizing her own womanly potential. From other women she learns of other possibilities which she either does not or cannot make her own. In Dream 6, there appears a child with whom she engages herself—indeed, chiefly cognitively and not deeply feelingly—and from whom she perceives the most diverse possibilities, among them the totality of the potential of a female human being, even if not thematically. She does not know what this has to do with her own existence and selfhood—to illuminate this is the task of further analysis.

In the dream events of the third, fourth and fifth examples of Martha's dreaming, there are progressive changes in respect to bodiliness, the kinds of animals appearing and her relation to sex. From an orientation to the bodiliness and nakedness solely of her mother, she becomes intimately concerned with her own. The animal forms of life become ever more highly differentiated and approach more closely human existence. Between the third and fifth dream happenings, she progresses from merely hearing of a cockroach in her mother's pubic hair to an involvement with a man.

This brings us to a consideration of Martha's changing relationship to men. In the first dream events, there are diverse relational modes toward men. She is open to the address of an unknown young man as a helper but in no other way. She refuses the proposal of the Prime Minister who has to climb *up* to her. Her own husband has gone off, and husbands in general are conspicuous for their absence.

In the fifth dream events, she at least dares a kind of "sexual intercourse," but one which is mutilating for the partners and reduced to a mere temporary exchange of small pieces of flesh. She feels only a sense of responsibility and burdensomeness. Again, further analysis is nesessary before Martha will be able to make those existential possibilities whose bodily sphere is made up of the sexual organs her own in her waking state.

In the course of her therapy, there are also radical changes in one of her deepest and most characteristic world relationships, one which determines how she has to exist, which limits her freedom to unfold her own existence and potential, viz., that world relation in which she exists in dependent modes—childlike and daughter-like. The overwhelming power of her mother in the second dream happenings and the mesmerizing power in the third no longer hold sway in the fifth and especially not in the sixth. In this last, she is no longer with her parents. She even discovers the possibility of a child's making decisions for itself and, more important, of its discovering itself as a being distinct from its mother, with a worth not dependent on its mother's judgment. Once more, Martha does not thematically know what such matters could have to do with her own existence. Here, too, further analysis is necessary.

In conclusion, then, a careful comparison of the existential understanding of Martha's diverse dreaming reveals that the perceptive world openness, as which she exists, has expanded, become more open and more free in its responsivity to encountered beings, human and nonhuman. In the course of our discussion, it has also been indicated just how the therapeutic application of an existential understanding of dreaming fosters immediately and directly such an expanding, opening and freeing of a human existence as world openness, as Da-sein.

GLOSSARY

Da-sein: literally, "Da" means "here," i.e., at a certain point in space, close to the speaker, in opposition to "dort" ("there," "over there," somewhere farther off; "sein" is "being"; "Da-sein" is "here being."

In its daseinsanalytic use, however, the "Da"—the "here"—came to mean something quite different. In this philosophical language, the term "Da-sein," or "being here," is exclusively used as the name for human existence. Its shortest definition: the human existence is "being *the* Here" (in German, "Da-sein" = "das Sein des 'DA' "). Now, the "here"—the "Da"—has become the title for the whole expanded openness or clearance, called "world," which is "inhabited" and pervaded by the unobjectifiable, understanding and responsive essence as which man basically is existing. Only then can human existence be claimed to serve as the luminated world-wide open dwelling place into which all that what has to be can enter. How could anything shine forth, come to be pre-sent, in short become a being, if there were no such openness and clearance—as is existed by man? All becoming *pre*-sent and shining *forth* presuppose an understanding open world realm into which the "pre-" and the "forth" may occur.

Daseinsanalysis: In this term the word "analysis" is not used in its meaning of the modern natural sciences, i.e., it does not mean the tearing of something into its elements. "Analysis" in the realm of Daseinsanalysis rather keeps its ancient and original Greek significance. In other words, analysis leaves here the being in question in its wholeness as that which it discloses itself to be and "only" that. Here, analysis simply means making the structure of something transparent as to its different members and in their belonging together.

Interpretation: (a) within the frame of references of the so-called depth psychologies, dream interpretation means the "undoing" of the hypothetical results of the unconscious covering up of the "dream work" and replacing the "manifest" but "symbolically" veiling and deceiving façade of an alleged "dream image" by the up-to-now hidden but "really meant" latent thing or content;

(b) within the frame of references of the phenomenological or daseinsanalytical approach, "interpreting" a dream's content first of all starts by *not* interpreting it in the psychoanalytical way and by not reducing a given thing to a mere intrapsychic image, but by letting it be in its own right as the being as which it shows itself to be within a dreamer's world. Daseinsanalytic interpretation "only" goes on to unfold and differentiate more and more succinctly the essence of a dream thing, meaningfulness and the significances which address a dreamer's understanding from the thing itself. Thus dream contents in the light of Daseinsanalysis never hide or cover up something else in a "symbolical" way—whatever the term "symbol" is supposed to mean. To the contrary, all dream things are always and from the onset by themselves and as themselves revealing, disclosing their proper meaningfulness to everyone who keeps to them, dwells with them and carefully looks at them.

Ontic: the philosophical term referring to those particular phenomena which can be perceived by our senses and may be scientifically described and registered.

Ontological: this term refers to the essential features of a given being which cannot be "seen" optically but which are nevertheless accessible by "insight," e.g., the very existence of something or the essential nature of space. Ontological and respective ontic phenomena always belong together in such a way that the former are pervading, permeating the latter as their essence without which these latter could never be what they are.

Phenomenology: a *scientific philosophy* which has been brought to its perfection by Martin Heidegger. The same term can, however, also be used as the name for a scientific approach to ontic beings which is based on phenomenological philosophy. In both cases, the phenomenological perspectives are in sharp contradiction to the natural scientific research methods. The latter—as best defined in their very nature by S. Freud—are not so much interested in the immediately perceptible phenomena. Instead, the natural scientific methods always try to proceed as fast as possible, turning their attention away from the immediately perceptible phenomena in order to derive speculatively from them a play of forces which allegedly exists behind them. The phenomenological research method, on the other hand, avoids going behind that which can be seen—optically and sensually, as well as by "insight"—and keeps strictly to the phenomena, until the phenomenological scientist has become clearly aware of all the manifold features and structures of significance and meaningfulness of which the dream phenomena are made up and which he is able to reveal to a careful and patient observer. Phenomenology is the only research method possible for use in Daseinsanalysis. The other way round: Daseinsanalysis is only possible as a phenomenological research method.

REFERENCES

Boss, M. (1958). *The Analysis of Dreams.* New York: Philosophical Library.

———— (1975). I Dreamt Last Night: A New Approach to the Revelations of Dreaming. New York: Wiley & Sons, 1977.

———— (1978). *Existential Fundaments of Medicine and Psychology.* New York: Jason Aronson Publishers.

Freud, S. (1900). *The Interpretation of Dreams. Standard Edition,* Vol. 4 & 5. London: Hogarth Press, 1953.

———— (1900). On dreams. *Standard Edition,* Vol. 5. London: Hogarth Press, 1953.

———— (1915-1917). Introductory lectures on psychoanalysis. *Standard Edition,* Vol. 16 London: Hogarth Press, 1963.

———— (1922). Dreams and telepathy, *Standard Edition,* Vol. 18. London: Hogarth Press, 1955.

———— (1933). New introductory lectures on psychoanalysis. In *Standard Edition,* Vol. 22. London: Hogarth Press, 1964.

Heidegger, M. (1962). *Being and Time.* Library of Philosophy and Theology. London: SGM Press.

REFERENCES

_____ (1969). *Zur sache des denkens*. Tubingen: Max Niemeyer Verlag.

Jones, R.M. (1970). *The New Psychology of Dreaming*. New York and London: Grune & Stratton.

Kluge, F. (1967). *Ethymologisches Worterbuch der Deutschen Sprache*, 20. Aufl. Berlin.

Masserman, J.H. (1972). Dream dynamics. Scientific proceedings, Academy of Psychoanalysts, *Science and Analysis*, Vol. 19, New York and London.

CHAPTER SEVEN

Gestalt Approach
RAINETTE EDEN FANTZ, Ph.D.

BASIC THEORY OF THE MEANING OF DREAMS
AND THEIR CLINICAL USE

The gestalt theory of dreams derives organically from the body of gestalt principles and methodology and is perhaps most representative of the difference which exists between the existential modes of therapy and the more traditional procedures. Two concepts which are central to the understanding of gestalt formulations are the idea of need fulfillment as a process of progressive formation and destruction of gestalten and that of differentiation and integration as exemplified by the work with polarities.

The notion of need fulfillment is a familiar one, encountered in many theories of psychology ranging from Freud to Rogers to Maslow, and differing chiefly in the importance granted to the specified needs. Perls' view of the patterning of needs was one of constant flux or movement; he did not see any one or two needs as preeminent, nor did he view them as necessarily hierarchical. Rather, he regarded them as a function of shifts in a figure-ground relationship. As one need became figural, perceived, paid attention to, expressed and satisfied, it promptly became destroyed or destructured, that is, it returned to the ground from which it came, and another need was then able to emerge, become figural and organize the individual's perceptual field into a new and energizing form. In the integrated individual this process from formation to destruction of gestalts proceeds smoothly with little or no interruption. New figures are always being formed. When the needs which regulate their formation are satisfied, they are destructured and new ones arise. It is only when the needs are blocked, repressed or not recognized that they cannot be discharged and so remain, not quite figure, not quite ground, to muddy the individual's perceptual field and prevent the emergence of a new need which might organize the field in a cogent and coherent manner. It is the task of gestalt therapy to make these blocked, repressed, unrecognized needs more flowing, conscious, reowned.

One of the chief modes of actuating this phenomenon is through the concept of polarities. Polar traits—or, more simply, opposing traits—in the individual may be viewed as dualities which fight and paralyze one another. But it is more viable to regard them as a starting point for the potential integration of the total personality. Perls' paramount philosophy—indeed, that of gestalt therapy—is one of differentiation and integration. Analysis as a modus operandi for the growth and development of latent power remains inadequate since it reduces all behavior to its smallest denominator and neglects the synthesis that would result in a more meaningful whole. The woman who has been in analysis for ten years only to discover after laborious and minute introspecion that her problems in social intercourse stem from her early absorbtion in masturbation has no tools with which to improve her social intercourse. On the other hand, the attempt to integrate polar traits by first separating them out, recognizing them as one's own in spite of their often paradoxical appearance and assimilating them in some compromise form, or as parts of the self that are appropriate to different life situations rather than as stereotyped or stimulus-response kinds of reactions, allows one to evolve a more comprehensive whole as well as a more suitable behavioral patterning. Instead of the individual refusing to confront particular needs because they are ostensibly contradictory to other needs which feel more ego-syntonic, he is able to allow room in his ever-expanding system of self for myriads of needs which, if expressed, can elicit from his environment sufficient nourishment to allow for increasing development.

Bearing in mind, then, the concept of the need fulfillment pattern of the individual as a process of gestalt formation and destruction and the concept of polarities as a process of differentiation and integration, we find ourselves possessed of a conceptual framework for the theory of dreams.

Unlike the Freudians, who regard dream work as an attempt to disguise the workings of the psyche and who consequently cut up the dreams into their component parts, which are then assigned a symbolic meaning, the same meaning for every individual—unlike the Freudians, who then resort to association and interpretation as a means of understanding the dream, the gestalt therapist views the dream as an existential message from the dreamer, a means of creative expression, much as a painting, a poem or a choreographic fantasy is a creative expression, which allows the dreamer to come into touch with the very personal, idiosyncratic parts of his being.

It is important to remember that gestalt therapy, and dream work as a part of that therapy, is an existential and phenomenological approach to the study of human behavior. It is inextricably anchored in the here and now; the only reality occurs where I am in this moment of time, and in this here and this now I am the ongoing process—never static, always becoming. And in this process, I move from the awareness to the satisfaction to the destruction of my constantly forming needs. Only when this flow is interrupted do I become static, confused, steeped in pathology. This "stuckness," this pathology, is clearly manifested in dreams as part of the total existence of the dreamer.

A very important function of the existential message of the dream is to present to the dreamer the "holes" in his personality. These present themselves in the dream as voids, or empty spaces. They present themselves as avoidances or as objects or persons with whom it is impossible or fear-provoking to identify. In other words, the dream work calls attention to those needs in the individual which have not been met because they have not been recognized. So the need fulfillment pattern is interrupted, and as a consequence we have recurrent dreams, often nightmarish in quality, which will continue to clutter up the dreamer's sleeping field until they are confronted.

Perls maintains that *everything* is in a dream—the existential difficulty, the missing and therefore limiting part of the personality, as well as the fully integrated and identified part of the self. The dream can be seen as a central attack directly into the midst of one's nonexistence. And as such it is a marvelous tool, a catalyst for becoming.

Now, the mechanism most central to the gestalt theory of dreams is that of projection. And like the various other resistances to contact, it may be viewed in its pathological sense and in its creative functioning. Pathologically, projection is seen as an impulse which by rights belongs to one's own organism or behavioral system but is disowned and put out into the environment, where it is then experienced as directed against the self by some person or object—usually forcefully. Creatively, projection serves as a basis for empathy inasmuch as we can identify in others only those qualities or emotions we have experienced ourselves. At its most inventive, projection is the source of all artistry—music, drama, painting, dance.

Another way of looking at this dichotomy, this division into pathological and creative projection, is to consider the projections as part projections as opposed to whole projections. The part projections, incomplete and fragmentary, are pathological. They stem from introjects which have not been thoroughly digested nor spit up, but rather remain as painful lumps in the psyche until they are projected out into the world. Let us take the example of the youngster who has introjected the judgmentalism of his stern but loving father. He is not comfortable with this judgmentalism, and, disliking it in his father, he will not accept it in himself. But the impulse toward judging is there, and so he attributes it to others in his world whom he then resents. The important thing to remember is that it is the judgmentalism, the undigested introject, which is projected rather than the *totality* of the stern but *loving* father. If on the other hand, the youngster grown to manhood can accept and understand in his father and in himself the sternness, the judgmentalism and the loving nature that comprise, along with many other qualities, the substance of their respective characters, he conceivably could create a novel which might utilize all the knowledge of fathers and sons garnered from intimate experience. This is the total projection, which fosters artistic endeavor, which allows for the total identification of the self with the other. Total projection is of necessity aware projection, projection that is deliberate and focused rather than capricious and sporadic—in a word, the very opposite of pathological.

In gestalt therapy we view dreams as projections—not only pathological ones in which the impulse is disowned and consequently projected onto the environment from which it in turn plagues the self, but aware, creative projections which pit the individual's recognized and identified facets against his repudiated ones in a confrontation which can lead to discovery and knowledge. The sleeping state of the dreamer is regarded as an immense and unending projection screen on which projections flicker and pass. In time the totality of one's existence is formulated there. The more fragmented the individual, the more nightmarish the dreams—the more filled with holes, with avoidances, with sterility. The more well-integrated the individual, the fewer the holes—the clearer the identification, the more generative the process.

If we accept the premise that the dream incorporates both the accepted and rejected parts of the self, it then becomes an instrument for exploring and consolidating those parts of our personality that as yet remain unrealized. As long as we are able to remember our dreams, they are still alive for us and pregnant with unfinished situations—situations which remain unassimilable. Of course, the more unassimilable the situations, the less likely we are to remember the dream and the more apt we are to be phobic. Those people who refuse to remember their dreams are, in essence, refusing to face their existence.

When Perls first began his work with dreams, he was content to have the dreamer speak of himself as each of the myriad parts of the dream. For example, if I dreamed of a red and orange afghan made of expensive wool, I might describe myself as soft, sumptuous and colorful, both a comfort to the touch and a delight to the eye. If, on the other hand, I dreamed of a black granite-topped table, I could describe myself as dark and cold, indestructible and perhaps useful for holding things.

As he delved deeper and deeper into the substance of dreams and their efficacy in effecting change and growth in the personality, Perls came to believe that it was essential for the dreamer not only to delineate himself verbally as the parts of the dream but to play out all the parts *actively*. Only through the playing out of the parts could any real identification take place. And it is this very identification that is a counteraction to the alienation that had been in existence. "That's not me, that's something else, something strange, something not belonging to me."

Central to Perls' trend toward a more active approach to the dream was the notion held by Hefferline and Goodman, as well as himself, that in this age of alienation the individual made *things* out of his own behavior, his own processes. Rather than functioning creatively, creativity becomes a dream to talk about; instead of vitally moving from experience to experience, vitality becomes a cause célèbre. As a consequence of never experiencing himself in action, man divests himself of the responsibility for those very actions. Even his language becomes impersonal and empty of ownership. "It's sad that he had to die" replaces "I am sad, and I am lonely." "There's a tightness in my stomach" substitutes for "I'm holding myself tight and giving myself a pain in my gut!"

By getting the dreamer to identify *actively* with each part of his dream, by inducing him to project himself *totally* into his alienated facets so that he in verity becomes that thing, that afghan, that granite tabletop, the dreamer is forced ultimately to reown, reintergrate and finally take responsibility for the sum of his existence. If I in turn were to become my afghan in action, I might drape myself over the legs or shoulders of someone in a group or the someone to whom I am telling my dream. In so doing I might come in contact not only with my own warmth but with the warmth—or coldness—of the person I touched. I might experience myself as instrumental in changing the physical or emotional temperature of someone else in the world. I might experience my power. If, on the other hand, I become my black, granite-topped table, I might actively stiffen up and discover how rigidly I force myself to hold back if I wish to keep myself dark and cold and unresponsive. I might discover the amount of energy I force myself to expend in the maintenance of a hard surface rather than an open vulnerability. I might be better able to assess the cost to myself of an unthinking way of being.

In this way the dreamer can experience his own reality much as Van Den Berg came to appreciate the reality of his patients through their view of their own worlds—through the phenomenological here and now. If one of his patients describes the people in the street as "hostile, meaningless puppets," who are separated from him by huge distances even though they brush against him in passing, Van Den Berg recognizes that this distance is the only way in which the patient experiences the presence of other people. He projects his own need for distance, his own hostility into the world around him. So, too, do I project my own warmth, softness, coldness, darkness into my dreams.

On the face of it, this process, the process of identifying with and reclaiming our own holes, our own rejected parts, seems simple enough. The paramount goal of the individual—at least in the eyes of Perls, Maslow, Rogers, May and certainly Goldstein, who believe it's the only motive that the organism possesses—is that of self-actualization. "Any need is a deficit state which motivates the person to replenish the deficit. It is like a hole that demands to be filled in. This replenishment or fulfillment of a need is what is meant by self-actualization." Unfortunately, the process of self-actualization, of becoming what we have the potential to become, is fraught with difficulty only partly of our own making. The individual happily and unhappily does not live in a vacuum. He lives instead in the teeming vortex of what we term "society." And it is when our own individual needs for becoming come into conflict with society's need for conformity and the status quo that we find ourselves at an impasse.

One way of viewing this impasse is to regard it as a pause in the maturation process. As we become more mature, more adult, we move from environmental supports to self-supports, or from obsolete self-supports to those that are more authentic or current. However, when environmental supports cease to exist, and self-supports, not fully developed, are insufficient to sustain the necessary activity of being in the world, we stumble, we panic, we freeze. We discover that our introjections, those pieces of our early environment that we've swallowed whole without assimilating, are forcing us into repetitive and stereotyped modes of behaving; our repressions, which in gestalt theory are viewed as comprised of muscular phenomena or motor processes, are forcing us into muscular contractions which prevent flowing movement and at their worst cause us to develop body symptoms and joint involvements. In other words, those resistances to contact which we have afforded ourselves in order to cope with the anxiety that is evoked by refusing to move from excitement to action are proving to be both ineffective and difficult and painful to maintain.

These pauses in the maturation process can be easily identified in dreams. One can see, for example, that part of the dream that is representative of the drive toward self-actualization. It could be something as obvious as running freely and easily in a sun-warmed meadow. One can see that part of the dream that depicts society's dictum to conform—something as simple as dreaming of oneself as part of a regiment clothed in uniforms that are absolutely identical.

Our introjections can be recognized through the identification of a mother figure or a father figure in a dream, by a policeman, by a judge. Our repressions can be perceived by difficulties in identification with persons who possess traits which we regard antipathetically—persons who are miserly, avaricious, hostile, self-pitying. The refusal to acknowledge these traits can do nothing to dissolve them. Only by reclaiming them, exaggerating them, becoming them in action can we assimilate them and so utilize them appropriately. After all, each of us can conceive of times when it might be advantageous and possibly powerful to be miserly, avaricious, hostile or self-pitying.

I would like to emphasize again that in our dream work it is not enough to recognize the parts of the dream or even to claim as one's own the characteristics which these fragments represent. It is vital to actually become *in action* one's myriad facets. It is imperative to *move* as does one's dream image, to use one's voice to sound one's moods, to sound whispery and seductive as the houri, to shout loudly and bombastically as the demagogue, to let one's voice break as the small child who has been punished or rejected. Only thus can one get in touch with the stark reality of those parts of the self.

Not only is it important to act out these manifestations of the self, it is revealing and exciting to develop scripts and to set the stage for a confrontation between two parts of the self that incorporate polar traits. The moment one parcels out opposing characteristics, and develops a dialogue between them—the moment these dissimilar and often disowned facets meet, not only do they become vivid and compelling, but an ascendency of one part over another becomes visible and often painful. One can recognize the autocratic part of the self as it rides roughshod over a less developed, as yet fragile part of the personality. One can quickly discover how one part doesn't listen to another part, or explains, or makes excuses, or becomes whining and self-deprecatory. One can capture the flavor of strength in the self that resists the autocratic manipulation and help kindle it into an effective, potent force in the dreamer's life field. By calling attention to the phenomenon of the immediate happening, the therapist can aid the dreamer in discovering how he uses his various parameters, in discovering what needs to be further developed or enriched, what needs to be argued with or cajoled into moving over temporarily, what needs to be recognized as obsolete, nonprofitable and interfering with one's maximum function.

If one continues to fight those parts of the self which one disparages, if one refuses to take responsibility for them and does not allow them to be incorporated, assimilated into the self, these parts will continue to exist—but chaotically and not subject to our rational control. They will appear when least useful and most inappropriate rather than as a part of a unified, acknowledged self that functions smoothly and appropriately and in a vital and exciting fashion.

In his later years, Perls used the working of dreams almost exclusively as his therapeutic approach, relying on the experience achieved by the dreamer in acting out the multiple dream fragments as revelatory and growth-producing. Most of the gestalt therapists with whose work I am familiar count on dream work as an important part of their armamentorium, but none of them use it exclusively. I, myself, move in cycles, sometimes devoting numerous therapy sessions to the exploration of dreams, sometimes never engaging a client in them at all. My reasons vary. With certain individuals there may be so much happening in the here and now that I am presented with a plethora of richness and feel no need to go on additional fishing expeditions. With others, though I would welcome the richness that accompanies the dream work, I find them extremely resistant to working a dream if they have one: "It's too silly; I'll feel like an idiot; it's childish!" Or, "I never dream, and if I do, I never remember them."

When a client is resistant to dreaming but still presents viable areas from his life space to pursue in therapy, I may never insist that he remember his dreams. This stems from some laziness on my part inasmuch as coaxing a noncooperative dreamer to first dream and then explore his dreams is really quite difficult work. However, if a client has reached a point in therapy where he is by no means at the point of termination but is stuck in a morass of noncommunication both with himself and with me, then I insist that he dream. I insist that he dream since everyone dreams, that he remember his dreams since one may do this merely by *not* moving one's head from the pillow, that he write down his dreams since anyone can put out a pad and a pencil before sleeping, and that he bring the dreams in with him to his next therapy session. He will.

It is not necessary that the dream be a complete three-act production. As a matter of fact, the longer the dream, the more difficult it is to engage it thoroughly since the therapy hour is limited. A very short dream, or even a dream fragment, can be most effective as a pathway to the hidden or disowned self. The important thing is to avoid getting sucked into the client's deprecating statements that the dream is too short or too undefined to be of value.

Very early in therapy with a twenty-six-year-old, shy, diffident, nonverbal man who, not unnaturally, had trouble communicating and often spoke in huge generalizations, he had his first dream. Say, rather, a dream fragment. He reported waking up early one morning tearing at his arms—he had a skin allergy which troubled him intermittently—with the word "around" in his head left over from a dream. I asked him to try to think of himself in some way as "a round," two words. He finally thought of himself as a circle, more particularly as being inside a circle and trying to scratch his way out. He then thought of himself as in a spotlight, a *round* spotlight. I asked him how he thought of this, and he replied, "When my skin's pretty bad, I think I look damn lousy. I give myself nicknames like 'Itchy, Goomey, Scratch.' And I remember how a kid in the lunchroom when I was a child got sick when he watched me scratch. It didn't make me feel so good. I'm uncomfortable shopping by myself, having to face somebody. I break out in a cold sweat from simple embarrassment." Now, this was the first time he had ever referred to his skin in therapy and the first time he had acknowledged the embarrassment that was manifest during interviews with me. He would squirm in his chair, rarely look at me and smile inappropriately down at his hands, which were red and raw. After he had shared his dream fragment with me, he was occasionally able to look at me. In effect, he had given me entrée into his *circle*, from which most of the world was excluded.

I could, of course, have had the young man be his circle; I could have had him position himself as one with his hands around his feet and his head down and turned away from the world, and so have him experience his closed-offness, his inability to see anything outside of himself. I could have had him exaggerate that turning away and experience the tightness of it and the energy needed to maintain that position. But it was early in the therapeutic process, and his way of getting in touch with himself, his world and me was more than adequate for where we were in that moment of time—and not so threatening. It is important to gauge an individual's readiness for experimentation and to move him toward the cutting edge of growth without causing him to take on risks for which he has as yet no supports.

Given, then, that I have as a client someone who generously or reluctantly presents me with his dream productions, how do we proceed clinically from manifest dream content to self-disclosure?

I ask him to start very simply by relating to me his dream in the first person and in the present tense, as if it were happening here and now for the very first time. By doing this, he virtually gets into the mood of the dream and finds it difficult to objectify it or to relate it as a story which does not pertain to himself. The actual telling of the dream in this fashion will often get the dreamer in touch with some important aspect of himself that eluded him while merely writing down the dream.

The next step for the dreamer is to actively become the different parts of the dream. I'm often asked, "What part do you start with?" "How do you choose among the manifold facets?" There are various ways. Sometimes I will ask a client to try to become that part of the dream which is invested with the most energy. This is a useful place because it quickly does away with whatever inertia may be present. On the other hand, it may be too emotionally laden for comfort, and a more neutral projection could be more comfortably portrayed. If the dream is not too long, I may suggest that the dreamer play out in order the varying parts of the dream. This has the advantage of including parts that the dreamer might otherwise neglect because he thought them unimportant or because he found it difficult to identify with them. It is of great moment that those parts of ourselves which we cannot or will not claim be dealt with, because they represent the holes in our personalities, our unrealized potential.

Say, for example, that a person dreams of an octopus and that he can in no way conceive of himself in that role. No problem. If he cannot see how he is like the octopus, he can express all the ways he is *unlike* the octopus. For example: "I am not dark; I am not ugly; I do not grab at things and people and squeeze the life out of them; I am not frightening; I am not rubbery." The important question to ask is, "Never?" On exploration the dreamer may realize that though his skin and hair are fair, he may be subject to dark moods which he finds necessary to hide because his mother might have told him when he was sad that he was just sleepy. He may discern that though his visage is handsome or comely, his disposition is occasionally frightful and that he shuts himself away from the world rather than share his unseemly self. He might speculate while squeezing the life out of a pillow that he does not allow himself to put his two arms around any person because if he did so he might encounter his overpowering need to hold someone close for warmth or comfort or support which for him could mean a denial of his manliness. He might recognize that he is *not* frightening because he hides his black moods and his sometimes ugly disposition through the fear of rejection and that in so doing he prevents himself from truly being known and abnegates his power. And finally he might contemplate the fact that through his body is firm and often rigid rather that rubbery, allowing it to occasionally go slack or to twist in rubbery gyrations might be exciting, graceful and vulnerable. By examining closely the things which he clearly claims as his non-self, he enables himself to identify in some new way with those disclaimed attributes, to reown them, to establish his own responsibility for them and to incorporate them into his behavior system in some productive way.

A next step in the dream work is the dialogue between different aspects of the dream. The dialogue sharply illustrates the divergence present in the personality of the dreamer, his opposing goals and motivations, his early training as contrasted with his current needs, his inability at first to pay attention to what one part of him wants.

One of my clients, who is an aspiring and very talented violinist but also a wife and mother of three children, dreamed of wandering in a city full of dark, square buildings silhouetted against a sky of intense and brilliant light. After having her experience herself as both the buildings and the light, I asked her to make up a dialogue between these two aspects of her personality. As the buildings, she sat squarely on my couch with her feet firmly planted on the floor, her hands primly folded in her lap and seriously said, "I am square and solid and deeply rooted, and I want to be allowed to remain as I am." As the light, she rose to her feet and moved gracefully around the room, replying, "I am intense and brilliant and very powerful, and I am going to illuminate you!"

BUILDINGS: "I don't want to be illuminated; I don't want to be visible to all eyes and stared at and judged—I want to remain inconspicuous and attend to my homey things."

LIGHT: "You're blocking me! You're preventing me from shining forth in full splendor; you're cutting me off."

BUILDINGS: "But you'll expose my imperfections—I don't want you to shine on me. Go away."

LIGHT: "No, I cannot extinguish my brilliance and leave you to your lethargy! I have a need to express myself, a need to expose you, let you be seen."

BUILDINGS: "But you would expose my most intimate being, the insides of me as well as my outer shape. I would be vulnerable—open to the world."

LIGHT: "That's true, but you have much to share. You have a depth of feeling that you could communicate to others and warm their lives for a little. You are being stingy by hoarding your emotions and not conveying them in your music."

BUILDINGS: "I hear some of what you're saying, but you scare me a little. I don't know what I would lose."

LIGHT: "You might lose your rootedness, some of your concrete foundation, but you could share my freedom, my limitlessness, my intensity, my power."

BUILDINGS: "Some of what you say sounds very attractive. Maybe I could let you illuminate me a little. I would really like to plumb my intimacy and share it in a meaningful way."

LIGHT: "What you really should do is go to the beach and just lie in the sun and absorb all my warmth into you."

BUILDINGS: "Oh, yes!"

With this exclamation, my dreamer grew rosy red almost as if she had been sitting in the sun, and her face was lovely and relaxed and illuminated.

Now, both of these aspects of the dreamer were not unknown to her. She had talked about them dispassionately many times, but the look of her as she became her light, the vibrancy in her voice as she spoke, the freedom with which she moved allowed her to experience this dimension of herself with an immediacy that effectively communicated with her more stolid, wife-mother entrenched self and loosened its position as an obstacle toward growth.

This particular dream vividly illustrates the importance of the setting of the dream, the place where the action begins to emerge. Phenomenologically, my violinist sees her world as a place of tremendous energy and light. She sees life as an illuminating experience made up in part of shelter, in part of sharing and exposure. It is possible to lift from the setting of any dream one view of the dreamer's world in microcosm. Life is a theater, life is a merry-go-round, life is a wake, a dull and dreary void, a Christmas tree loaded with presents. And it may be any of these things at any one point in time and all of them ultimately. What the dream does is say, "Here's where I am now, today, this minute. And here is the place from which I must move."

Clinically, then, the dream may be used to enable the client to encounter both the alienated and accepted parts of the self, to rediscover lost areas and develop neglected ones, to redefine both one's self and one's objectives through open and impactful interchange between the fragments of the self in dialogue, and to recognize one's statement of one's own existence.

In addition, it may present a vehicle for communication with the therapist and an instrument for the elimination of paranoid projections which may abound. If the therapist is merely the recipient of the dream, it is very possible that the dreamer may experience him eventually as a voyeur and try to close him out of his world. Carl Whitaker, to counteract this, used an approach which he termed "forced fantasy." In this, he had the dreamer invent a role for the therapist in the dream. Often when a dream appears unfinished, I will ask a client to complete it in fantasy and to involve me somehow in the outcome of the dream. Needless to say, I sometimes meet up with unrecognizable views of myself. One of my clients dreamed that she was walking along a lonely stretch of beach immersed in her inward musings and conscious only of the savage pounding of the surf. She was at that time closed off in a rather sterile world unlit by human companionship which she tended to discourage by her impenetrable façade. I asked her to continue the dream with me in it as another solitary stroller and continue to move from there. She then had us approach each other in the sand and both of us pass each other by, eyes averted. I was astounded. I was tremendously fond of this particular woman and sad that she apparently was unaware of my feeling. I asked her to role-play the meeting in the sand with me. In so doing, I was able to convey the real pleasure that I experienced in meeting her in a place full of loneliness and beauty, and she was able to express to me with her tears the meaning this had for her. An impactful and exciting experience.

So far, I have discussed dream therapy in the gestalt mode as a one-on-one experience. Potent as it is, this is not the only approach. Dream work in a group can be not only powerful for the dreamer but revelatory to the individuals in the group who play out the various roles. Joseph Zinker calls this group participation "dreamwork as theater," and indeed it is. There are various ways of setting the stage. The dreamer may be the director and cast the parts according to his own perceptions of the people participating. He may take one of the parts for himself or merely orchestrate the others, calling for more violence, more passion, less closeness, less antagonism—stopping the play to better delineate a role as he sees it or to catch his breath as the visual and auditory happenings move him.

Another way to cast the parts is to have each member of the group—including the dreamer—choose to be a part of the dream that he feels lies closest to his own mode of being and to have the therapist direct the production in such a way as to make it most potent. Whether or not the group members pick their own roles, there is always something that may be garnered from the acting out of the dream. We are each one of us a part of the human community and as such share in the archetypes that contribute to the manifest dream. We all share in the power, the weakness, the glory and the degradation that permeates the body of a dream. Even when the elements cast are not human, even when they are in truth "elemental," we can get in touch with some of our basic ways of feeling and behaving as we act out our scripts.

In a recent workshop I did, one of the participants, a priest who was having huge conflicts about remaining in the priesthood, had a dream which shook him to his very foundations. He dreamed that he was alone in the center of a torrential storm. The rain was beating down, the lightning was flashing and the thunder rending. The wild waves beat and clamored against the shore, and the darkness cast its pall over the land.

He was ambivalent about acting out the dream in the group. One part of him was very eager to explore all the avenues of meaning, whereas another part of him was most anxious about making contact with the clearly overpowering aspects of his being. He finally decided to play himself in the dream and to parcel out the other roles among the various members of the workshop. Two of the women were designated as rain, a man and a woman as lightning, two men as thunder, a man and woman as the waves, one tall, serious-miened man as the darkness, and a man and two women as the ground. I was a part of the ground as well as the director, inasmuch as the dreamer wanted to experience the full impact of the onslaught. I got the raindrops to pitter-patter at the beginning and gradually to increase in sound and fury and to hurl themselves at the dreamer in the height of the storm. The two lightnings flung themselves about in forked movements, lashing in and out of the melee, while the thunder rumbled and roared, soaring in a crescendo above the head of the crouching dreamer, who was desperately holding onto the three bodies which comprised the ground. The waves threw themselves bodily at the ground and at the dreamer attached to it, then rose and fell away, only to return in greater violence. Through the entire action the ground rested steadily and sturdily unmoving, while the darkness, coat thrown over his head as a cape, hovered closely over the dreamer, rain, lightning, thunder, waves and ground. The sound in the room was deafening, the movement was abandoned, and the dreamer, rocklike throughout, was never swept away.

The effect of the production on the entire company was powerful. All the moving players got in touch with their potency, their potential for violence, wildness and freedom. The man who played the darkness particularly enjoyed his ability to push down on others and to resist being pushed down in turn. And the dreamer, though he could acknowledge each of the players as a reification of his own projections, could also accept himself as able to maintain both control and solidity in the face of manifold emotions. This discovery was of profound significance to him inasmuch as it signified an ability to make rational decisions although buffeted by strong passions. A very good thing to know.

Very well, then, given that we can get a person to remember his dreams, to identify both in words and action with manifold parts of his dream, to engage in a dialogue between the polarized traits of the dream and even to play out the dream as one actor in a group of peers, we discover that we have a peerless tool for the exploration of the developing self.

Dream work extends the boundary of the self, allows those shadowy parts barely perceptible or totally invisible to be experienced, tried on for size in a low-risk situation, and subsequently developed into full-flown parts of the personality. In the process the rigid structure of "character," so stultifying to full expression, is destroyed.

INTERPRETATION OF MARTHA'S DREAMS

Theoretical Understanding

As we move from the gestalt theory of dreams, from the conceptual underpinnings of structure to the more or less objective overview of Martha's specific dreams, we encounter a problem characteristically pertinent to the gestalt discipline. Gestalt therapy with dreams requires three elements, without any one of which we have an incomplete whole. It requires a client, a therapist and a dream. What we are presented with at this moment in time is a therapist and a series of dreams; the dreamer herself is conspicuously absent. Her own idiosyncratic way of perceiving, feeling, communicating is markedly lacking.

Believing as I do that the dreams one dreams are projections of the self, both the alienated parts of the self as well as the recognized and identified facets, and believing too that only by becoming these parts in action as well as fantasy can one fully experience their meaning, I find it virtually impossible to present a "theoretical understanding" of Martha's dreams in the abstract. To attempt to do so would be at least paradoxical, at most an abandonment of my position as a gestaltist. My basic concern is that Martha encounter at first hand her own total self, rather than be forced to move from any preconceived notions of my own, any fixed symbolization.

What I *can* do is share my impressions of Martha's dreams as they occur to me and as they present to me images which I might use later as points of departure in her working of the dreams. Bearing in mind the idea of need-fulfillment as a process of progressive formation and destruction of gestalten, I can pay attention to the "holes" in the fabric of her dream paintings, the underdevelopment of certain aspects of herself, the "stuckness" from which she has not moved. I can focus on those features of the dream which strongly suggest polarities and the consequent possibilities for differentiation and integration. I can also share my sense of her dream progression, her movement in the dreams as a reflection of her movement in therapy and relatedly in life.

Bear in mind, however, that these are *my* impressions—all, it is true, evolving from Martha's pictorializations—but mine nevertheless, and that were Martha truly my client, she would be free to disagree with any and all of them and would be more apt to initiate directions of her own. The working of a dream is a very intimate and personal travail, and the same object in two persons' dreams can have two utterly divergent meanings. So, never forgetting this caution, let us move to Martha's dream progression.

Dream No. 1

If one views Martha's first dream as representative of her state of being at the time she first entered therapy, and if one accepts the fact that each part of her dream is a portrayal of some part of herself, several possibilities present themselves for consideration. One may regard Martha as unsure of herself (rickety and shaky), old-fashioned (dressed in period costumes), covered up rather than open and revealing (wearing pantaloons and long dresses) and certainly out of date (exemplified by her wedding gown). None of these ways of being are inconsistent with her presentation of herself to the therapist in her initial interview. If one is rickety and shaky in one's existence, one certainly has the tendency to be anxious and tearful in one's manner. Almost immediately we are presented with a "hole." Martha dreams of a rickety, shaky balcony, but she does not dream of tall and stately pillars to support it, nor of a sturdy house to which it is anchored. Where are her supports? Has she never had them, or is she somehow overlooking them and focusing on something else?

Martha sees herself in the dream as "tall and lanky like Katharine Hepburn, but not particularly attractive," the opposite of what she actually looks like—an interesting polarity to explore. To me, the presence of Miss Hepburn in Martha's dream suggests the potential for competence and assertiveness, and it is telling that Martha finds it difficult to identify with this part of herself. Her own view of herself is that she is old and therefore removed from the action—in actuality, she is only thirty-three—and that the action from which she has removed herself is explosive and dangerous.

There are numerous paradoxes in Martha's dream—polarities, in gestalt terminology. There is her immobility as contrasted with her explosiveness, her fear of explosions as well as her attraction toward them, her notion of everything being over for her as opposed to her sense of being at the beginning of things (marriage), and her feeling of deadness as counterbalanced by her burgeoning via the little children in her dream. A continual balancing of the scales between curtailment and progress. A veritable treasure trove of potential to explore.

Finally we are confronted—here, at the beginning of things—with Martha's notion that age gives one a privileged position, the opportunity to be indulged without the burden of responsibility. It is interesting that Martha's mode of dress, slightly old-fashioned, and her excessive weight would tend to make her appear older than she is. With the hope, perhaps, that she could thus be more indulged and less responsible? Certainly she indulges herself in the eating; she makes herself less responsible for her attractiveness.

Dream No. 2

Seven months later we encounter a Martha becoming aware of the permeability of her boundaries, her sense of being invaded and her abandonment of control. We could consider her mother to be an introject, the part of herself that is hurt, tearful, rarely angry, that she might like to spit up. The door in her dream could be regarded as one of the boundaries between different parts of herself and the ineffectiveness of the lock as a clue to her lack of armor. Martha begins to get in touch with her own anger in conjunction with being spied upon; she also begins to realize the lack of power that she brings to that anger, a realization that could be used to advantage in the dream work.

Dream No. 3

In her third dream, nine months later, we meet a Martha who is naked and in my parlance more vulnerable; she has stripped away some of the coverings, trappings of respectability, and so has become more visible, less defended. This dream is the first one she has had which is representative of her cockroach phobia and as such can be regarded as a clue that she is capable of working with it. The dream suggests to me the beginnings of an awareness that truth can be frightening but also the rudimentary ability to face that truth. Martha's associations to her dream highlight the awakening of her youthful sensuality and the mockery that was associated with it.

Dream No. 4

In this dream, again nine months later, Martha encounters her phobia head-on. We find her in a vulnerable position in the tub, naked, completely unprotected and accessible to her most feared attacker. But interestingly that same attacker is now half dead, clearly lacking in vitality. Manifestly, one part of Martha which had frightened her previously is no longer so potent.

It is tempting to view the spray can in the dream, as might the analysts, as a penis symbol, particularly when one considers the propellant spray, but to do so would be to disregard the more useful and more inclusive possibilities that it suggests, namely, assertiveness or even aggression. The use of the spray can or, in other words, the use of assertiveness is accompanied by movement up the phylogenetic scale from insect to chicken to dog to human and is indicative, perhaps, of her own movement. This progression would be interesting to explore in the dream-work and might get Martha in touch with her different modes of behavior or possibilities for behaving. Still evident in this dream, or at least in the associations to the dream, is Martha's antipathy toward unpredictability and aggressive play, but the very expression of this distaste augurs well for the possible emergence of that which is now distasteful.

Dream No. 5

Martha's fifth dream, almost two years later, is laden with fantastic imagery. To me, it suggests that Martha is progressing more and more distinctly and specifically toward an awareness of her own sexuality and responsiveness. Her symbolization is powerful and evocative, which in itself supposes an ego better able to confront that which might have been titillating and therefore scary. Martha appears more in touch with the presence of her own boundaries and their inviolability; in consequence, she has less of a sense of invasion. In addition, she is more conscious of her own potential for being hurtful and of the possibility of utilizing her own self as a weapon. Again, the whole concept of castration when considered in Freudian terms is too puny to be serviceable. The mechanism of cutting off or curtailment could be more aptly applied to the total function of self rather than merely to the sexual functions.

Dream No. 6

Martha's sixth dream is for me an exciting and vivid exploration of her total self, both external and internal. It clearly depicts the façade she has built up over the years as well as the richness that lies at the center of her being. At the heart of her dream there is an encounter with her child self as it really was as opposed to how she has disguised it through the years with her introjects—for me, a particularly poignant meeting. Finally there is an open acceptance of herself.

The whole dream progression from shaky, rickety Martha at the start of therapy, a Martha unsupported and vulnerable, attracted and repelled by involvement and excitement, through a Martha unsure of her own boundaries and beginning to contact her own anger, through a Martha more vulnerable

yet more candid, to a Martha in touch with her own aggression and assertiveness, her own sensuality and responsiveness and ability to hurt, to the final
Martha both knowing and accepting of herself in her many facets and permutations is a remarkable reflection on the ability of the therapist who
abetted her progress and evidently supported her struggles and a tribute to
Martha, the woman, who worked diligently to attain her manifold potential.

Clinical Use of the Dreams

Before dealing with each of Martha's dreams individually and in abundant detail, I want to emphasize once again that what I will be presenting are
my own imaginative forays into the world of Martha which in no way should
be taken as the gestalt translation of symbols. There *is* no one way to translate
symbols according to gestalt parlance.

By the same token, the reader could more accurately regard any and all
of the work that follows as more applicable to me than to Martha—except for
the fact that the dreams themselves are Martha's own. Lacking Martha, this is
the best approximation I can produce. At the same time, there is a good possibility that my projections are accurate ones, as many projections are.

Finally, I would like to stress the sheer impossibility of writing up all the
elements of the dreams, much less the permutations that would evolve for
dialogues given those same numbers of elements. As a consequence, I have
tried to pay attention to those parts of Martha's dreams that offer most opportunity for drama and illumination. In the process, I am sure to have neglected
other avenues which could have been at least as productive.

So, to the dreams...

Dream No. 1

When I hear Martha's first dream, I am impressed both by the imagery,
which is vivid, and by the polarities which it suggests. I am also intensely
aware that Martha's relating it in the past tense permits her to maintain a
sense of distance and objectivity from the dream which is at cross-purposes
with my own intentions, namely, to get her involved in her own projections
and consequently better able to claim her disowned attributes and emotions.

My first request is that she repeat the entire dream to me in the present
tense. My assumption is that she would have no trouble doing this. In the new
format, then, the dream would progress as follows. "I am sitting on a rickety,
shaky balcony. Everybody is dressed in period costumes with pantaloons and
long dresses. I am the opposite of what I actually look like. I am tall and
lanky like Katharine Hepburn, but not particularly attractive. I look down
below and there are explosions and black clouds of smoke. I am watching
from the balcony. There are people jumping off the balcony and running off

toward the explosions. I call out to one person not to go because it looks dangerous, but she runs off. I stay in that chair for twenty years.

"When I decide to come down, I am fifty years old and all of that activity is over. I have no emotions, and when I go down, I look quite a distance. Before I go down, I have to get out of the chair, which is on a shaky and narrow balcony. I need some help to get out of the chair. Everybody seems to be young and I'm regarded as old. One young man wearing an open jacket, which just now reminds me of your jacket, graciously comes up. He holds out his hand and helps me to jump down. I can jump because fifty isn't really that old.

"I am wearing a wedding gown. My husband has gone off. The Prime Minister climbs up and asks me to marry him. But I refuse.

"I am now on the street walking with the people. My wedding gown is out-of-date, so I cut off a little to make it shorter. The people are nice and friendly. I ask about children and husbands, but everybody is dead. They do have grandchildren and nieces, so I am pleased."

I would anticipate that as Martha relates the dream in the present tense, her voice would take on more emotion and that she would be struck by the immediacy of some of her statements. For example, "I stay in that chair for twenty years" might certainly impress her with her own immobility and might force her to take a closer look at her own lack of movement, her lack of decision-making and ability to follow through.

With this long and involved a dream, I might ordinarily ask Martha to choose that part of the dream for exploration which seems to have for her the most energy. I could guess that the people running off toward the explosions might afford some excitement. But since this is Martha's first dream in therapy and since we do not have the restriction of the fifty-minute hour, I will ask her instead to identify with each important part of the dream as it presents itself and to become that part of the dream in action.

To begin with, I would ask her to become the balcony in her dream and to tell me about herself in the first person. I would expect her to say, as she did in her presentation of the dream, "I am rickety and shaky," and perhaps to continue with "and unsupported. I do not experience myself as solid nor as affording a firm foundation for anyone else. I am shaky and narrow, unsure of myself and constricted in my point of view." I might ask her to add, "And this is my existence." This phrase is very effective in getting a dreamer to experience just exactly what he is saying about himself, and I would anticipate that Martha might become somewhat tearful and agitated in the expression of it. We could then explore her feeling of lack of support, which I expect she might describe as environmental, stemming in part from her mother's hurt and tearfulness and inability to keep a secret, which Martha may have regarded as a betrayal. It might be pertinent to mention at this point, even though it may have been stressed earlier, the absolute confidentiality of the client-therapist relationship. This is one way of building in new environmental support without which it is difficult to move toward self-support.

Another and perhaps more dramatic direction to take when Martha becomes tearful and agitated is to dispense with the verbal exploration of lack of support and ask her instead to really *be* the rickety, shaky balcony and give herself up to her agitation until she veritably starts to shake. At this point, I would expect a certain amount of resistance. Both her painstakingly slow and careful speech and her decision to come into therapy because she wasn't controlling her life indicate a tremendous need for control, and my asking her to abdicate it suddenly might be experienced as an attack. If this were to happen, I might reduce the risk level by asking Martha to fantasize what might happen if she permitted herself to really shake. I imagine she would reply that she might not be able to stop and that she would certainly burst into tears that would be endless. "And then what might *I* think?" I could softly ask. Chances are she would expect that I would look on her with disfavor and perhaps contempt. Since that is clearly not what my reaction would be, I would assume that Martha was projecting and ask her to own her own statement by saying it about herself. She might demur at first, but on my insistence she might venture, "If you were shaking and crying uncontrollably, I would be contemptuous of you!" She might continue with "Just as I was contemptuous of my mother when she was so easily hurt and tearful and of my father when he was boorish and tended to exaggerate! And as I am contemptuous of myself when I lose control and give way to emotions." If she were able to say these things, we would be well in touch with a part of Martha that was always present but not manifestly acknowledged.

If, on the other hand, Martha offers no resistance to my suggestion that she go with her agitation until she starts to shake, I would expect her to discover the actual control that is present when one *allows* an action to proceed untrammeled, to discover that that action eventually runs its course and leaves one in a genuinely more stable position. That, in effect, one does not fall apart but instead reaches a new plateau with new awarenesses of freshly formulated needs. In the process, she could discover that I was fully supportive of her emotion and certainly far from contemptuous. A very good thing to know.

Once Martha experienced herself as her balcony, rickety and unsupported, I might point out the clear absence of support for her structure in her dream. I would share with her my sense that all balconies are either an outcropping of some more grounded structure, such as a house, or are supported by tall and stately pillars. So where Martha's supports should be, there is a "hole." Those things which should hold her up and solidify her position are lacking in consciousness. I might ask her to fill in these holes, experience herself as the pillars. She might disclaim the ability to do so—after all, the pillars are my idea, not hers—but again upon my urging she might be willing to try.

I would ask her to get up out of her seat and to stand tall in front of me with her feet planted solidly on the floor; I would ask her to stretch gradually toward the ceiling and to experience the entire length of herself. And then to share her feelings and identity with me. She might say, "I am tall and strong and solid. I take a *stand*, a *position* [probably uttered with some surprise] and staunchly never budge! It is difficult to move me because I am well-grounded and solidly based. I am capable of holding up more than a fragile, incipient idea!"

At this point, I would share with her my delight over her experience and then explore how she keeps herself unaware of her supports and her groundedness. We could reexamine her academic record, which is indeed good but somehow doesn't bolster her self-image. We could explore the fact that she is really doing well at a graduate level, which certainly indicates that she falls within the top 2 percent of the population, but that somehow she negates this information—perhaps through some identification with her father, who was uneducated. We could have her list the subjects in which she is grounded and how she could use them to support herself in finding a new job. Hopefully, Martha would experience herself as more solid and more grounded as she progressed in her statements. She might also become increasingly aware that she can obtain actual support from her own body when she really gets in touch with it instead of scrunching up to hide it.

The next facet of the dream to explore is the part of Martha represented by the period costumes complete with pantaloons and long dresses. It is tempting to view Martha's costumed self as an easy example of Jung's concept of "persona." The word derives from the use of the mask in ancient Greek theater which portrayed a particular personality and has come to mean the more or less organized social face we present to the world and even at times to ourselves. On the face of it, Martha projects the image of the old-fashioned girl—modest, demure, certainly nonradical, again a view of herself which is in synchrony with her actual appearance. But I am interested in exploring this disguise further, and I would ask Martha to be her period costume.

One possibility is that she might say, "I give the illusion of something which is not true. I appear to be modest and old-fashioned whereas underneath I am really quite liberated and modern." I remember at this point that Martha had a sexual experience while she was abroad in which she was orgasmic and felt free. I might allude to this and wonder if that might be possible to explore further here. I expect that she might indicate that it would be difficult in her present milieu, where she anticipates censure. I would ask her to continue to be her costume and say more about herself. She might reply, "I am a disguise; I am a cover for what's underneath. With my billowing pantaloons and long skirts, I mask the Martha underneath—I don't let her be seen in her nakedness and vulnerability." If she were able to verbalize this clearly, I might press her further to discover what disguises she uses in actuality besides her old-fashioned clothes. Given her history of obesity and her mother's guarded and evasive approach to sex, which often fosters the belief that sexual activity and everything pertaining to it are bad, I could entertain the possibility that she might respond with, "I disguise the possibility of my own attractiveness with excess weight. I can thereby protect myself from advances which I would not be able to handle here and now. I also protect myself from the possible discovery that I wouldn't be regarded as attractive even if I were thin!"

Conceivably it is too early in therapy, depending on what work has transpired prior to her first dream, for Martha to come up with so major an insight. But it may not be too early for her to realize that she uses her weight as an armor to protect her very vulnerable self. This second expression of self is in itself a very important one and would be indicative that Martha was willing to be somewhat exposed and vulnerable in therapy. I would be openly appreciative of this.

If, on the other hand, Martha did not experience her excess weight as either a disguise for attractiveness or a protection against vulnerability, I would be inclined to mention her obesity myself and remark that her cumbersome body was at odds with her attractive face and occasional sparkle. Certainly, I would expect her to fall back on her long history of overweight and the fact that both her mother and sister were fat. But this historical perspective would not satisfy me, and after saying so I would ask Martha to be Katharine Hepburn.

Again I would anticipate some resistance, such as "But I'm nothing like Katharine Hepburn; I can't even imagine being her!" To which I might reply, "Not in any way?" Once again we are working with a "hole," an entity which Martha finds ego-alien, and it is important to pursue it despite protestations. She might start out with "Well, I'm *certainly* not long and lanky—I look like a pig!" I could ask her what it might cost her to be long and lanky, and she might reply, "Inveterate discipline! When I feel anxious and depressed, I go on wild eating sprees and I feel absolutely helpless about controlling them." If she says this, we could explore the meaning of food for her, the possibility that her eating sprees are gifts that she gives herself when she is feeling most deprived. Chances are good, considering the abundance of avoirdupois on the female side of her family, that her mother used food as a reward when the children were little and possibly used the bottle as a pacifier when the girls cried. So food becomes a palliative, a substitute for other things that are desired but harder to come by. Such as attractiveness or affection. Inveterate discipline might enhance Martha's attractiveness and better her chances for receiving affection, but she would then, of course, be faced with the responsibility of that attractiveness and the responses she might elicit.

But we're by no means finished with Miss Hepburn. Even if Martha answers with "inveterate discipline," it's important to examine other ways in which she fails to exercise discipline. In the failure to make decisions, for example, or the inability to carry them out. For fear, perhaps, that she would then be judged as right or wrong? Or that she could be held responsible? The energy that could be expended in the execution of a decision is therefore blocked; no action is taken, and the concurrent excitement is replaced by anxiety. How would the incomparable Kate handle a decision? If encouraged, Martha, as Kate, might say, "I have infinite faith in my own competence. I know clearly what's right and appropriate for myself and even those around me! I do *not* cater to the public wishes. I'm independent, I take myself seriously, and I make whatever decisions concern my own life with aplomb and assurance!" The possibility that Martha could say these things about herself is still remote, but she could say them about Miss Hepburn and at least empathize with the wish that they might one day be true of her.

After exploring the first three elements of Martha's dream, we already find ourselves possessed of some expanding knowledge of her personality. But we have as yet to handle the frightening image of her explosion. I say "frightening" because this has been my general experience with this particular component of a dream. Individuals are reluctant to be their explosions, much less to explode per se. Often in clients who dream of explosions the polar need for excessive control is present in their waking selves. This is certainly true of Martha.

I would ask her to be her explosion, immediately anticipating that she would tighten up. If she started to do so, I would try to have her heighten her experience by tightening up even more until she is completely folded in upon herself and aware of the accompanying aches and strains. In other words, I would heighten her resistance. Once she had suffered the pain that attends the deliberate rigidifying of the musculature, I would suggest that she explode out of her chair. Again I would expect reluctance, perhaps in conjunction with words such as "But I would look so ungainly! Like a pig jumping for the moon."

At this point, I might back off a bit and suggest to Martha that she describe herself as if she were an explosion. She might start out with her most available fears, namely, that she would split into infinitesimal fragments, never again to be restored to her original form. A frightening concept. And one with which I can sympathize. But to allow Martha to remain with the global image of explosion would be nonproductive. I would press for a more varied phenomenological approach, taking into account the onslaught upon the senses. She might respond with "I assail the ears with deafening sounds." "Whose ears?" "Your ears. I blaze forth in colors of red and orange and gold. I blaze forth in auroral splendor. Oh, but I'm beautiful to behold! And scary. People are both attracted and repelled by my tremendous energy." To which I might add, "And so are you," bringing in at that point the information from her dream that people were running toward her explosion at the same time that she was trying to prevent them from doing so.

The important happening at this point is her own contacting consciously, for perhaps the first time, the beauty and power of her own lack of control, her own release of energy. It is the element of beauty, color and light in explosiveness that is so often blocked out by those people who desperately need to be in control. Once Martha has experienced this, I would again ask her to tighten up in her seat and spring out of her tight circle into an open and stretched-out stance, releasing at the same time the shout of her phenomenological explosion. If she were able to do this, we would have made a giant step into a new way of being. If not, I might ask her what she might like to explode into. She *could* reply, "Dancing." This would not surprise me. Many heavy people have it in themselves to be amazingly graceful but restrain themselves because of their abhorrent imagery—in Martha's case, the pig. I would offer to twirl with her about the room, perhaps ending spent and giggling upon a heap of pillows. A possible pleasant moment.

Of course, in handling the explosion itself as an entity, we have not incorporated the black clouds of smoke. Once again I would ask Martha to become her smoke and to speak of herself out of that projection. She might respond, "I am dark and cloudy and unresolved as to edges; I hide what's going on around me." I would ask her to continue on her feet, moving as she spoke. And to lift her arms as she moved. I would expect her to start out gingerly but to gradually gain grace and momentum and say, "I billow and swell and cover up the burning. Oh, I am light as a cloud—I float!"

At this point I think I might have her engage in her first dialogue, one between the explosion and the black clouds of smoke. I think she might venture thus.

EXPLOSION: "I want to burst my boundaries, explode into the world with color and light and beauty. I'm tired of being contained."

SMOKE: "I cannot permit you to be seen! People would be upset—you'd rattle their cage."

EXPLOSION: "What do I care about other people? What did they ever do for me? I want to flame and rage and be expressive!"

SMOKE: "No way! Once you burst out of your tight containment, you'll never be able to put yourself back together. It'll be one wild burst of glory and then dead ashes."

EXPLOSION: "Dead ashes! You've never even let me put forth with a few live coals. I want to be seen; I want to affect my environment, not be encapsulated by it. I want to be joyous and dramatic."

SMOKE: "Well, maybe I can let you be seen a little at a time. I can hover over you and cover your more blatant aggressiveness and perhaps experience my own ebb and flow."

EXPLOSION: "You're wafting on my parade. But I guess something is better than nothing. Still, I want you to remember that without me you wouldn't exist at all. If I didn't explode, you'd have no excuse for being."

SMOKE: "I hear you. But maybe you could think of me as a reality factor—letting you be seen in tolerable doses till you learn to be a little less scary."

EXPLOSION: "Okay. But you might remember that your blackness and smokiness make me more scary!"

SMOKE: "You have a point there."

Clearly this type of dialogue has no final resolution, but it does illuminate the two sides of Martha that are in opposition to each other—the part of her that is eager to be seen, heard, paid attention to, and the part of her that denies this need with the rationale that it would scare people away and might result in her own eventual destruction. The second part is very likely an introject, stemming from her parents' inability to express any affection toward one another and probably to the children as well. This introject would certainly be worth exploring in the therapeutic process.

If Martha were willing to generate the kind of dialogue fantasized here, it might not be necessary to reify the part of the dream which depicts people running toward the explosion and Martha trying to restrain them. A similar dichotomy could be elicited. If, however, she is unable to converse with herself as the explosion and smoke, I would suggest that she explore the projection of people running toward the explosion with all the curiosity and excitement and "scared" involved, and the projection of the restraining Martha with the accompanying fear of danger and disaster. I have little doubt of her ability to so do.

In either case, whether she does the dialogue or explores the attraction-repulsion dichotomy, I would then insist that she be herself sitting in the chair on the shaky, rickety balcony for twenty years. I would ask her to move from my comfortable sofa to my hard-backed chair and experience her own immobility. And I would ask her to remain silent for a while and then speak out of that immobility. She might venture, "I'm unmovable. I sit here on my ass on this hard, uncomfortable chair, with only shaky supports under me, and I do not budge. I sit and I sit and I sit. I feel myself rigidifying in this damn chair while the world explodes in chaos around me and I simply look on, unmoving, taking no part in the action. I am apart from it all, untouched by it all—and if my balcony doesn't crumble, I can sit here forever!"

I would point out that in the dream she veritably remained in that chair for twenty years. And she might add, "While my life went on without me. While I did not explode but only watched. While my emotions drained from me and left me unchanged but empty. Removed and empty and old." Perhaps with a touch of tears, a poignancy for the unspent years.

If this happened, I would let her sit with it a moment, feeling myself flooded with empathy at the possibility of such waste. I would then refer to her expressed need for help to get out of the chair and the young man who helped her to jump down. Martha might spontaneously define that help as the therapeutic process and the young man in the open jacket as the therapist—in this case, me, female gender. I could accept this as a sign of trust and hope-fullness and respond to it with some warmth. I would then ask Martha to become the open sports coat to get in touch with her own opening self. If we've come this far, she certainly should have no trouble and might simply state, "I am no longer tightly closed and buttoned up. I am still protective of what goes on underneath me, and I'm still keeping certain things under wraps, but I'm letting some things hang out and be seen." In Jungian terms, one might say that Martha had loosened her mask.

If Martha were indeed in therapy with me, I would be singularly tempted to leave the dream at that point. We have made a multitude of discoveries and have achieved a certain amount of closure. We could at least leave the end of the dream to a future session.

If, in that session, she were still involved with the drive toward completion, I would have her experience herself first as her wedding gown. Once again I would anticipate a rush of resistance, Martha's protest that she is in no way like a wedding gown—she is more like a blue serge suit. But I would gently persist and suggest that she try it on for size. She might start haltingly, "Well—I'm a wedding gown. I'm white and I symbolize virginity (in no way am I a virgin!)." To which I'd reply, "In no way?" "Well," she might say, "maybe when it comes to dealing with people and situations and expressions of my own anger and excitement. Okay. I'll go overboard—but I don't believe this. I'm white, and sumptuous and decorative, and I feel satin-smooth to the touch." At this point Martha might begin to blush slightly as she started to get in touch with her own sexuality, and I might smile slightly and nod in some acknowledgment. "Well, I guess I am," she could add, "although I don't think of myself that way often." And I might venture that it was indeed a neat way to think about herself. And after all, it was her dream!

We could then move to her husband—her absent husband. Once more with a modicum of difficulty, since he certainly wasn't there to be counted. "Well," Martha might begin, "I'm the man of the house. It's my responsibility to earn the money, and pay the bills, to make all the major decisions and keep a stiff upper lip. We all know men don't cry. Wow! What a stereotyped picture of a male! Talk about male chauvinists!" I might wonder aloud whether any of her stereotypic notions could pertain to herself. And she might answer that they were the very qualities with which she had trouble coming to terms. That, indeed, it was her responsibility to earn money—from which she was absenting herself because of having no job. That, indeed, she had to make major decisions about her own life—from which she was absenting herself by never following through on a decision once made. That, indeed, she tried to keep a stiff upper lip, but lost herself in tears and anxiety. In a word, she was sabotaging the masculine side of her nature. Another important thing to know.

Once Martha identified with her masculine component, her assertive, active self, or in Jungian terms, her animus, we could move to her version of the Prime Minister. By this time Martha should be well-versed in the process of becoming the various parts of her dream and might easily say, "I am the Prime Minister. I am *first*; I am important. I am the head of my government. I hold sway over my cabinet—I hold sway over Martha! Oh dear, I don't know what to do with that; I don't know what to tell Martha to do except to make decisions and be responsible and we just went through that. You know something! My Prime Minister is the exact opposite of how I think of myself at fifty. After all, fifty years old entails a privileged position *without* much responsibility. People smile the way they treat someone who is older. You're indulged—treated special. It's the way I felt overseas—it's tempting."

If Martha were to make this sort of statement, I would be tempted to point out that "prime" was only half of "Prime Minister" and that she might consider the other half. I would expect her to look a bit confused for a moment and then to brighten up with the new possibility. "Oh, to minister is to aid! To take care of someone! But damn, that's more responsibility—and one of the things that stops me from developing my full potential."

My reaction would be to ask her how she might aid or care for Martha. This might be a whole new notion and might take some thinking about, but it certainly has possibilities. Martha could consider ways in which she might indulge herself, ways in which she could care for herself, ways in which she could give herself pleasure—sexually or otherwise. This train of thought could lead to many pleasant fantasies. At the end of which I would suggest that Martha, as her Prime Minister, ask herself, as her fifty-year-old, to marry him—a possible integration of the polarity. Somewhat bemused Martha might begin, "Martha, Martha, will you marry me (with my musket, fife and drum)?" Perhaps in some spirit of playfulness. "We could have a neat life; I'd trade you my importance for your irresponsibility. I'd care for you and indulge you if you come down from your balcony and help me make my way in the world. I'll allow you to be fragile and female at times if you at other times cooperate in the making of decisions. How can you possibly say no?" But chances are good that Martha still can. She is as yet tentative and scared and not certain enough of the strength of her assertive self.

If I was wrong about her reluctance to marry with her more powerful self, I would be pleased since it would mean that she would be better able to enter into the world in a decisive fashion. If I was right, I would continue in pursuit of her dream.

We would return to her out-of-date wedding gown and have Martha play out its significance. Starting simply with "I am a wedding gown, and I am out-of-date. And this is my existence!" I would have her repeat that statement and try to taste the flavor of it. I expect she might experience it as distasteful. She could continue with "I am disguised as a virgin and I'm not a virgin. I do have some experience—good experience—and I'm acting as if I don,t. I'm really out-of-date. I'm acting as if this were the beginning of the century instead of 1970 and as if women were still supposed to be shy and re- tiring and sedate. Women today are beyond that. They can be in the forefront of business and politics and have important lives of their own rather than existing as a satellite for some important or unimportant man. Wow—I sure have a long way to go!" I could agree with that but also appreciate that in her very recognition of her backward state she is taking a step forward.

This would lead me into the death of the children and husbands in the dream. And how she had killed off the child in herself. We've already dealt with the husband. I think she would look wistful and remark that she had killed off all her exuberance and spontaneity because a part of her was always striving for control and because no one in her home had responded to her af- fectionate overtures. And I would be most delighted to point out that she had left herself some grandchildren and nieces to work with.

In other words, although she had temporarily blocked off some of her verve and fresh energy, she still had stores of it available to herself should she care to draw upon it. In the midst of death there was life.

As can be seen, Martha's first dream lays the foundation for a rich and varied therapeutic process. It illustrates with vividness some of the important holes in her personality structure and the need to confront consciously her numerous "stucknesses." And it does this in a way which is not at all mys- terious or abstract but pictorially clear and personal. In the same fashion, it points up her various polarities and the need for really emphasizing their dif- ferences before they can be integrated into a more comprehensive gestalt. In addition, her dream work has provided a milieu through which Martha and I have been able to develop a kind of rapport that might have been more diffi- cult otherwise. Finally, when we pay attention to the context or setting of Martha's first dream, we focus in on Martha's sense of her own life at that mo- ment in time, i.e., "Life is a shaky thing at best in which immobility is essential to escape the explosive happenings around one."

Dream No. 2

Martha's second dream, seven months later, occurs after she has obtained a new and better job. Once again I would ask her to relate it in the first person, present tense, and it would accordingly be changed as follows:

"I come home and go into my room. My mother is in there, going through my purse. She doesn't look like my mother. I don't want this, and I tell her to go away or get out. She has found a check written to you. I am angry and want to express more anger than I feel. I scream. It never seems to be loud enough." I ask her to change "it" to "I," which she does. "*I* never seem to be loud enough. I grab her by the hair and throw her out. She lands at the bathroom door and falls. I lock my door and feel afraid that she has hurt herself. I sit down on the bed, but my mother comes in again right through the locked door. She asks if I want anything—that is more like my mother, solicitous. The only difference is that she doesn't sound wounded."

To begin, I would ask Martha to be her room. Now, clearly I have no direct knowledge of what Martha's room is like physically, but there are things I know about it just from the dream itself. It's reasonable to assume that she might say, "I am Martha's room. I am a private place for her, away from the hustle and bustle of the rest of the household. It is in me that Martha keeps her intimate belongings, does her intimate things and thinks her intimate thoughts. I try to keep myself closed off from my family, but this is hard to do." To which she might add, "Yes, it certainly is!"

I think I might then ask her to skip to her purse, which I regard in some sense as an extension of her room, rather than identify immediately with her mother. In the Freudian sense, both her room and her purse can be categorized as symbols of the vagina and as such are pregnant with sexual implications—to say nothing of incest and homosexuality if we consider the mother's entry into them. I would prefer that Martha develop her own symbolization, however, and if sexual implications follow, fine.

As her purse she might venture, "I am closed and dark and I hold things of value as well as a lot of junk; I have special compartments for different things and I'm usually filled so full that I'm in a jumble." I might question if that were true of herself as Martha as well as her purse, and she might reply that it was, that she really has a lot of knowledge about important things but that her head is also crammed with useless tidbits. And that in truth she has never separated out the things she really thinks and feels from the values of the people around her.

I would then ask her to play her mother—anticipating resistance. I would expect her to say, "But I'm not like my mother! I'm not snoopy and invasive; I don't pry into things that are no concern of mine. I respect people's privacy." I think I might respond with "You sound as if you don't approve of snooping and invasion. What are your objections to that kind of behavior?" Martha might look startled and reply, "But no one likes you if you're snoopy and intrusive!" To which I might add, "That's not necessarily true; you don't like it when your mother behaves that way. That doesn't mean that no one else ever would. What do you lose by never snooping or prying?" To which she could answer, "Well, I don't know, I never thought much about it. I guess there are lots of things about people I never discover because it's impolite to ask."

At this point I'd ask her to really give herself permission to be a "snoop," to poke and pry into the things in my office that she's curious about. I'd surmise that she'd be reluctant but that soon her eyes would begin to sparkle and she'd get up and move slowly around with the beginnings of enjoyment. She'd unlatch my carved wooden priest from Mexico and laugh at the discovery of the Scotch kept there for medicinal purposes; she'd lift the cover of my long ceramic cigarette box and find the many colored crayons I keep there for clients who want to sketch during the therapy hour; she'd press the button on the key chain lying on the coffee table and delight in the Mozart melody that tinkled forth. She'd ask me where I got my Colombian hanging and who gave me the poster with the lamb on it and the description "It's ewe I love." She'd know me considerably better, and I think she'd be surprised and pleased at her ability to participate in contacting me through my things and at my response to her efforts.

Once she began to explore her possibilities for being curious, I'd ask her to develop a dialogue or perhaps a "trialogue" between her purse and her room and her mother/curious self. Again I think she'd need time to regroup and pick out the proper chairs for the particular parts. She would start hesitantly.

ROOM: "I want to be alone, to be private. I want you to respect my boundaries; I feel assailed when you act as if I don't have any!"

MOTHER: "But, my dear! You're a part of me, a very important part, and I'm curious about what you're like in there."

ROOM: "It's none of your business—my private things, my intimate thoughts and feelings are my own, and I don't want to share them with you. Go away!"

PURSE: "Hey, wait a minute! There are some valuable things inside us. If we don't let anyone in, no one will ever know about them."

ROOM: "Well, that's their loss."

PURSE: "Maybe, but it's our loss, too. I'll bet we have things in us that even *we* don't know about."

MOTHER: "Well, certainly *I* don't know about them, and I feel cheated."

ROOM: "Mother, I couldn't care *less* if you feel cheated—there are certain things I simply don't want you to know. Hey! I really feel that. I feel myself setting my own boundaries. That's neat."

PURSE: "But wait a minute—it's okay to keep things from *her*, but what about keeping them from ourselves? I know I'd really like to explore our sexuality more and really experience it. And I'd like to discover what part of us has real value and what crap it's time to throw away. What do you suppose we're in therapy for, anyway?"

ROOM: "Wow, I never thought of it that way. The whole thing about going into therapy is that you're snooping into parts of yourself that you're not acquainted with! That's heavy. There's a part of me that isn't sure I want to know all about me."

ME: "I hear you. It can be a little scary, and I can understand how you may need to move slowly at times. But I won't push you harder than you can handle. I have some respect for your boundaries, too. I'm glad you do."

Now, in an actual therapy session the completion of the "trialogue" would be a splendid place to stop. Also, in an actual therapy session Martha's words would never have flowed so easily. There would be pauses and ramblings that do not occur when I try to telescope happenings into a package that has some cogency. But in our abbreviated version Martha has confronted several important facts about herself: her need for privacy, her battle to maintain it, her sense of her own value and the possibility of opening up and sharing that with others, her need to separate out her valuables from her junk—in other words, the necessity of either assimilating her introjects or of spitting them out—and the really positive aspects of being a snoop. In addition, she has confronted her own ambivalence about psychotherapy, her reluctance to explore the hidden parts of herself as well as her real eagerness to systematically search out those same parts. In the process she has heard me acknowledge her need for certain boundaries and perhaps has given me a modicum of trust.

Martha's second dream, however, has a great vein of richness remaining to be mined. And it warrants further effort at another session. The bathroom door appears to be the focal point of a good bit of activity, so when we start work again, I would ask Martha to be her bathroom door. I would ask her to stand up, experience her structure and describe herself to me. My assumption is that she could do so. She might begin, "I am my bathroom door; I can be locked so that I close people out. I represent the boundary between my bedroom and my bathroom, between the place where I sleep and go to for privacy and the place where I perform some of my elementary functions and my ablutions. I try to keep these separate. Ha! Between the place where I rest and the place where I produce! That's funny!"

I would inquire into the "funny" and Martha might respond that she associates production with "work" and that work is really a public function rather than a private one but one which would have to tap her private place

where her creativity lies in order to be first-rate! A reason to keep her boundaries pregnable to herself—to allow for communication within her own
system.

Of course, there's a good chance that Martha would not view her door as
a block to communication. She might experience it instead as a very flimsy
structure which allows anyone or anything to pass through it. She might regard it as no boundary at all. If this seems more pertinent, we might explore
the disadvantages of no boundaries. Martha might realize that she is exces-
sively permeable, that she is easily influenced and consequently more like a
weathervane than a polestar. She might also suspect from this that it is difficult for her to take a stand or indeed be her own person. She could tie this in
with the difficulty she has with decision-making.

The question then becomes "What could you do to shore up your boundaries against outside attack or cajolery?" One possibility is to continue as she
has, superficially rigid. With some reflection, however, she might revert back
to her dream and hesitantly mention the phenomenon of her anger. If she
brought this up on her own, I would suggest that she reenact the anger scene
in her dream using a sturdy pillow as her mother. I would anticipate that she
would balk at my suggestion. After all, the expression of anger easily could
connote to her a substantial loss of control. I would point out the lack of risk
in the situation, the fact that no one could really get hurt since the object of
her anger was not in the room, and the actuality of my support.

If she is convinced, she might start out by softly saying to her mother,
"Get out of my room. I don't want you here; I don't want you going through
my things." The pillow wouldn't move. I'd ask her to switch to being her
mother—hurt, tearful, not openly angry—and answer herself. To which, moving to a different chair, she might reply, "I'm only looking through your
things because I care about you. How can you treat me this way?"

MARTHA: "There's no way to make you respect the integrity of my
things. No way at all!"

MOTHER: (with sob in her voice) "You never share anything with me. I'm
your mother—I deserve better than this."

MARTHA: "You're a whiny, tearful martyr—I really don't like you at all!"

ME: "Martha, do you recognize that hurt, tearful part of yourself?"

MARTHA: "I don't like to think about it. Yes, I suppose it's there. I feel
like picking it up by the scruff of the neck and shaking it!"

I'd tell her to say this to the pillow.

MARTHA: "I'd like to shake you—pummel you. There's no way to make
you respect my integrity."

The pillow wouldn't move. I'd ask her to repeat her lines louder. She
might venture them with somewhat more volume. The pillow still wouldn't
move. I'd ask her to pick it up and start shaking it at the same time that she

screamed at it, mother, to get out. By this time she might be getting into the swing of things, and I would encourage her to breathe so that she could free up her voice as well as get in touch with her own excitement. It's important to remember that unless one breathes and relaxes the throat muscles, screaming can be very painful. Martha, of her own volition, might finally throw the pillow at the door and stand there, legs apart, eyes shining, breathing heavily. I would applaud her successful exertions and suggest that she be her mother in a heap by the bathroom door. I think she would look at me askance and indicate that she didn't feel one whit like her mother. I'd pursue nonetheless and tell her that she couldn't feel like Martha/mother, recumbent, in the stance of Martha, the aggressor, and that she should try it from the crouching position. With some reluctance Martha might take her position huddled against the door.

She could look up at the place where the angry Martha had been and say, "You hurt me! But, that's funny, I don't feel hurt. I'm lying here and looking at you and feeling, wow, that's queer, a kind of admiration for you! You certainly have a lot of energy when you're riled. What do you usually do with it?"

ME: "Be the other Martha."

1ST MARTHA: "I use it to keep my emotions under control, my passion, my anger, my exuberance."

MARTHA/MOTHER: "What a shame! You're a lot more exciting the other way. I'd hate to tangle with you, but, you know, it might be fun!"

At this point Martha and I might grin at one another and agree that in truth it could be more fun, both for Martha and whoever was involved with her. I would also point out that since her mother in the dream was simply another facet of herself, it was very likely that she, Martha, did not respect her own integrity, and that in order to assert it she might very possibly have to get angry on occasion. At this point Martha might agree.

We might then shift our emphasis. It could be useful to have Martha play her mother coming through the locked door, solicitous, unwounded, refusing to give up. Martha might object to being solicitous—after all, being solicitous is very likely a quality of her mother's which she does not find endearing. But how about being solicitous toward herself, how about finding out what *she* wants? It would certainly facilitate the making of decisions. Once more she could engage in a dialogue.

MOTHER: "Martha dear, is there anything you want, anything I can get you?"

MARTHA: "Mother, no, you're always asking what I want. I don't want a thing."

MOTHER: "But, dear, you're sitting on that bed looking so woebegone; I'm sure you must want something. I'd really like you to have it."

MARTHA: "But that's the problem in a nutshell! I don't *know* what I want. If I did, things would be a hell of a lot easier."

MOTHER: "Well, dear, you must have some idea. After all, you're thirty three years old and you've been to college and have a decent job as an editor. What's missing for you?"

MARTHA: "I guess most of all I want to be my own person. I want to stand for something—to be financially and intellectually independent, and to really stretch my limits."

MOTHER: "Sounds as if you really *do* know what you want. That sounded pretty clear to me."

MARTHA: "Hey, you know, you're right! Now all I have to do is augment it a little!"

Once again we would have come up with some concept of boundary, Martha's wish to really have a sense of herself, to be independent and to grow. We could tie this in with her need to be assertive, the excitement that accompanies her successful expression of it and the difficulty of keeping her boundaries both permeable and impenetrable as suits her need.

Finally, we could take a look at Martha's association to anger toward the therapist. If it was indeed me toward whom she was angry—and expressing more than her anger warranted—I would ask her to try to get into it again and observe when the anger was real and when it was exaggerated. When it seemed to her to be "locking horns." In the process we might discover that the locking of horns could represent a need or demand for physical contact and that if the only way to obtain contact was through anger, even hollow anger, then angry she would appear! If this turned out to be true, we might examine other ways of making contact physically. Perhaps a simple hand-shake. Perhaps a small hug at parting. The important thing is for her to recognize her need and to take whatever action is necessary to satisfy it.

I might, for example, ask Martha to stand up and experience the distance between us, to move away from me and toward me until she discovers the space in which she is comfortable. If her real need is for contact, and she is able to acknowledge that, I might hold out my hand and see if she can take it. If she can, we've moved one step forward. If she can't, I might let her explore the consequences of taking my hand in fantasy.

If, on the other hand, she is not able to acknowledge her need for con-tact, I would propose that she be her check—the check made out to me that her mother found. She could start out with "I am Martha's check. I am worth something; I am of value!" I'd ask her to repeat her statement—after all, being of value is an important thing to know. She might repeat, "I am of value, and I'm giving myself to *you!* Oh, my God, and someone is watching!" At which point we have two directions in which to go: one, the fear of being watched or spied on in an intimate interaction; two, the very consequential recognition of her giving herself to me.

I think the fear would have to be dealt with first—the fear of what people would think, her parents' lack of demonstrable affection which could have been introjected as "any show of palpable affection is bad," her probable anticipation of rejection by me. All these aspects of her fear might take some time to deal with, but once we had made some inroads into her resistance and stressed once again the lack of risk in the therapy situation, I could ask Martha in effect to be her check and give herself to me. If our foregoing work was really effective, she might indeed approach my chair, sit down on the floor and put her head on my lap. With my hand resting on her shoulder, I would ask her what she felt at that moment in time. She might reply, "Soft, and vulnerable, and open—I've really been sharing so many intimate things with you—and safe." This would bring us to the end of another session.

During the exploration of the second half of Martha's dream, we would have touched on the permeability of her boundaries, the expression of anger as both a boundary and contact function, her admiration for her own anger, her distaste for the hurt and tearful part of herself, the realization that she wants to be her own person, and finally her need and fear of contact.

I would like it to be borne in mind that the illumination of any one of the above facets could in actuality have taken a considerable amount of time and that I, in effect, have, as I said before, telescoped them for the purpose of cogency and impact. Even so, the dream is still a shortcut to discovery.

Dream No. 3

With Martha's third dream we become privy to her cockroach phobia. As with her other two dreams, I would ask her to repeat it in the present tense, and it accordingly would proceed as follows:

"I walk into a room and my mother is standing there naked. She explains that she told me something that wasn't true because she thought the truth might frighten me: that a cockroach was walking across her pubic hair. I think she was right—it would frighten me."

Now, in this dream, the first really short one, we have only four elements to deal with: a room, Martha's naked mother, a cockroach and pubic hair. However, at least three of them are very powerful images. Although we know next to nothing about the room, not even what kind of a room it is, it presents a nonthreatening starting place. I would therefore ask Martha to begin by being the room. She, too, might be somewhat vague as to its specific qualities, but she might venture, "I am a room. I have walls, and a floor, and even a door and windows to let in light and people on occasion. I have boundaries and a foundation, and I can either make people welcome or shut myself up."

If Martha said the above, I would be apt to commend her perception of her own boundaries and the options she could choose to exercise in regard to them. I think that might please her and enable her to continue with the other, more loaded imagery. She might immediately add, "And at the moment I contain a naked woman and a cockroach! Fantastic. That reminds me of the lady and the tiger." I'd very likely laugh and ask her to become the naked woman.

She might begin, "I am Martha's mother—" but by this time she would probably know enough about dream work to change her opening to "No, I am Martha, standing here naked, vulnerable, without armor, unencumbered but exposed. I feel kind of light and airy, but at the same time I feel like hiding. I'm not sure I'm ready to be this vulnerable yet. Maybe because of the cockroach."

So I would ask her to be the cockroach. I imagine she'd make a möue of distaste and shake her head as if to rid it of the image. I would press her to continue and she might really balk, saying, "No way—I'm nothing like a cockroach, dirty, lowdown little beasties." I'd ask her to tell me more of how she conceives of cockroaches and she might reply, "Well, they're insects, dirty, salacious, close to the floor, pests!" I'd wonder aloud whether any of those words had ever described her, and she might answer that perhaps she had been a pest when she was a kid, asking questions, trying to climb on her daddy's lap when he didn't want to be bothered. Neither of her parents had expressed affection to one another and Martha had finally become inhibited in expressing her own. I'd ask her how she felt, remembering this lack of affection. She might respond that it made her feel sad to think of missing it but that it also made her think of herself as bad for demonstrating any affection herself. Bad, dirty, perhaps like a cockroach! That might certainly be some sort of revelation.

At this point she might remember her early fear of cockroaches, the old neighborhood and a game she once played with some children a little older than she. She would tell me how, one at a time, the girls went into a room where some boys waited. "I went into the room when it was my turn. The boys tickled me and then I went out. After the game, they all laughed. One of the boys said that they had just tickled me."

This story might touch off some further associations, particularly if she tied it in with her image of her mother, naked and, as Martha earlier described her, overinvolved. Martha might venture, "You know, if I really allowed myself to be involved—not overinvolved, but just involved—and exposed, vulnerable, tickled, you know, really letting down my hair and being merry, people might laugh at me." I would agree; they might, indeed, laugh at her. But what are some other possibilities? She might consider that they might laugh *with* her, that they might regard her as really fun to be with, and that just possibly they might get turned on to her. Perhaps a promise, perhaps a threat.

Before we finally left the cockroach, I would ask Martha to actually get down on the floor, to crawl around on her hands and knees, and virtually become her insect. She might be absolutely unwilling to try this. After all, it would be undignified and childlike. If she in reality refused to get down on the floor, I would lower the risk and suggest that she try the experiment of being the cockroach crawling on the floor *in fantasy*. Perhaps with me in the fantasy as someone to crawl on. We then would work with the ensuing developments, possibly with repugnance, possibly with delight or at least interest.

If, however, Martha could get down on all fours and *be* her cockroach, she might really get a new perspective on the room and me in it. A child's-eye view, as it were. The furniture would stretch up in long lines above her; she would have to look upward to see my face; the walls might loom interminably, and the carpeting would be fuzzy under her. All resulting in very mixed feelings. On the one hand, she might feel dwarfed and insignificant, in touch perhaps with her own child-self, underfoot and about to be stepped on. She might even focus on her own fragility as Martha/cockroach and the necessity for an exoskeleton—in her case, armor. This could lead to an exploration of her own current defenses and some sense that because of her increase in size and strength and knowledge some of them were a bit antediluvian.

On the other hand, Martha might experience the real support that the floor offers her—the solidity of the world under her body and the textural richness of the carpeting. I could induce her to take off her shoes and feel the pile of the rug under her toes as well as her fingers and to move around on hands and knees, possibly even tickling my toes in the process. She might be able to capture a long-lost childlike quality and be able to enjoy the human contact. She also might become embarrassed—to me, an indication of suppressed excitement—and once again associate to the scene with the boys tickling her and the possibly concomitant sensuality. If she did become embarrassed, I would suggest that she allow herself to experience her own embarrassment for a while, and then I would comment on the aliveness of her face as she flushed and smiled slightly. I expect we would both end up smiling at one another. And that she might decide that embarrassment was quite tolerable after all.

Which would leave us with the pubic hair to work on. This, too, could prove discomfiting to Martha, but given that she had survived, unscathed, the discomfiture of the tickling episode, she might be amenable to dealing with it. Accordingly, she might begin, "I am a brush of pubic hair. I am thick and coarse and springy. I am both a protection for Martha's genitals and an invitation to someone to enter me. Hey! The cockroach! But that's me, too. Oh, my." Now, if Martha were able to come up with the above statements about her dream projections, she might very well proffer some associations to her own masturbation conflicts. As the cockroach, she might have wanted to crawl up inside her own genitals, explore her own "thickness," her own turgidness. As the young Martha, she might have been hesitant or guilty about the activity because it was thought to be "dirty," "salacious," possibly forbidden. The important factor for us to deal with is that Martha, as a woman rather than a child, is in a position to make her own decisions as to masturbation—or any other type of sexual activity, for that matter. She can allow herself to dwell on the intrinsic pleasure of the behavior as well as the real or imagined condemnation of it. She can choose it for herself or not.

In spite of the real possibility that, given Martha's symbolization, masturbatory associations are quite likely, she might, nonetheless, not come up with any. Instead, she might view the encroachment of the cockroach/herself into her own nakedness, her own vulnerability, as an entry into the dark and bright secrets of her inner self with a certain accompanying fear, trepidation and burgeoning excitement. She might experience herself on the verge of discovering who she truly is. In any event, the phobic quality of the cockroach symbol may have been somewhat dissipated. The possibility that truth, though frightening, can be faced with awareness may have emerged.

Dream No. 4

Martha's fourth dream, in which, as I noted previously, the phobic content is manifest, occurs after over two years of therapy and after she appears better able to cope with its "loathsome" content. As always, I would have Martha repeat the dream in the present tense to get a more immediate, here and now, perspective. It would thereby read as follows:

"The thing occurs in a dream that I am most frightened of. I am in a bathtub and a cockroach is there. It is half dead. It gets on my leg. I don't panic." I would ask her to repeat "I don't panic" one more time to actually get the feel of the words, and Martha would do so with more emphasis and perhaps a look of considerable conviction. She would then continue, "I get out. It crawls onto the wall near my bed. A girl is there and she goes over to kill it, but it is too big and won't quit." I would ask Martha to change that to "I won't quit" and once again would do so with a small smile. And would I add, "And this is your existence." She would repeat, "This is my existence—I do not quit." Again she would continue, "I take a can of spray and give it one long spray. As I spray, it gets bigger, turns into a chicken, then into a dog. I stop spraying since I don't want to kill a dog. It has some human characteristics, too. It asks to leave. I open the door and apologize for spraying."

Now, clearly, this particular dream is so loaded with diverse projections that in actual therapy we might not deal with all of them even in several sessions. I do think, however, that we would start, as does the dream, with the bathtub since it appears to depict a side of Martha not dealt with previously. I would, accordingly, ask her to experience herself as her tub, and she might sit for a while to get the feel of herself and then say, "I am hard, and cold, and smooth. But when someone decides to fill me up, I am full of warm liquid. I am a place for someone to relax in, to be cleansed in, to be soothed. Hmm—that gives me goose bumps, both because I feel really sensual when I say that, but also because I'm aware that unless I let someone fill me up, or somehow fill me up on my own, I'm going to remain hard and cold, and I don't think I like that." If Martha replied in the above fashion, it would be the first time in her dream sequences that she expressed distaste for her veneer, and I would be careful to point out that she could choose whether or not she would let someone enter her world or even whether or not she would dissolve her own armor. I'd allow her to sit with that notion for a while and then suggest that she play out her half-dead cockroach. She might move her shoulders slightly with aversion and then slouch down low in her chair with her legs out straight in front of her and her arms dangling lackadaisically at her sides and in a lackluster voice begin, "I'm so lacking in energy that I feel half dead. People think I'm dirty and loathsome and are scared of me, and I really don't have the strength to assert myself. I think I'll just crawl up on Martha's nakedness and rest for a bit. Ugh!"

I would assume that Martha's "Ugh" would be emitted by the naked Martha rather than the cockroach, so I would ask her to switch roles and become her naked self stretched out in the tub. She could this time stretch out on my love seat in an open, vulnerable position and softly say, "I'm lying here in a vulnerable position, naked, open to attack, with no protection against anyone or anything that wishes to invade me. Oddly enough, I don't panic. Even though that cockroach is repugnant and filthy and utterly loathsome, I don't panic. Even as it crawls on my leg, I don't panic. I simply get up and get out of the bathtub and remove myself from its vicinity. You know, that's really funny. Something which always threw me into a panic before no longer has the power to do that to me." I would acknowledge the verity of her observation and suggest that perhaps we could discover the reason for her changed attitude by continuing with the dream. I'm sure she would acquiesce, and I would ask her to be the girl who goes over to kill the cockroach.

As the girl, she might get up from the love seat, plant her feet firmly on the floor and, facing the cockroach on the wall, say, "I'm going to kill you; you'd better watch out for me!" The cockroach grows bigger. I think she might suddenly do a double take and say in a voice full of wonder, "Wait a minute—it's as if one part of myself, the self I'm used to, is trying to kill another part of myself—my dirty self—but it's too big. The more I try to squelch that part of myself, the larger it grows!" I don't think I could resist saying, "Jung stressed that the basic aspects of the psyche which the person has denied in his conscious living"—much as she has denied her more sensual self—"tend to grow in the unconscious as a shadow tends to reflect the mass of the *real* thing." Unless that part of the self is ultimately dealt with, it becomes too fearful to handle. She, as the spray can, is trying to keep it in check. Perhaps she could be the spray can. I think Martha might demur. She might protest that the spray can as presented in the dream is an instrument of destruction, possibly even lethal, and that she is quite unlike that. I would point out that, after all, it's her dream and that if she is refusing to look at her possibility for destructiveness or even assertiveness, she may be neglecting an extremely important facet of her own personality. I might further wonder, out loud, how this neglect conceivably might handicap her in her current existence. She might consider my statement for a moment and then tentatively reflect that her inability to take a stand or assert who she is in the face of someone's more vocal needs or demands might actually interfere with her development or potency. She might also contemplate the possibility that her lack of aggression in demanding what she needed for herself led to her compulsive eating sprees which engendered in her such helplessness and hopelessness. There's no question but that I would acknowledge the soundness of her observations.

Again I would urge her to be the spray can and be as aggressive or vituperative as possible toward anyone in her life space. I would ask her to engage in this transaction standing firmly planted on the soles of her feet with her finger leveled toward the object of her anger in an attitude of *"J'accuse!"* and the words pinging from her mouth like the spray from the can. It's very possible that she would start out with her mother. With some encouragement, I think she might get into a veritable diatribe, beginning with her anger concerning her mother's invasion of her privacy, her resentment about her mother's evasive, subtly intrusive manners, her inability to keep a secret. Martha's anger would crescendo when she attacked her mother's guarded attitude toward masturbation which resulted in her own feelings of guilt and would diminish and be transmuted to sadness when she spoke of the absence of demonstrations of affection between her father and her mother which somehow tempered her own affectionate nature.

Martha might actually begin to enjoy herself as she allowed all her old angers to surface. She might get in touch tangibly with the vitality that accompanied the expression of her anger and with the energy that was involved in the restraint of it. She might be willing to take on more of her world—perhaps her father, perhaps her boss. She might not. I rather imagine that I'd think her mother was enough for one day and ask her to explore the other relationships at some future time. She might be eminently relieved.

At some point it would be incumbent upon us to return to Martha's use of the spray can vis-à-vis the transmutation of the cockroach into first a chicken and then a dog. Once again I would have her contemplate herself as the spray can and report out her imaginings. Somewhat reluctantly she might venture, "Well, I'm a container, sealed up pretty tightly and under extreme pressure—wow, that's a pretty accurate description—I'm filled with liquid that can rigidify, halt something in its tracks. I'm irritating, polluting, potentially poisonous! God, when I'm like this, I'm even worse than the insect I'm afraid of—now that's a paradox. Wait a minute, the more suppressive one part of me becomes, the more growth occurs in another part of me—what I thought was my dirty, unacceptable self. Perhaps if I can really express my aggression, I can express my humanness, too. I know what I'm saying is similar to what I said when I first tried to kill my cockroach, but I feel as if I've taken an additional step."

I could easily agree with Martha's assessment, mentioning that therapy is often a spiral process and that we frequently return to what we've already encountered on a slightly different level. I would then suggest that she try a further step by becoming the chicken. Martha could laugh a little and remark that she didn't think too highly of chickens, silly cackling things. But with a show of good will she might continue, "Well, I'm pretty predictable—we used to have chicken for dinner every Friday—you can almost set your calendar by me, and I scratch in the dirt for my sustenance. Maybe that's what I do. Look in sterile places for nourishment—that might be why I don't get huge amounts. Possibly I should spend more time with the roosters instead of the hens. Though you've got to admit there are a lot more hens in a barnyard!"

I'd ask her if she had to remain in the barnyard. That would certainly be a *predictable* thing for a hen to do. I suspect she'd reply that she wasn't sure yet whether she was ready to move. I would also ask her if she liked being predictable. To which she might respond that it was a lot better than running around like a chicken with its head cut off! I wouldn't be able to resist that and would urge her to conjure up that chicken, headless, out of control. I rather expect Martha would find that shocking and much too threatening to attempt at this time. If I was wrong and she was willing to attempt it, I'd direct her to get down on the floor and let her limbs thrash around until she went limp with exhaustion and experienced the relief that comes with giving in to something that scares you without reaping any dire consequences. That would be quite a step forward.

If I was right, however, and Martha was unwilling or unable to enact her uncontrolled self, I believe we'd explore the possibility that there are numerous steps between complete predictability and utter loss of control—playfulness being one of them. We would then proceed to her dog.

I would ask Martha to become her dog and really play him out. I imagine she'd grimace and respond, as she did in her free associations, "I don't like dogs. When they're near, they slobber on you. They're a threat to pantyhose. They're unpredictable and they jump even in play." I'd laugh a little and suggest that some of that sounded rather like fun. Martha might react indignantly and proclaim that it certainly was *no* fun to be slobbered on. I'd pursue that possibility and ask her where some slobbering might occur that possibly could be tied in with pleasant things. After a while she might consider that it *could* be a part of sexual play—though in no way tidy. On the other hand, she might not think of any way at all in which slobbering was acceptable—it might simply be associated in her mind with her father's "boorish" eating habits. In which case, I might drop that mode of exploration and ask her once more to be her dog. She might capitulate and say, "I'm a friend of man! I'm unpredictable, I'm powerful, forceful—when I jump, I knock people down." I'd laugh again and ask her if she'd ever knocked a man down. She might laugh, too, and say, "No, but if I ever fell on one, I could!"

Martha's saying that would make me think of her uncontrollable eating sprees, which predictably happen when she's anxious or depressed, and I would ask her if she saw them as predictable, too. I think she might say that she indeed saw them that way. To which I might respond that that would be an excellent area in which to be unpredictable.

Finally, I'd remark that I certainly would find her jumping unpredictable, that I truly doubted that she had tried it in years, and that I'd like very much to see her be her dog and jump up and down until she was out of breath. I'd expect a flat out "No." Followed by "It'd be more like a whale jumping out of water!" But I wouldn't settle for that; after all, even dolphins are noted for their graceful leaps. If I could convince her, I think she might jump up and down till she was breathless, till her face was flushed and her body was loose and unarmored. I think she might like the breathlessness, the flushedness, the looseness. I think she might collapse in a heap and grin.

I'd ask her how it was for her to be unpredictable. I'd tell her it was delightful for me to see her be so. Possibly she would say that it was fun. Embarrassing, but fun, and certainly different. We then might explore other ways to be unpredictable. Like her taking the lead in the therapy hour, or asking a man to dinner, or coming in late for work. Or having a riproaring argument with her mother. Or sitting in her father's lap. Some of the behaviors risky, some of them rewarding, all of them unexpected. I'd suggest that she try some of them before the next session. But before she left I would ask her to apologize again to the dog for spraying it. I think she might say, "I am really sorry for attacking you so unmercifully. I can see now that you share with me some human characteristics, that you like to play and romp and frolic, and that I might benefit from following your exanple. I certainly don't want to continue to suppress you until you're big enough to devour me in the night. Maybe we could make a pact so that I sometimes play with you and you in turn let me sleep quietly."

Now, you'll notice that I did not deal with the projections of the wall and the bed, which I see as somewhat polar traits. To me, the wall was similar to the bathtub in that they are both smooth and hard; similarly, the bed shared with the water the components of softness, warmth and the ability to envelop. If Martha had not dealt with the bathtub and the water, I would have asked her to be her wall and her bed and would perhaps have elicited such qualities as perpendicularity and uprightness as well as the other properties mentioned above. There's really no limit to the number of directions we can pursue, each with a possibly different though equally productive outcome.

What we did do is move from the energy that was tied up in the maintenance of her inviolability, her smoothness, her coldness, through the potential dissolution of her armor to a state of vulnerability but no panic. We considered the conflict between her "dirty" perhaps sensual self and her more controlling, society-oriented side, noting in the process how her "dirty" self expanded as she tried to hold it in check. We dealt too with the possibilities of developing Martha's incipient assertiveness, the vitality that accompanies anger and the energy that is required to restrain it. Finally, we played around with predictability versus unpredictability and the acceptance of playfulness and its concomitant sensuality.

In the process we may have laid to rest her cockroach phobia.

Dream No. 5

Almost two years later, Martha dreams a dream which is most evocative of sexual imagery. Once again I would have her relate it to me in the present tense, and it would proceed as follows:

"I am living with my parents somewhere. There is a fellow here who was somewhere at a nearby island. It is a different type of environment, but not too far from where I am. I am supposed to join him there in a few days for the weekend. Before he leaves for this island, he cuts off his penis and a nipple of my breast and we exchange them. This is supposed to be temporary. And they are supposed to reattach themselves.

"I also have the razor blade. It isn't painful. I don't want my mother to see the razor blade and penis in my hand. If she does see, she doesn't bother me. I am wearing a loose shirt. The breast is healing, but it is irritating me." I would suggest that she change "the breast" to "I," and she would repeat, "I am healing, and it is irritating me." To which she might add, "It's true, I am feeling better, but the process can be irritating!" She'd then continue, "If that is bothering me, he must be really uncomfortable. Is it healing right? Am *I* healing right? I am supposed to join him on Friday night. I would rather join him on Saturday, but I am concerned about getting the penis back for it may start rotting. I have to get it back to him."

I expect that Martha might have related her dream with some embarrassment over the graphic content, but inasmuch as we have known one another for four years and have shared many experiences, I doubt that she would have too much trouble dealing with it. My temptation might be to treat the dream as a whole and somehow short-cut the various elements—perhaps starting with "Life is an island." But I imagine I would resist that and, as I mostly do, have Martha become each one of her projections. Accordingly, I would ask her to start by being her island. I would suggest that she walk to a point in the room where she could feel more island-like and really experience that. I think she might move as far away from me as possible without moving too close to a wall and after a short silence say, "I am surrounded on all sides by water; I'm alone here, cut off from the mainstream. And I'm a little lonely, but I feel good about myself, too. 'No man is an island,' hmm." I would mention that she had considered her island to be a different type of environment from where she had been, and I would wonder in what ways it was different—in what ways *she* was different. She might start musingly, saying, "Well, perhaps more secluded than I was—with more of a sense of my own boundaries; I really stop at the water's edge. Maybe a bit more independent, a bit more self-contained—not as anxious. I'm not all that different from how I was. Maybe that's the direction in which I would move if I cut off my responsiveness. I would truly be isolated then—more than I am now."

If Martha spoke in such a fashion about herself, I would ask her what had evoked the comment about responsiveness. By this time she clearly might be able to relate it to either her nipple or the penis or both, and she might say, "When I think of myself as my nipple, I think that I can be responsive, that I can become stiff and engorged and excited—even capable of arousing excitement in someone else. I can also provide sustenance—even my excitement is sustaining! The same kind of thing is true of me when I become the penis; I'm tumescent, capable of arousal, responsive—but sometimes I feel as if my own responsiveness is a burden, one that could cause me to get into situations that perhaps I couldn't handle. That makes me restive sometimes.

"So I tend to 'cut off' my own responsiveness, hoping that I'll have it available when I really want to use it. But, you know, it's irritating to me to be minus a part of me—my responsiveness—at least while I'm still in touch with it; later I may no longer notice the lack. That's a little scary!" I would agree that it was indeed scary.

Now, it's quite plausible that Martha would have been able to move into the above reifications of her nipple and penis on her own. By this time she would have been more than sufficiently familiar with the dream technique. But I rather imagine the concept of the razor blade might pose a problem. I doubt that she would bring it up on her own and I would point out the lacuna. If she then were able to identify with the razor blade, fine; if not, I would suggest that she do so. She might start in haltingly with "I am sharp-edged, dangerous, cutting, steely—I am *not!* Well—I am slim, finely honed. Wait a minute—if I were thin and sharp, I would be dangerous! I could both elicit and cut off the responsiveness in others. That sounds pretty powerful. It might not be such a bad thing to be." To which I might reply, "Why not? It would only take a loss of about forty-five pounds." I suspect she would parry my question, but it wouldn't matter. After all, she had made her point and I had made mine.

I might then ask her to try a dialogue between the razor blade and the nipple/penis, in large part because they appear so utterly antithetical. Again I would expect a hesitancy, followed by "Well, let me position myself. As the nipple/penis I think I'll just recline here on this couch, and as the razor blade I think I'll stand erect in front of my other self and look sharp." Here she might laugh a little and say that perhaps she should have worn a different outfit.

NIPPLE/PENIS: "I'm resting here, uninvolved, but with the potential for being excited, engorged, erect."

RAZOR BLADE: "I'm standing here at the ready, about to prevent you from becoming!"

NIPPLE/PENIS: "That's a dumb thing to do! Here I am, all ready to give out with all sorts of pleasure, and you want to stop me in my tracks. What'll it get you?"

RAZOR BLADE: "Never mind what it'll get me! Martha can't handle that kind of excitement. She likes things cool—under wraps, like that silly loose shirt she's wearing so that no one can see what she really looks like."

NIPPLE/PENIS: "You're sidetracking me. Martha's wearing that shirt so she won't irritate *me.*"

RAZOR BLADE: "Exactly! She doesn't even want to know you exist. Soft, vulnerable thing. Now me, I can take care of myself. I'm a mighty dangerous fellow and you'd better look twice before you tangle with me."

NIPPLE/PENIS: "Who wants to tangle with you? I think you'd be great if someone were threatening us, but I can't see that anyone is right now. Maybe you could go out and carve a niche for us in the world and I could reap the benefits. You forge ahead, and I'll follow and be excited and exciting. We could both have a ball."

RAZOR BLADE: "You make out quite a case. You're a great defense attorney. Maybe we could go into partnership?"

Martha might end that dialogue laughing. Perhaps having skirted some of the more loaded issues like the dangers that accompany being sharp and aggressive and out to cut a swath. But we could tackle that another day.

What would remain to be dealt with in the present is the disconnected penis that is subject to rot. I would simply mention that we had not dealt with it, and I think Martha might just as simply reply, "If I cut off a part of myself and don't use it, it will atrophy; it will rot. I don't want that to happen." A very good place to stop for the day. I would say so.

What I did not do is have Martha identify either with the fellow at a nearby island or with her mother. The first omission stems from my lack of clues about the kind of fellow he was. I could, of course, have worked from a stereotype, but I felt that that was better dealt with through the vehicle of the razor blade. My second omission stemmed from my sense that Martha's clarity about boundaries, which I picked up from her identification with the island, obviated the need for the identification with a mother who did not seek to change these boundaries or need to load her views of the world on Martha.

As can be seen, even without my direction, Martha did tend to deal with her dream as a whole. She started out by being aware of her own potential for isolation, a being cut off from the world. At the same time, she was in touch with a sense of independence and a distinctness of boundaries within herself. This was augmented when she became cognizant of the fact that her lack of responsiveness could be seen as cutting her off from the people around her. This was followed by her recognition that she was unwilling to cut off part of herself and that she could use her potency or aggressiveness to shape the world to her needs. In effect, she could forge an alliance between her excitement and her assertiveness so that no part of her need rot.

Dream No. 6

The last of Martha's dreams which we are about to explore was experienced by her as a breakthrough. If we listen to Martha relate it in the present tense, which for the first time she does almost without prompting, we hear: ".My friend Eileen takes me to an enormous building, very old and dingy. It looks like an old railroad station but it is supposed to be a cultural or amusement area. Although it has been in operation a long time, I don't know about it.

"When we enter the building, we go down hundreds or thousands of feet, down many, many steps. The inside is rather like a shell, very dark, and if you fall off a staircase, you can drop down to the bottom.

"When we get to the bottom, it is even darker. Some men are laying a cement floor in one room. The atmosphere is a little creepy, but I'm not frightened.

"In the middle of the basement is an open place with sunlight. It seems to be an amusement area. People are there, and there are amusement park rides. I see a little girl, perhaps five or six years old. She is a pretty child, with a round full face, dark hair with bangs, and dark eyes. She is here in spite of her mother, who tried to keep her back. I spent some time with her, and, after getting to know her for awhile, I say to her, 'You're not evil, no matter what your mother told you.'

"I start back to the ground level alone. It's a long way back up and sometimes a little dangerous. I walk cautiously, but again I'm not really frightened.

"When I get out, I realize that it's early and I could have stayed longer, but it's a long trip down again and it doesn't pay to go back so late in the afternoon."

To have Martha begin by experiencing herself as her friend Eileen might not be overly rewarding, inasmuch as I know next to nothing about Eileen. I do know, however, what the dream relates, and at least that much Martha could tell me. She might say, for example, "I am the kind of person who brings Martha into situations that are deceptive, that cannot be taken at face value, that have to be thoroughly explored before she can see the excitement under the unprepossessing surface. I may even have been the part of her that brought her into therapy so that she could do just that!" I might nod in agreement and, if she doesn't do so herself, suggest that she be the unprepossessing surface starting with the building. Of course, at this point in time Martha might move into being the parts of the dream with little or no help from me.

As the building, Martha might start by saying, "I am old and enormous and dingy," and I might add, "and this is my existence!" Martha might repeat rather grimly, "and this is my existence. I look old because I'm enormous and because I've been here a long time. I have kept myself enormous and dingy—fat and dowdy—so that I would remain unaware of my potential for pleasure. As long as I present myself as huge, old and noncolorful, I *cannot* realize my potential for pleasure. People use me as a railroad station, a means of getting somewhere else, but not as a source of edification or pleasure." With that, she might turn to me and rather explosively say, "Damn it, I've got to lose some weight. This hugeness is really weighing me down. I'm suddenly realizing that all the facilities for amusement and pleasure have existed in me a long, long time, but I was hardly ever cognizant of this and so did nothing to develop myself." She might stop at this point a little bemused and perhaps need a bit of encouragement to proceed.

I think I might mention softly that I had been aware of her potential for amusement and pleasure for some time, and then ask her if she could be her staircase. I suspect she'd nod and say, "I go down hundreds or thousands of feet into the center of my being. If you enter me, you will go down, down,

down into the center of my being. The inside of me is shell-like, smooth as the inside of a shell, and dark, dark. If you lost your supports—controls—you would sink into the depths of me" and, with a little twinkle, "not a bad way to die!" To which I might grin in response and then remark that one could sink into the depths of her quite deliberately, one step at a time, without losing control at all! At which point she might laugh and say, "Yes, I know; it was like that when I was abroad."

I would ask her next to move to the part of her dream which encompassed her basement and cement floor. In a rather deliberate way she might say, "As my basement I am dark, but extensive. This is the part of me that underlies the rest of my structure, the foundation on which the rest of me is built. I am no longer frightened of my own darkness. I'm not, you know! I'm no longer frightened of my own darkness—I've learned to live with it, and at times to brighten it. Hey! I want to be my cement floor." I would nod, and she would continue, "Instead of being rickety and shaky as I once was—oh my, was I—I am now building myself a solid foundation. I, the cement, will harden so that I can support the weight of my total being—my plethora of rooms, of divergencies." While saying this, I think Martha might rise to her feet and walk about the room, pacing out her space and balancing easily on the balls of her feet, sometimes raising her arms to the ceiling and standing on tiptoe. I'd ask her how it felt to experience the height and breadth of her, and she might nod and reply, "Really good, supported and alive."

Then she might sink down to the floor and, sitting cross-legged, say, "In the center of my being there is openness, warmth and sunlight. *I* am open, warm and sunny. When I am with a friend, like Eileen, for example, I can experience my warm, open sunniness without fright. I can do that here with you. That part of me which I grew up thinking of as creepy has become the opposite." I would nod, and I imagine we might both sit quietly for a moment thinking of the past few years.

After a bit I would ask Martha to be her amusement area. She might smile and say, "Deep in the core of me there is a fun place; I don't mean just sexually, although that's there, too. But I offer thrills and excitement and welcome to people. Maybe I scare them a little, too, but only enough to make life interesting. Hmm, I wonder if I would frighten people if I showed all my own excitement and warmth. Perhaps I would, perhaps it's just a projection. Perhaps in either case it would be worth it. More so than being dull and dingy and just overlooked!"

I would agree that it certainly sounded more profitable to me. Then I might wonder out loud about her little girl. A look of wonderment might pass across her face and she might say, "Here in my fun place I have discovered the child in me—pretty, round-faced, dark of eye and hair. I *am* pretty, round-faced, dark of eye and hair. I, the child in me, have discovered my capacity for having fun, for being excited and exciting in spite of my mother's warnings to stay away from those characteristics in me.

"I, Martha, say to my child, 'You're not evil—your darkness is not evil, your excitement is not evil; they are vital and expansive and drenched in the life-giving warmth of the sun.'

"My child looks at me with wide dark eyes and says, 'I know that now. Thank you. I'm so glad we could meet at last and that you could come to like me.' I'm glad, too. I'm looking forward to sharing all sorts of new experiences with her."

I think Martha might then look at me and say, "That was a long journey down into the parts of me that I'm just beginning to know. It takes a while to get back to the current realities—to what, indeed, I want to do with my life. It takes a while, and I'm not going to leap into anything suddenly, but I'm not frightened of what's to come. There are some things I know.

"I know I want to be fully Martha, to know where I stop and someone else begins. I want to be independent, but not alone. I want to be aware of my potential for excitement and assertiveness, for sensuality and sharpness. I want to be unafraid of my own vulnerability, my own candor, my own anger, my own warmth. In short, I want to *be*. I think I've learned some of the ways."

And given the work that we would have shared together, I, too, believe she would have learned some of the ways.

It is now necessary, however, to leave the world of fantasy and imagination, the fictional world of Martha, which in essence I have woven from whole cloth. The woof of the dreams was given, but the warp was entirely mine, and in order to illustrate the way in which a gestalt therapist works with dreams, I allowed myself huge liberties. I find it imperative once more to issue a caveat, namely, that I have been playing both parts—the part of the therapist and the part of the dreamer. And playing, what's more, the part of a dreamer whom I have never seen. What one is possessed of is a kind of map of an unexplored terrain where only certain landmarks are known. At any point Martha's rivers could have taken a different turning, her mountains could have risen to a different height, her caves could have remained hidden. There is no guarantee that any of the directions I followed would have led us to our current journey's end. But it's possible. The projections I worked with could have been my projections rather than Martha's, but let us not forget that a good projector generally picks a good projection screen, and Martha at times could have reacted as I reacted for her.

The important thing to remember is that someone, Martha or no, could have responded in the ways I have depicted to the kinds of suggestions or directions that I used. And in so doing could have enriched and broadened his world. The beauty of the method lies in the fact that any response of the dreamer can be followed through to an exciting or illuminating closure, either through the identification of the dreamer with a particular fragment of the dream or with the polarity of that fragment. There is no way in which any area can be neglected if the dreamer and the therapist have patience enough, perceptivity enough, and time. Huge dollops of time.

Finally, I would like to say that although dream work is an exhilarating and valuable tool for plumbing the depths of a personality and widening the scope of the self so that choices can be made, it is only one tool in the arsenal of a gestalt therapist. There are therapists who work *solely* with dreams and use them beautifully and productively, but I believe that in order to develop a relationship, which for me is the core of psychotherapy, more than dreams are needed.

From the therapist are needed sharing, and commitment, and love, and a history of living that allows for the understanding of pain and fear, and the reluctance to move, and growth that evolves by inches.

From the client are needed trust, and the determination to grow in spite of pain and fear, and the reluctance to move. For this, more than dreams are needed. Yet "We are such stuff as dreams are made on; and our little life is rounded with a sleep."

REFERENCES

Fantz, R. (1975a). Fragments of gestalt therapy. In *Gestalt Therapy Primer*, ed. F.D. Stephenson, pp. 80–86. Springfield, Ill.: Charles C. Thomas.

——— (1975b). Polarities: differentiation and integration. In *Gestalt Therapy Primer*, ed. F. D. Stephenson, pp. 87–96. Springfield, Ill.: Charles C. Thomas.

Hall, C. S., and Lindzey, G. (1957). Organismic theory. In *Theories of Personality*, p. 304. New York: John Wiley & Sons.

Munroe, R. L. (1959). Other psychoanalytic approaches (Adler, Jung, Rank). In *American Handbook of Psychiatry*, ed. S. Arieti, p. 1459. New York: Basic Books.

Perls, F. S., Hefferline, R. F., and Goodman, P. (1951). *Gestalt Therapy*, p. 215. New York: Julian Press.

REFERENCES

——————— (1969). *Gestalt Therapy Verbatim.* Lafayette, Calif.: Real People Press.

Van Den Berg, J. H. (1955). *The Phenomenological Approach to Psychiatry,* p. 12. Springfield, Ill.: Charles C. Thomas.

Whitaker, C. A. (1966). Training for the unreality experience. *Voices,* Vol. II, No. 4.

Zinker, J. C. (1971). Dreamwork as theatre. *Voices,* Vol. VII, No. 2.

CHAPTER EIGHT

Comparison And Synthesis

JAMES L. FOSSHAGE, PH.D.
and CLEMENS A. LOEW, PH.D.

BASIC THEORY OF THE MEANING OF DREAMS

Since theory serves as the foundation of dream interpretation, we asked the contributors to present their respective theories of the meaning of dreams. In response, they have provided us with a panorama of theoretical approaches, all of which have their particular formulations, terminologies and emphases. In this chapter our primary aim is to clarify the similarities and differences within these six theoretical approaches. To make our task manageable we have chosen for purposes of comparison a limited number of basic dimensions and concepts which, in our judgment, are critically important for the understanding of dreams and substantially affect the clinician in the dream interpretive process.

Psychological Function of the Dream

One of the most important questions for interpretation is what psychological purpose or function the dream serves within the personality. The theoretical notions, whether articulated or not, about the dream's purpose structures the analyst's hypotheses about the meaning of the dream, his investigative questions and his cognitive organization of the patient's associations.

For Freud, the primary function of the dream was to provide discharge for unconscious impulses and thereby, secondarily, to serve as the "guardian of sleep." During sleep the mind regresses to the early developmental form of drive discharge, that is, hallucinatory wish fulfillment. The wish is defined as an unconscious impulse and must be of infantile origin in order to instigate a dream.

My supposition is that a conscious wish can only become a dream-instigator if it succeeds in awakening an unconscious wish with the same tenor and in obtaining a reinforcement from it.... a wish which is represented in a dream must be an infantile one. (Freud, 1900, p. 553f.)[1]

Although the dream is an attempt to gratify repressed infantile wishes, the dream work (the processes of condensation, displacement, symbolization and secondary revision) "disguises" the dream content in order to meet the demands of the "censor" (later referred to as ego defense mechanisms). Hence the dream as a final product is a compromise formation (just as in a neurotic symptom, a joke and a slip of the tongue) or, in other words, is a disguised attempt at wish fulfillment. We refer to this as essentially a *discharge-conflict model* of dreaming in which the unconscious impulses push for discharge but encounter the conflicting repressive forces of the censor.

How do the contributors view the function of dreams? Garma maintains Freud's conflict model of dreaming but places less emphasis on the discharge function. For him the day's events stir up a repressed childhood conflictual or traumatic situation. Due to repressive barriers, the conflictual situation typically remains unconscious. These repressive forces are alleviated during sleep but continue to operate through the dream work to disguise the painful traumatic material. Garma deviates from Freud in that for him the material defended against is not an infantile wish but a repressed conflict (which may involve an infantile wish) or a traumatic situation.[2] He hypothesizes that traumatic situations are the basic material of dreams to explain the often distressed quality or affect of dreams.

The dream, then, is a compromise between an expression of the trau

---

[1]In his interpretation of dreams Freud took license with his theory of dream formation in that the latent wishes often do not appear to be repressed infantile ones (Jones, 1970). Although these wishes may be viewed as derivatives of repressed infantile wishes, in many of his examples of dream interpretation Freud neither spoke of nor sought the infantile origins.

[2]Currently with the shift from what has been called "id analysis" to "ego analysis" many Freudian psychoanalysts, including Garma, focus less on the wish or the unconscious impulse seeking discharge and emphasize instead the more comprehensive intersystemic conflict which may or may not involve an id impulse (see also Arlow and Brenner, 1964). Theoretically this change in clinical practice is based upon a shift from topographical (conscious, preconscious and unconscious systems) to structural theory (id, ego and superego systems).

matic conflictual situation and its repression (for Freud, a compromise between the infantile wish and its repression). The dream work attempts to
conceal from consciousness the conflictual material in order to preserve sleep.
The dream may include a "fictitious solution" or wish fulfillment in order to
alleviate the traumatic conflict. Here, the wish is conceived as part of the defense rather than as the repressed wish of infantile origins which is seeking
discharge. (Examples of the wish as a defense can also be found in Freud's
works, although they deviate from his theory of dream formation; see footnote 1.)

For Garma, conflicts cannot be resolved unconsciously. Dreams offer no
solutions but only present the traumatic conflictual situations, "creating fantasies about them—arriving, at the most, at fictitious and deceptive solutions."
Dreams for this reason are always nightmarish in nature, while positive
dreams are viewed as defensive: " . . . one must basically consider dreams not
beautiful but rather as bothersome nightmares whose contents have been disguised in an infantile, deceptive way." Hence the function of dreams for
Garma is to express, disguise and attempt to make pleasant (fictitious solutions) unconscious traumatic conflicts which the day's events have stirred up.

Importantly, the "fictitious solution" for Garma is viewed as a defense.
Using structural theory as the basis for understanding dream formation, we
could theoretically deduce that the ego in its mastery-competence (adaptive)
function (Bellak et. al., 1973) is also involved in dreams in attempting to *work
through* and resolve conflicts. However, this ego function is generally not alluded to in Freudian discussions of dreams, for it is posited that a high degree
of regression occurs during dreaming which precludes the operation of more
mature ego functions. Nevertheless, as Freud pointed out in 1917, Fenichel in
1945, and Arlow and Brenner in 1964, the degree of regression of each mental
structure fluctuates within the dream and from dream to dream. Hence the
mastering and adaptive capacity of the ego could be functioning to a considerable extent in some and to a limited degree in all dreams. In contrast, post-
Freudian theorists stress the ego's adaptive or working-through function in
dreams, which accounts for some of the major differences in the clinical practice of dream interpretation.

Padel, in his integration of British object relations theory with the classical Freudian psychoanalytic paradigm, "look[s] less for the wish . . . than for
the attempts to deal with bad or threatening object-relationships and to put
right what went wrong." Fairbairn assumed that "dreams are representations
of endo-psychic situations over which the dreamer has got stuck (fixation
points) and *often included some attempt to move beyond that situation.*" (Italics ours) Hence the function of the dream is to work through bad object
relationships or fixation points. To view the dream as often including "attempts to move beyond" is significantly different from what Garma calls

"fictitious solutions." This view implies that the dream is less deceptive and potentially more constructive which, as we will see, corresponds with the other contributors' conception of dreams.

Whitmont sees the dream as directly presenting "an objective reality, external and/or internal, that corrects and compensates our subjective distortions and blind spots." He continues, "... *the dream is a function of a self-healing balancing process.... it compensates the one-sidedness of the conscious position and its deficiencies.*" (Italics ours) To quote Jung, "The dream ... presents the inner truth and reality as it is ...." Hence the function of the dream is to compensate or add to the conscious state. Dreaming involves no repressive barriers aimed at concealing but is engaged in its primary purpose of revealing. We refer to this conception of the dream as a *self-balancing model* of dreaming in which dreams are viewed as attempting unconsciously to heal or balance the personality and to work through unresolved conflicts.

Bonime, from the culturalist perspective, states that the dream "is an unguarded symbolic expression of the self.... The dream is not a disguise, but probably the most authentic presentation of personality." In agreement with the Jungian approach, Bonime views the primary function of dreams to be integrative in nature and not solely problem or conflict-oriented. The culturalist's concept of integration and the Jungian concept of compensation are equivalent. Hence Bonime also posits a self-balancing model of dreaming.

Boss[3] focuses entirely on the existence of the dreaming experience, i.e., the dream just "is" and, accordingly, refers to his as the *phenomenological model* of dreaming. Boss does not directly discuss the function of the dream. From his theoretical perspective, he would most probably view our discussion of the psychological function as an attempt to impose a "waking structure" onto the dreaming experience which would jeopardize the full experience of the dreaming world. However, *clinically* Boss perceives and uses the dream as revealing "previously unknown significations and referential contexts" to the dreamer. Accordingly, a self-balancing model is implied.

The primary function of the dream for the gestaltists, as presented by Fantz, is "to present to the dreamer the 'holes' in his personality.... The dream work calls attention to those needs in the individual which have not been met because they have not been recognized." Her conceptualization of

---

[3]In order to facilitate our discussion we have taken the liberty of referring to the Boss and Kenny Chapter by the name of the first author only.

the dream function corresponds with the Jungian concept of compensation and the culturalist's concept of integration. Thus she also utilizes a self-balancing model for dreaming.

In summation, it is clear that the contributors differ in the conception of the function of the dream. The Freudian discharge and conflict model (Garma) stands in contrast to the self-balancing model of the other contributors (Whitmont, Bonime and Fantz; Padel seems to straddle these two models) and to the phenomenological model (Boss). According to their respective theories, upon hearing a dream Garma would look for the latent repressed infantile traumatic conflict situation and would view a dream solution to be fictitious and defensive; Padel would be prone to see the dream as a struggle with bad objects and as an attempt to move beyond that situation; Whitmont, Bonime, Fantz and also Boss would wonder what new material, whether conflictual or additive, is emerging for integrative and self-balancing purposes, with Boss and Fantz emphasizing the dreamer's experience of the dream as it is. This is not to say that these psychotherapists would be totally confined to these notions but that their theories would sensitize and cognitively structure them to understand the dreams in these respective ways.

Manifest and Latent Content vs. Manifest Content

Garma presents the classical Freudian view that the original content of dreams (latent content) is unpleasant or unacceptable and is, therefore, disguised through the dream work. The disguised content is the manifest content or the manifest dream and must be penetrated in order to arrive at the true meaning of the dream.

Freudian psychoanalysts, as previously pointed out, have noted in dreams fluctuation in the degree of regression of ego functions, primarily related to the defense mechanisms and to the observing function. In their application of structural theory to dreams, Arlow and Brenner (1964, pp. 136–37) describe how in some dreams the ego function of reality testing remains intact so that the manifest dream element may be taken at face value. For example, a dreamer's thought, "This is only a dream," is a valid observation. Whereas within the topographical theory every dream element is the result of condensation and displacement which conceals its true identity, within the structural theory the possibility of the validity of a manifest dream element emerges. *Although Freudians predominantly view dreams as disguised content, the structural theory with its increased emphasis on ego functions has potentially moved the Freudians in the direction of the other contributors in accepting the validity of the manifest content as a direct (undisguised) expression of the dreamer's personality.* In this vein, Erikson (1954) has noted how the manifest surface of the dream reveals the dreamer's individualized (ego) modes of experiencing and relating to himself and his world. And more recently, Kohut (1977) in his development of a psychology of the self has described a type of dream, called "self-state dreams," in which the healthy sectors of the personality are clearly and *manifestly* reacting to and attempting to deal with an uncontrolable tension-increase or a dread of the dissolution of the self.

Jung was first in proposing that the meaning of a dream is apparent on its manifest level. The dream is valid as it appears and is neither censored nor disguised. Only the conscious position may resist the "truth" of the dream. Whitmont writes: "The seeming illogic of the dream is . . . an expression of a preconceptual psychic stratum that operates in terms of images rather than thoughts." "Because the dream does not conceal or censor but reveals the 'situation as it is,' the image in its immediate allegorical or symbolic context presents the meaning directly." Hence the task in dream interpretation is to understand these images as they present themselves, not to consider them standing in lieu of more anxiety-producing material.

Bonime also states that the "dream is not a disguise but probably the most authentic presentation of personality." The dream is an "unguarded symbolic expression of the self." Essentially in agreement with the Jungian approach, Bonime notes: "The manifest dream does not *tell*—it presents to the dreamer accurate information about his own attitudes, in the form of oneiric images, actions, and emotions." The concept of the censor is rejected. Only figurations"dream report. Any other distortion in the dream comes about during the reporting of the dream, when the symbolic language of the dream is translated into the discursive mode of waking mental activity.[4]

Although Padel does not directly discuss the manifest-latent content issue, we sense less distrust and a greater reliance on the manifest level of dreams as they portray the struggles with internal and external object relationships. These struggles are apparently less concealed and appear more directly in the dream. However, in his interpretation of Martha's dreams, it seems equally clear that he differentiates between manifest and latent content along classical Freudian lines.

Boss "accepts all phenomena showing themselves in a dreaming state as being nothing but what they reveal themselves immediately to be." Thus he, like the Jungians and culturalists, rejects the concept of a censor and accepts

---

[4]Bonime uses the term "latent content" to refer only to the dreamer's unrecognized attitudes about himself—a very different meaning from that of Freud.

the manifest level of the dream as the most salient experiential level of the dream. Boss states that "the modern dream theories," in contrast to his, accept the concept of the dream censor. However, all the contributors in this book, apart from the Freudian and object relational representatives, actively reject this concept.

Fantz also rejects the concepts of censor and disguise and views the dream instead as an existential message to the dreamer. The dream is what it is.

In summary, while the Freudians (including Padel) maintain the premise that dreams are disguised and, therefore, the true meaning of the dream is discovered in the latent content, all the other contributors propose that dreams give direct authentic presentations of the personality and that the meaning of dreams, although in symbolic form, is immediately and manifestly evident.

Symbolism

Dreams are rarely discussed without reference to the concept of symbolism. However, authors differ sharply as to their definitions of a symbol as well as to the existence and the explanation of the universality of symbols.

Garma views symbolism as a special form of displacement. Displacement refers to the representation of one thing for something else through the transfer of energy from one mental image to another. The connections between the manifest representations and the latent meanings depend on the individual's particular psychology. In contrast, a symbol is a "displacing representation" which has a constant unconscious meaning for a majority of people. For this reason symbols occur not only in dreams, but also in mythology, folklore, religion and literature. (Garma uses the term "symbol" in a more limited fashion; for, typically, within the Freudian framework, the terms "symbol" and "universal symbol" are used respectively to denote the above distinction.) Although Garma does not address the issue of the origin of universal symbols, the traditional Freudian explanation is that universal symbols are the product of a primitive part of the psyche common to all and involve the basic preoccupations in life.

In the Jungian approach, symbols are not viewed as a form of displacement, for the dream does not emerge in disguised form. Instead, dreams are a product of a "preconceptual psychic stratum that operates in terms of images rather than thoughts." These dream images are symbols which at the deepest level touch the "transpersonal dimension of life." A symbol is not an intentional sign for something else which is known, but is "the best expression possible, yet it ranks below the level of the mystery it seeks to describe" (Whitmont quoting Jung). Jung also writes:

It is far wiser in practice not to regard dream symbols as signs or symptoms of a fixed character. We should rather take them as true symbols—
that is to say as expressions of something not yet consciously recognized or
conceptually formulated. (Jung, 1933, p. 21)
Since a symbol is the best possible expression, its "mystery" or meaning is not
fully knowable or fully translatable into a conceptual form. (Boss makes essentially the same point.)

In the Jungian formulation universal symbols are called archetypes and
appear in dreams, myths, religion and literature. Archetypes are " 'a priori'
motivational energy configurations" analogous to instinctual behavior patterns which are the product of a primitive psychic structure called the
collective unconscious.

Bonime's references to dream symbolism once again strike a chord very
similar to the Jungian approach. Bonime views the dream as "an unguarded
symbolic expression of the self." Symbols are condensed images of cognitive
and affective responses presented in the "representational" mode. They offer
as yet unknown information about oneself and, in so doing, serve an integrative function.

Bonime differs from Garma and Whitmont in his view that all symbols
are personal and never universal with fixed meanings. According to his view,
symbols at times have a common meaning for individuals, but it is the result
of a common cultural heritage, not an in-built psychic structure.

Padel does not directly discuss symbolism. However, he points out that
Fairbairn viewed dreams as representing "firstly statements about the present
lives of his patients, secondly situations from the past, especially the oedipal
period, and thirdly the 'state-of-affairs' of the inner object-relations." Accordingly, dream images appear to reflect more directly the psychological state
than to represent something else. In viewing dream symbols as a sign for
something else versus a condensed image that is the best unguarded expression possible of information unknown to the dreamer, Padel seems to be at a
midpoint with Garma at one end of the continuum and Whitmont and
Bonime on the other.

Boss, in contrast to the Jungians and culturalists, accepts rather than
redefines the Freudian conceptualization of symbolism and then rejects the
concept as invalid. The concept for him implies a deception and veiling.
Dream beings or personages "neither 'mean' nor are they 'in reality' anything
other than what they reveal themselves to be." Instead of using the concept
of symbolism, Boss states that dreaming and waking are analogous since they
are based upon the same existential structure of personality. For example, in
treatment dreams are used as an analogy to increase consciousness or "the
world openness of the waking state" (e.g., "Do you perhaps have an inkling
now, in your waking state, of an analogous position?") Boss's views of the

"realness" of the dream personages and of the correspondence between dreaming and waking activity are certainly congruent with the Jungian and culturalist approaches.

Fantz, similarly to Boss, also rejects the Freudian concept of symbolism. Instead, she views the dream as an existential message to the dreamer. The dream images simply are what they are, not stand-ins for anything else. Her views are congruent with the Jungian, culturalist and phenomenological approaches.

In conclusion, within the Freudian theory of dream formation, symbolism is a part of the dream work used to disguise the latent content. In contrast, within the Jungian, culturalist, phenomenological and gestalt approaches, dream symbolism is viewed not as a disguised representation of something else, but as the best possible expression of itself. Although both Freudians and Jungians posit the existence of universal symbols based upon a primitive psyche common to all, because of their different personality theories their interpretation of these symbols would differ considerably.

Dreams: Perceptions of Reality or Hallucinatory Experiences

When confronting the task of understanding and interpreting a patient's dream, a basic question emerges: Does the dream reflect a realistic perception of an external situation (e.g., a memory as compared to a fantasy), an intrapsychic event, or both? For example, when a patient dreams about the therapist (or about any other known person), does the representation of the therapist correspond with reality, i.e., an accurate perception, or is it shaped primarily by projection? In the case of projection, the dream image is clearly reflective of an intrapsychic state. Moreover, the projection may involve an aspect of the self, i.e., an aspect which is experienced as part of the self, in other words, a self representation,[5] or may involve an object representation which is not experienced as part of oneself but as part of the other. In the situation where the dream image corresponds with reality, it may involve only a perception of the external situation or it may in addition reflect an intrapsychic state, i.e., either a self or object representation. Hence, in this latter case, a correspondence exists between the external and internal realities (e.g., an object representation or the expectations of a patient based upon past

---

[5]Self representations refer to the unconscious, preconscious and conscious representations of the bodily and mental self in the ego system (Hartmann, 1950; Jacobsen, 1964; see also Sandler and Rosenblatt, 1962).

experience are confirmed or reinforced within the current object relationship).

Although Garma does not directly address the above issues, his position is evident. A present-day conflict which serves as the manifest content of the dream (called the day residue) must always trigger a repressed childhood traumatic situation in order to instigate a dream. The dream personages may be present-day figures who become sufficiently potent for appearance in a dream *only* because they trigger active unconscious object "representations of the real and imagined parents in childhood and also those persons who are psychically important" and followed the parents. With the emphasis on projection and displacement or, in sum, transference, the theoretical and therapeutic emphasis is on past rather than present-day figures. Even when present-day figures are realistically portrayed and are obviously not the product of projection, Freudians would view these figures as causing conflict because of displacement of affect from past childhood figures. (In contrast, Whitmont and Bonime might conceive this portrayal as a presentation of new information about the current situation for the purposes of integration into consciousness.) Thus for Garma the dream may include self and object representations either of which may be realistically accurate or imagined, but the emphasis is on the transferential reactions which are based on the past and are living in the present. The therapeutic task, therefore, is primarily to unravel the underlying traumatic situation from the childhood past (genetic reconstruction) in order to determine the effect of the past on the present.[6] In this way the interpretive focus shifts significantly from the current interpersonal encounter to the internal world of the patient and its genetic past.

In the Jungian approach, the historical past is deemphasized and the present-day external and internal realities are viewed as the primary instigators of dreams. Perhaps from this vantage point the need to differentiate between the external and internal representations in the dream increases. Accordingly, Whitmont is the most explicit of all the contributors in differentiating between "an outer 'object' reality" and "an inner 'subject' level." By subject level interpretation Whitmont means that "every object or person of the dream represents an aspect of dynamism of the dreamer's unconscious psyche." In order to determine the level of interpretation, the

---

[6]In the treatment of the more disturbed personality, particularly the borderline, classical psychoanalysis has been modified so that in all clinical material including dreams genetic reconstruction receives less emphasis and present day conflicts are focused on more exclusively (Kernberg 1975).

dream is first assessed as to whether or not it corresponds with external reality. In Jungian theory the dream is always presenting new information for assimilation into consciousness. If the dream presents new information about a reality situation, an object level interpretation is warranted. However, if the dream restates an already known situation, the interpretive focus is shifted to the subject level. When the dream deals with people or situations which are not currently relevant in the dreamer's external life, a subject level interpretation is called for. "When people or situations in a dream evoke strong affect in the dreamer, they tend to show up projections and hence call for subject level interpretation, regardless of object level relevance." Apart from these guidelines, the overall criterion which Jungians use is whether or not the interpretation is compensatory and has a healing effect.

In the case of subject level interpretation, the Jungian tendency to view dream personages as projections of the self in combination with the greater focus on the present situation results in minimal focus on the transference.

In dream interpretation, Bonime, like Whitmont, attempts to address both the inner and outer situations. He perceives dream personages as representing either personality aspects of the dreamer or qualities about others which the dreamer consciously rejects (which correspond to Whitmont's subject and object levels, respectively). Thus, when the therapist appears in the dream, Bonime focuses on the patient's reactions to the therapist in the ongoing process which may or may not be based on misperceptions. When misperceptions emerge, Bonime also looks to the historical past to identify their source, but he views these misperceptions typically as the functioning of characteristic personality patterns rather than as manifestations of projection and displacement. Generally, Bonime, like the Jungians, emphasizes unraveling the present in contrast to the Freudian, more pronounced focus on genetic reconstruction.

From the object relations point of view, Fairbairn, as has been previously stated, took dreams to represent "first, statements about the present lives of his patients, second, situations from the past—especially the oedipal period—and, third, the 'state of affairs' of the inner object relations." Hence Fairbairn emphasized it all—the inner and the outer, the present and the historical. Dream personages can be viewed either as self representations or at other times as object representations. Repressed object relationships emerge in dreams during the psychotherapeutic process and become manifest in the transference. Padel points out the need for the dreamer to view dream figures at times as part of the self or as aspects of himself and at other times as part of the other person in order to promote greater self-object differentiation which for Padel is a major therapeutic goal.

In Boss's phenomenological approach, dream figures and situations occur in the dreaming state itself and may or may not be related to the waking state. Since the dream images do not refer to anything other than what they are, there is no theoretical need to differentiate between inner and outer or self and object representations. However, in determination of the analogous relationship between dreaming and waking, Boss in practice does differentiate between self and object representations on the basis of their actual manifestation in the dream (e.g., only those figures which directly refer to the self are viewed as self representations). In the same vein, Boss does not use the concept of transference and focuses exclusively on the present.

From the gestalt perspective, all dream figures are viewed as projections and as belonging to the self. To restate, the dream includes "the existential difficulty, the missing and therefore limiting part of the personality, as well as the fully integrated and identified part of the self." Hence gestaltists consistently view dreams as referring to the inner psychological situation where dream figures are seen always as part of the self and not of the object. Since dream personages do not involve an interplay between self and object representations, the need for immediate and more distant historical investigations wanes. The primary emphasis is on the present (in therapy) experience of these various aspects of the self.

In conclusion, when the effect of the childhood past on the present receives greater focus, the external or interpersonal events manifest in the dream become deemphasized since they serve as the vehicle for the latent conflicts (Garma). Clues to the external situation of the childhood past may be evident in the dream (differentiating memory from fantasy). However, the focus of dream interpretation is predominantly intrapsychic. In contrast, when the present events are emphasized, more credence is given to the dream as possibly portraying unknown elements of the current outer reality as well as the inner reality (Whitmont, Bonime and to some extent Padel). An exception to this generalization is the gestalt approach wherein the existential moment is emphasized, yet dream interpretation has a total but limited (only self representations) intrapsychic orientation.

Finally, dream figures may be viewed as self and/or object representations (Garma, Whitmont, Bonime and Padel) or solely as parts of the self (Fantz and Whitmont's subject level interpretation). From our perspective, to view all dream figures as aspects of the dreamer's self may help the dreamer to reown projections and, therefore, to differentiate himself from the external world. However, the exclusiveness of this position may have the unintended effect of making it difficult for the patient to differentiate himself from others since representations of others do not exist in dreams.

Sexuality in Dreams

One of Freud's legacies in dream interpretation is his emphasis on sexual symbolism and instinct theory. Although many therapists today reject the omnipresence of sexual symbolism, clinicians differ sharply as to the emphasis of sexuality in dreams. This emphasis, of course, is integrally related to the respective personality theories.

Since the psychosexual developmental model is basic within the Freudian paradigm, the Freudians view dreams as typically having sexual references. In his discussion of symbolism Garma's emphasis of sexuality is well-documented (e.g., "the table and the eating constitute the very frequent symbol of bed and intercourse"). In his discussion of Martha's dreams Padel also refers frequently to the latent psychosexual material.

Other contributors who do not retain Freud's psychosexual developmental model typically view sexuality as one of many motivating forces in personality and dreams. Consequently, any image, whether sexual or not, for Whitmont and Bonime may imply sexual as well as relationship problems. In addition, for Whitmont, on the "subject" level, sexual and nonsexual images may refer symbolically to the female and male aspects of the personality. These are major differences from the Freudian approach.

Repetitive Dream Themes

All of the contributors agree that repetitive dream themes indicate no change within the personality has occurred. For Garma, the traumatic conflict remains consciously unresolved; for Whitmont, the dream message has not been sufficiently understood or assimilated. Bonime suggests that change in personality can be monitored by change in dream themes as well as in individual dream symbols. And recurrent dreams for Fantz point to the fact that the need fulfillment pattern, which triggers the dream, remains interrupted. Here, there is agreement that repetitive dream themes indicate no movement in the respective area of the personality.

This concludes our comparison of some of the basic theory of the meaning of dreams.[7] Before observing the impact of these theoretical differences on the interpretation of Martha's dreams, we will compare the principles on the clinical use of dreams.

---

[7]See the following chart, "Summation of Some Basic Theoretical Principles."

Summation of Some Basic Theoretical Principles

Category	Garma	Whitmont	Bonime	Padel	Boss	Fantz
Function of dream	To express, disguise and attempt to make pleasent repressed traumatic situations: conflict model	To correct, compensate or add to the conscious state: self-balancing model	To integrate aspects of the personality: self-balancing model	To work through bad-object relations: a combination of a conflict and self-balancing model	Dreaming just *is*: phenomenological model (concept of function is not applicable; but, a self-balancing model is implicit)	To present the "holes" in the personality for integration: self-balancing model
Manifest and latent content	Manifest content is the disguise of the latent content	Manifest content is valid; the dream is not a disguise but occurs in images rather than thoughts	Manifest content is valid; the dream is not a disguise but occurs in images rather than thoughts	Apparently differentiates between manifest and latent content although greater reliance on former as representing struggle with inner object relations	Manifest content is valid; the dream is not a disguise	Manifest content is valid; the dream is not a disguise
Censor	A concept of a mental agency which requires dream distortion.	Rejects concept	Rejects concept	Uses concept to a lesser degree	Rejects concept	Rejects concept

Symbolism	*Symbol:* a displacing representation, it refers to or stands for something else, and has a constant unconscious meaning for most people ("The unconscious meaning for most people" is typically reserved for the concept of universal symbol).	*Symbol:* "the best expression possible, yet it ranks below the level of the mystery it seeks to describe."	*Symbol:* a condensed image which offers as yet unknown information about oneself and in so doing, serves an integrative function	*Symbol:* not directly discussed but appears to be viewed at times as referring to or standing for something else	*Symbol:* when they refer to or stand for something else, they imply a "deceiving and veiling." Rejects the validity of this concept for dreaming and does not redefine or use the concept of symbolism	*Symbol:* rejects the validity of the concept when it is defined as referring to or standing for something else and does not redefine the term
Universality of symbols	Universal symbols exist: there is a constant unconscious meaning for most people; they are based on the primitive psyche common to us all. (Actually Garma reserves the term "symbol" for universal symbol)	Universal symbols exist: called archetypal symbols (archetypes are "a priori motivational energy configurations" common to us all)	Universal symbols do not exist: common symbols are the result of a common cultural heritage and not of an in-built psychic structure	Not discussed	Does not apply: see above	Does not apply: see above

PRINCIPLES CONCERNING THE USE OF DREAMS IN TREATMENT

The common purpose of all six therapists in their clinical work with dreams is to help the patient contact the inner experience and to expand and enhance the dreamer's waking view. As is clear from the contributors' sections on Martha's dreams, each therapist expects the patient to experience dreams in such a way as to accept responsibility for them, to share his feelings and associations to the dreams and to understand that the meaning of his dreams lies within. In addition, all the therapists anticipate using their fantasies and associations generated by the dreams as helpful clues for understanding the dreamer's personality and dreams. Of course, the importance of the dream as a vehicle of change, the kind of material that a therapist focuses on and the way in which dreams are utilized and worked with vary. In this section we will compare the theories of the technical use of dreams.

Importance of the Dream in Treatment

Despite the fact that all contributors emphasize the therapeutic usefulness of dream material, differences emerge in their general attitudes toward dreams and overall evaluation of the importance of dream material in the therapeutic encounter.

According to Garma, the dream is "more valuable than any other product which he [the dreamer] could invent while awake," for it provides an inroad into unconscious conflicts. During difficult treatment moments, Garma likens "the emergence of a dream to finding a strong rock in a storm." Dreams "give an urgency for investigation" and it is only when "deep dream interpretations are realized that treatment progresses well." For Garma, dreams in contrast to other clinical material provide a direct inroad into unconscious conflicts and, accordingly, are given priority in the analytic session.

However, Freudians disagree as to the evaluation of dream material. While many Freudian psychoanalysts (e.g., Altman, 1969; Garma, 1966; Greenson, 1970) continue in the tradition of Freud to regard the dream as different from other clinical material in that it provides ready access to unconscious material, other Freudians now argue strongly that a dream is no different and clinically no more important than any other piece of verbal or nonverbal behavior. This difference derives in part from Freud's two conceptualizations of mental structure. Within the context of his topographical model, dreams which are a product of the unconscious become highly esteemed in the primary therapeutic task of making the unconscious conscious. With Freud's later structural theory, the therapeutic focus shifts from making the unconscious conscious to intersystemic conflict and to the analysis of defenses. These intersystemic conflicts (which may be unconscious or even conscious) are readily accessible in any of the patient's behaviors, including dreams. Hence dreams are viewed as neither more nor less important than any other piece of clinical material (Arlow and Brenner, 1964; Waldhorn, 1967).

Within the Jungian approach, the dream is supremely valued for its healing and balancing function and for its (at times seemingly omniscient) objective presentation of inner and outer reality. Thus, according to Whitmont, dream interpretation is the chief therapeutic modality. Analysis cannot be conducted in depth without the use of dreams. The dream is accorded center stage in Jungian analysis and serves as the "guide for insights" and as the "director" of the therapeutic process. From this position, the dream has an equalizing effect on the patient and analyst, for only the dream can objectively indicate what is awry and what changes are needed. In accordance with this primary focus on dreams, the patient is instructed to keep a dream journal in which he records dreams immediately upon waking. No other therapist makes that request as a routine treatment procedure, and no other therapeutic approach elevates the dream and the unconscious psyche to this level of importance.

Bonime, from the culturalist position, considers the dream to be of equal importance to other behaviors, all of which can serve as departure for investigation of the personality (corresponding to those Freudians who emphasize structural theory). However, Bonime's view of the dream as "the most authentic presentation of personality" appears to heighten his evaluation of the dream. Bonime also finds the dream to be facilitative in introducing the patient to the free associational process and in establishing (similar to Whitmont) an equalizing collaboration between patient and therapist.

Padel states that the therapist should focus on what is foremost in the patient's mind rather than concentrate on the dream per se. For Padel (as for other Freudians and Bonime), the dream is not prized over other associational activity. Like Whitmont and Bonime, Padel stresses that the dream can be used as an objective third term which both patient and analyst may use for consensual validation. The dream, therefore, has an equalizing effect on the patient and analyst and aids the patient in overcoming his placement of the analyst in an omniscient position. For this reason, working with dreams is viewed as essential for analysis.

Boss argues that dreaming is as "real" and valid as waking experience. He states, "There is always the dreaming human being. At one time he exists as a dreaming being, at another, as a waking being." He decries that the dreaming experience is typically relegated to a secondary position (clearly the opposite is true for the Jungian approach) and interpreted with a biased rational conscious attitude. Since the same existential psychological structure

may determine both dreaming and waking thought, both the dream or waking experience can serve equally as points of departure for analysis of the
personality (like Bonime). Similar to all of the contributors but in his own terminology, the dream is important in that it may bring forth for the first time
new "signification and referential contexts... in a massive ineluctable way"
which can clarify and broaden the patient's "waking existential state."

Boss's initial claim that dreaming is as valid as waking places the dreaming experience on an equal footing with conscious experience. However, his
ultimate judgment is that the waking mode of existence achieves "the highest
rank." This view does not simply refer to the therapeutic goal of consciousness common to all of these theorists, but involves perceiving the
waking world as offering a richer, more varied and more open experience of
being in contrast to the relatively constricted experience in dreaming. Boss's
view of dreaming as a relatively constricted experience contrasts with the
others' and particularly with the Freudian conception of dreaming, in which
the constraining forces of the ego and superego relax sufficiently to allow for
more unrestrained expression of id impulses.

Fantz views the dream as equally important as other behavior for experiencing and investigating the personality (similar to Bonime, one Freudian
camp and Boss). However, Perls, the founder of gestalt therapy, out of his
conviction that "everything" (the existential difficulty, the missing part of the
personality and the integrated self) was in the dream, used dream analysis almost exclusively. Here, the approaches of Perls and Jung converge.

In summation, all the contributors might agree, but Whitmont, Bonime
and Padel in particular stress the use of the dream in the therapeutic session
as an equalizer between patient and therapist. Despite some advantages provided by the dream, Bonime, Padel, Boss and Fantz value the dream equally
with all other behavior for therapeutic investigation. Boss rallies behind the
dream experience itself but awards the highest rank to the waking mode.
Whitmont elevates the dream to a position of unequaled importance as a representative of a "superior, archaic intelligence." And lastly, Jung and Perls
looked to use dreams as the primary therapeutic vehicle, a practice which apparently is still true for Jungians today but not for gestalt therapists.

We wish to note that in our judgment the dream journal which Jungian
analysts recommend enables the patient to contact the inner world and to
view dreams seriously. However, the patient may use the dream journal during the analytic hour in the service of defense (often intellectualization) and
in avoidance of the affective dream experience and the therapeutic moment.
Also, according dreams and "the unconscious" excessive authority may create
dependency on this hypothetical internal authority and, consequently, may
reinforce passivity and undermine the conscious ego. Jung (1916) was clearly
aware of this danger: "However much people underestimate the psychologi-

cal significance of dreams, there is an equally great danger that anyone who is constantly preoccupied with dream-analysis will overestimate the significance of the unconscious for real life" (p. 256).

Lastly, we agree with Boss that the imposition of overly rational conscious attitudes may jeopardize the dream experience. However, we also believe that despite all efforts to the contrary we (including Boss, which is evident in his interpretations of Martha's dreams) can never completely abandon conscious and unconscious (theoretical) notions and attitudes about personality psychodynamics and development—nor should we, for these notions are invaluable inputs which our patients can use to make emotional and cognitive sense out of their dream experiences. Only when these notions become too rigid and unbending do they become obstructive to the therapeutic process.

The Task of the Dreamer

Each approach makes explicit or implicit requirements of the dreamer's participation in the therapeutic process. Each requires the patient's associations; however, each engages the patient in a different associational process.

Garma specifies that the dreamer is to associate freely either through the continued expression of his thoughts and feelings following the dream report or through association to specific dream elements. In either case, free associations may appear to move away from the manifest elements of the dream but are considered to be meaningful and related to the latent content. According to the Freudian point of view, any material presented during the session in which a dream is reported is considered to be dream-related. The dreamer learns in his work with a Freudian analyst to decode the disguised content through the free association process and through the search for genetic sources of the present conflicts in the historical past.

Because the dream appears in an undisguised symbolic form, Whitmont asks the patient to associate as directly as possible to the dream images themselves in order to clarify the meaning of the dream. "Free" associations are viewed as not helpful since they lead away from the direct message of the dream. Whitmont also requests the dreamer to provide explanations, i.e., functional definitions of dream images. In turn, the therapist may amplify the meaning of the dream through reference to related themes in mythology, religion and literature—the "traditional associations of mankind." Thus the Jungian approach to dream interpretation is far more focused and structured compared to the Freudian approach.

Although Padel works with dream material essentially as a Freudian, he asks the patient "to play" with dream images and themes. Stressing Winnicott's idea, Padel encourages therapists to think of patients as people who in childhood forgot or never developed the knowledge of how to play. Hence the dreamer's task is to play in thoughts and images (free association) and Padel uses himself as a model to facilitate the dreamer's ability to play.

For Bonime, the patient's task is similar to that of Padel and Garma in that the patient learns to use the free associative style of thought. Although the dream is not disguised, free association is used for the translation of symbolic language into the discursive mode. However, Bonime attempts to maintain more of a focus of attention on the dream itself (similar to Whitmont). He also consistently inquires about the dreamer's affects during the dreaming experience.

Boss requests the patient to describe in as much detail as possible the dream with all its particular features and meaningful references. He seeks a description of the mood and of the emotional relationships within the dream. Through this endeavor, the patient and the therapist become aware of the analogous relationship between the dream's events and mode of waking existence (similar to Whitmont and Bonime).

For Fantz, the task of the dreamer differs considerably from the others. Fantz requests the patient: (1) to relate the dream in the first person and in the present tense; (2) to actively become the different parts of the dream, i.e., to role-play the various dream elements; and (3) to engage in dialogue between different aspects of the dream.

Interpretive Focus

Dream interpretation in a general sense is the clarification of the meaning of a dream either by the patient or by the therapist. Interpretation has a specific meaning and the interpretive focus differs for each approach.

For Garma, interpretation involves transforming the dream from manifest to latent content. That is, it involves reversing the process (dream work) by which conflicts were disguised. Since dreams reported in analytic sessions are viewed as "always" revolving around the psychoanalyst, transference interpretations are central. The successful interpretation occurs when the patient realizes the transformation from manifest to latent content. However, the unconscious defenses which were responsible for the disguise of the dream are reactivated in the transference relationship and hinder the process of associating and understanding a dream and, therefore, serve as resistance to the analytic process. Thus, to make a successful interpretation, both the manifest content and the patient's resistance have to be penetrated.

Whitmont sees interpretation in terms of helping the dreamer to understand the dream's unconscious symbolic language and to relate these images and feelings consciously to the dreamer's life. Since the dream is viewed as a function of a self-healing process and since the dream reveals the "situation as it is," there is no censor or resistance for the therapist to circumvent. Whitmont uses the term "resistance" to refer specifically to a patient's objection to an interpretation (which from a Freudian view may or may not be defensive). For Whitmont, such a resistance "indicates the therapist's approach is inappropriate if not in content then at least in timing, attitude or emotional stance or insufficiency of rapport."

Padel's view of dream interpretation is essentially classical Freudian. However, Padel differs from Garma to the extent that he relies more on the manifest level of the dream in its portrayal of object relations and places less emphasis on transferential interpretations. For him, the interpretive focus more generally involves undoing the repression of "bad" and threatening objects.

For Bonime, interpretation involves, as for Whitmont, the translation, elaboration and understanding of the dream's symbolic, imagistic and affective language. The purpose of these interventions is to establish connections between dream and personality elements with the intention of modifying personality through the ongoing patient-therapist relationship (not through the analysis of transference). Resistance to interpretation stems chiefly from anxiety related to change. Because Bonime does not see himself as a parental surrogate in the analytic situation, no transference resistances exist. Bonime stresses, as do Whitmont and Padel, that interpretations are hypothetical and can be made by the therapist or patient.[8]

According to Boss, to interpret is to do "violence" to the dream. Abstract models of "dream interpretation" will disappear if all dream phenomena are approached phenomenologically. The daseinsanalytic "interpretation" accepts all phenomena in the dream as being whatever they reveal themselves to be and consists of unfolding and differentiating all the meaningful references which make up the dream. Boss theoretically uses neither the concept of transference nor that of resistance. However, he does recommend focusing on dream elements which "resist against closeness with something or somebody." The therapist needs to deal particularly with those dream elements which show fear or disgust or which barricade against something.

Like Boss, Fantz does not use the concepts of interpretation, transference or resistance. Dream work involves enabling the patient to identify and

---

[8]As the manifest level of the dream is accepted as symbolically valid, so also is the patient's interpretation, for it follows that defenses do not operate as globally to distort either the dream material or the patient's perception of it.

take responsibility for each part of the dream and ultimately to reown and integrate the sum of its existence. "It is vital to become *in action* one's myriad facets." Hence the therapist actively directs the patient to role-play each dream element and to develop scripts and dialogues between the various elements.

To summarize, most of the contributors (Garma, Whitmont, Padel and Bonime) view dream interpretation as a critical tool in enhancing and expanding the patient's self-understanding, while others (Boss and Fantz) see interpretation as an antitherapeutic distortion of the dream experience itself.

Resistance, particularly as it is manifested in the transference relationship, is of paramount importance for Garma and to a lesser extent for Padel. Resistance related to anxiety about change is also important to Bonime. Whitmont speaks of resistance in a far more limited way, i.e., rejection of interpretations. Boss and Fantz reject the concept of resistance but refer to barricades, restrictions and blocks to change and engagement with people, all of which would be included in the Freudian concept of resistance and is similar to Bonime's use of the term.

Garma's view that all dreams reported in analysis involve the analyst is the most extreme and perhaps the most accepted position within the Freudian school. However, many Freudians would not agree. For example, Padel indicates that the British analysts also focus farily exclusively on the transference but warns against it. We also question the therapeutic value of such exclusive transference interpretations, which we treat more thoroughly in the discussion on Transference in the following section.

In our theoretical comparison of the meaning of dreams and the principles concerning the use of dreams in treatment, many substantive theoretical differences have emerged. The question remains: To what extent do these theoretical differences affect the understanding and evaluation of the same dreams? To answer that question, we turn to a comparison of the contributors' actual interpretations of Martha's dreams.

INTERPRETATION OF MARTHA'S DREAMS

All contributors emphasize that their understanding and interpretations of Martha's dreams would normally derive from the patient's more complete associations and from the full experience of the therapeutic context. Nevertheless, the dreams, limited associations and case material have provided sufficient data for our contributors to generate extensive hypotheses about the dreams, the patient's psychodynamics and the progression of treatment. Again, we are concerned not with the accuracy of these hypotheses for this particular patient, but with how these hypotheses exemplify the various therapeutic approaches to understanding and working with dreams.

Out of the vast array of interpretive hypotheses, we selected for purposes of comparison specific dream images and events which, we feel, are particularly useful in assessing similarities and differences in the contributors' interpretations. In addition, we chose several dimensions, namely, transference and progression of treatment, for extensive comparisons.

Throughout our study we will focus both on the specific understanding of the dream imagery and on its evaluation. Evaluations of dream personages and events are based largely on the patient's affects and associations, but are also in part determined by the therapist, especially in those cases where dream material remains obscure. The therapist's internal evaluations serve as a basis for his interventions and often are communicated implicitly or explicitly to the dreamer. These messages further the ongoing process of the dreamer's evaluation and affective coloration of these internal images and events, e.g.s, the dream figures may be experienced positively or negatively, the dream events as psychologically progressive or regressive. Thus, the patient-therapist evaluations are one of the more crucial aspects of the dream interpretive process.

Dream Imagery and Events

Dream No. 1

Perhaps the most striking aspect of the dream material is that, despite the array of interpretations, all contributors perceive very similar and at times identical basic psychodynamic themes and problems. This is particularly true for their understanding of the *"shaky, rickety balcony"* image in the first dream. The contributors interpret this image unanimously to be a reflection, at the beginning of treatment, of Martha's psychological state of insecurity, withdrawal, detachment and grandiosity. They all agree that Martha had to give up her defensive "balcony" posture toward life in order to become more solidly human and vitally alive. Accordingly, they interpret her departure from the balcony as a harbinger of change. They agree more generally on the basis of the case material and imagery in the first dream that Martha avoided sexuality and marriage.

This degree of commonality in understanding the first dream is rather remarkable in light of the distinct theoretical differences and outspoken interschool schisms. All the contributors—including Garma, who theoretically differentiates between manifest and latent content—interpret the balcony symbol literally (manifestly) as representational of Martha's psychological state. Garma's view of the balcony image as indicative of Martha's psychological instability would not be expected if this were a "disguised" image and a product of "dream work" (although from the Freudian perspective the manifestation of an undisguised image is the result of the failure of defensive functions). Here is an example where clinical practice does not conform to a major theoretical proposition.

However, the contributors do differ significantly in their interpretation and evaluation of other dream elements. We have chosen three elements in Dream 1 to demonstrate the interpretive and evaluative variations: the "Prime Minister," the "young man," and the "explosions and black clouds of smoke."

Prime Minister. Garma suggests that the Prime Minister represents an idealized, yet mocking image of the therapist. Martha's refusal of the Prime Minister "signifies her anxiety about intercourse and also about progressing in her therapy which causes her to return to her fixation on her forbidding parents." Hence her rejection of the Prime Minister is viewed as a defense against her sexuality and its sublimated aspect, the therapeutic working relationship. Her refusal is naturally seen as a regressive move. The progressive move would have been to psychologically embrace this internal figure. In contrast, Whitmont views the Prime Minister as a glamorous figure who "seeks to replace the realistic life expectations (the ordinary husband who has left in the dream). Her refusal of the Prime Minister is prognostically promising." Her action is viewed as a momentary turning away from her projected grandiosity and, therefore, as a progressive move. For Boss, the Prime Minister episode implies that her "dreaming existence is not attuned to love, but rather to matters of status in society." Her "narcissistic self-love" and grandiosity is also apparent in that the Prime Minister "has to climb up to her" and then she refuses him. Boss evaluates her rejection as a continuation of her grandiosity and, thus, as a negative action. For Fantz, the Prime Minister becomes the special (prime) and responsible (minister) aspects of Martha which need to be owned and integrated. Fantz suggests that the potential marriage is a possible integration of the polarity between the fifty-year-old (a place of specialness) and the Prime Minister (the responsible head of state).[9]

In summary, Garma interprets the Prime Minister as the therapist, an example of what Freudians mean by "symbol" (i.e., the dream image stands for something else) and the focus shifts to the therapeutic relationship and to its transferential aspects. Whitmont, Boss and Fantz, on the other hand, attempt to amplify the image instead of translating it in order to determine its psychodynamic meaning. However, their amplifications differ sharply.

Young man. Martha reported the appearance of a young man who wore an open jacket similar to that of the therapist and who helped Martha jump

---

[9]Bonime and Padel did not specifically address this image.

down from the balcony. Garma states that the therapist's sports coat and possibly his hand symbolize "the therapist's penis, which he exhibits. (On a deeper level, it represents her parents' genital organs.) At this point the dream creates a more permissive atmosphere in which her instincts can function better, and this takes the form of orgastic acceptance of the genital relationship . . . . " "Jumping down" symbolizes the attainment of a genital relationship and, therefore, is progressive for Martha. For Whitmont, the association to the therapist's clothing "emphasizes the need for the contemporary (sports coat) way of meeting reality presented by the therapist. The reference to the need for the therapist's help as early as in the initial dream may be compensatory to the therapeutic resistance alluded to in Dream 2 and perhaps 6 . . . . "[10] Bonime and Padel view the image as a warm acceptance of the therapist's help and her readiness to come down to the human level. Bonime points out her acceptance of only "the necessary amount of assistance—without expecting him to lift her down, she jumps down on her own feet." Boss stresses that the young man is unknown, even though in waking and dreaming she is now aware of being helped by a man through the analysis. He warns against prematurely equating the figure with the therapist: "To interpret the young man as the analyst would be to overlook the human distance which Martha still maintains from him. Only if the unknown young man is allowed to remain what he is—unknown—does it become visible how the behavioral possibilities of a young man, as being helpful and gracious to a woman, have hitherto been unknown to her." Fantz sees this image as a "sign of trust and hopefulness." Considering this image also to be a projected aspect of Martha's self, she would have Martha "become the open sports coat to get in touch with her opening self."

Thus Garma translates the helping young man image into sexual terms reflecting the potential genital relationship to the therapist (object representation), the transference (object representation) and the greater acceptance of her sexuality (self representation). Whitmont, Bonime, Padel and to a limited extent Fantz interpret the imagery literally to refer to Martha's relationship to her therapist (object representation). Whitmont and Fantz also view the young man and his clothing as an aspect of Martha (self representation). Boss

---

[10]Although Whitmont in his theoretical section limits the scope of the concept of resistance, in his clinical work with Martha's dreams he refers to her resistance to the treatment process which corresponds with the much broader meaning of the Freudian conception of resistance.

works with the dream image on a dreaming and waking interpersonal level (object representation) as presented by the dream. Apart from Whitmont's reference to resistance, all view this episode as a momentary progression for Martha and her treatment and as prognostically favorable.

Explosions and black clouds of smoke. Garma views this imagery to be a "regressive anal expression of genital activity which she feels to be dangerous." This imagery also suggests to Padel that the pathology began in anal experience. Bonime, on the other hand, sees the explosions as anger and does not relate them to psychosexual development. Fantz relates to the frightening power contained in the image and does not define it further. Boss takes at face value Martha's view of the world as potentially explosive and dangerous. And Whitmont feels that the explosions represent either a potential psychological breakdown or a projection of her explosiveness onto the outer world. Thus the Freudians (Garma and Padel) interpret the imagery in terms of psychosexual development, while the other contributors, particularly Boss and Fantz, remain closer to the manifest level of the dream. Whitmont alone suggests that the image could reflect a potential psychological breakdown.

Dream No. 2

Garma interprets the latent contents of Dream 2 to be masturbation and the psychotherapeutic investigation of her mind which, in turn, stir up sexual contents (a good example of latent versus manifest content). The exciting genital and forbidding aspects of her internal objects, mother and therapist, motivate masturbatory fantasies. He writes:

> The act of masturbation is quite clearly represented in the dream, when it is seen that the mother, as a genital object, also symbolizes Martha's genital organs ("I grabbed her by the hair and threw her out. She landed at the bathroom door and fell"). These sentences describe Martha masturbating, her desire to achieve an orgasm and her retreat from sexual excitment when she has done so. To land "at the bathroom door" expresses once again the anal component of masturbatory excitement, but at the same time it also refers to Martha's superego causing her to evaluate masturbation as dirty, as well as something which might harm her ("I was afraid that she had hurt herself").

> ... masturbation in the dream represents both direct genital behavior and also its sublimated aspect of psychotherapeutic treatment. Martha undertakes treatment in an atmosphere of favorable excitement, but she also tries to destroy it. "My mother was in there, going through my purse" symbolizes her therapist helping her to explore her mind, and this exploration excites her and encourages her to become sexually excited.

In accordance with his theory, Garma translates the dream symbols into sexual terminology. He focuses on the internal struggle between her genital strivings and the exciting and forbidding aspects of her introjects (mother and therapist) and on their manifestations in the transference.[11]

With variations, all the other contributors, except for Fantz, understand the dream on its manifest level to involve essentially Martha's repressed, uncontrollable, impotent rage at her mother's intrusiveness (Bonime, Padel and Boss) and at her mother's internalized standards and attitudes (Whitmont and Bonime). Fantz initially views the dream as also portraying Martha's struggle with her maternal introject, but then shifts the focus to an internal struggle with an aspect of herself: "I would also point out that since her mother in the dream was simply another facet of herself, it was very likely that she, Martha, did not respect her own integrity and that in order to assert it, she might very possibly have to get angry on occasion." Although Fantz momentarily differentiates between self and object representations, she clinically emphasizes, in accordance with her theoretical position, that the dream figures are self-representatious.

Padel relates Martha's repressed anger toward her mother to toilet control and suppression of early masturbation: "Throwing her mother against the bathroom door indicates the place in which the main traumas occurred; the sense that there was no way to make her observe the integrity of her things indicates the nature of the traumas." Rather than translating the dream imagery into sexual terms, Padel focuses on the internal and external object relational struggles. Thus he shows greater reliance, as we sensed in his theory, on the manifest level of the dream and translates dream imagery to a lesser degree that Garma into psychosexual terminology.

Padel and Bonime also note how Martha's object relational (Padel) or interpersonal (Bonime) struggle with her mother impinges upon the therapeutic relationship as indicated by Martha's reference to her treatment of the therapist. Padel calls this impingment transference and Bonime refers to this as the manifestation of the same personality pattern in relationship to both her mother and therapist.

---

[11]Object relations theory permeates many of Garma's formulations. However, for Garma, the object relational struggles typically revolve around sexuality and are viewed in terms of psychosexual development.

Dreams No. 3 and No. 4

In Dreams 3 and 4 Martha directly confronts her phobic object, the *cockroach*. Garma connects her cockroach phobia to an infantile era in which she fantasized masturbation both by herself and her brothers. Her internalized parental attitudes (superego) prohibited such fantasies, resulting in conflict. "The latent symbolism of cockroaches for Martha was the wish for the fingers of her parents, brothers and sister, a substitute for their penises, touching her genital organs and other parts of her body to excite her and make her pregnant and also to control her and punish her; in other words, making superficial, cutaneous, sexual caresses, which were 'dirty' like the cockroaches, by which Martha felt both attracted and nauseated."

Padel also relates the cockroach to sexuality:

> The cockroach in both dreams has a transitional quality; also, it is a devourer, it is dirty, and it is lively—characteristic of oral, anal and phallic sexuality, respectively. But what is it that the mother won't tell and that the girl doesn't wish to know? Not the role of the male but the female's own sexual activity, so that the cockroach stands both for the labia and clitoris and for the fingers. The defense against knowing this is very strong, and, once the cockroach phobia is dealt with, its transformation will be the razor blade and the fear of her mother's comment.

Whitmont says that cockroaches "are usually associated with dirt. They are animal life, drives, that are hidden from the light and feed on refuse; psychologically upon what is 'refused' by consciousness, instinctual urges considered dirty. Often the allusion is to sex. In view of the context of this dream (pubic hair) and of the indication of forbidden play in Dream 6, the reference to sexuality in its playful aspect would probably apply."

Bonime suggests that the mother's concealment that a cockroach had crossed her pubic hair might represent that "the facts of life (father's cock penetrated mother's genitals to produce Martha) had been hidden from Martha. Did the withholding occur because that action represented to the mother, and perhaps also to Martha, something base, forbidden and repulsive?" For Bonime, the meaning of symbols may change during one's lifetime so that at one time roaches might have referred to "the sperm that initiated the frighteningly uncontrollable process of pregnancy" and perhaps at other times the "urgency of the excited 'cock' .... Did she hate and feel repelled by the 'cock' because her own uncontrollable sexual urges 'degraded' her to the level of other women? ... Did the roaches symbolize also the unbearable borrishness of her father and the debasement of her mother?"

Boss describes the cockroach as cold-blooded, unchangeable, "bound to limited instinctive, unfree modes of behavior" and a carrier of disease. And for him the dream imagery clearly indicates that Martha equates the cockroach with sex. He writes:

> Of all the possible forms of life that could appear in connection with the pubic hair of her mother, it had to be a cockroach. How much Martha knows about cockroaches would have to be explored, but in any event she certainly knows them as bringers of plague and disease, as strange, distant, unfamiliar beings living in secret nooks and crannies, as things invoking panic. In her dreaming state, Martha's existence is open for the perception of mature womanly sexuality only from the bodily appearance of her mother, and then only in the closest connection with all those characteristics and significations properly belonging to a cockroach.

Fantz sees the cockroach as a projection of Martha's self—possibly "a pesty girl (due to the lack of affection in the family)"—and related to masturbation conflicts. "As the cockroach, she might have wanted to crawl up inside her own genitals, explore her own 'thickness,' her own turgidness." She then relates the cockroach more generally to sensuality: "We considered the conflict between her 'dirty,' perhaps sensual self, and her more controlling, society-oriented side, noting in the process how her 'dirty' self expanded as she tried to hold it in check."

Although coming from different vantage points and navigating through the dream imagery in varying ways, all contributors arrive at the same symbolic relationship between the cockroach and Martha's sexuality.

In contrast to the cockroach image, the understanding and evaluation of the *sequential events* in Dreams 3 and 4 differ considerably. In Dream 3, when the cockroach first appears, Martha reports, *"She [mother] explained that she had told me something that wasn't true because she thought the truth would frighten me: that a cockroach had walked across her pubic hair. I thought she was right—it would have frightened me."*

Garma views this episode as Martha's submission to her superego mother, who frightens the girl about her sexual fantasies, and as her consequent attempt not to understand the cockroach phobia, "i.e., the sexual and superego fantasies of her childhood." Padel, Boss and, to a limited extent, Whitmont also view this dream episode as Martha's defensive attempt not to recognize her own and her mother's sexuality.

Bonime notes the possibility of denial of "degrading" sexual urges, but also mentions the possibility of Martha's "appreciation of her mother's candor, even though her mother lied to her at an earlier time. There is now, however, a more accepting attitude toward her mother, in contrast with the violence of the second dream. This interesting shift of feeling appears in a dream invoking two symbols (mother and roach), presumptively connected with feelings of rage and terror. The emotions evoked are nevertheless gentle, empathic and trusting. The changed feelings suggest the possibility of new insight and maturation." In a similar vein, Fantz writes: "The dream suggests to me the beginnings of an awareness that truth can be frightening but also the rudimentary ability to face the truth."

Our contributors also differ as to their understanding and evaluation of other imagery in these two dreams. In Dream 4, "... a cockroach was there. It was half dead.... I took a can of spray."

In their respective terminologies, Garma and Boss related the half-dead cockroach to her half-dead instinctuality. Bonime and Fantz, on the other hand, suggest that Martha's terror of the attacking cockroach was half dead. Garma also notes this possibility and relates the half-dead cockroach to her incipient understanding of the cockroach phobia.

Whitmont and Boss see the spray can episode as a continuation of her hostile and repressive attitude toward her instinctual life, although they see the outcome of this encounter ("As I sprayed, it got bigger....") as progressive. Fantz, too, sees Martha attempting "to keep it [the cockroach] in check," but also feels that some initial assertiveness is contained within that anger.

In contrast, Bonime evaluates the episode more positively as "the real Martha tackling her problem in a more [as compared to the other girl] self-contained fashion—using an insect spray. She gave it 'one long spray.' This may possibly refer to her awareness of taking a good long look at her own problem of wanting to control." Padel concurs with the positive evaluation: "A sign of recovery is taking the can and giving the creature one long spray. As so often with an hysteric, recovery seems to start from recollections of initiative and independence over urination." And Garma considers both regressive and progressive possibilities: "The girl in the dream might be Martha feeling that she is still too babyish to be able to face up to her adult conflicts. She might also symbolize Martha's genital organs, and in that case 'spraying' to kill might symbolize the opposite, the lubrication of her vagina because she is excited by a sexual object ('... a cockroach.... got on my leg')."

Dream No. 5

Viewing the dream as a whole, Garma, Bonime and Fantz are very similar in their central psychodynamic formulations. They note Martha's more direct attempts to deal with her sexuality, her destructive potential and her compassion toward men. Somewhat related is Padel's "main interpretation ...of a masturbation fantasy in which the penis is appropriated and internalized; concern for the male is marked. . . . " Boss focuses on Martha's dependency relationship (living at home) and on her sexuality, i.e., sexual intercourse is conceived but in terms of mutilation rather than love. Whitmont also focuses on the dependency struggle with mother and then, in Jungian terminology, on the intergration of the animus (others might refer to this as the integration of assertiveness): ". . . by renouncing her identification with mother's attitude she may avail herself of her phallic assertive potential. By getting away from being mother's daughter, who shuns the risks of living, she can assert herself and rely upon her own mind and power of judgment." Whitmont is the only one who does not focus on sexuality in this dream, but instead interprets the phallus to be a symbolic expression of the animus.

Dream No. 6

Dream 6, which Martha as well as some contributors considered to be a breakthrough, is discussed extensively in "Progression of Treatment." We have chosen, therefore, to focus here on the understanding and evaluation of the following single dream image: *"In the middle of the basement is an open place with sunlight. It seems to be an amusement area."*

Garma feels that this image "could symbolize the capacity of the female genital organs to produce children. And in its sublimated aspect it would symbolize psychotherapeutic ability to 'clear' the mind and help a person to be fulfilled positively." Hence the image is positive, as it shows greater acceptance of her sexuality and both sexual and emotional procreativity.

Whitmont equates the sunlit amusement area with liberation: "The liberating experience rests upon conscious awareness of these oppressive restrictions upon the child and her ensuing ability to substitute her own for her mother's value judgment."

Padel writes: "An area of sunlight in the middle sounds promising. Father's potency penetrates even as far as this and ensures that the area has been and can still be used for amusement and not only for cultural activity (the latter I interpret as the *procreative* aspect of sexual intercourse)."

Considering the amusement area, Bonime ponders: "Is she on the brink of discovering unknown potentials and pleasures? . . . she is finding new illumination, a more crystallized insight. All is not pathology. There are pleasures and solidity to be found."

Fantz also views this as an increased awareness of "her potential for amusement and pleasure."

Although Boss seems to evaluate the amusement park as a trivial place "for the amusement of anonymous masses," he reacts favorably to the sunlit area: the sun "allows the beings of our world to appear before our physical eyes so that we may see and, seeing, understand what is revealed in its light."

The light brings greater openness.

Although Garma and Padel translate the sunlight image into sexual terms and, therefore, differ as to their understanding, clearly all contributors reacted favorably to it.

Summary.

While the contributors often differ considerably in their understanding and evaluation of dream images, they not infrequently focus on the same central psychodynamic themes. For example, all view Martha at the beginning of treatment to be insecure, withdrawn and detached, with elements of compensatory grandiosity. In addition, all focus on the dependency struggle with the mother and with the fear and avoidance of sexuality.

Despite these striking similarities, the contributors vary as to their primary focus and as to their specific formulations. From Garma's viewpoint, most of Martha's difficulties are related to conflicts about genital sexuality, including the regressions and self-protective maneuvers she developed to deal with these anxieties. Psychodynamically, Garma perceives the basic conflict as between her internalized persecutory parent (superego) and her genital strivings (a structural construction) and between the genitally exciting and forbidding aspects of her internalized parents (an object relational view). In accordance with the theory, these dynamics are seen as emerging constantly in the transference and its interpretation essential to the treatment process.

Garma's consistent translation of the dream elements into sexual imagery, his differentiation between manifest and latent content and his continued utilization of massive transference interpretations cause his interpretations to be strikingly different compared to those of other contributors. In contrast, Padel's greater emphasis on the object relational struggles which are not solely involved with sexual conflicts, his increased reliance on the manifest content and his diminished use of sexual symbolism move him in the direction of the other contributors.

Whitmont, Bonime, Boss and Fantz stress the validity of the manifest content and attempt to amplify rather than translate the imagery for determination of its meaning. Accordingly, they emphasize more equally the dependency and sexual struggles in Martha's dreams. Whitmont stresses Martha's struggle with her internalized mother's attitudes, which intrude upon her individuality, pleasure and sexuality, and the therapy itself. Bonime often formulates Martha's problems in terms of attitudes (e.g., grandiosity) and behavior patterns (e.g., competitiveness). For Boss, the primary dynamic is Martha's lack of an active engagement with life. Many of Boss's interventions are made in the context of the intimacy-distance dimension (e.g., it is the cold-blooded cockroach that walks through the pubic hair, not a "loving man"). Fantz focuses on the many aspects of Martha which the dream figures represent. Her exclusive interpretation of dream figures as self representations is a major deviation from the other contributors.

Transference

Transference within the Freudian paradigm is central to dream interpretation and the therapeutic process. Transference refers to the patient's displacement and projection of feelings, ideas, object representations, etc., derived from previous figures in the patient's life onto the analyst. Transference is also used more generally to refer to the patient's emotional attitude toward the analyst which is always determined by the past (see Rycroft, 1973). As presented in the theoretical section and specifically discussed in the Prime Minister and young man dream images, the other contributors typically do not interpret the dream images as relating to the therapist unless the therapist is explicitly mentioned. When the therapist does appear in the dream, the focus tends to be on the here and now relationship with the therapist, with minimal reference to the past, and on the intrapsychic representation of an aspect of the dreamer's personality (for Whitmont, the subject level; for Fantz, the therapist is a projection of an aspect of the self).

Good examples of the differences in the use of transferential interpretations are the way in which the contributors deal with the mother and the check (written to the therapist) images in Dream 2. For Garma, the "dream appears to describe something which is happening in Martha's mind, i.e., in her internal fantasy world. 'I came home and went into my room' symbolizes Martha turning inward to examine her mind." Both a genital mother and a persecutory mother emerge in the dream "which are also two aspects of Martha's internalized analyst . . . . " Hence he interprets the mother image as the introjected mother and as the internalized analyst. In turn, the check "represents the excitement Martha feels toward her therapist. This excitement is sexual, and the sublimated derivation of this sexuality is intellectual, i.e., Martha's interest in her therapy. This excitement is both accepted and criticized by Martha's internal mother and therapist. A consequence of this ambivalence is that her excitement acquires the anal characteristic of money . . . . " Garma's understanding focuses on the transferential relationship (the internalized mother-therapist equation) and on the patient's intersystemic conflict with her sexuality.

Padel also views these dream images as the intrapsychic continuation of past struggles with mother and father. Martha's repressed anger and violence is directed toward her mother "presumably over toilet control and over suppression of early masturbation . . . . " At times, she may have experienced the sessions as putting pressure on her, like her mother; but she also admits that "she has acted toward him [the therapist] (investigating and trying to get things out of him) as her mother had acted toward her." Martha's "growing feeling for her therapist will be resurrecting her early devotion to her father and her brothers...." and "...the check for the therapist indicates Martha's old secret that she felt close to her father because her stool could be equated with his penis." In his work with her, he would "acknowledge that she regarded her relationship with me as a private possession which she apparently wished to keep unscrutinized by her mother, as she had perhaps wished to keep her relationship with her father and with her brothers and sisters free of her mother's scrutiny and control." Thus the focus is on the intrapsychic continuation of the past relationship with mother and father, the therapeutic relationship and its transferential dimension. In a far more limited way than Garma, Padel focuses on the transference primarily when the dream imagery or associations directly refer to the therapist and correspond with past object relationships. This is in keeping with his point that extensive transference interpretations are oppressive.

Whitmont notes: "In presenting a figure who is not the actual person it purports to be, the dream points to an entity 'like mother' from the outset, this is, to subject level significance. It refers to 'mother in her,' to whatever qualities, values or attitudes mother engendered in her." These mother attitudes are the intruders. The implication of mother's concern with the check ("energy or libido") is that she "questions the libido given to therapy. Perhaps the mother's value system considers analytic work an indulgence or immoral?" Whitmont focuses on the struggle with internalized mother attitudes (a less cohesive force than what we usually refer to as an introject) and their relationship to therapy. Hence therapy and the potential resistance to therapy are important and may be related to the Freudian concept of transference; but it is clear that Whitmont does not emphasize transferential interpretations.

Bonime also refers to the fact that the dream mother "didn't look like my mother" and interprets the figure as possibly resembling "a kind of person Martha would not like to acknowledge as mother. If she can avoid seeing what her mother really is like, or her true feelings about the woman...." Here Bonime views the dream as possibly presenting a previously repressed perception of reality. Bonime focuses on the interpersonal struggle with the mother and on Martha's attempts to control both her mother and her anger. He does not address the check image specifically. He also attends to the therapeutic relationship: "The parallel between Martha's hostility to her mother and her spontaneously associated hostility (locked horns) toward the analyst offers, also, an opportunity to discuss with Martha the singleness and unity of her own personality.... In her relationship with her parent, she tried to force her mother to stop being intrusive; in her relationship with her analyst, she tried to force him to answer questions. There is one Martha, battling two separate and unrelated people. Competitiveness and controllingness are pervasively present, dominant aspects of her personality." Whereas the Freudians would work with this dream material in terms of displacement and projection, Bonime relates to the material in terms of personality aspects and patterns.

The fact that Martha's dream mother does not look like her mother indicates, for Boss, that "Martha does not recognize this behavioral modus as belonging immediately to her existential relation to her mother, in which she herself exists as a helpless, defenseless daughter." Like Bonime, Boss feels that Martha has not recognized this aspect of her mother and its impact in her waking state. In the dream, Martha's anger and violence is provoked in part by the mother's intrusive penetration of her relationship with her therapist. Boss writes:

> There is no justification for designating Martha's dreaming of her analyst's bill and her mother's discovery of this bill as a "transference dream" in which the analyst "in reality" means her father and the dream events represent the "oedipal constellation." Such an "interpretation" would not be an interpretation of the dreaming, but rather the arbitrary substitution of one thing for another. In the dream events, there may indeed be parallels to the kind of relationship that Martha had to her mother and father when she was small—perhaps five or six years old. Nevertheless, in her present dreaming, it is the relationship to the analyst that is penetrated by her mother. It is not that the analyst represents her father, but rather that Martha has stagnated so that she still exists as the childlike "field of seeing" as which she has already existed as a child. Consequently, she is able to perceive only the paternal and maternal traits of grown-up human beings and possibilities of relating to these grownups only as a child even in her present dreaming. If these dream events were simply "interpreted" as a replay of past events in masquerade form, their impact for the presently living Martha would be greatly weakened. She would be distracted from experiencing fully her actual and concrete emotional attachment to her therapist. On the other hand, when she becomes aware of the childlike character of her present existing, those events of the past speaking in her present relational modes will begin recurring to her with full relevance.

Thus through the dream events Boss focuses primarily on the current interpersonal arena and the ongoing therapeutic relationship and secondarily on the related events of the past.

Fantz writes: "We would consider her mother to be an introject, the part of herself that is hurt, tearful, rarely angry, that she might like to spit up."

Elsewhere she notes: "I would also point out that since her mother in the dream was simply another facet of herself, it was very likely that she, Martha, did not respect her own integrity and that in order to assert it, she might very possibly have to get angry on occasion." She addresses neither the issue of the dream mother looking different from the mother nor that of the check. Thus Fantz works with the mother as a projected aspect of the dreamer and does not focus on the interpersonal struggle with the mother (although indirectly her work would have an impact on this relationship).[12] She brings up the therapeutic relationship not with the check in the dream, which directly refers to the therapist, but only with the association which directly reveals anger toward the therapist. At this point, the focus is on dealing with the anger in the here and now relationship, with no reference to the past or to the transferential dimensions of the relationship.

In conclusion, it is clear that the inclusion and importance of the transferential dimension in dream interpretation as well as its definition vary considerably. Whereas Garma views all dreams as involving transference, Padel alludes to transference only when the dream imagery or associations lead directly to the therapist. Whitmont focuses on the internal struggle and does not often refer to the transference. Bonime emphasizes the unity of Martha's personality so that she reacts to her therapist out of the same behavior pattern as she established with past objects—a somewhat modified meaning of the Freudian concept of transference. Boss's focus on the actual dream figure and reluctance to equate the figure with the therapist unless they are one and the same within the dream resembles Bonime's concept of the "unity of personality"; in this case, the "unity" is manifested in the dreaming and waking states. Bonime and Boss arrive at a

---

[12]To role-play the mother facilitates bringing the unconscious projection into consciousness. However, a potential risk, in our opinion, is that the internal mother may become a more cohesive dynamism (introject). We also sense that to view the mother immediately as part of the self could impede the process of self-object differentiation and could be generally isolating (e.g., "I am but full of internal parts struggling with one another").

In contrast to her theory, Fantz in her work with Dream 5 also was concerned about Martha's self-object differentiation. Fantz did not choose to have Martha role-play the mother since "...my sense that Martha's clarity about boundaries, which I picked up from her identification with the island, obviated the need for the identification with a mother who did not seek to change these boundaries or need to load her views of the world on Martha."

similar emphasis of the internal and external interpersonal arena and of the ongoing therapeutic relationship. In her consistent intrapsychic focus on aspects of the self, Fantz does not utilize transferential interpretations and does not seem to actively utilize the past for understandings.

In our opinion, whenever we make transference interpretations and utilize the concepts of projection and displacement (e.g., "You are angry with me as if I am your intrusive mother"), we chance moving away from the immediacy of the ongoing patient-therapist relationship and diminishing the potency of that experience. The manner in which we phrase and utilize transferential interpretations increases or decreases this risk. This risk is what Bonime and Boss warn against and attempt to avoid. We agree with Padel that constant transference interpretations, particularly when the therapist is not directly manifest in the dream, are oppressive. Such exclusive focus potentially makes the patient more dependent on the therapeutic relationship to the exclusion of other life involvements. Despite these potential pitfalls and regardless of how transference is conceptualized, the connections between past and present, which are embedded in transferential interpretations, enhance perspective and potential for psychological freedom.

Progression of Treatment

Therapists frequently use dreams to evaluate progression of treatment. We will compare our contributors' more salient evaluations of Martha's progression and regression in terms of specific elements in each dream, changes from dream to dream, overall changes manifest in the dream series and the status of treatment at the time of the last dream. Some contributors will not be mentioned in the discussion of each dream, as they did not specifically allude to progression or regression in all of the dreams. In addition, at the risk of redundancy, those dream images which have previously been examined will be briefly discussed again for their progressive or regressive evaluations in order to provide a complete picture. For purposes of accuracy, quotations will be used extensively.

Dream No. 1

As we have noted, all of the contributors see Martha in the first dream as a precariously withdrawn, detached and defensively superior individual with some progressive movement in her coming down from the balcony to join the human family. Her ambivalence about this incipient change was apparent to all.

Dream No. 2

In Garma's view, Martha's conflict between acceptance and rejection of her genital strivings and its sublimated derivative, e.g., psychotherapeutic investigation, results in a regressive "retreat from fantasies of intercourse into fantasies of masturbation ('going through my purse')....A consequence of this ambivalence is that her excitement acquires the [regressive] anal characteristic of money ('a check written to you')....Martha undertakes treatment in an atmosphere of favorable excitement, but she also tries to destroy it." Martha wants her therapist to "help her progress in her treatment and her genitality ('I felt I was forcing you to answer questions and clear up the confusion')."

Whitmont senses ambivalence or resistance in the check incident: "The implication is that she intrudes upon or questions the libido given to therapy. Perhaps the mother's value system considers analytic work as indulgence or immoral?...an ambivalence about if not outright resistance is intimated." Martha's attempt to deal with her internalized mother's attitudes through anger is "unsuccessful," implicitly maladaptive, and "the problem comes back as overt solicitousness."

Comparing the second dream to the first, Bonime writes: "The clear identification of the interpersonal relationship, and the sharper focusing on and recognition of feeling, all indicate therapeutic progress." He also notes treatment movement in Martha's "spontaneous independent focusing when she correlates her own dream activity (forcing respect from her mother) with her remembered activity in a previous session (forcing answers from the analyst)." However, he senses there might be denial: "Possibly the dream mother 'who didn't look like my mother' resembles a kind of person Martha would not like to acknowledge as her mother." Similarly, "She reported that the mother 'had hurt herself,' thus evading a clear statement that she, Martha, had hurt the mother. This shielded her from facing the full intensity of her own rage." And, "I would point out also that she appeared to me to be denying her true feelings toward me when she said, 'I was expressing more anger than I felt toward you'...."

Padel, like Bonime, notes that "it is a good sign that she recalls how she has recently treated her therapist." He states: "Even at the first interview Martha had been well aware of her mother's intrusiveness; she is now beginning to be aware that her own relationship to the males of the family did not develop enough because it could not go unobserved by her mother." He sees Martha's potential resistance to the maternal transference, her tendency to regress in the face of enforced passivity and her "use of self-imposed passivity as a defense against powerful control by parent figures." However, he senses Martha's hope to have her mother discover "the fact of her therapy as a relationship that she could not control" and Martha's vision of a more compassionate mother-daughter relationship.

Fantz sees Martha as "becoming aware of the permeability of her boundaries, her sense of being invaded and her abandonment of control . . . . Martha begins to get in touch with her own anger in conjunction with being spied upon; she also begins to realize the lack of power that she brings to that anger . . . . "

Dreams No. 3 and No. 4

The cockroach appeared in Dreams 3 and 4, and all the contributors perceive changes in Martha's relationship to her phobic object. Although Garma perceives Martha resisting the latent meaning of the cockroach, he assesses her sexual fantasies to be maturing. He writes: "The dream may indicate that Martha is more able to face up to these worrying contents ('I didn't panic'), although it may also be a negation. At the same time, it shows that these contents are becoming more and more conscious ('it got bigger') because of her treatment." Garma also perceives Martha as moving toward "more adult sexual fantasies, represented by the cockroach turning into an erect penis and a pregnancy ('a cockroach . . . . it got bigger'). In this positive sense, the half-dead cockroach could mean that Martha had begun to understand the latent meaning of her cockroach phobia."

Whitmont evaluates Dream 4 as showing "an unsuccessful attempt to deal with the roach problem by doing away with it, by willful repression." However, in the transformation of the cockroach into a chicken and then a dog, he notes change: "They reveal themselves and move nearer to consciousness (the progression from insect to humanoid animal) as she unsuccessfully tries to fight it. This progression is accompanied by a shift in attitude toward greater willingness to accept these aspects."

Bonime perceives Dream 3 as showing more gentleness, empathy and trust toward the mother, which is indicated by the absence of fury toward her and Martha's acceptance of her mother's "good intentions" on concealing the truth. (However, he points out that the latter could also be denial.) About Dream 4 he writes: " . . . she seems to carry forward a salutary development from the dream of nine months earlier. There is a degree of mastery of her phobia, an absence of rage, a transformation of feelings in the direction of humanity and compassion . . . . There is, overall, the aura of an integrating personality." As evidence, he refers to the half-dead roach, which "may reflect (except for the possibility of denial) her feeling that its power to terrify her is half dead. Possible confirmation comes: 'I didn't panic.' That this long-standing anxiety-producing symbol does not bring on panic can be seen as her own recognition of the alteration of her anxiety." The transformation of the cockroach may allude to "Martha's developing capacity to see others as more than insects...." However, Bonime notes "alternative interpretive possibilities. The Friday night chicken dinners may represent an oppresive family ritual. The spraying of the chicken may indicate a continuing desire to get rid of certain aspects of the mother."

Padel sees "clear progress" from Dream 3 to Dream 4 "since in Dream 4, Martha faces her phobic object and the object changes and gives rise to quite different lines of association." "She can now face the worst not only in its symbolic form, but also the worst about herself." "A sign of recovery is taking the can and giving the creature one long spray. As so often with an hysteric, recovery seems to start from recollections of initiative and independence over urination." Padel also stresses in both dreams the manifestation of a "strong defense against entertaining serious thoughts of male sexuality.... The main point of this defense would be to make the therapist responsible for thoughts of male sexuality and to keep females (especially Martha's mother and herself) innocent and unaggressive." At one point, Padel equates the "growth in size of the object sprayed with the growth in size of the genitals when stimulated." However, he adds:"...the paucity of associations and the fact that Martha opens the door and apologizes to the dog suggest she holds fast to her virginal primness."

Boss finds the appearance of the mother naked in Dream 3 as progressive, for it indicates "the possibility of living out fully the existential potentiality of a grown mature woman." Yet Martha remains in the dependency relationship with her mother and denies sexuality (she thought the mother was "right"). Turning to the cockroach in Dream 4, Boss perceives movement in her therapy: "Here, this living being concerns Martha directly, in the moment when she is engaged with her own bodiliness and nakedness. No longer does she have to perceive it only from a mother outside herself, while she just looks on. Her own relation to this being of her own world is in the foreground, even though it is half dead. She does not panic, contrary to what would have been expected at such a waking encounter with a cockroach." With regard to the transformation of the cockroach, Boss writes:

> In the wake of her encounter with the cockroach, albeit a hostile encounter, her existence as world openness expands to such an extent that it allows ever more differentiated animal forms of life to shine forth into it and come to be present. A living being that is absolutely stagnant in its evolutionary development undergoes first change to a chicken and then to a mammal—to a dog, "man's best friend." Martha is prepared to let this living being go free in her dream world and even shows regret at having tried to kill it. She is, though, still far from welcoming the immediate presence of this warm-blooded animal and becoming familiar with its bodily

intimate and playful but unpredictable behavior. In her encounter with the dog, she is free enough to willingly permit an animal form of life to remain in the openness of her existence. This is far different from her response to animal ways of beings when they could only disclose themselves to her from the ever disappearing, hated and despised cockroach. Now that they can appear revealed to her from a dog with human characteristics, they come much closer to her human existence, even though a considerable aloofness still remains.

In Dream 3, Fantz sees Martha as less defended and more vulnerable, able to face the cockroach in her dreams for the first time, and with a beginning awareness that "truth can be frightening but also the rudimentary ability to face that truth. Martha's associations to her dream highlight the awakening of her youthful sensuality and the mockery that was associated with it." Fantz sees Martha as encountering her phobia head-on in Dream 4: "We find her in a vulnerable position in the tub, naked, completely unprotected, and accessible to her most-feared attacker. But interestingly that same attacker is now half dead, clearly lacking in vitality. Manifestly, one part of Martha which had frightened her previously is no longer so potent.... The use of the spray can or, in other words, the use of assertiveness is accompanied by movement up the phylogenetic scale from insect to chicken to dog to human and is indicative, perhaps, of her own movement."

Thus all contributors, except Whitmont, note progress in the direct appearance of Martha's phobic object, the cockroach, in Dreams 3 and 4. Despite differences in their specific understandings, all see positive movement in the transformation of the cockroach.

Dream No. 5

In the fifth dream, Garma notes an increase in Martha's sexual responsibility and freedom, and a diminution in the persecutory aspects of her internalized mother:

> In this dream, Martha tries to deal with her sexuality by herself. She is making an effort to understand that the damage to her objects and her own sexual tendencies are the cause of her destructive behavior ("I also had the razor blade"). She therefore feels the need to make amends ("...I was concerned about getting the penis back for it might start rotting. I had to get it back to him").

> Martha is now stating that rather than her parents having been the cause of her sexual failure, it was caused by her own castratory tendencies

toward her sexuality. In this dream, her mother seems to oppose castration ("I didn't want my mother to see the razor blade and penis in my hand"). "If she did see, she didn't bother me" indicates that in the course of therapy, Martha's internal mother—who is transferentially also her psychotherapist—has become more cordial toward Martha's sex life. This gives Martha more sexual freedom ("I was wearing a loose shirt").

As the internal images of a persecutory mother and psychoanalyst grow weaker, Martha feels that she must make the effort to mature sexually. But she feels that she is not yet capable of doing so because of these superego objects ("It was...a responsibility...a burden, like walking around carrying too many packages").

In very different terms, Whitmont appears to perceive further movement in the separation process and in the integration of her assertive potential:

The underlying theme is breakup and reunion in a new form, analysis and synthesis, termination of unviable states for the sake of reorganization and renewal. In this dream, the reorganization involves a temporary exchange between the dreamer—the conscious personality who is still in the world of her parents' attitudes—and the unknown man on the island. He is in a "different environment", an as yet unknown orientation. An island, solid ground separated from the larger continents by water, depicts an autonomous personality fragment in the midst of the unconscious, an autonomous complex. The male on the island is a consciousness potential within this complex, an animus figure. The animus represents those drives in the feminine psyche that strive for assertiveness, positive accomplishment, discernment and rational judgment....

The penis she receives refers to an assertive or discrimination potential that needs to be actualized. This again is merely a general statement, without the specific qualities associated to this man or a person resembling this man.

The phallus is also, as in our previous example, an image of creative renewal. Lacking specific associations to breast and nipple one might speculate in general archetypal terms that by renouncing her identification with the mother's attitude she may avail herself of her phallic assertive potential. By getting away from being the mother's daughter, who shuns the risks of living, she can assert herself and rely upon her own mind and power of judgment.

But eventually the phallus is to be returned to its rightful owner if she is to receive back the integrity of the breast, that is, to find her own femininity. This I take to refer to the necessity of relating to the animus as an autonomous function of the non-I rather than identifying with it. It means being responsive to the impulse for assertion and discrimination—but in a woman's way as opposed to a male's, deliberately or unconsciously.

Bonime perceives in Dream 5 maturation as well as continued ambivalence in Martha's relationships to men and to her sexuality:

Martha is apparently dealing with her relationships with men, with problems of intimacy, sexuality and commitment. The element of compassion, which appeared in her third and fourth dreams, seems involved here in her relationship with men.

A maturing sexuality is suggested, even though it is represented in bizarre fashion.... While the total dream suggests intense physical involvement with a man, specified in genital and mammary terms, and although there are plans for her to live with the man over a weekend, Martha's lingering immaturity is indicated by her conceiving of herself as still, or again, residing with her parents. Her continuing insularity from men is implied in her boyfriend's being "somewhere on a nearby island." Her ambivalence about venturing too far from her familiar ways is indicated by her description of the man's island as being different, "but not too far from where I was." Does this mean not too far, developmentally, from where she is? Not too far (any longer) from the "security" of life within the encirclement of her parents? Does it promise imminent change?

Now she is presumably more independent, not embattled with her mother, and is arranging to go off with a man.... Furthermore, noticing the mild irritation of her breast, she becomes aware of her boyfriend's probably greater difficulties (from sexual detachment or involvement): "If that was bothering me, he must be really uncomfortable."

Padel notes psychosexual development as well as postponement in her heterosexual relationships:

I like the way in which Martha becomes more able to accept her penis envy through envisaging the man's envy of female organs. I notice that her readiness to postpone heterosexual relations a bit longer comes up as "I was supposed to join him on Friday night. I'd rather have joined him on Saturday...." Perhaps this also refers to her reluctance to depart from the Sabbath observation appropriate to her Jewish background.

For Boss, Martha continues in her dependency relationship to her parents: "Martha is still living with her parents. Where there are parents as parents, there are children. Martha remains, then, in a parent-child way of existing to her world." Boss also perceives that the possibility of a loving union between a man and a woman emerges but is far from being realized. He writes:

> Indeed, in the exchange of fragments of bodily organs with such rich significations and referential contexts, there is a direct—but from Martha totally hidden—limit at the possibility of a man and a woman sharing in each other's specifically manly and womanly existential possibilities through intercourse with one another.

Fantz writes about the integration of her sexuality, the consolidation of her ego boundaries and the realization of her hurtful potential:

> ...Martha is progressing more and more distinctly and specifically toward an awareness of her own sexuality and responsiveness. Her symbolization is powerful and evocative, which in itself supposes an ego better able to confront that which might have been titillating and therefore scary. Martha appears more in touch with the presence of her own boundaries and their inviolability; in consequence, she has less of a sense of invasion. In addition, she is more conscious of her own potential for being hurtful and of the possibility of utilizing her own self as a weapon ....The mechanism of cutting off or curtailment could be more aptly applied to the total function of self, rather than merely to the sexual functions.

Although in Dream 5 all contributors perceive varying degrees of psychological growth in the separation process and in Martha's integration of her sexuality, Garma, Padel, Bonime and especially Boss point out her reluctance to move on.

Dream No. 6

Four and a half years into treatment Dream 6 occurred, the last dream of the sequence and a dream which Martha considered to be a breakthrough. All contributors addressed the issue of progression of treatment and the current status of treatment, i.e., whether or not termination was in sight. Some also note the overall progress from the first to the sixth dreams.

Garma views Dream 6 essentially as an exploration of her genital organs, particularly her vagina: " ...we can suppose that owing to the therapist's work, Martha is beginning to feel a sexual rebirth. She reactivates fantasies of genital exploration, of masturbation and intercourse, and finds them interesting and pleasant, although also very dangerous...."She feels more capable sexually, which in turn creates further resistance. " 'Some men are laying a cement floor' could signify increased repression as psychotherapy delves deeper." Her premature return to the surface indicates her resistance and fear of further psychotherapeutic investigation.

Garma concludes:

> In synthesis, on a superficial level in the latent content of this dream, Martha feels herself to be quite capable both in her sexuality and in her psychotherapeutic progress. This signifies that she realizes how much she has improved, but it also reinforces her resistance to further improvement. On a deeper level, to which Martha has more resistance, she is afraid because she feels threatened by her persecutory parents and by her therapist when she undertakes sexual and psychotherapeutic activities and hopes to improve. These fears could make her interrupt her treatment too soon. She can do this either by stopping treatment or making by making sure that her sessions are not productive.

Whitmont writes: "This dream features the classical archetypal motif of the descent into the underworld of the unconscious which enables the dreamer to confront a core problem and thereby attain a degree of liberation." He, too, senses resistance:

> The ending of the dream appears to imply that more could have been assimilated. She "could have stayed longer" but it does not pay to go back again. Is this an insufficient willingness to work upon her development in depth, perhaps as a result of the mother's (in her) interfering with therapy as foreshadowed in Dream 2? We can only speculate; the answers would have to arise out of a personal confrontation of therapist and client.

Bonime views this dream as Martha's "greater courage in exploring herself, a discovery of potential pleasures in the 'depths,' and the suggestion of a new firm basis for further development (men laying a concrete floor)." The little girl indicates that a new young Martha "is coming into existence, a new personality emerging from nearly five years of analytic work." Martha's spontaneous association ("I was struck by what I had said to the child. I felt it applied to me") suggests to Bonime Martha's sense of her own progress. He, as do Garma and Whitmont, understands Martha's comment, "I could have stayed longer...." as an expression of her ambivalence (which he sees as her fear about her new sense of self) and possible wish to terminate analysis prematurely. Despite her ambivalence, he feels that treatment has resulted in a major change in the intensity of her problems, in her manner of dealing with them and in her view of herself. He compares the first and sixth dreams:

> Dream 1, showed her great insecurity, her anxiety about controlling her emotions, and her desire to avoid involvement in ordinary life. Instead of moving off her rickety balcony to examine the distant explosions (possibly her angry outbursts), she stayed behind and waited (slept?) in her chair for twenty years. In Dream 6 she went almost fearlessly into an exploration of her self and her current life—going down a great many steps, even though there was still insecurity in doing so with no apparent protective banister.

> In Dream 1, she trivialized her analyst—he was a nice young man. She was ambivalent about ordinary marriage; her own marriage was seemingly husbandless and was immediately followed by a proposal from a VIP, the Prime Minister. In Dream 6, the men at the bottom of her exploration were laying a concrete base that may have symbolized a new view of her analyst and of other men—as human beings who helped her to create her life's solid foundation.

> In Dream 1, Martha became a fifty-year-old "old lady" who had stayed in a chair for twenty years. In Dreem 6 (even though she left the situation, perhaps anxiously, earlier than necessary), she had found herself to be a solid and likable "child," with life ahead of her.

Viewing the explored space in the dream as Martha's "innermost world," and also "Martha's mother's inner world," Padel states:

> I fully share Martha's own appreciation of this dream as a breakthrough. Whatevertechniquesmayhaveledtoithavebeenjustifiedbythefactof the dream experience and its quality. In the dream, the relationship between the patient and her friend, Eileen, makes the exploration possible and not terrifying. I remember that in the first dream, there were explosions and black smoke *down below* and that a female friend joined the people running toward them and was warned by Martha of the danger. "Down below" now has a different and fuller meaning; there is still risk, but Martha is taken by her friend to the very bottom *and comes up alone.* Both the unknown friend who ran to see in the first dream and Eileen in dream 6 represent aspects of Martha's ego . . . but the different use made of this maneuver indicates that the self-splitting can now be used constructively and is far less compulsive; independence has grown.

Men laying a concrete floor "is a good constructive symbol for the anal aspect of Martha's parents' intercourse." He likens the little girl to Winnicott's concept of the *true self*. And the "mild contradiction about the time of day—'early' yet 'so late in the afternoon'—reveals different ways of viewing her stage of life now that treatment is drawing to its close. 'Early' means that she has enough time left for making something of her life but 'so late in the afternoon' means that being in her late thirties she can't afford to spend longer on her self-analysis (if she's going to have a family), however enjoyable it has been." Accordingly, Padel feels that termination is appropriately at hand. "If Martha did not make the link herself, I should make sure that we both accepted that the dream of exploration referred to the main business of the therapy as completed. . . . From then on, I should look out for opportunities to help Martha deal with her feelings about ending treatment and about leaving."

According to Boss, Martha in Dream 6 fearlessly "gets down to the bottom of things" where men are constructively laying a floor. Here, there is new unexplored space, lit by sunlight (insight), and an intimate human encounter occurs. Yet Boss is pessimistic about her early return:

> Martha undertakes the ascent to the surface of the earth alone and despite a little danger is not afraid. It seems a matter of course that she leave this realm of light, where an intimate encounter takes place. Martha's world relationship in these dream happenings are such that her "getting to the bottom of things," reaching the fundament, occurs far away from the place where she habitually dwells on the face of the earth. The question of staying does not occur to her, which is surprising when we compare these two worldly dwelling places, the one barren and comfortless, the other bright, open, lighted by the sun—a place where she discovers a child. Martha just goes back to her old habitual abode. Not until she is outside again does she realize that she has not used her available time to the best possible advantage. She could have stayed longer in the open, lighted realm where an important human encounter took place. Rather than undergo the hardships of the return to this realm, she chooses to remain comfortably on the surface of her world. Martha's passivity and lethargy come once more to the fore.

In comparing the first and sixth dreams, Boss perceives growth in more consciousness, openness and active engagement with life, but he still sees the need for further analysis. His comparisons in summary form are:

> In the first [dream], she is spatially above and isolated from the world below her. . . . In the sixth example, she reaches to the secret depths of her world, arriving at the fundament . . . . Between the first and sixth, Martha's worldly dwelling place becomes ever more personal, stable and open in a

specifically human way.

In the first.... Martha herself lives a monotonous, never-changing present of twenty years' duration.... In the last dream events, there is, in the form of the solid, likable girl-child, a promise of a full womanly future....

In the first described dreaming events, Martha responds to her world as a passive, languid, anxiously shrinking spectator.... In the sixth, she penetrates actively into the depths and commits herself in a human encounter, even though this encounter remains limited in character and duration....

...In Martha's first reported dreaming, the events present themselves as distant, dangerously explosive and obscured behind clouds of smoke. In her later dream happenings, the events are even more differentiated and personal. This change in the general character of the events of her dreaming indicates a maturing of Martha's Da-sein....

In the dream events of the third, fourth and fifth examples of Martha's dreaming, there are progressive changes in respect to bodiliness, the kinds of animals appearing and her relation to sex....

This brings us to a consideration of Martha's changing relationship to men.... She is open [in the first dream] to the address of an unknown young man as a helper but in no other way. She refuses the proposal of the Prime Minister who has to climb *up* to her. Her own husband has gone off....

In the fifth dream events, she at least dares a kind of "sexual intercourse," but one which is mutilating for the partners and reduced to a mere temporary exchange of small pieces of flesh.... Again, further analysis is necessary before Martha will be able to make those existential possibilities whose bodily sphere is made up of the sexual organs her own in her waking state.

In the course of her therapy, there are also radical changes in one of her deepest and most characteristic world relationships... that world relation in which she exists in dependent modes—childlike and daughter-like. The overwhelming power of her mother in the second dream happenings and the mesmerizing power in the third no longer hold sway in the fifth and especially not in the sixth....

Boss concludes: "...a careful comparison of the existential understanding of Martha's diverse dreaming reveals that the perceptive world openness, as which she exists, has expanded, become more open and more free in its responsivity to encountered beings, human and nonhuman."

Fantz writes about Martha's movement:

Martha's sixth dream is for me an exciting and vivid exploration of her total self, both external and internal. It clearly depicts the façade she has built up over the years as well as the richness that lies at the center of her being. At the heart of her dream, there is an encounter with her child-self as it really was as opposed to how she has disguised it through the years with her introjects—for me, a particularly poignant meeting. Finally, there is an open acceptance of herself.

The whole dream progression from shaky, rickety Martha at the start of therapy, a Martha unsupported and vulnerable, attracted and repelled by involvement and excitement, through a Martha unsure of her own boundaries and beginning to contact her own anger through a Martha more vulnerable yet more candid, to a Martha in touch with her own aggression and assertiveness, her own sensuality and responsiveness and ability to hurt, to the final Martha both knowing and accepting of herself in her many facets and permutations is a remarkable reflection on the ability of the therapist who abetted her progress and evidently supported her struggles and a tribute to Martha, the woman, who worked diligently to attain her manifold potential.

In conclusion, wide discrepancies in the selection, interpretation and evaluation of dreams elements emerge. All note resistance, but Boss and Whitmont seem to stress it. All detect psychological growth, but the range varies considerably from Whitmont's occasional notation of progress to Bonime's appraisal of consistent growth from dream to dream. Because the contributors rather frequently view similar psychodynamic themes in the dream material, they often perceive growth in the same areas. Examples include the separation-individuation process, the integration of her sexuality and her relationships with men. In addition, clearly some dream images and sequences are sufficiently potent and lucid to provoke in therapists of all persuasions similar evaluations. For example, all contributors view the descent into the building basement in Dream 6 as indicative of a considerable move from her shaky balcony position in Dream 1.

With regard to termination, Whitmont, Bonime and Boss interpret Martha's early ascent as premature and indicative of resistance. In sharp contrast, Padel views this ascent in positive terms as related to Martha's need at this time to leave therapy and to proceed with her life. Whereas Whitmont and Bonime express concern about a premature termination, Padel feels that Martha is appropriately nearing termination and would have aided and abetted that process.

While disagreeing about Martha's readiness for termination, the contributors' agreement as to the fact of Martha's progress is rather remarkable and reassuring in light of their varying orientations, metapsychologies and interpretations. Because of different therapeutic approaches, our patients, as we have shown, will develop significantly different cognitive and even evaluative understandings of themselves and their dreams. However, our differences in cognitive systems and evaluation of specific dream events notwithstanding, we, as clinicians, can agree to some extent on an overall sense of a person's psychological and therapeutic movement.

CONCLUSION

In the theoretical section we examined the most significant similarities and differences in six theories of the meaning of dreams. We questioned whether the contributors' actual interpretations of the same sequence of dreams would correspond to their respective theories. In addition, we wondered how similar or dissimilar the contributors' understandings and evaluations of the same dream material would be.

All the theories of the meaning of dreams were clearly evident in the respective hypothetical interpretations. Specifically, the material suggests that the more elaborately detailed and restrictive a theory is, the more a theory shapes interpretations. For example, in keeping with Freudian theory, Garma consistently translates dream imagery into psychosexual developmental terminology with transferential references. Similarly, theory sculptures Whitmont's interpretation, particularly noticeable in Dream 5, in which his use of the Jungian term "animus" results in a significantly different focus from the other contributors. However, even when the theory of the meaning of dreams is less systematized, it still substantially influences dream interpretation. For example, even though the phenomenological and gestalt approaches stress close adherence to the dream imagery itself for the determination and integration of its meaning, their theoretical notions nevertheless clearly emerge in their psychodynamic formulations and understanding of the dream material (e.g., Boss's focus on the intimacy-distance dimension).

All dreams, particularly those whose meaning is obscure, require the use of our respective theories, whether articulated or not, in conjunction with patient's associations to facilitate cognitive and affective understanding of dreams. Only when our theory becomes too restrictive and inflexible does it jeopardize the dream experience and the collaborative working relationship, and potentially foster an undesirable patient-therapist dependency relationship. Certainly close adherence to the dream data which Boss and Fantz underline and to the patient's associations (which all contributors emphasize) decreases the potential for distortion of dream material through the excessive imposition of theory. But despite our efforts to be "objective," we necessarily rely on our theories to provide understanding of dreams.

The primary differences which emerge in both the theory of the meaning of dreams as well as in the hypothetical interpretations are as follow:

(1) The most important theoretical distinction is the Freudian differentiation of dream content into manifest and latent levels, while all other contributors (Padel, as we have pointed out, is in-between) stress the validity of the manifest content (i.e., the dream is not disguised). This theoretical difference is apparent throughout the hypothetical interpretations of Martha's dreams, although Garma at times (e.g., balcony image) and Padel often (object relational struggles) interpret more directly the manifest level of the dream imagery. Interestingly, through object relations theory, ego, psychology and, now, the psychology of the self Freudians have inched more closely to the perception of the dream as an "authentic presentation of personality" rather than as a disguised product.

(2) Distinctive to the Freudian approach is the Freudians' consistent translation of the dream imagery into psychosexual terminology. This translation is abetted by the manifest-latent content differentiation, for regardless of the manifest form of dream imagery latent psychosexual references can always be assumed.

(3) Garma's theory and hypothetical interpretations consistently emphasize the transferential dimension in contrast to the other contributors. Again the manifest-latent content differentiation allows for any number of transference interpretations since the therapist, regardless of his actual manifestation in the dream, can always be assumed to be latently present in the dream.

(4) Lastly, distinctive to the gestalt approach is the theory that all dream figures are self representations, which is clearly functional in Fantz's interpretations. Whitmont, in his Jungian subject level interpretations, similarly views all dream figures as self representations. Accordingly, the manifestation of the therapist on a subject level would be viewed as an aspect of the self rather than related directly or transferentially to the therapist. On the basis of these primary theoretical and applied differences, as well as the contributors' personal styles, Martha would have experienced very different understandings and evaluations of herself and her dreams.

However, differences in the interpretations must not be overstressed. Although the specific understanding and evaluation of dream content varies considerably, the contributors often relate to similar psychodynamic themes and problems in Martha (e.g., problems with isolation, compensatory grandiosity, dependency, sexuality and heterosexual relationships). In addition, potent, definitive images (e.g., a rickety, shaky balcony; a cockroach; an open place with sunlight) engender strikingly similar responses and understanding in the contributors and, presumably, in clinicians at large. The lucidity of these images, in contrast to the obscurity of others, cut through the different metapsychologies and result in similar evaluations. Hence, despite the differences in the specific understanding of dream content, dreams are often sufficiently definitive and potent to communicate to therapists and patients as well the primary psychodynamic struggles and the overall progressive and regressive psychological developments.

Obviously, dream interpretation is not an exact science. In recognition of this fact, the contributors, out of their openness and keen interest in dreams, have shared with us much wealth about dream interpretation. They have been willing to expose and share with us their internal conjectures and feelings during the dream interpretive process. Whatever their convictions, they have joined us with an investigatory spirit in a comparison with other approaches which they knew could possibly be quite foreign to theirs. What is clear is that we may explore in different ways, take different paths and use different terminologies and psychodynamic formulations, but we may arrive at and work with, perhaps more frequently than we would have thought, similar general psychodynamics with which a person is struggling to grow.

REFERENCES

Altman, L. (1969). *The Dream in Psychoanalysis*. New York: International Universities Press.

Arlow, J. A., and Brenner, C. (1964). *Psychoanalytic Concepts and the Structural Theory*. New York: International Universities Press.

Bellak, L., Hurvich, M., and Gediman, H. (1973). *Ego Functions in Schizophrenics, Neurotics, and Normals*. New York: John Wiley and Sons.

Blanck, G., and Blanck, R. (1974). *Ego Psychology: Theory and Practice*. New York: Columbia University Press.

Erikson, E. (1954). The dream specimen of psychoanalysis. *J. of the American Psychoanalytic Association*, 2:5-56.

Fenichel, O. (1945). *The Psychoanalytic Theory of Neurosis*. New York: W. W. Norton.

Freud, S. (1900). *The Interpretation of Dreams*. In *Standard Edition*, Vol. 4 & 5. London: Hogarth Press, 1953.

————— (1917). A metapsychological supplement to the theory of dreams. In *Standard Edition*, Vol. 14:67-102. London: Hogarth Press, 1953.

Garma, A. (1966). *The Psychoanalysis of Dreams*. New York: Jason Aronson, 1974.

Greenson, R. P. (1970). The exceptional position of the dream in psychoanalytic practice. *The Psychoanalytic Quarterly*, 29:519-549.

REFERENCES

Hartmann, H. (1950). Comments on the psychoanalytic theory of the ego. In *Essays on Ego Psychology*, H. Hartmann. New York: International Universities Press, 1964.

Jacobsen, E. (1964). *The Self and the Object World*. New York: International Universities Press.

Jones, R.M. (1970). The New Psychology of Dreaming. New York: Grune & Stratton.

Jung, C. G. (1916). General aspects of dream psychology. In *The Collected Works of C. G. Jung*, Vol. 8:237-280. New York: Bollingen Series by Pantheon Press, 1960.

———— (1933). *Modern Man in Search of a Soul*. New York: Harcourt, Brace & World.

Kernberg, O. (1975). *Borderline Conditions and Pathological Narcissism*. New York: Jason Aronson.

Kohut, H. (1977). *The Restoration of the Self*. New York: International Universities Press.

Rycroft, C. (1973). *A Critical Dictionary of Psychoanalysis*. New Jersey: Littlefield, Adams and Co.

Sandler, J., and Rosenblatt, B. (1962). The concept of the representational world. In *The Psychoanalytic Study of the Child*. New York: International Universities Press.

Snyder, F. (1969). The physiology of dreaming. In *Dream Psychology and the New Biology of Dreaming*, ed. M. Kramer. Springfield, Ill.: Charles C. Thomas.

Waldhorn, H. F. (1967). Reporter: *Indications for Psychoanalysis: The Place of the Dream in Clinical Psychoanalysis* (Monograph II of the Kris Study Group of the New York Psychoanalytic Institute), ed. E. D. Joseph. New York: International Universities Press.

EPILOGUE
James L. Fosshage, Ph.D.

We felt it would be meaningful and fitting to conclude with a brief, more recent statement about Martha and to present four subsequent dreams which Martha has had in the past year and a half.

Martha has just begun her third year of law school and, despite its travail and pressures, she reports considerable satisfaction with herself and her studies. She experiences moderate anxiety, but no longer panics before exam time. She was recently elected to an office of an honor society at school. In addition, she has left her editorship and is currently an assistant in a law firm.

Martha is generally more engaged with men. Although she has been having an affair, she has yet to become involved in what she considers a serious relationship. However, she is much less anxious about this situation.

Because of the pressures of finances and of her school and work schedule, Martha has reduced the frequency of her sessions. Nevertheless, the therapeutic work continues uninterrupted. The topic of termination surfaces periodically, but termination is not immediately at hand.

Because our contributors have provided us with a wealth of understanding and because Martha's dreaming is clearer as she becomes more lucid about herself, we have chosen to present the following dreams without associations or additional comments:

Dream No. 7 (six and a half years after the beginning of treatment; approximately two years after Dream No. 6)

I meet a man somewhere. I think he's wearing some kind of military uniform. He's not handsome but is particularly pleasant and comfortable. We like each other right away and feel an attraction—though none of this is overwhelmingly passionate.

I feel that his manner is making a suggestion that we have a sexual relationship, and I sort of am responding affirmatively. It's not that the suggestion and response aren't clear, just that they're made easily, not dramatically, and more or less without a lot of forethought—mostly it's fun.

Next, we have come to New York, and I'm supposed to go visiting my parents briefly. I think I suggest or have in mind that we not start anything until I pay the visit; then we can be at ease in the privacy of my apartment.

Next, we are in my apartment, lying on my bed, and we start to make love. I would rather not do it just then: I think I want to get the visit over with first. I ask him if he'd mind waiting. He's good-natured about it, and we get up and are dressing when my mother walks in (or both parents?). Probably I hadn't thought to lock the door.

But I'm not upset. It's compromising, but I just laugh and think " that's what they get for barging in." Probably the consequences will be that they'll assume this relationship is very serious and that this is a future son-in-law. I don't care. I'm feeling good-humored and am enjoying it all.

Dream No. 8 (two weeks later)

I am sitting at a table with a few people, next to a man who is ordinary looking—not in a negative sense. I am aware that he's not perfect—some kind of imperfection is noticed. I feel easy with him and attracted—I feel he is, too. Impulsively and easily, I lean forward and take his hand. It lets him know my response, and he responds to it.

Dream No. 9 (three months later)

I'm in a bedroom. My father is in another room down a hallway. I'm inviting sexual advances from him. He comes into my room. We are both naked. He puts his arms around me, though our bodies are not touching, and he says something. I'm not sure whether he means it sexually or not, and I don't want to risk jumping to conclusions. I say, "What do you mean?" He says, "You want me to say I love you and that you are beautiful." My arms are around his waist as he says this, and I realize he means this like a father and I feel that his body feels like a father's and not a lover's—it's soft and old.

Dream No. 10 (seven months later; a recent dream after seven years of treatment)

In my dream, I saw the one kind of cockroach that still bothers me a little—the element of horror is gone. I noted to myself: "That's the last one." And I tried to step on it.

INDEX

Abraham, K., 125, 133
abstract representation (of conscious mind), 20,21
actual conflict, 18, 31, 33
affect
  affective coloration of dream images, 265
  distress, 244
  fuzzy terminology, 89
  healthy affect in dreams, 99
  intensity, 106-108
  multiple, 89
  stimulus to dreaming, 83
  stimulus to recall, 88, 100
  See feelings, emotions
aggression, 19
  See death wishes
"aha" reaction, 54, 68
alienation, 194
allegory, 55, 57
ambivalence, 127
  as sign of progress, 93-94, 115
  concerning growth and change, 116, 119
amplification, 54, 55, 60, 63
anality, anal experience, anal symbolism, 35, 137, 139, 140-147, 268
analyst's subjectivity, 86, 292-294
  as constructive element, 84, 86, 102
  as obstacle to therapy, 90-91, 95
anima, animus, 62, 65, 73, 74, 76, 217, 273, 292
anxiety
  associated with terminal phase, 122
  diminution with new exprience, 93
  dream threat to self-image, 88
  pursuit of, 93
  related to personality change, 91, 116
archetype(s), 59, 65, 69, 72, 73, 203, 250
association(s), 54-55, 84, 86, 87, 94, 117, 261, 262
  See associative activity, free association, silences

associative activity, 84, 85, 107, 116-117, 261, 262

Balint, M., 125
boundary, 206, 224, 236
  See self-object differentiation
Brierley, M., 125
Britain, 125
  British object relations theorists, 4

censor, 17, 81, 244, 248, 249
  See disguise
character, 204
childhood conflicts, 18, 23, 24, 244, 245
cockroach
  dream image, 35, 36, 44, 71-73, 108-115, 139-140, 145-146, 206-207, 225-233, 270-272, 283, 294
  phobia, 8
collaboration, 82, 84
  competitiveness and cynical distrust, 92, 96
  counter to cultural trends, 91-92
  diminution of shame, 90-91
  dissolution of hierarchial barrier, 85
  and interpretation, 84, 90, 97-98, 113
  and progress, 96, 108-109
combined parents, 146
communication, 126
compensation, 60, 63, 246
competitiveness, 92
  and affection for analyst, 96
  cultural, 87, 91
concrete representation (of unconscious mind), 20, 21
concretization, 20
condensation, 20-22, 28, 244
conflict model of dreams, 17-18, 244, 247
consensual validation, 90